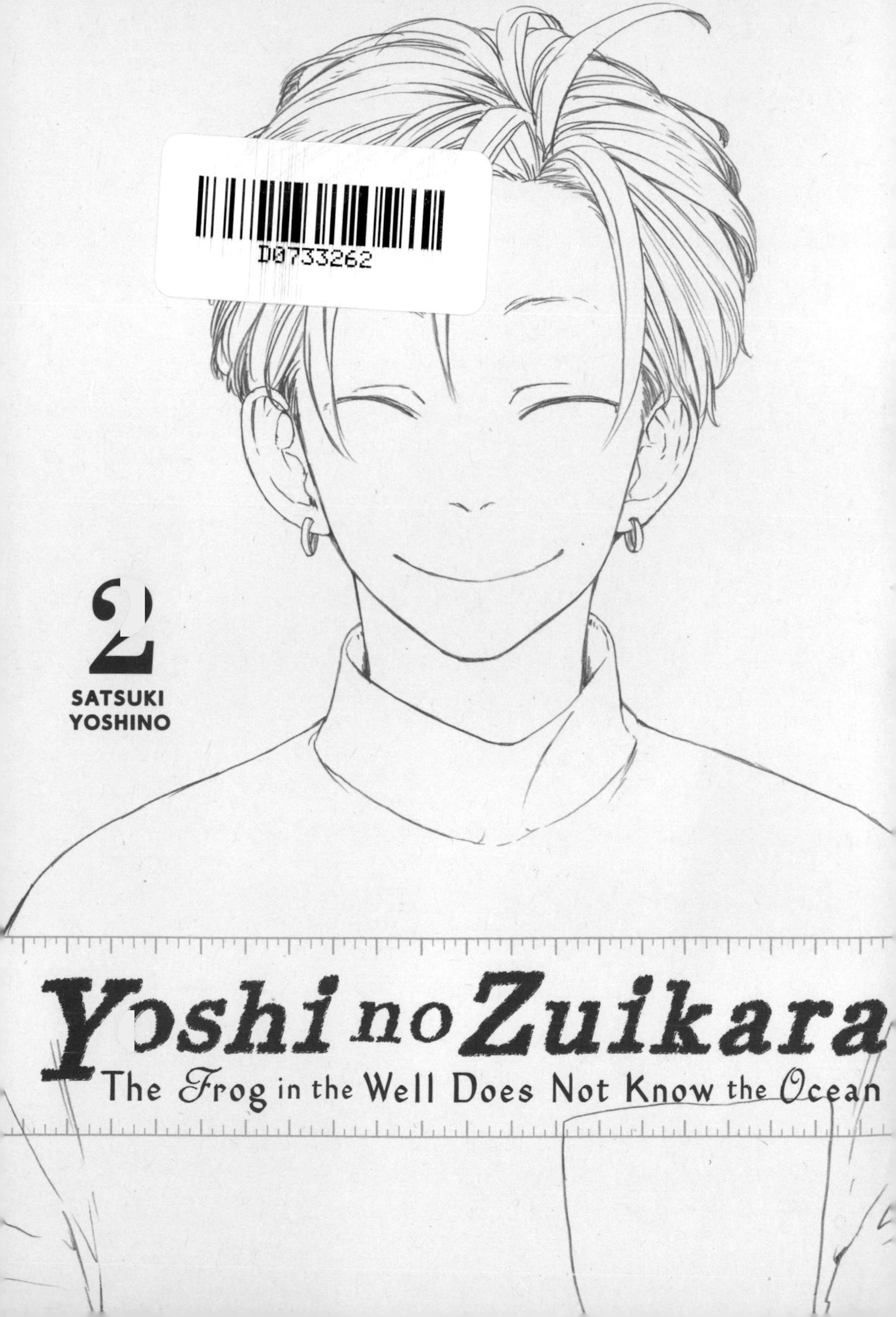

2

SATSUKI
YOSHINO

Yoshi no Zuikara
The Frog in the Well Does Not Know the Ocean

CONTENTS

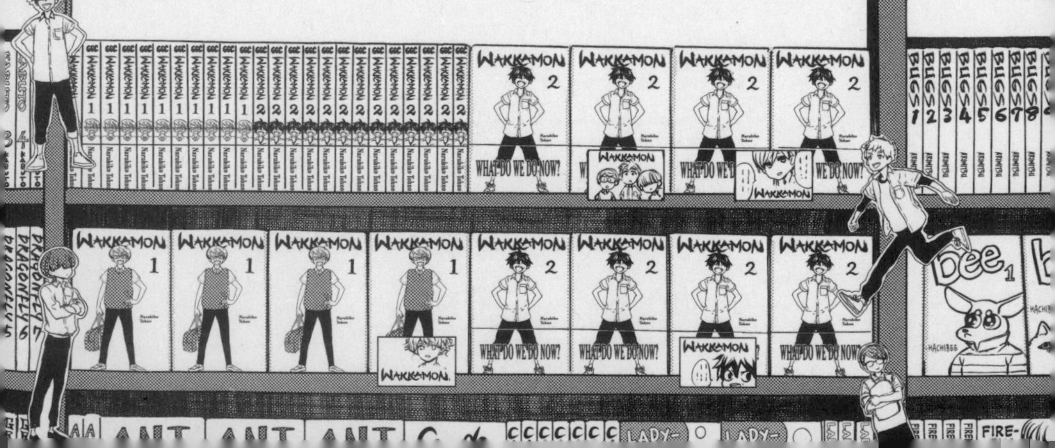

WAKKAMON 2
WHAT DO WE DO NOW?
BUGS 1 2 3 4 5 6 7 8
WAKKAMON 1
bee 1
HACHIBEE
DRAGONFLY 6
DRAGONFLY 7
ANT
LADY-
FIRE-

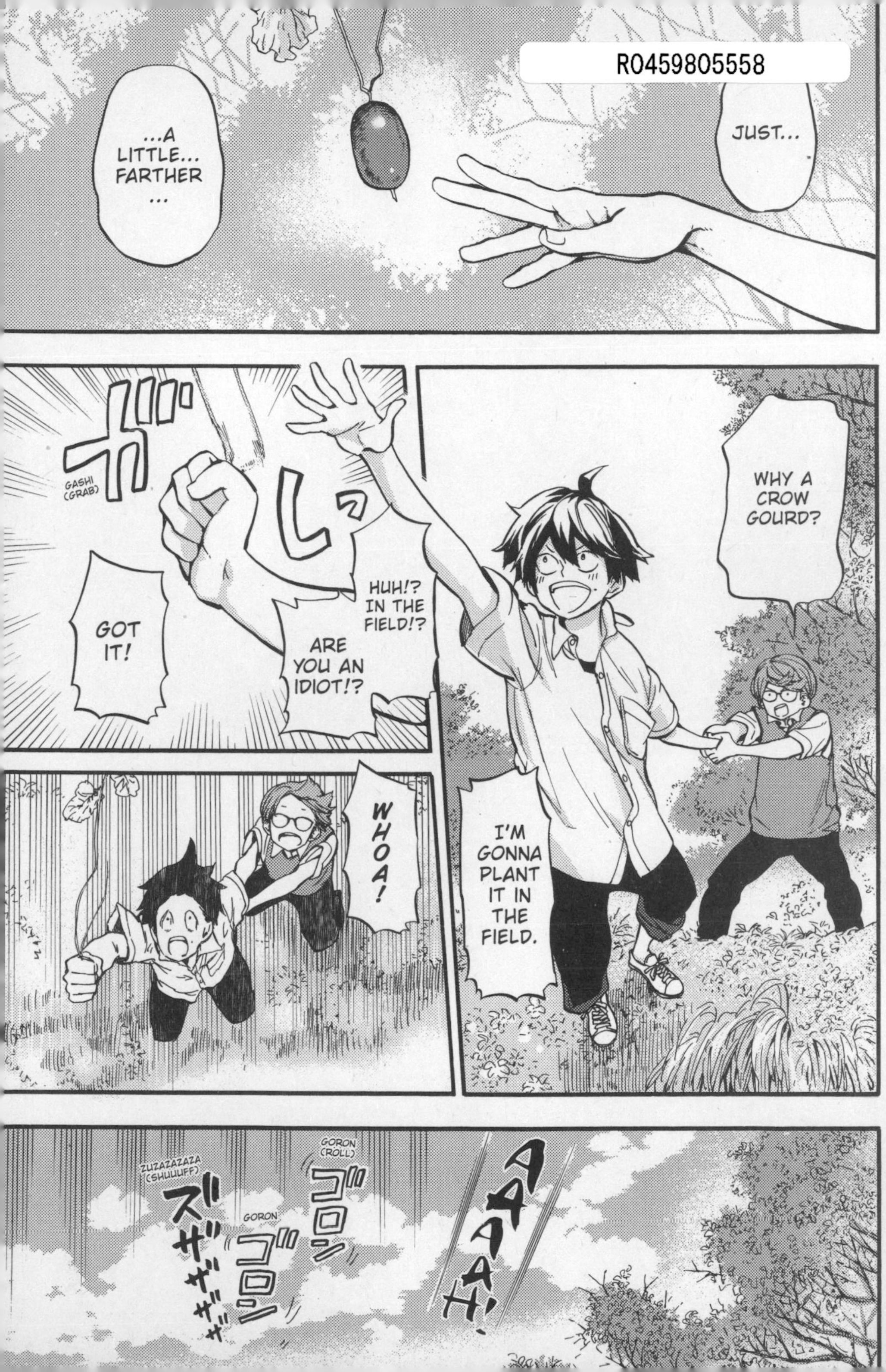
JUST...
...A LITTLE... FARTHER ...
WHY A CROW GOURD?
I'M GONNA PLANT IT IN THE FIELD.
HUH!? IN THE FIELD!?
ARE YOU AN IDIOT!?
GASHI (GRAB)
GOT IT!
WHOA!
AAAAH!
GORON (ROLL)
GORON
ZUZAZAZAZA (SHUUUFF)

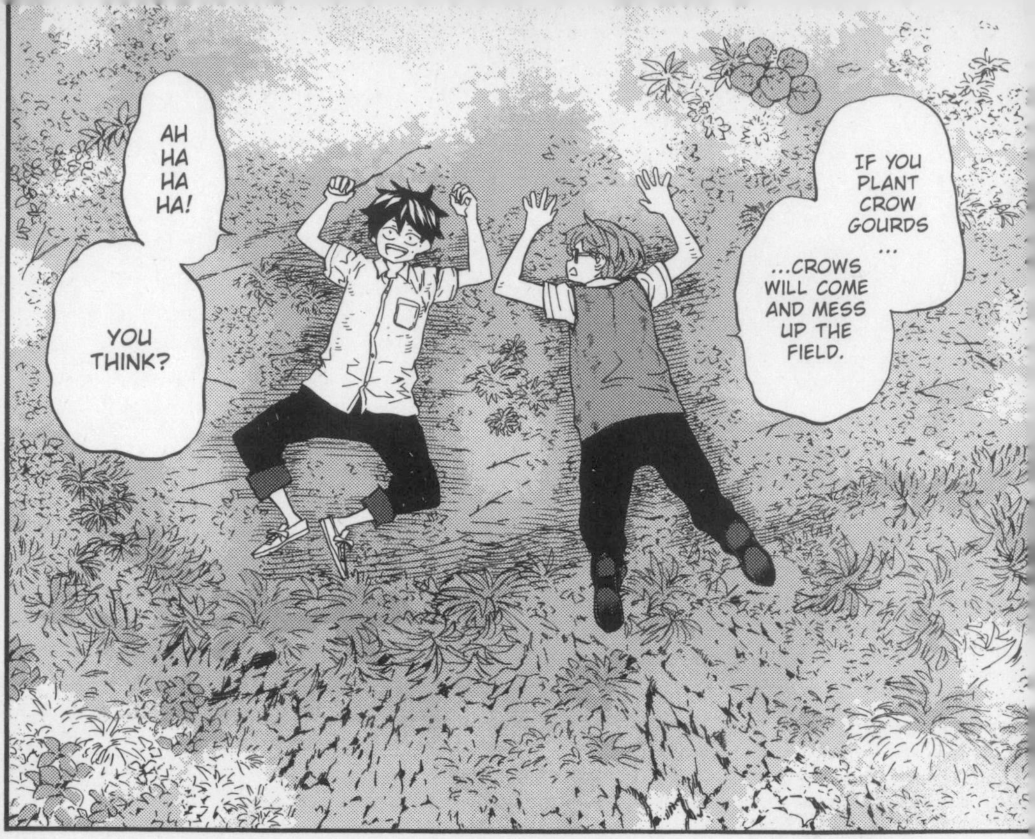
IF YOU PLANT CROW GOURDS ...
...CROWS WILL COME AND MESS UP THE FIELD.
AH HA HA HA!
YOU THINK?

Act. 8

ITSUMANDEN

(translation: Forever)

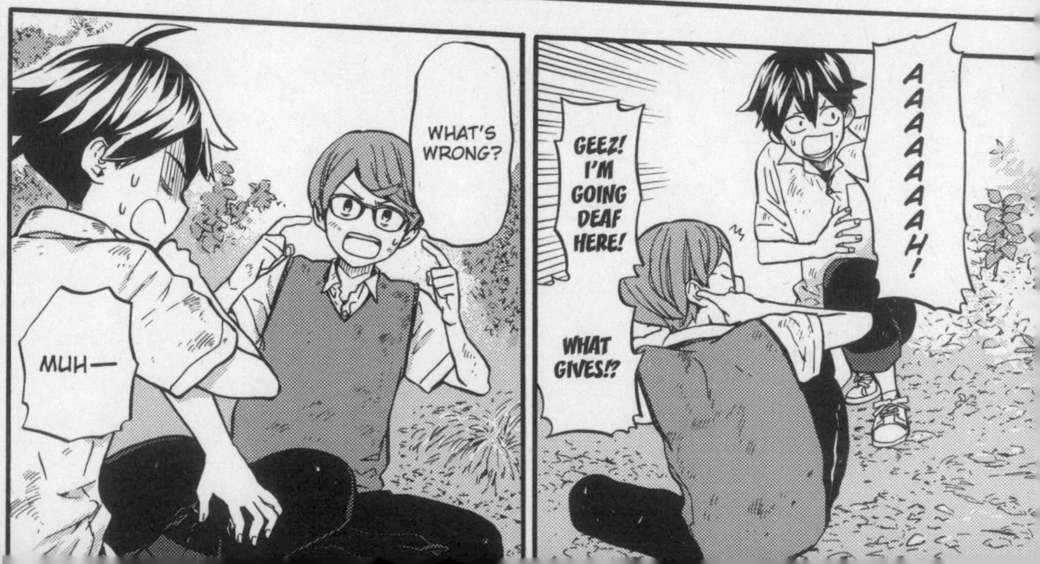
AAAAAAAH!
GEEZ! I'M GOING DEAF HERE!
WHAT GIVES!?
WHAT'S WRONG?
MUH—

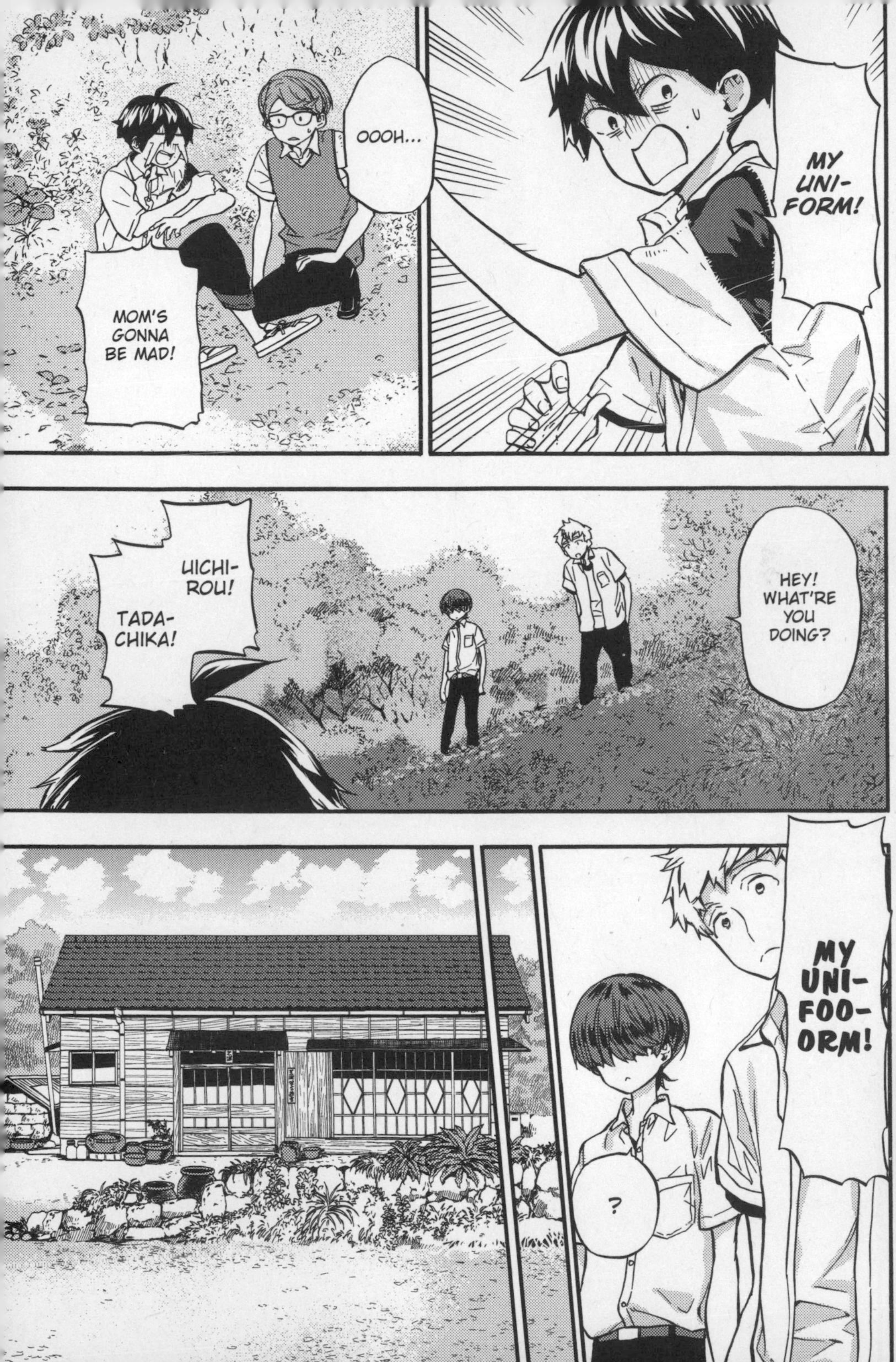
MY UNI-FORM!
OOOH...
MOM'S GONNA BE MAD!
HEY! WHAT'RE YOU DOING?
UICHI-ROU!
TADA-CHIKA!
MY UNI-FOOO-ORM!
?

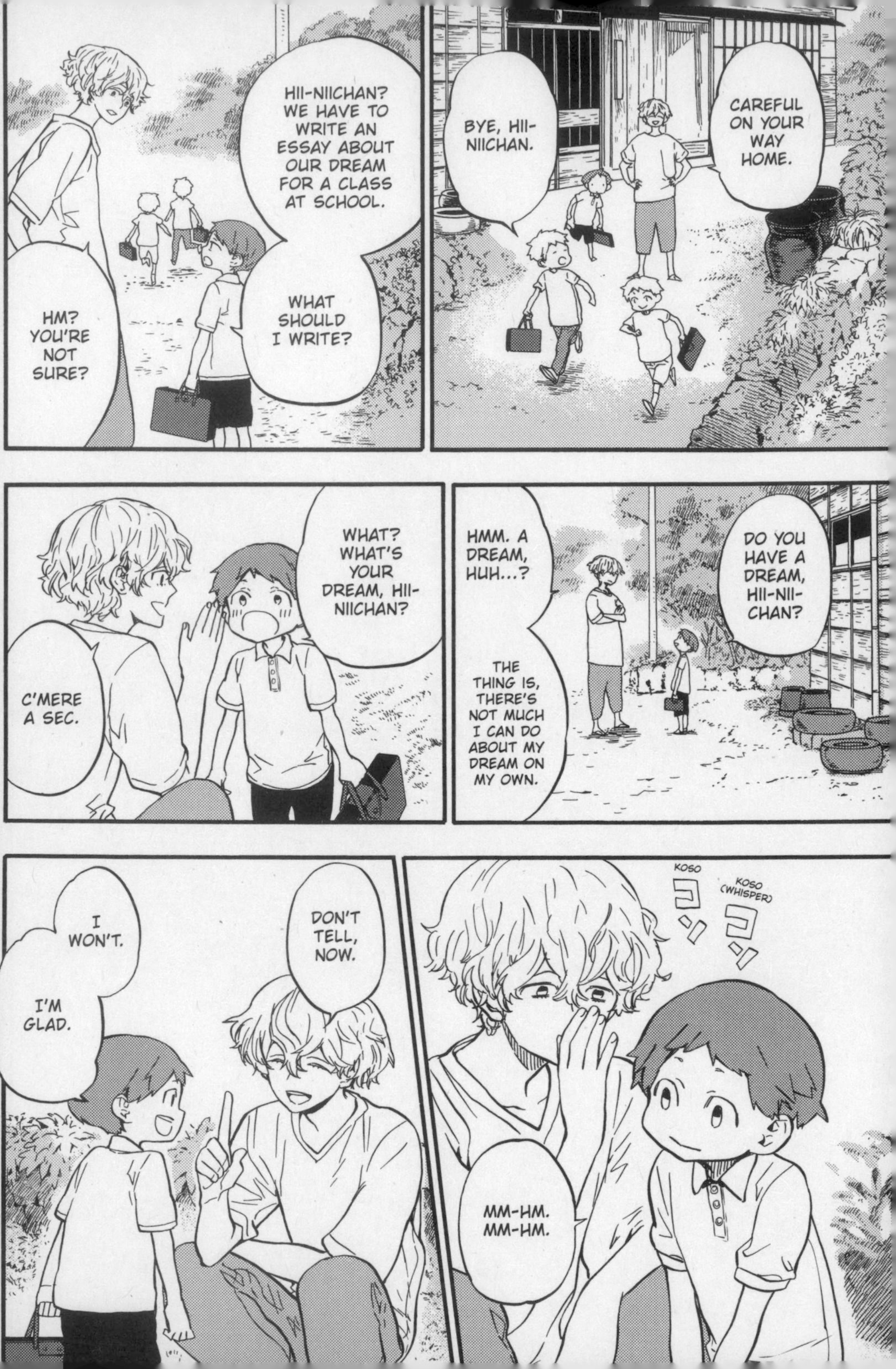
CAREFUL ON YOUR WAY HOME.
BYE, HII-NIICHAN.
HII-NIICHAN? WE HAVE TO WRITE AN ESSAY ABOUT OUR DREAM FOR A CLASS AT SCHOOL.
WHAT SHOULD I WRITE?
HM? YOU'RE NOT SURE?
DO YOU HAVE A DREAM, HII-NII-CHAN?
HMM. A DREAM, HUH...?
THE THING IS, THERE'S NOT MUCH I CAN DO ABOUT MY DREAM ON MY OWN.
WHAT? WHAT'S YOUR DREAM, HII-NIICHAN?
C'MERE A SEC.
KOSO
KOSO (WHISPER)
MM-HM. MM-HM.
DON'T TELL, NOW.
I WON'T.
I'M GLAD.

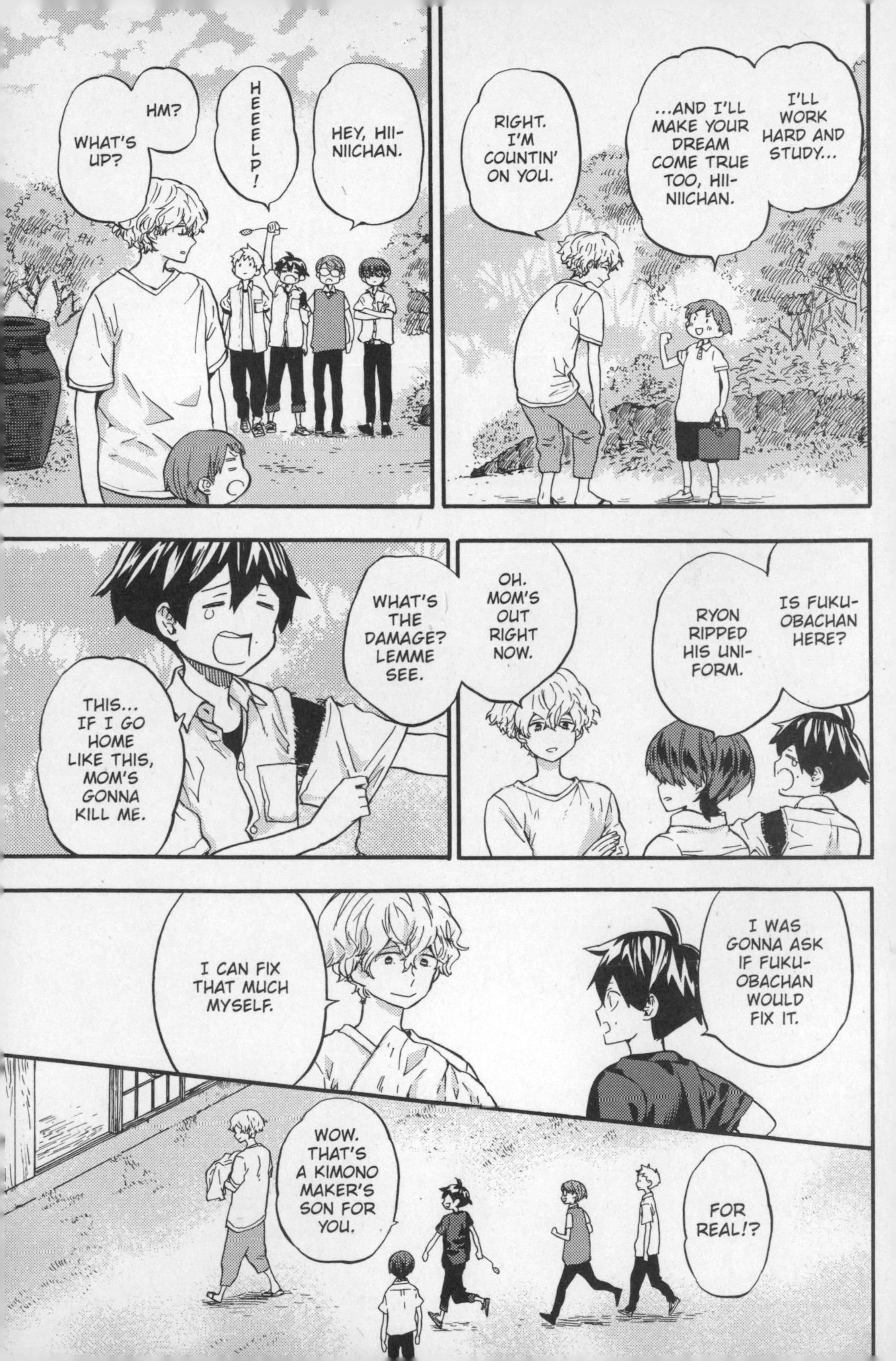
I'LL WORK HARD AND STUDY...
...AND I'LL MAKE YOUR DREAM COME TRUE TOO, HII-NIICHAN.
RIGHT. I'M COUNTIN' ON YOU.
HEY, HII-NIICHAN.
HEEEELP!
HM? WHAT'S UP?
IS FUKU-OBACHAN HERE?
RYON RIPPED HIS UNI-FORM.
OH. MOM'S OUT RIGHT NOW.
WHAT'S THE DAMAGE? LEMME SEE.
THIS... IF I GO HOME LIKE THIS, MOM'S GONNA KILL ME.
I WAS GONNA ASK IF FUKU-OBACHAN WOULD FIX IT.
I CAN FIX THAT MUCH MYSELF.
FOR REAL!?
WOW. THAT'S A KIMONO MAKER'S SON FOR YOU.

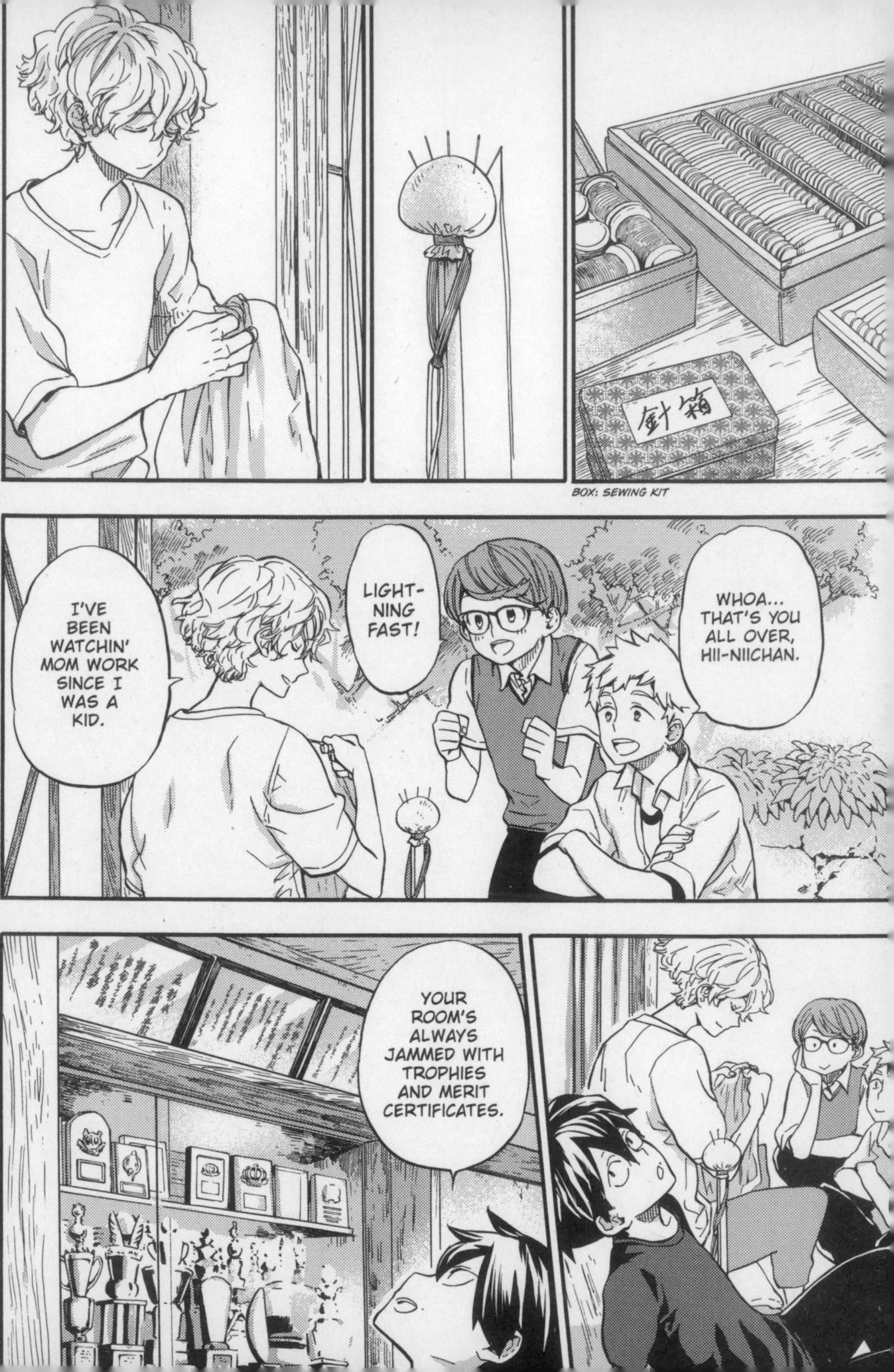
針箱
BOX: SEWING KIT
WHOA... THAT'S YOU ALL OVER, HII-NIICHAN.
LIGHT-NING FAST!
I'VE BEEN WATCHIN' MOM WORK SINCE I WAS A KID.
YOUR ROOM'S ALWAYS JAMMED WITH TROPHIES AND MERIT CERTIFICATES.

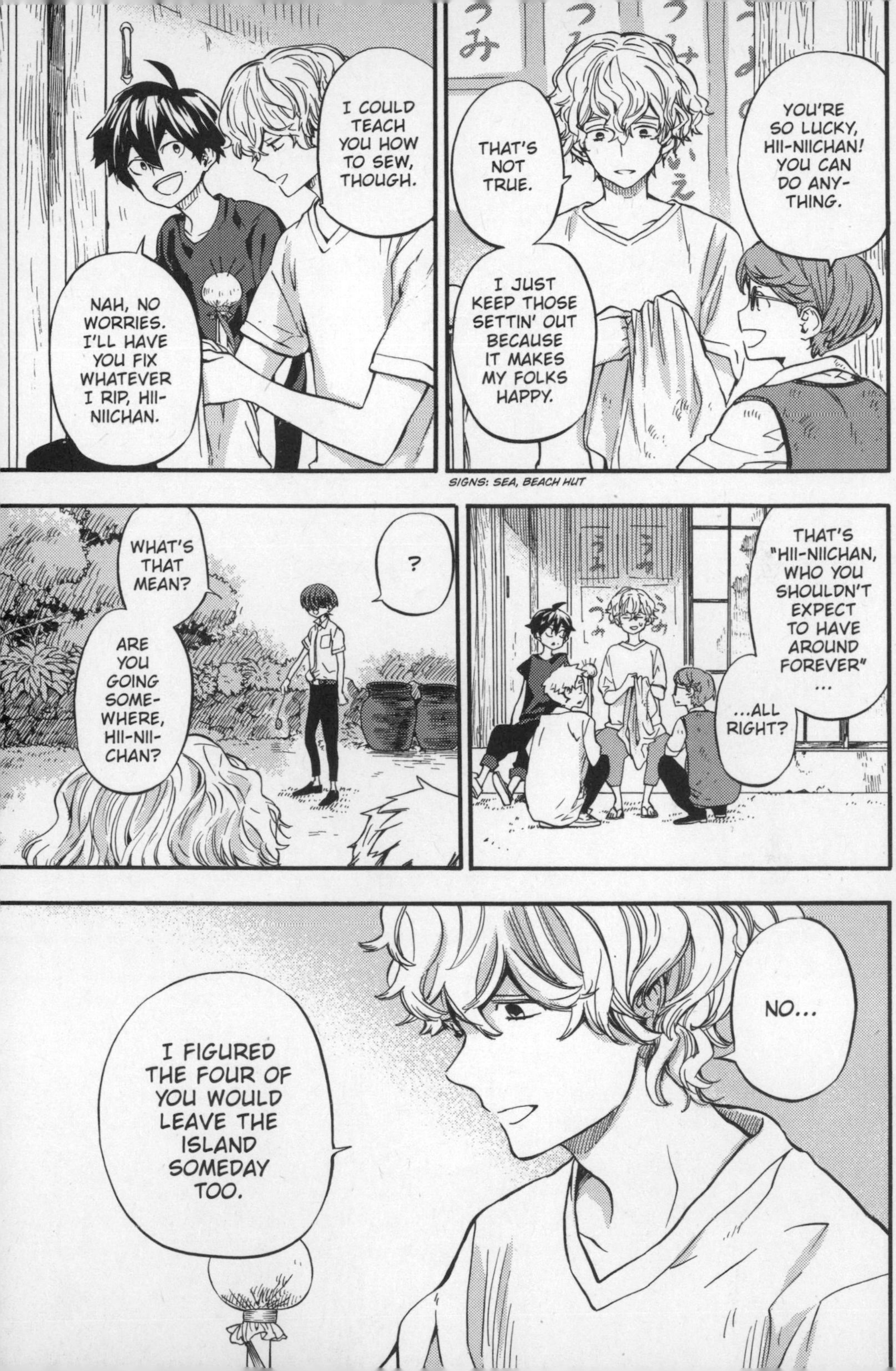
YOU'RE SO LUCKY, HII-NIICHAN! YOU CAN DO ANY-THING.
THAT'S NOT TRUE.
I JUST KEEP THOSE SETTIN' OUT BECAUSE IT MAKES MY FOLKS HAPPY.
I COULD TEACH YOU HOW TO SEW, THOUGH.
NAH, NO WORRIES. I'LL HAVE YOU FIX WHATEVER I RIP, HII-NIICHAN.
SIGNS: SEA, BEACH HUT
THAT'S "HII-NIICHAN, WHO YOU SHOULDN'T EXPECT TO HAVE AROUND FOREVER"...
...ALL RIGHT?
?
WHAT'S THAT MEAN?
ARE YOU GOING SOME-WHERE, HII-NII-CHAN?
NO...
I FIGURED THE FOUR OF YOU WOULD LEAVE THE ISLAND SOMEDAY TOO.

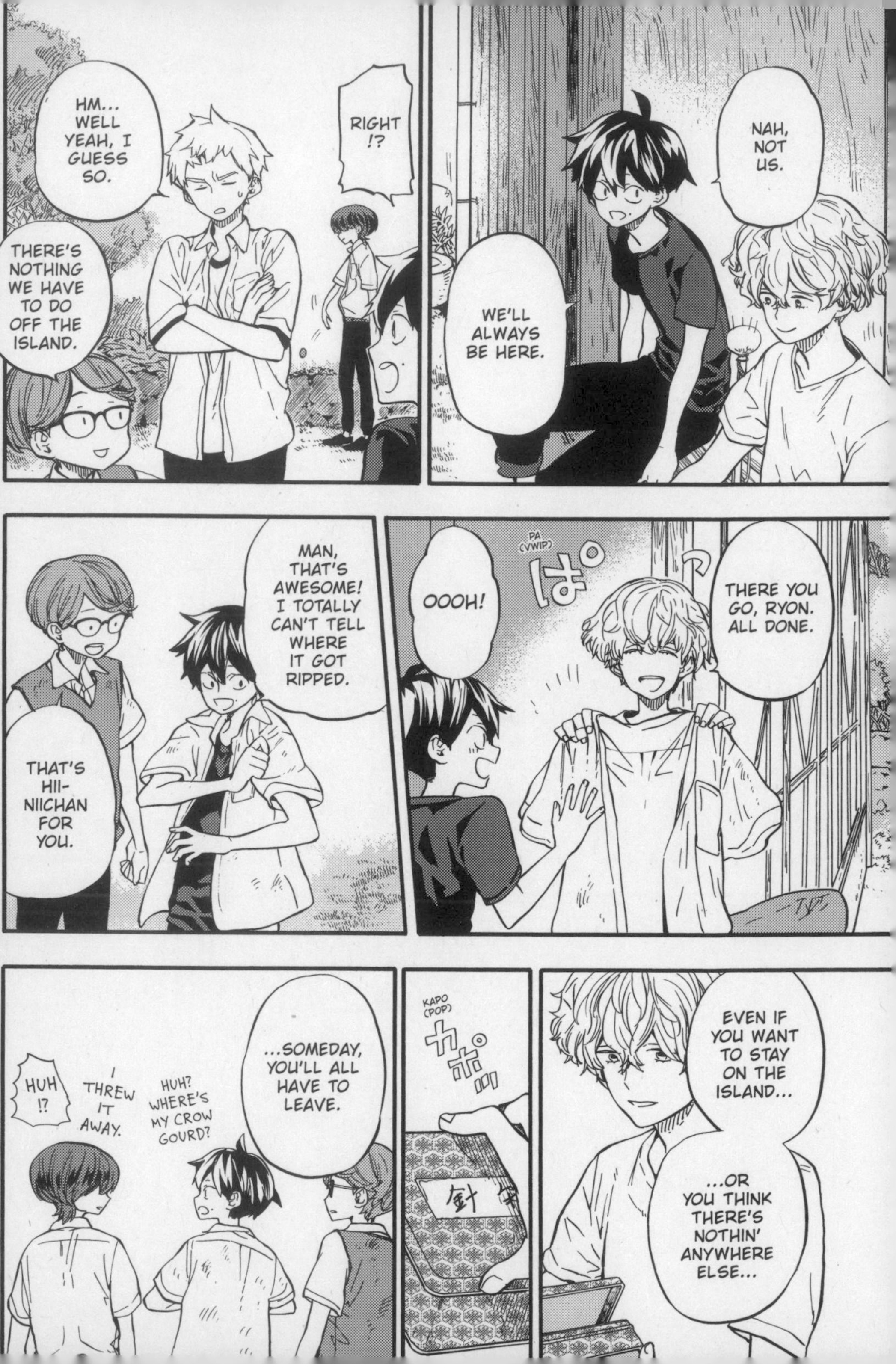
NAH, NOT US.
WE'LL ALWAYS BE HERE.
RIGHT !?
HM... WELL YEAH, I GUESS SO.
THERE'S NOTHING WE HAVE TO DO OFF THE ISLAND.
THERE YOU GO, RYON. ALL DONE.
PA (VWIP)
ぱっ
OOOH!
MAN, THAT'S AWESOME! I TOTALLY CAN'T TELL WHERE IT GOT RIPPED.
THAT'S HII-NIICHAN FOR YOU.
EVEN IF YOU WANT TO STAY ON THE ISLAND...
...OR YOU THINK THERE'S NOTHIN' ANYWHERE ELSE...
KAPO (POP)
カポッ
...SOMEDAY, YOU'LL ALL HAVE TO LEAVE.
HUH? WHERE'S MY CROW GOURD?
I THREW IT AWAY.
HUH !?

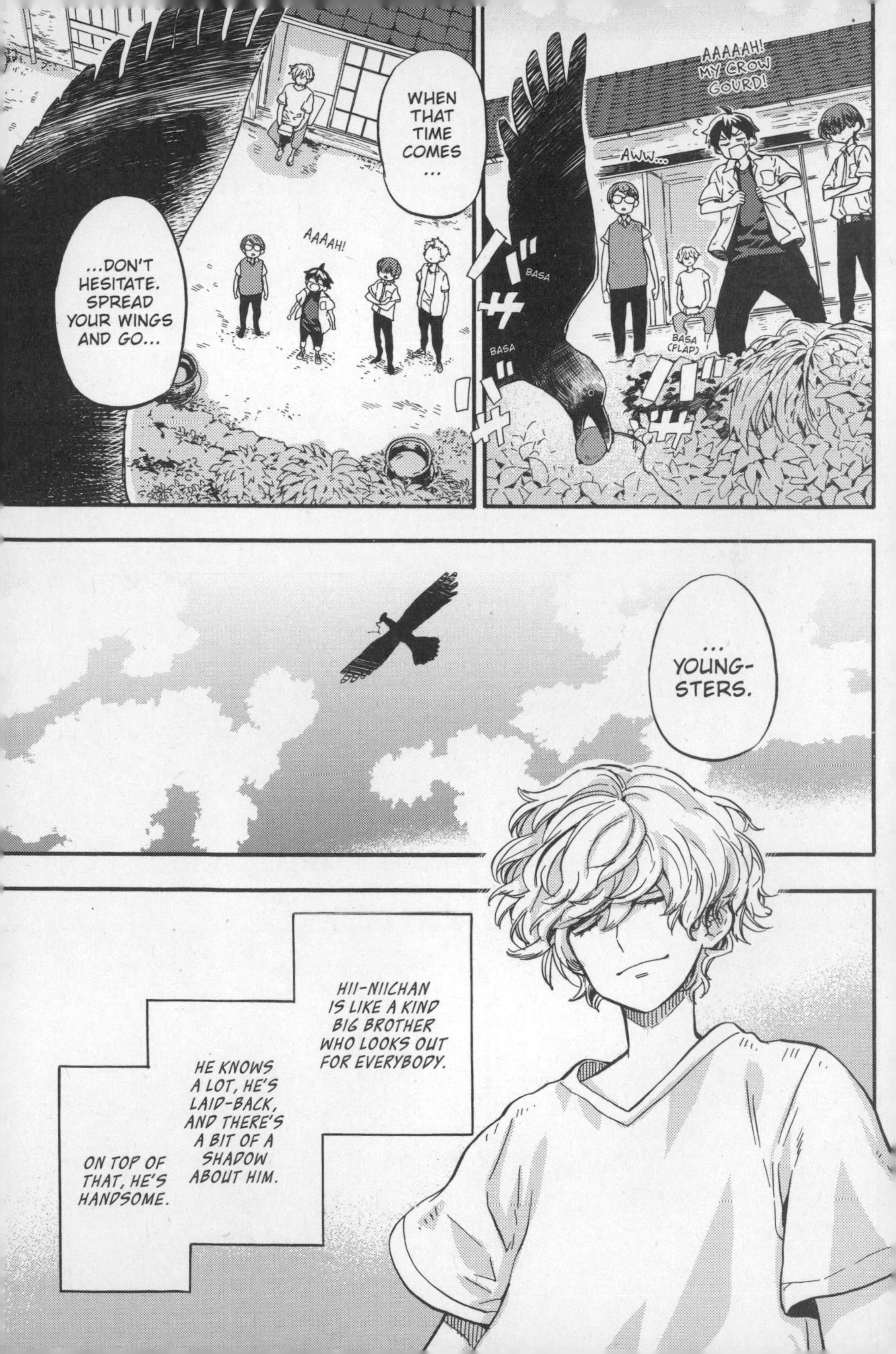
AAAAAH! MY CROW GOURD!
AWW...
BASA
BASA
BASA (FLAP)
WHEN THAT TIME COMES ...
AAAAH!
...DON'T HESITATE. SPREAD YOUR WINGS AND GO...
... YOUNGSTERS.
HII-NIICHAN IS LIKE A KIND BIG BROTHER WHO LOOKS OUT FOR EVERYBODY.
HE KNOWS A LOT, HE'S LAID-BACK, AND THERE'S A BIT OF A SHADOW ABOUT HIM.
ON TOP OF THAT, HE'S HANDSOME.

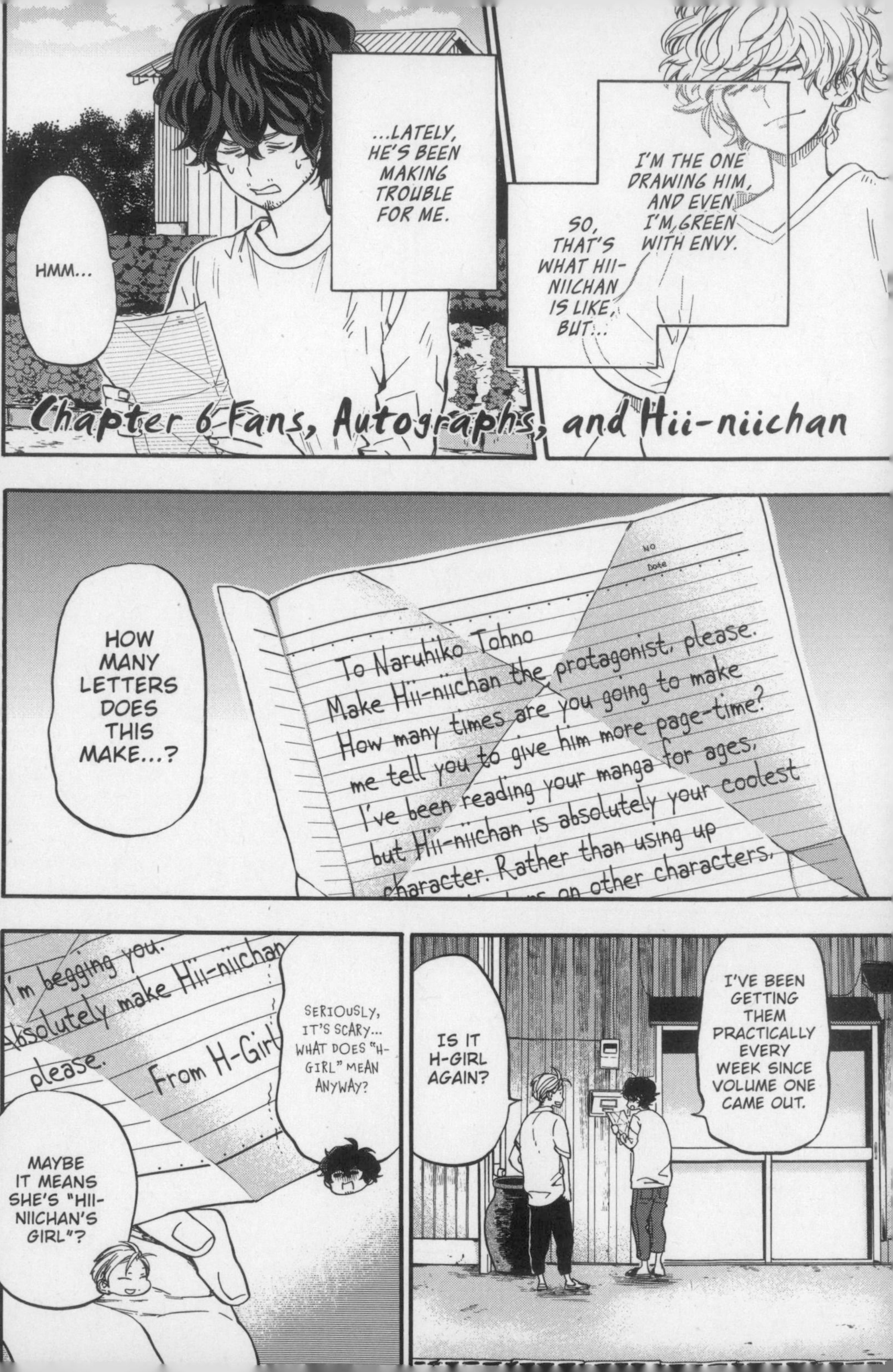
I'M THE ONE DRAWING HIM, AND EVEN I'M GREEN WITH ENVY.
SO, THAT'S WHAT HII-NIICHAN IS LIKE, BUT...
...LATELY, HE'S BEEN MAKING TROUBLE FOR ME.
HMM...
Chapter 6 Fans, Autographs, and Hii-niichan
NO
Date
To Naruhiko Tohno
Make Hii-niichan the protagonist, please.
How many times are you going to make
me tell you to give him more page-time?
I've been reading your manga for ages,
but Hii-niichan is absolutely your coolest
character. Rather than using up
HOW MANY LETTERS DOES THIS MAKE...?
I'VE BEEN GETTING THEM PRACTICALLY EVERY WEEK SINCE VOLUME ONE CAME OUT.
IS IT H-GIRL AGAIN?
I'm begging you.
Absolutely make Hii-niichan
please.
From H-Girl
SERIOUSLY, IT'S SCARY... WHAT DOES "H-GIRL" MEAN ANYWAY?
MAYBE IT MEANS SHE'S "HII-NIICHAN'S GIRL"?

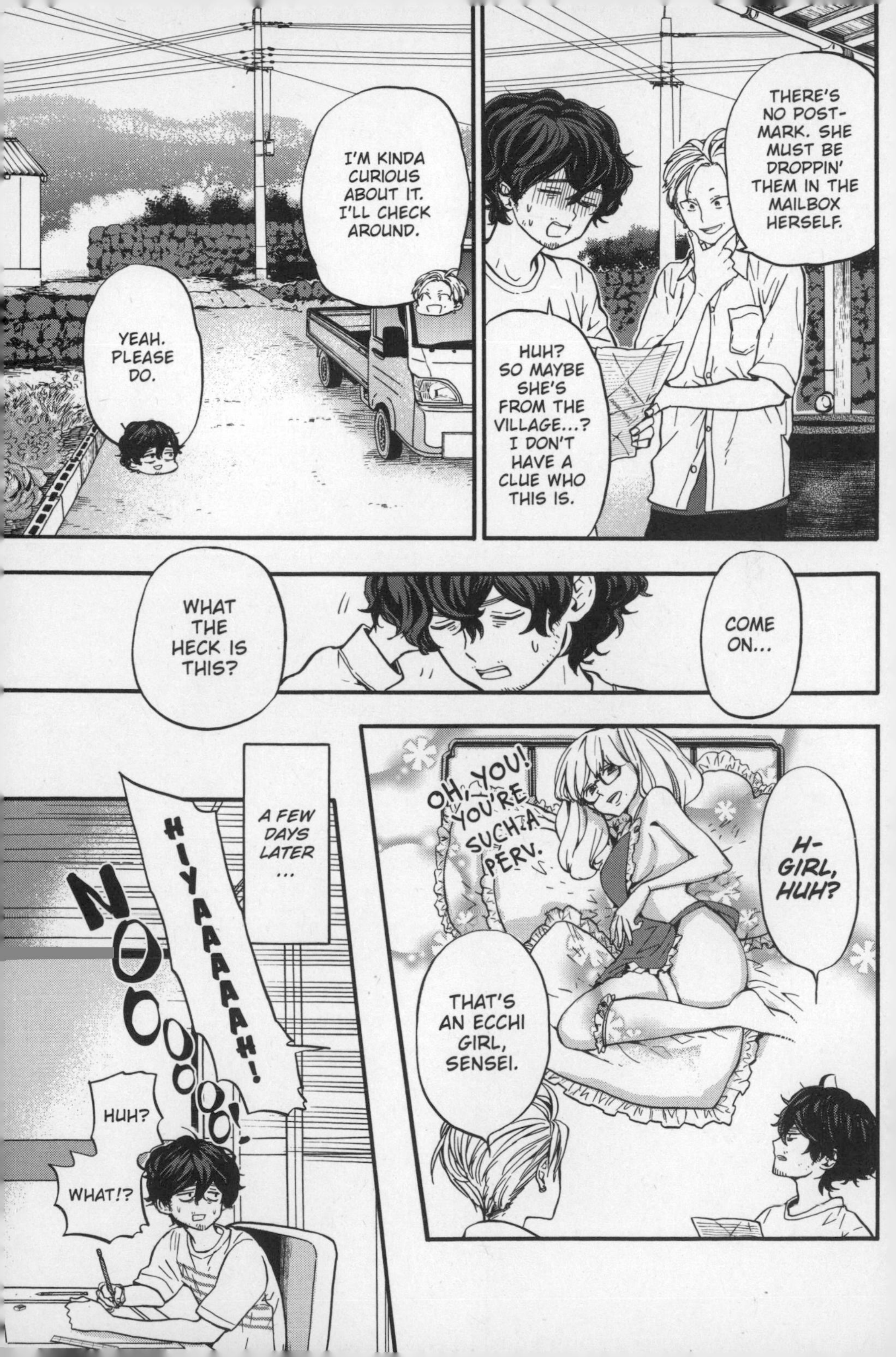
THERE'S NO POST-MARK. SHE MUST BE DROPPIN' THEM IN THE MAILBOX HERSELF.
HUH? SO MAYBE SHE'S FROM THE VILLAGE...? I DON'T HAVE A CLUE WHO THIS IS.
I'M KINDA CURIOUS ABOUT IT. I'LL CHECK AROUND.
YEAH. PLEASE DO.
COME ON...
WHAT THE HECK IS THIS?
H-GIRL, HUH?
OH, YOU! YOU'RE SUCH A PERV.
THAT'S AN ECCHI GIRL, SENSEI.
A FEW DAYS LATER ...
HIYAAAAAH!
NOOOOOO!
HUH?
WHAT!?

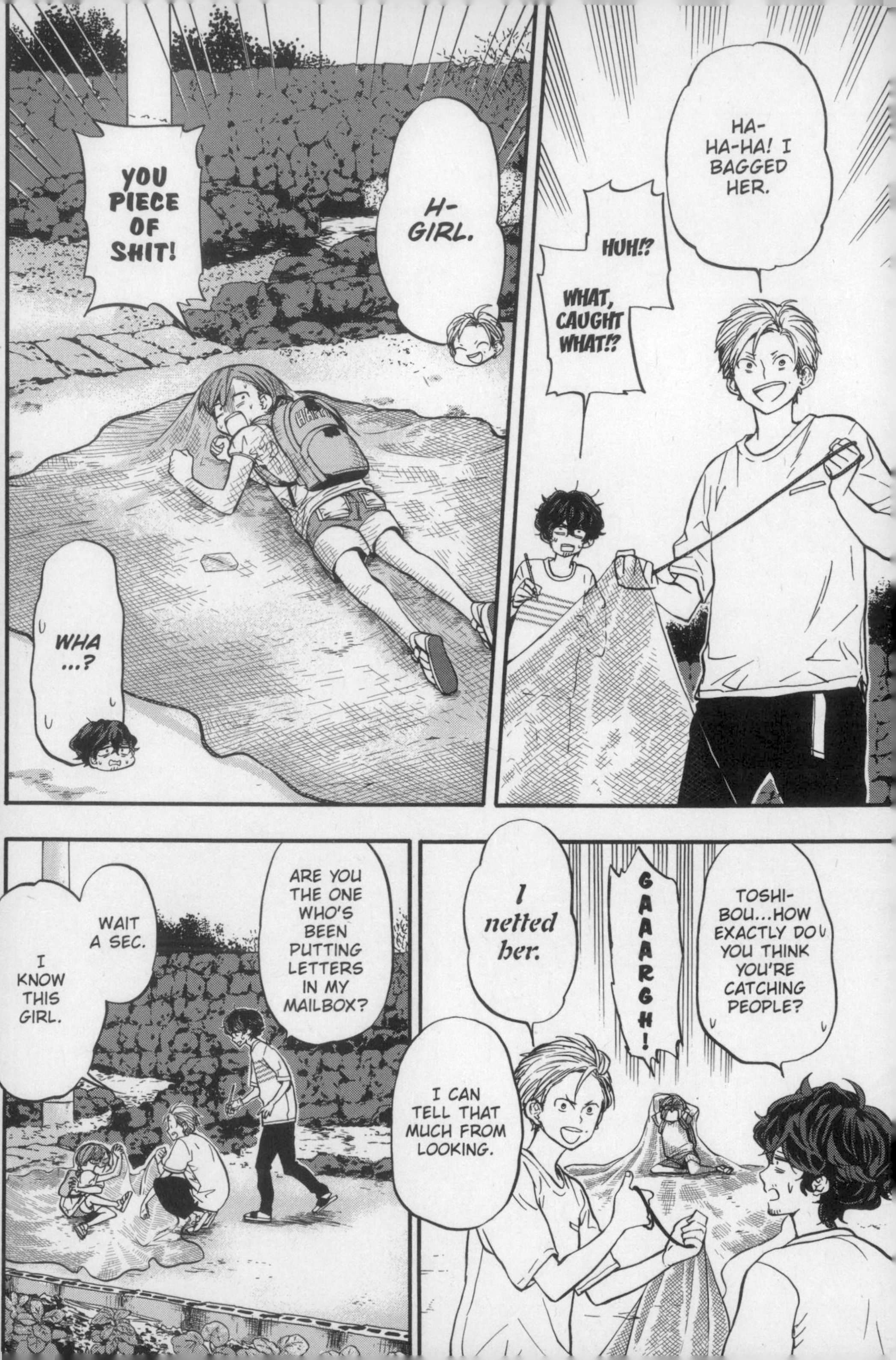
HA-HA-HA! I BAGGED HER.
HUH!?
WHAT, CAUGHT WHAT!?
H-GIRL.
YOU PIECE OF SHIT!
WHA...?
TOSHI-BOU...HOW EXACTLY DO YOU THINK YOU'RE CATCHING PEOPLE?
GAAARGH!
I netted her.
I CAN TELL THAT MUCH FROM LOOKING.
ARE YOU THE ONE WHO'S BEEN PUTTING LETTERS IN MY MAILBOX?
WAIT A SEC.
I KNOW THIS GIRL.

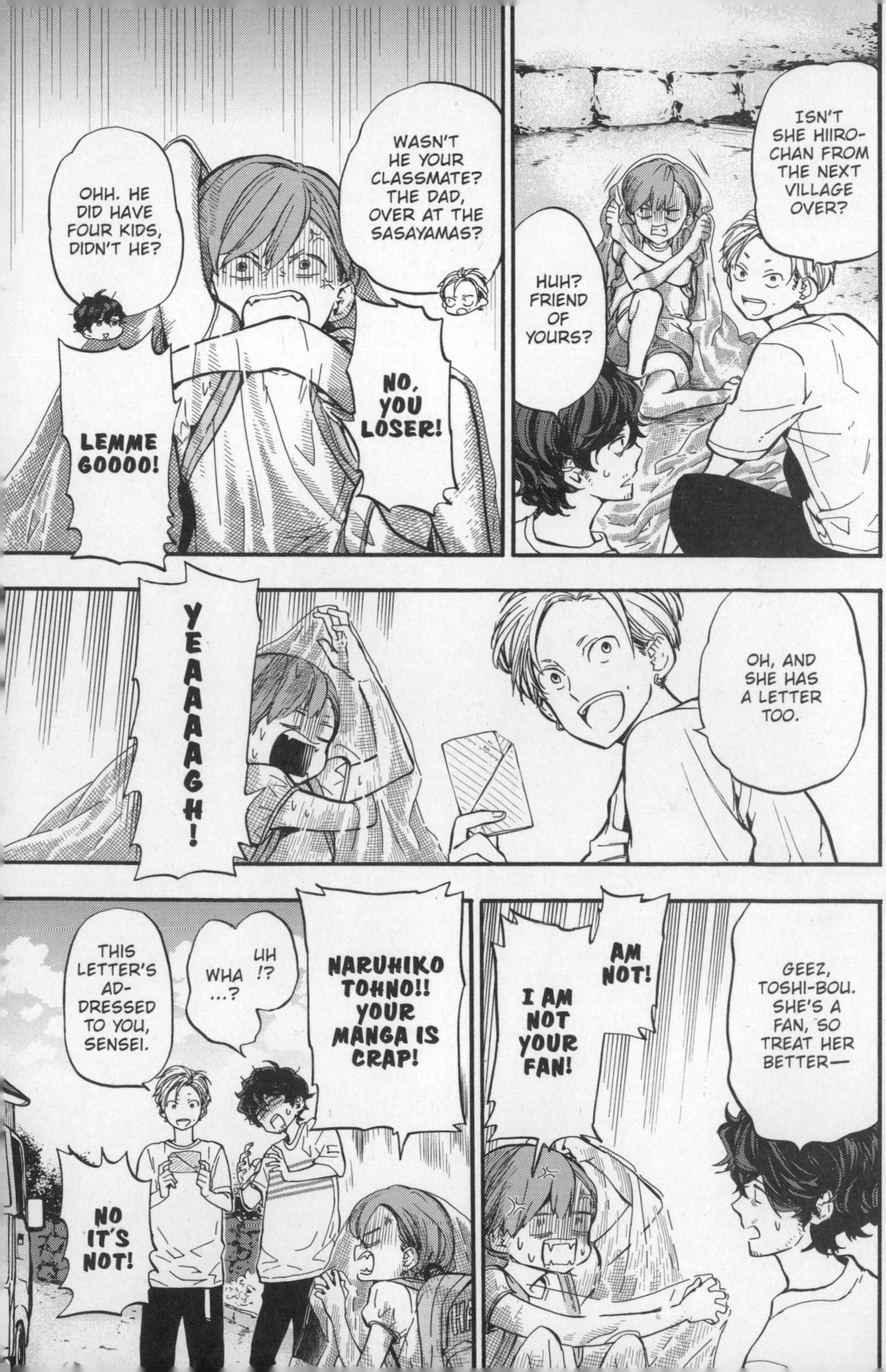
ISN'T SHE HIIRO-CHAN FROM THE NEXT VILLAGE OVER?
HUH? FRIEND OF YOURS?
WASN'T HE YOUR CLASSMATE? THE DAD, OVER AT THE SASAYAMAS?
OHH. HE DID HAVE FOUR KIDS, DIDN'T HE?
NO, YOU LOSER!
LEMME GOOOO!
OH, AND SHE HAS A LETTER TOO.
YEAAAAAGH!
GEEZ, TOSHI-BOU. SHE'S A FAN, SO TREAT HER BETTER—
AM NOT!
I AM NOT YOUR FAN!
NARUHIKO TOHNO!! YOUR MANGA IS CRAP!
UH !?
WHA ...?
THIS LETTER'S ADDRESSED TO YOU, SENSEI.
NO IT'S NOT!

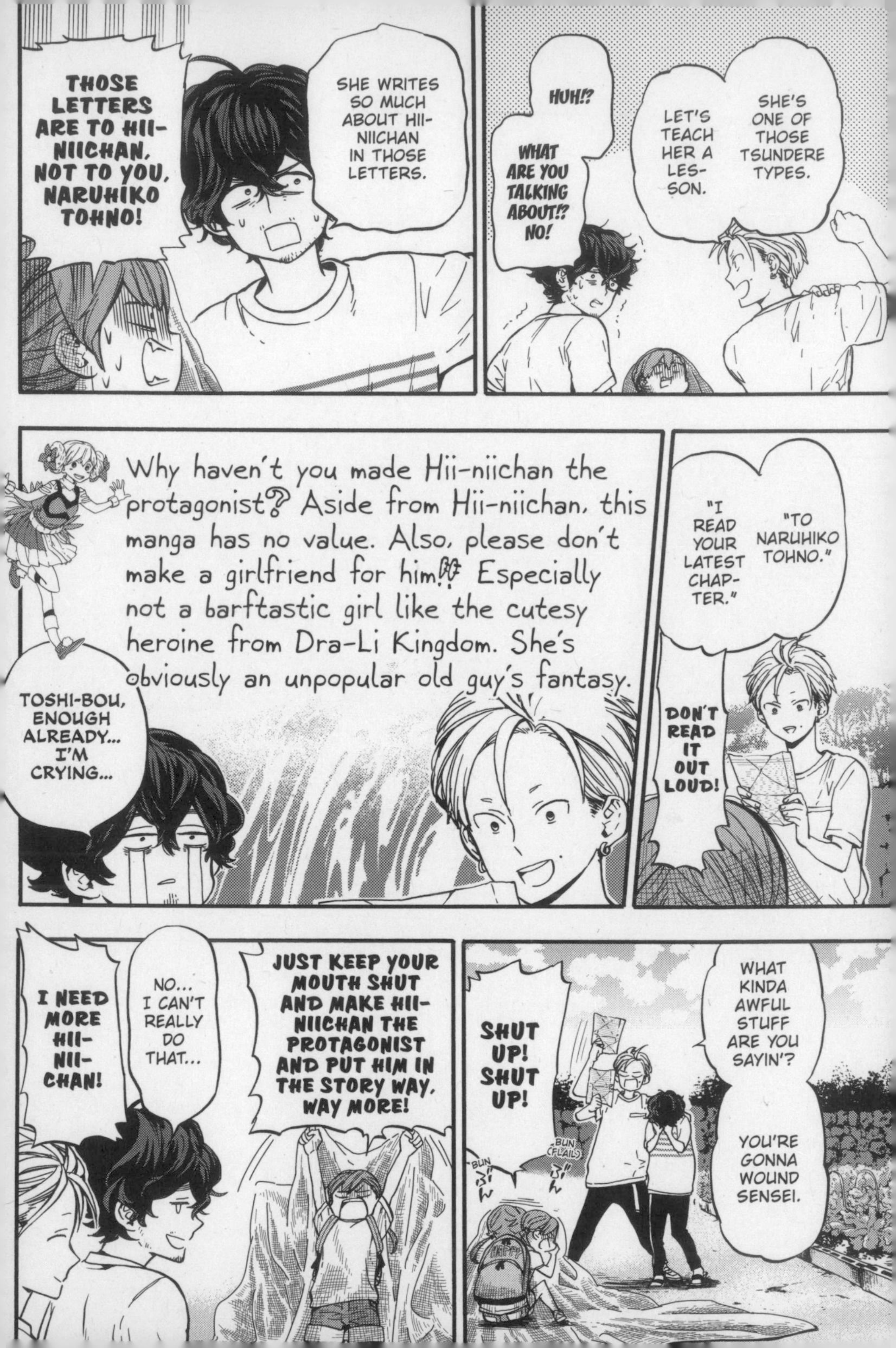
SHE'S ONE OF THOSE TSUNDERE TYPES.
LET'S TEACH HER A LES-SON.
HUH!?
WHAT ARE YOU TALKING ABOUT!? NO!
SHE WRITES SO MUCH ABOUT HII-NIICHAN IN THOSE LETTERS.
THOSE LETTERS ARE TO HII-NIICHAN, NOT TO YOU, NARUHIKO TOHNO!
"TO NARUHIKO TOHNO."
"I READ YOUR LATEST CHAP-TER."
DON'T READ IT OUT LOUD!
Why haven't you made Hii-niichan the protagonist? Aside from Hii-niichan, this manga has no value. Also, please don't make a girlfriend for him!! Especially not a barftastic girl like the cutesy heroine from Dra-Li Kingdom. She's obviously an unpopular old guy's fantasy.
TOSHI-BOU, ENOUGH ALREADY... I'M CRYING...
WHAT KINDA AWFUL STUFF ARE YOU SAYIN'?
YOU'RE GONNA WOUND SENSEI.
SHUT UP! SHUT UP!
BUN (FLAIL) ぶん
BUN ぶん
JUST KEEP YOUR MOUTH SHUT AND MAKE HII-NIICHAN THE PROTAGONIST AND PUT HIM IN THE STORY WAY, WAY MORE!
NO... I CAN'T REALLY DO THAT...
I NEED MORE HII-NII-CHAN!

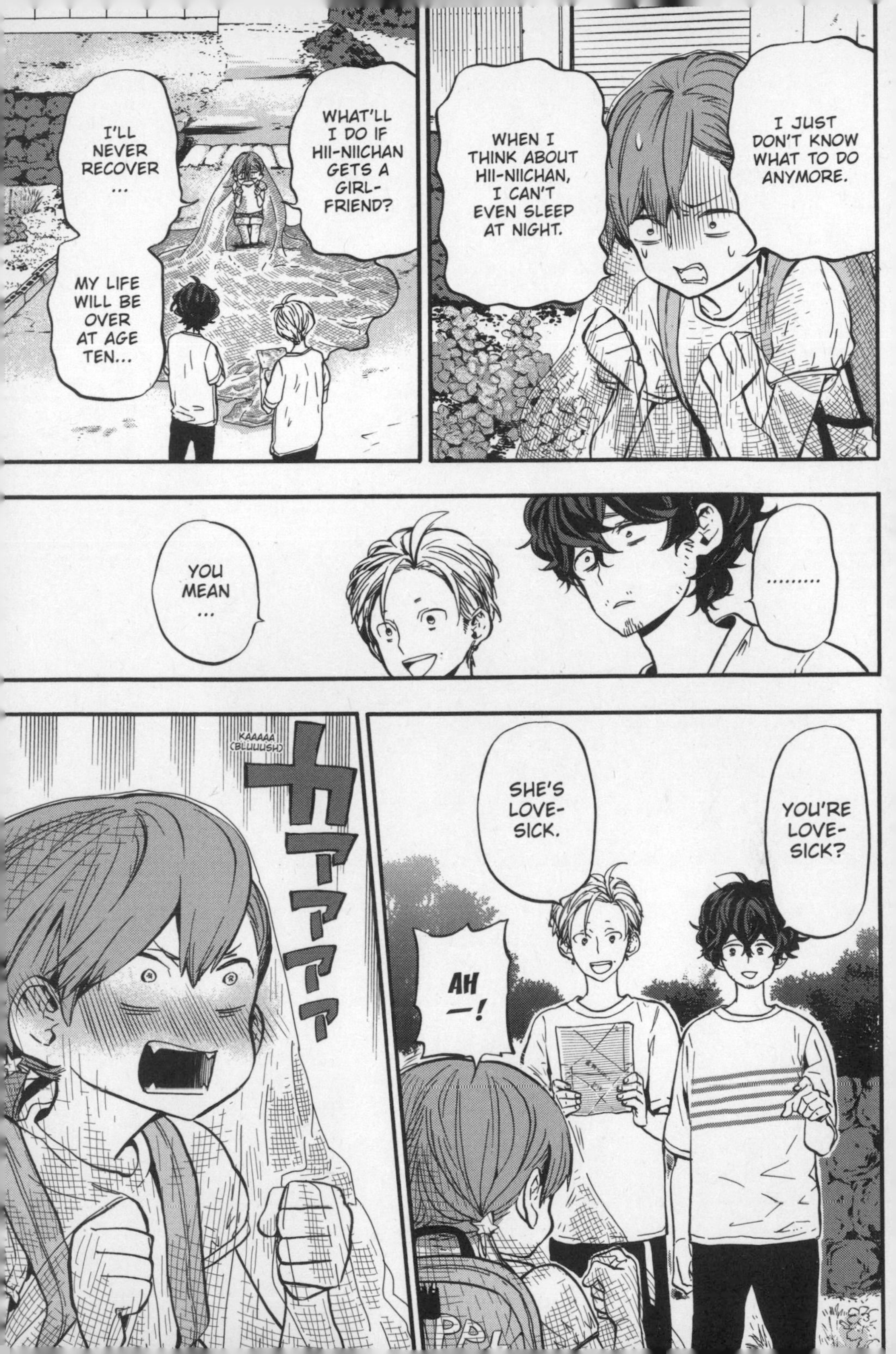
I JUST DON'T KNOW WHAT TO DO ANYMORE.
WHEN I THINK ABOUT HII-NIICHAN, I CAN'T EVEN SLEEP AT NIGHT.
WHAT'LL I DO IF HII-NIICHAN GETS A GIRL-FRIEND?
I'LL NEVER RECOVER...
MY LIFE WILL BE OVER AT AGE TEN...
....
YOU MEAN...
YOU'RE LOVE-SICK?
SHE'S LOVE-SICK.
AH—!
KAAAAA (BLUUUSH)
カァァァ

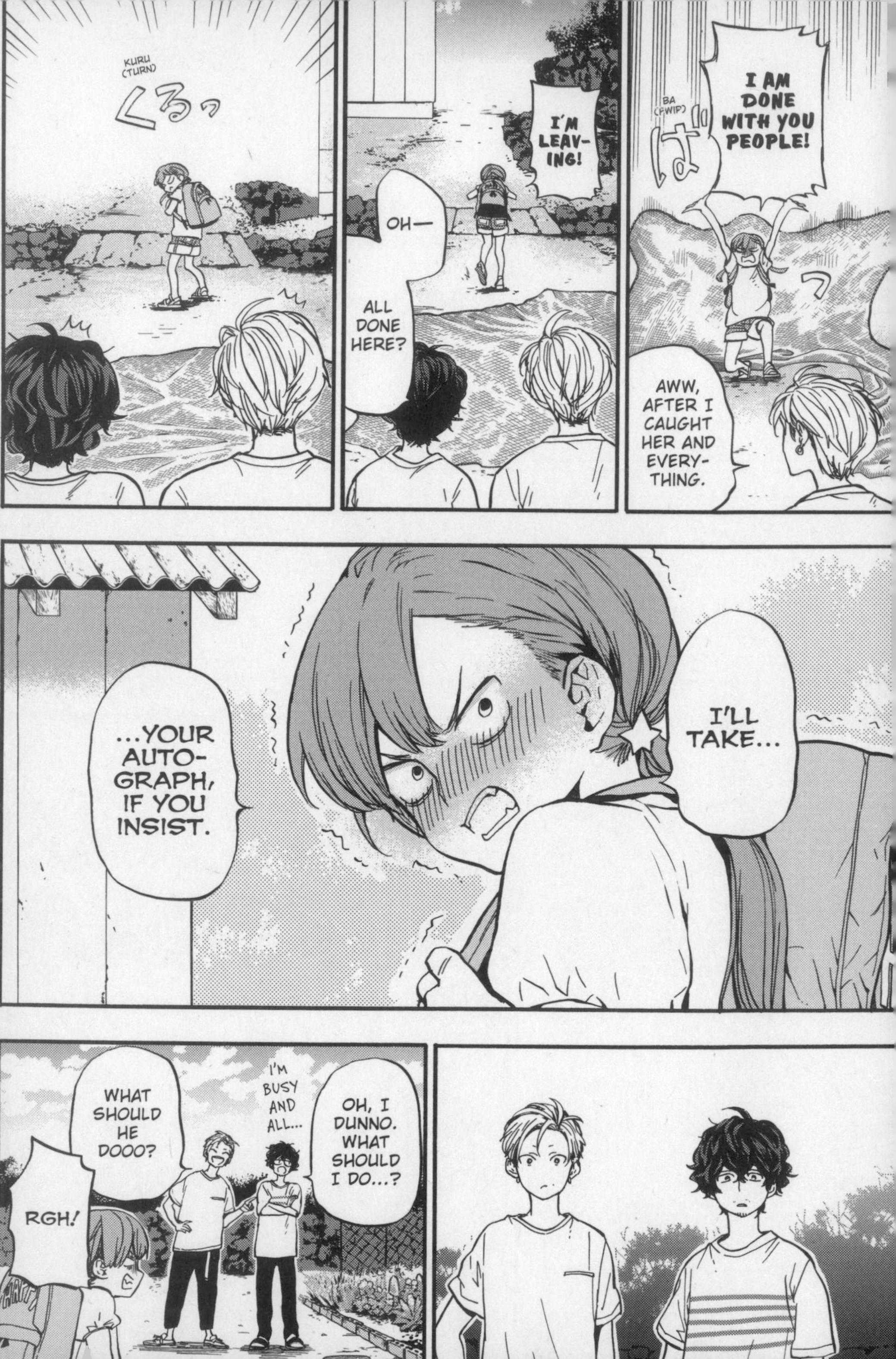
BA (FWIP)
ば
I AM DONE WITH YOU PEOPLE!
AWW, AFTER I CAUGHT HER AND EVERYTHING.
I'M LEAVING!
OH—
ALL DONE HERE?
KURU (TURN)
くるっ
I'LL TAKE...
...YOUR AUTOGRAPH, IF YOU INSIST.
OH, I DUNNO. WHAT SHOULD I DO...?
I'M BUSY AND ALL...
WHAT SHOULD HE DOOO?
RGH!

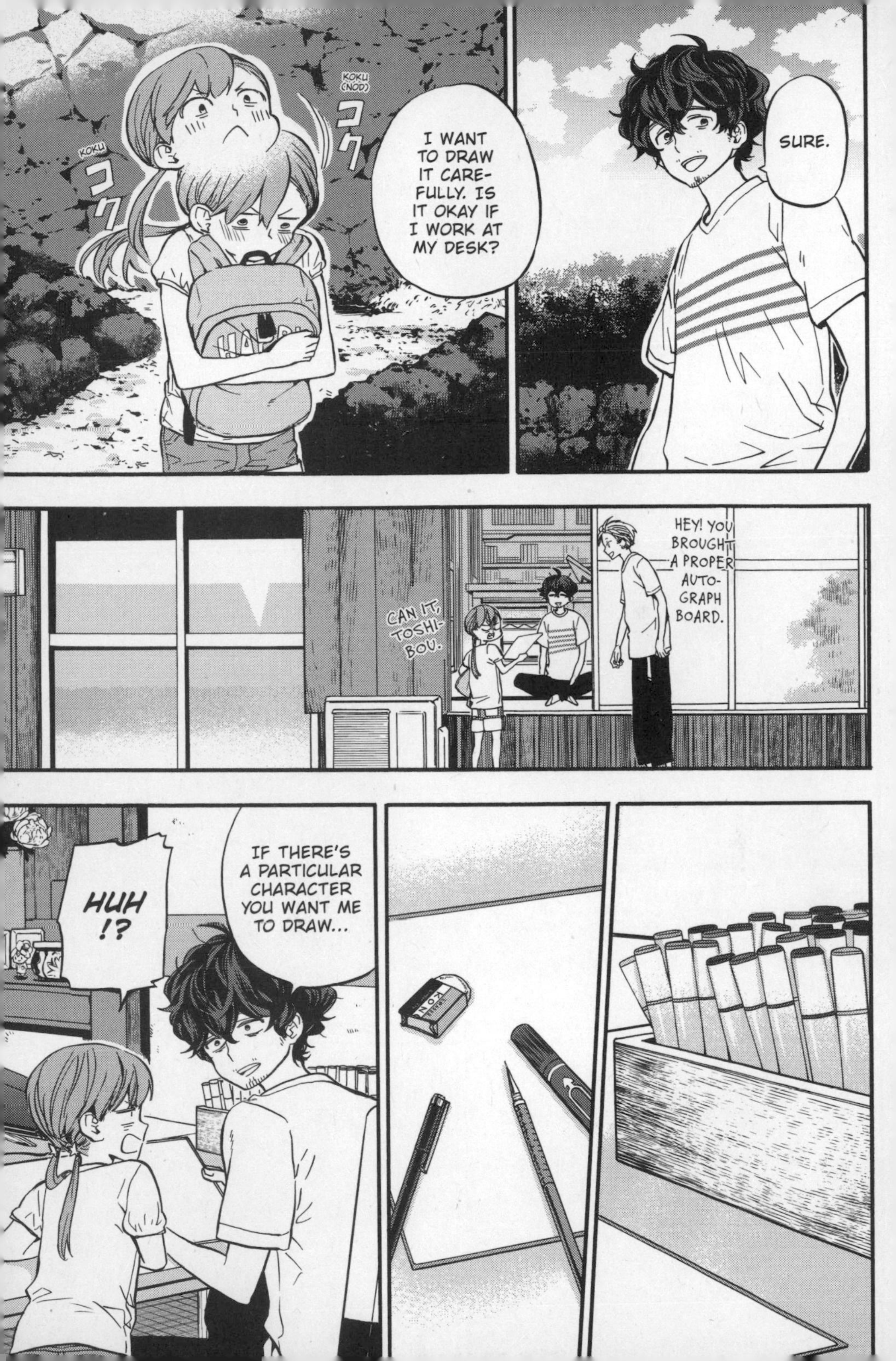
SURE.
I WANT TO DRAW IT CAREFULLY. IS IT OKAY IF I WORK AT MY DESK?
KOKU (NOD)
コク
KOKU
コク
HEY! YOU BROUGHT A PROPER AUTOGRAPH BOARD.
CAN IT, TOSHIBOU.
IF THERE'S A PARTICULAR CHARACTER YOU WANT ME TO DRAW...
HUH!?

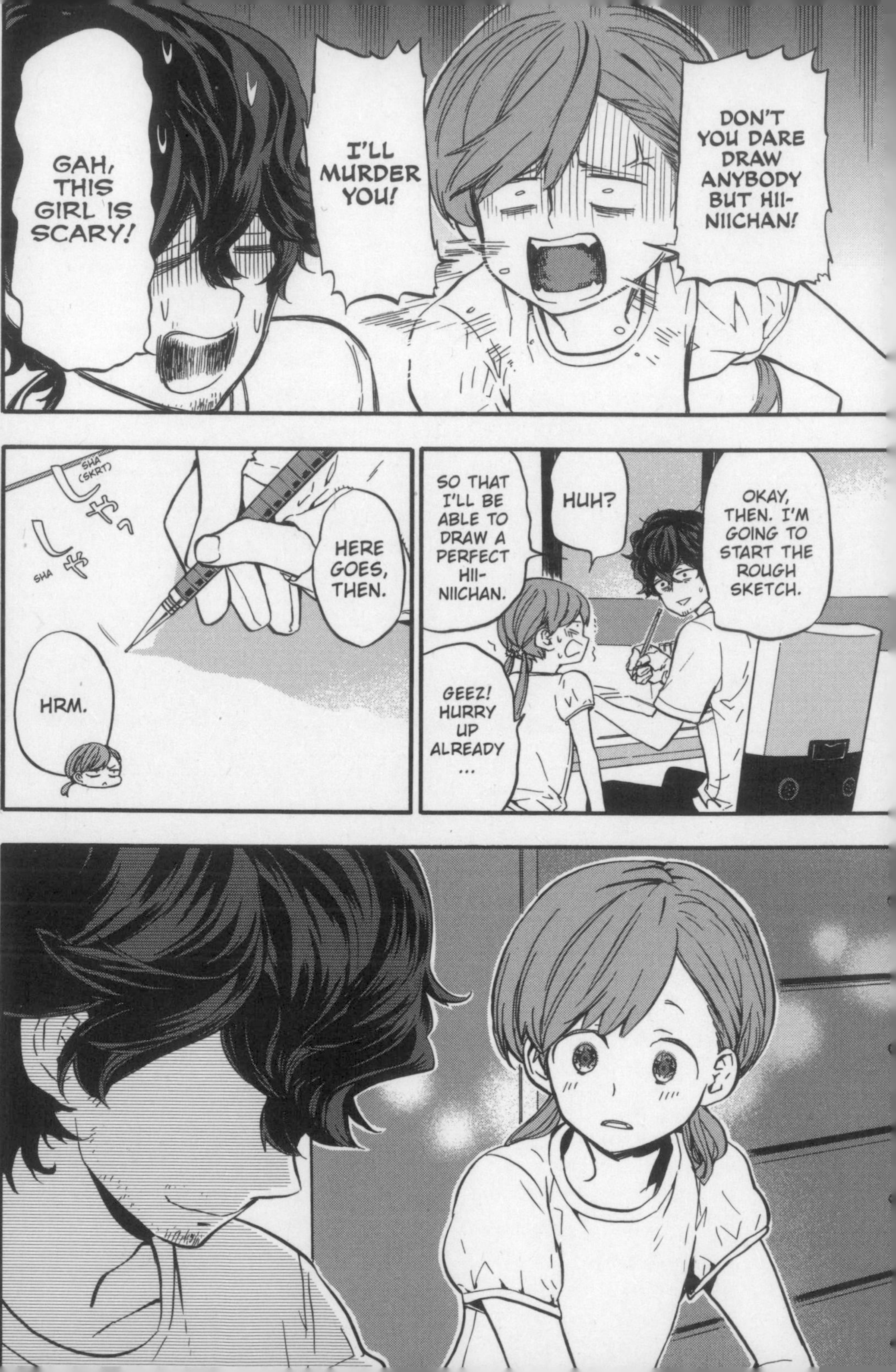
DON'T YOU DARE DRAW ANYBODY BUT HII-NIICHAN!
I'LL MURDER YOU!
GAH, THIS GIRL IS SCARY!
OKAY, THEN. I'M GOING TO START THE ROUGH SKETCH.
HUH?
SO THAT I'LL BE ABLE TO DRAW A PERFECT HII-NIICHAN.
GEEZ! HURRY UP ALREADY ...
しゃっ
SHA (SKRT)
しゃ
SHA
HERE GOES, THEN.
HRM.

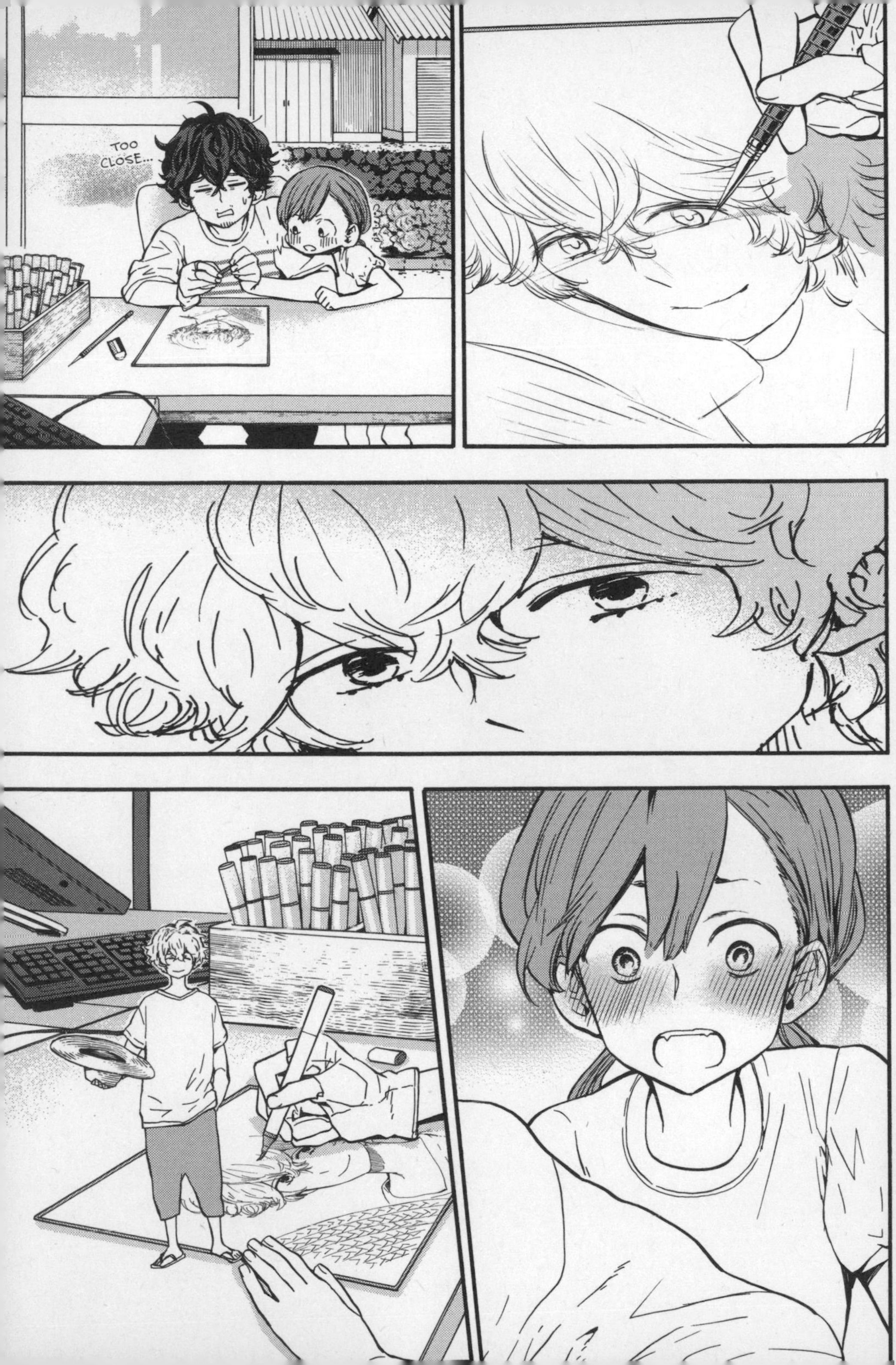
TOO CLOSE...

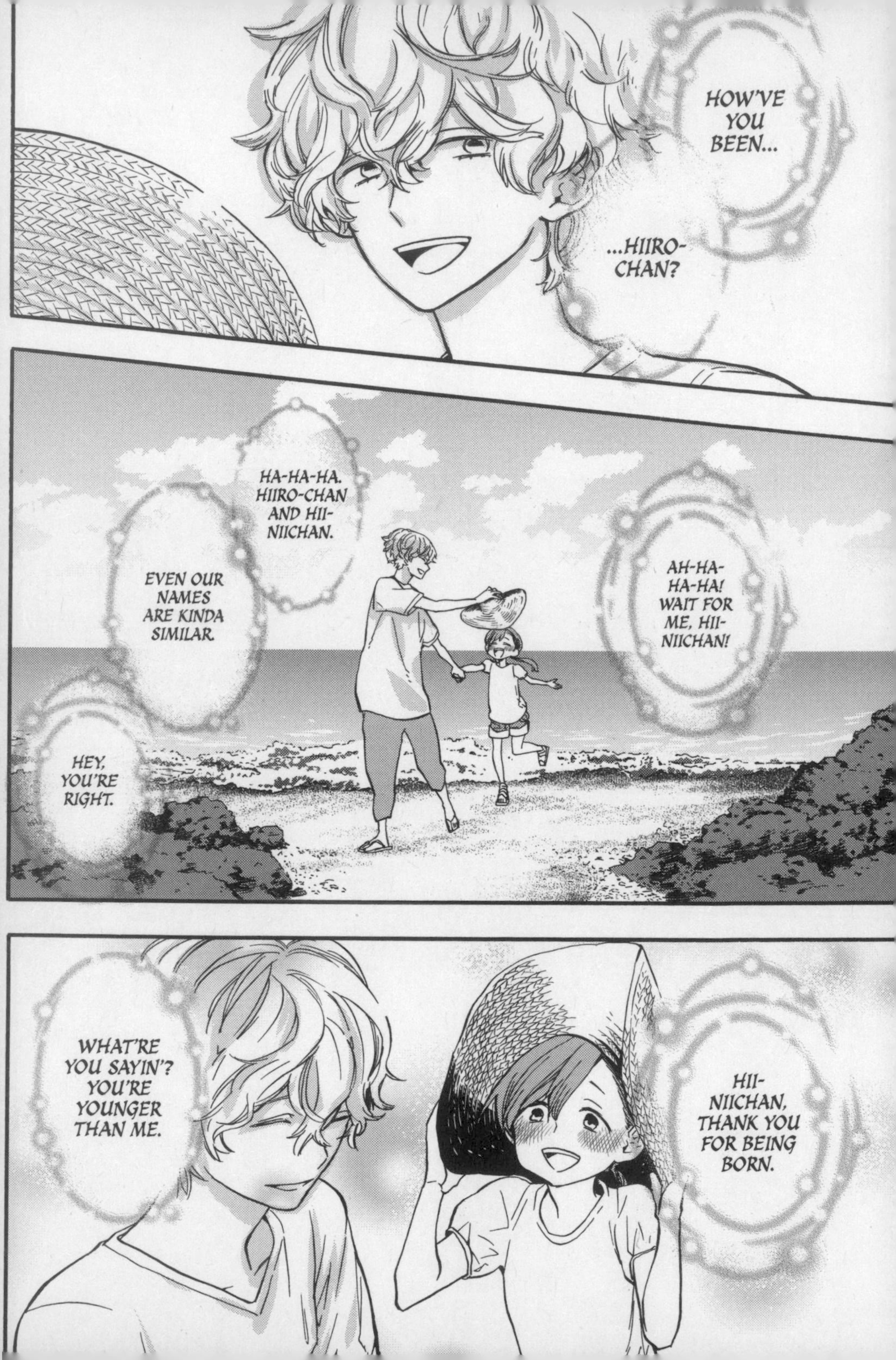
HOW'VE YOU BEEN...
...HIIRO-CHAN?
AH-HA-HA-HA! WAIT FOR ME, HII-NIICHAN!
HA-HA-HA. HIIRO-CHAN AND HII-NIICHAN.
EVEN OUR NAMES ARE KINDA SIMILAR.
HEY, YOU'RE RIGHT.
HII-NIICHAN, THANK YOU FOR BEING BORN.
WHAT'RE YOU SAYIN'? YOU'RE YOUNGER THAN ME.

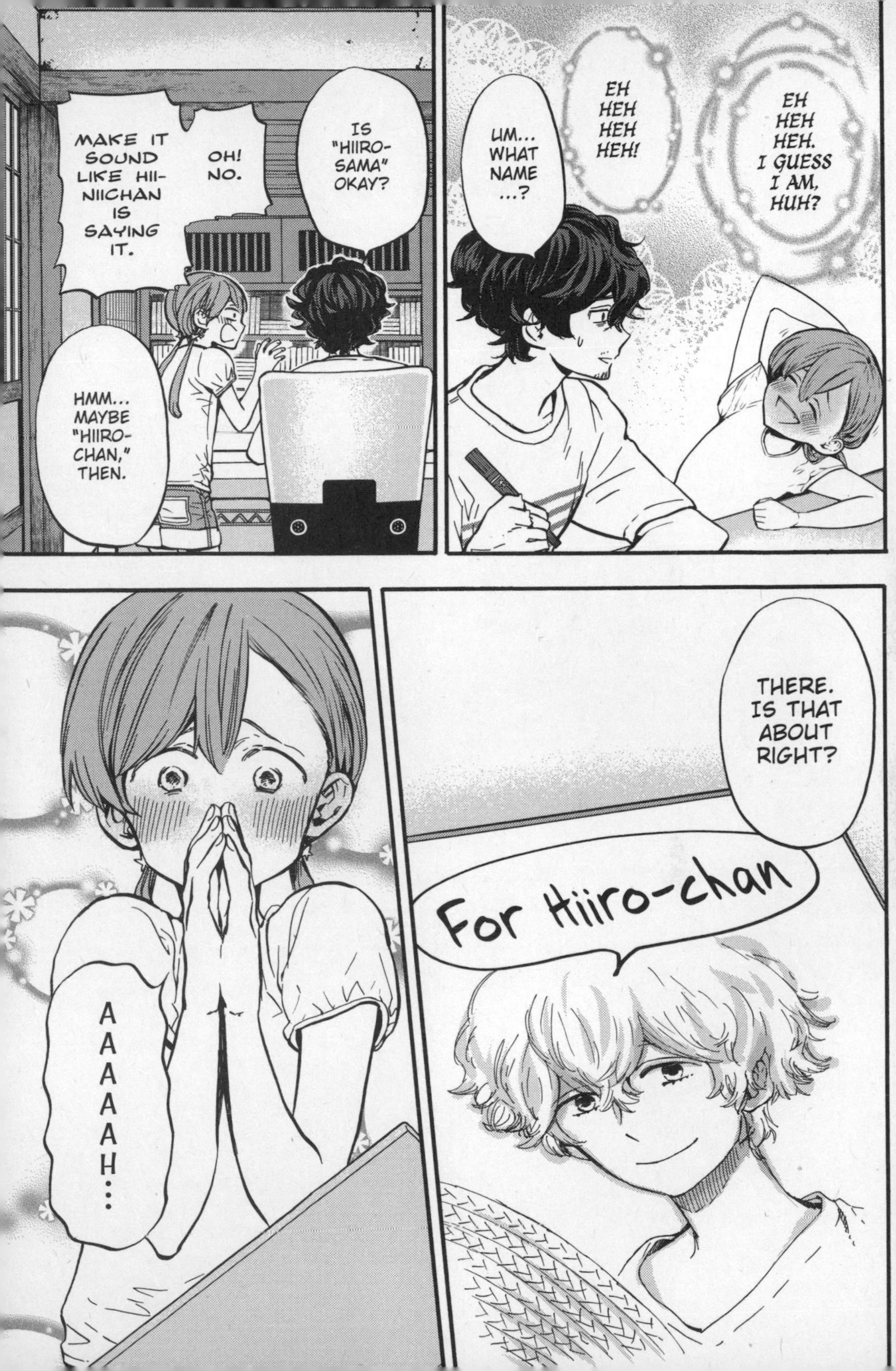

EH HEH HEH. I GUESS I AM, HUH?
EH HEH HEH HEH!
UM... WHAT NAME ...?
IS "HIIRO-SAMA" OKAY?
OH! NO.
MAKE IT SOUND LIKE HII-NIICHAN IS SAYING IT.
HMM... MAYBE "HIIRO-CHAN," THEN.
THERE. IS THAT ABOUT RIGHT?
For Hiiro-chan
AAAAAH...

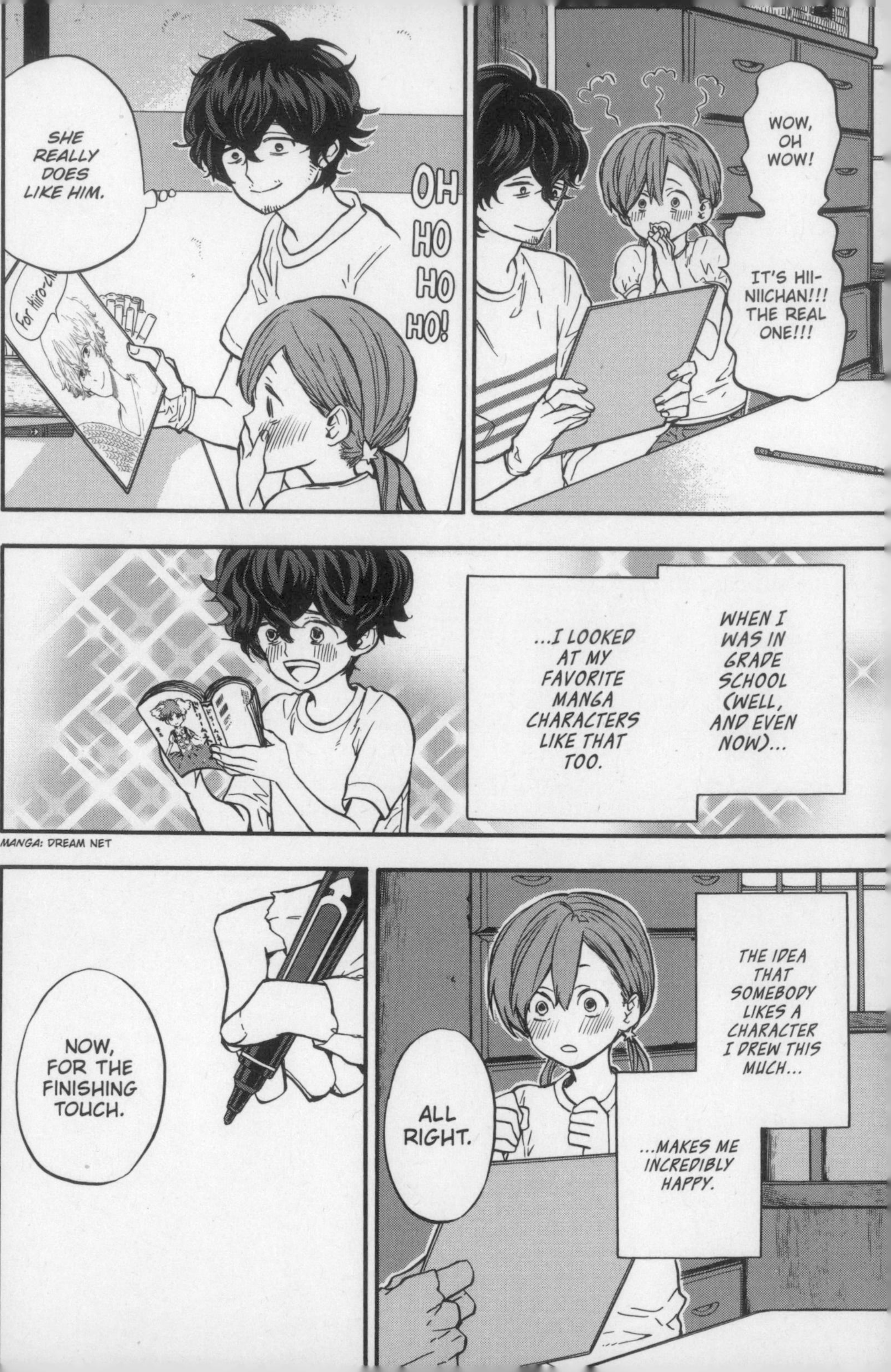
WOW, OH WOW!
IT'S HII-NIICHAN!!! THE REAL ONE!!!
SHE REALLY DOES LIKE HIM.
OH HO HO HO!
WHEN I WAS IN GRADE SCHOOL (WELL, AND EVEN NOW)...
...I LOOKED AT MY FAVORITE MANGA CHARACTERS LIKE THAT TOO.
MANGA: DREAM NET
THE IDEA THAT SOMEBODY LIKES A CHARACTER I DREW THIS MUCH...
...MAKES ME INCREDIBLY HAPPY.
ALL RIGHT.
NOW, FOR THE FINISHING TOUCH.

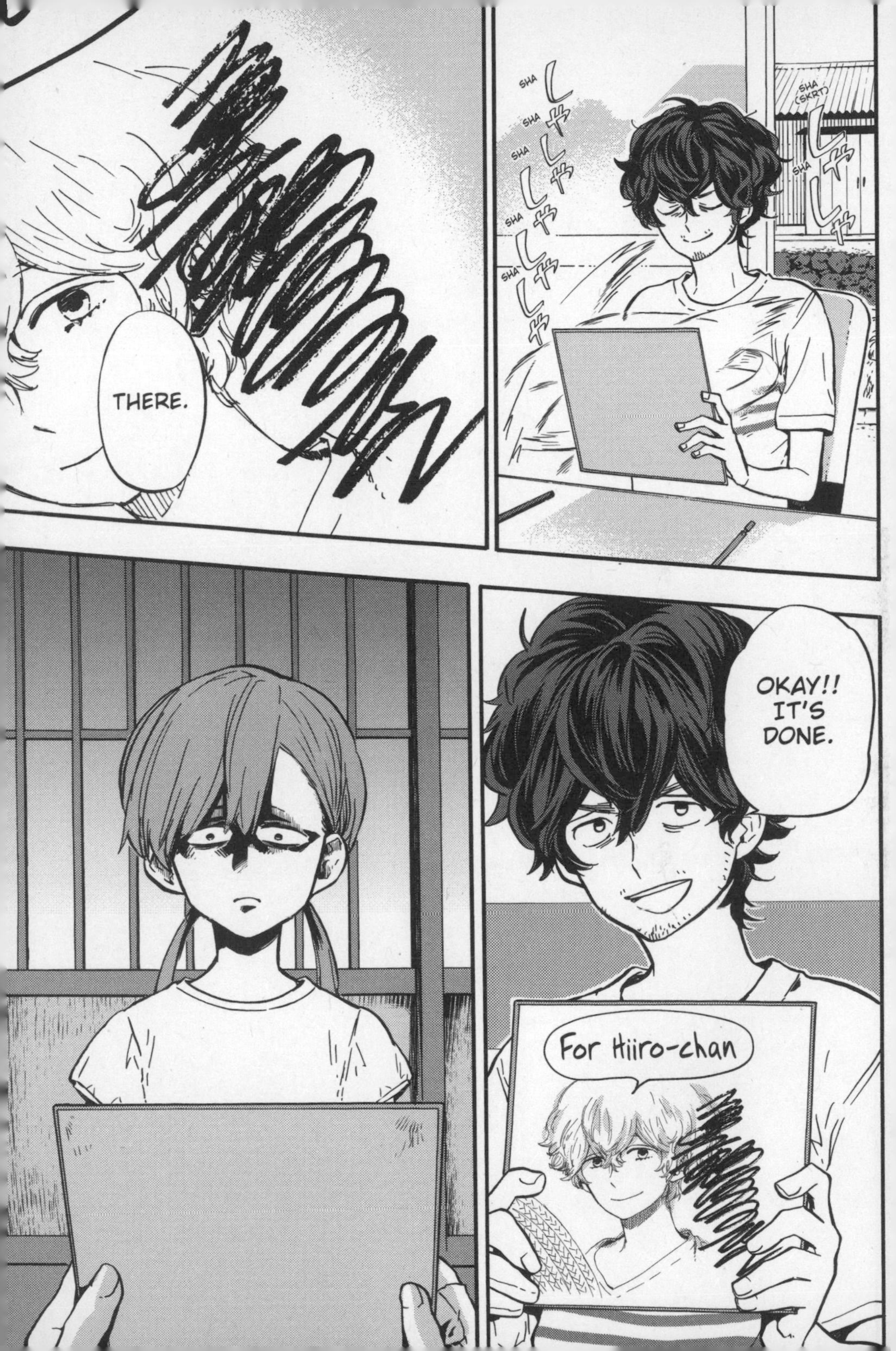

SHA (SKRT)
SHA
しゃしゃ
SHA SHA SHA SHA SHA
しゃしゃしゃしゃしゃ
THERE.
OKAY!! IT'S DONE.
For Hiiro-chan

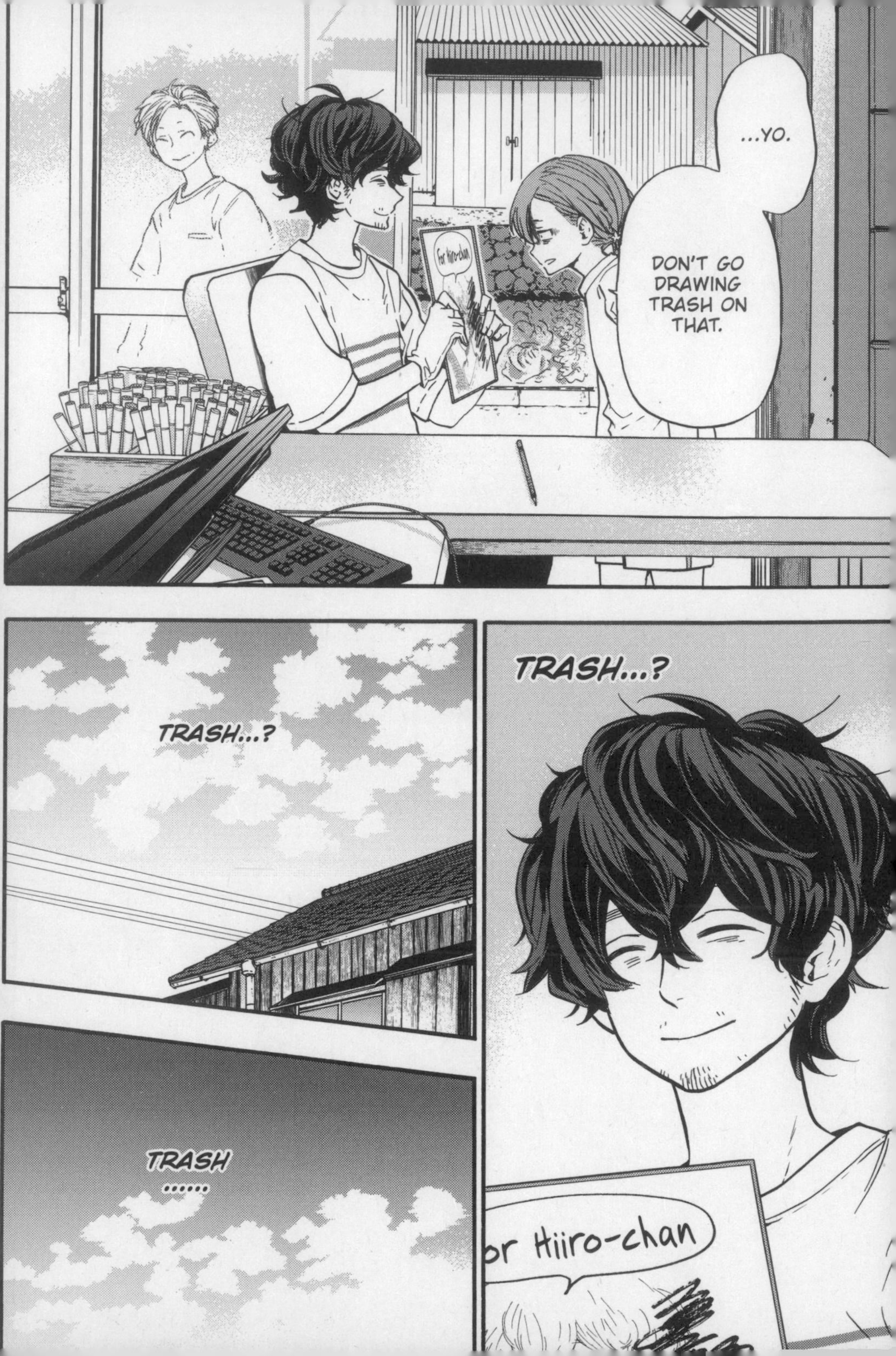
...YO.
DON'T GO DRAWING TRASH ON THAT.
TRASH...?
or Hiiro-chan
TRASH...?
TRASH ......

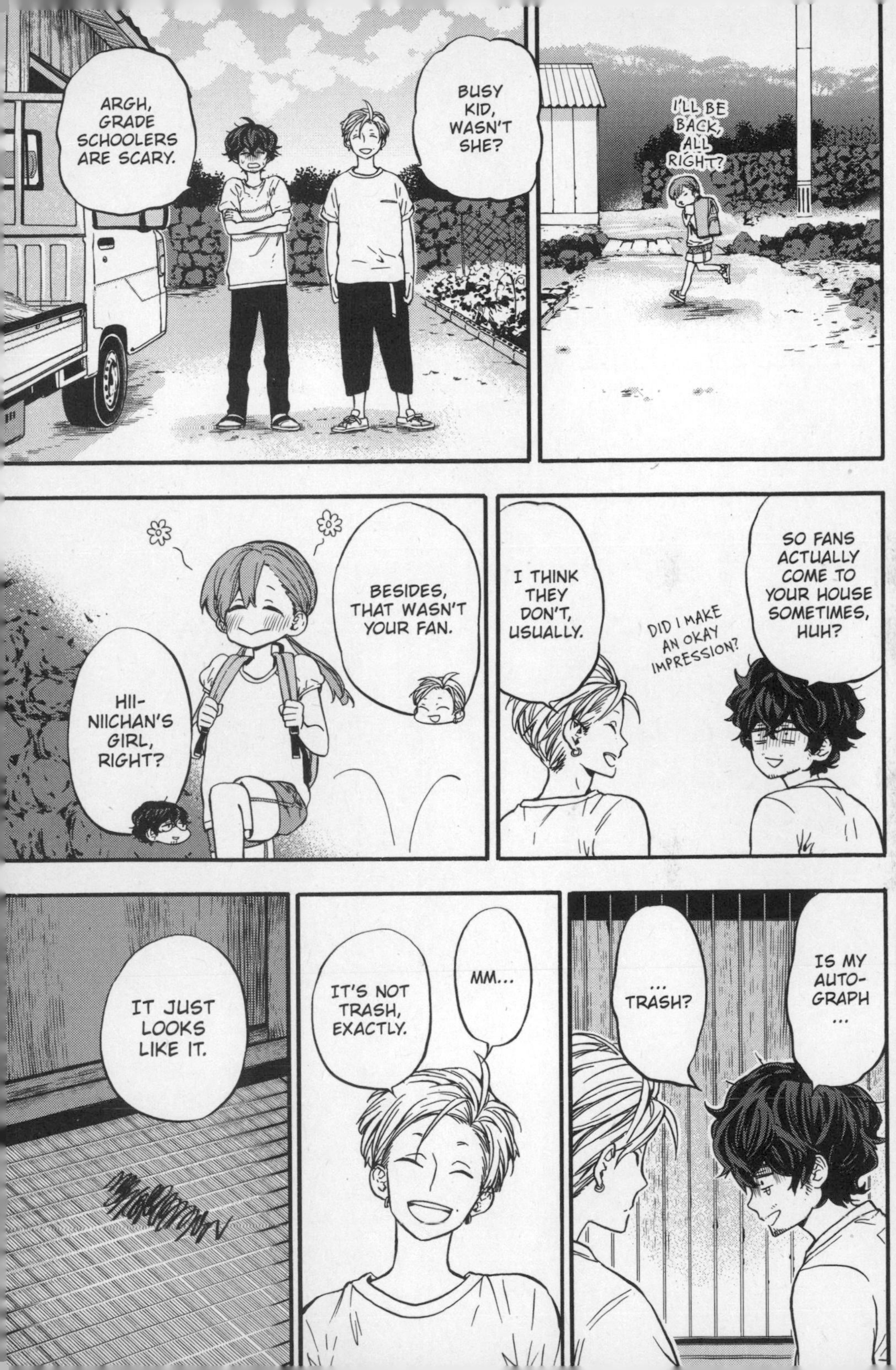
I'LL BE BACK, ALL RIGHT?
BUSY KID, WASN'T SHE?
ARGH, GRADE SCHOOLERS ARE SCARY.
SO FANS ACTUALLY COME TO YOUR HOUSE SOMETIMES, HUH?
DID I MAKE AN OKAY IMPRESSION?
I THINK THEY DON'T, USUALLY.
BESIDES, THAT WASN'T YOUR FAN.
HII-NIICHAN'S GIRL, RIGHT?
IS MY AUTO-GRAPH ...
... TRASH?
MM...
IT'S NOT TRASH, EXACTLY.
IT JUST LOOKS LIKE IT.

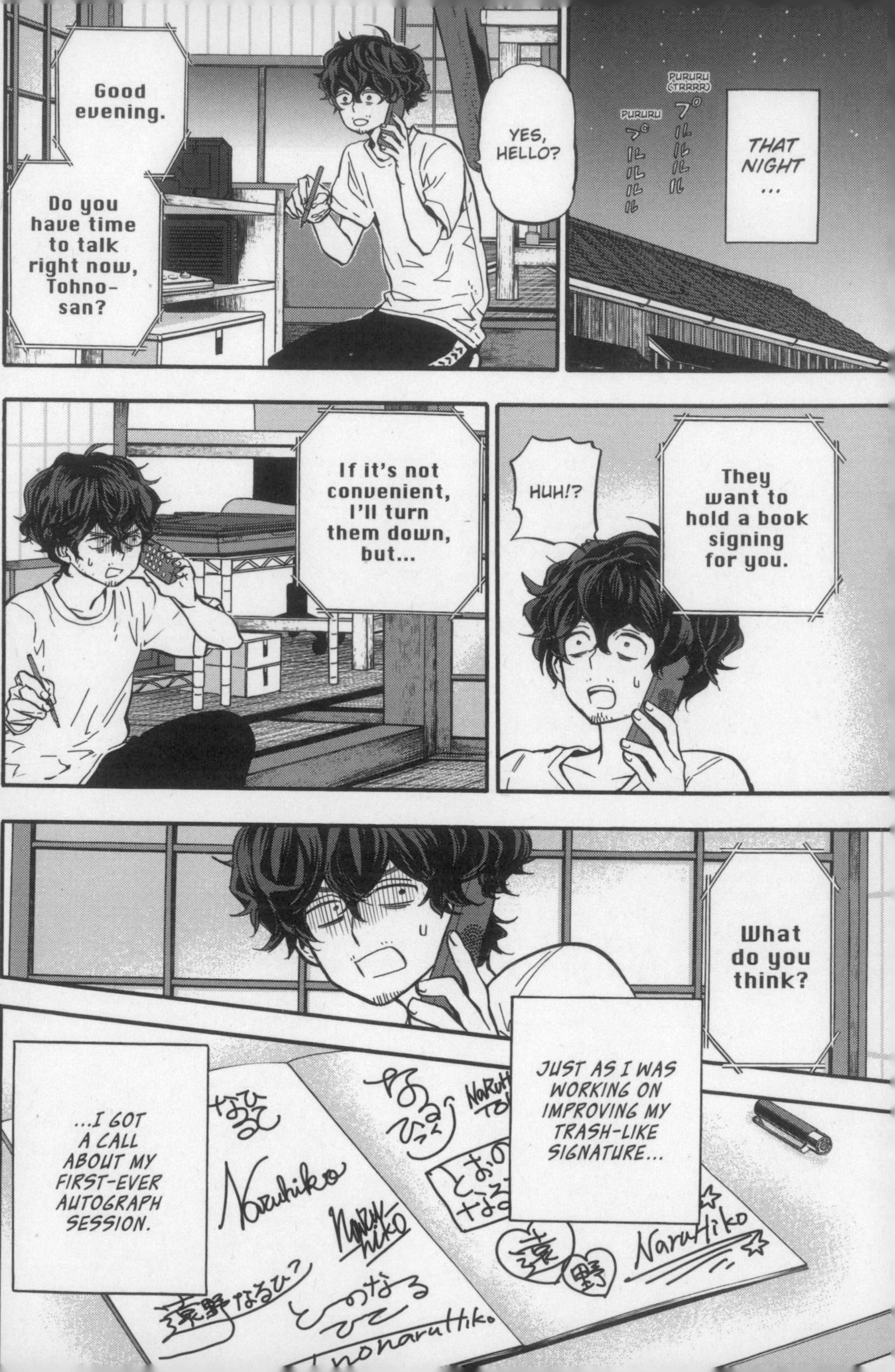
THAT NIGHT ...
PURURU (TRRRR)
プルルル
PURURU
プルルル
YES, HELLO?
Good evening.
Do you have time to talk right now, Tohno-san?
They want to hold a book signing for you.
HUH!?
If it's not convenient, I'll turn them down, but...
What do you think?
JUST AS I WAS WORKING ON IMPROVING MY TRASH-LIKE SIGNATURE...
...I GOT A CALL ABOUT MY FIRST-EVER AUTOGRAPH SESSION.

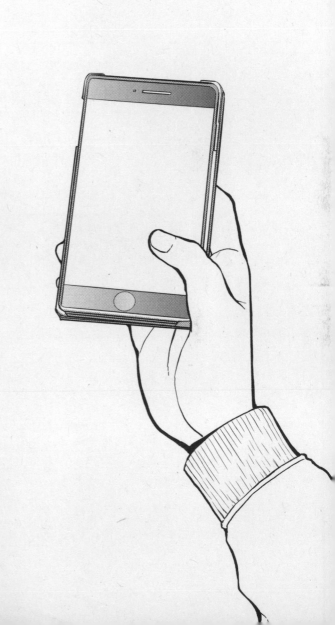

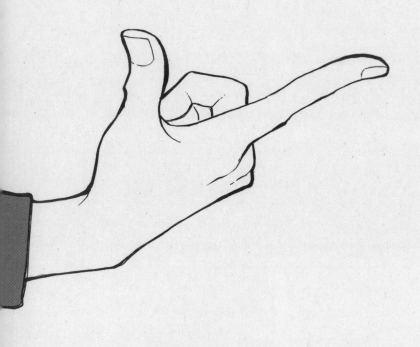

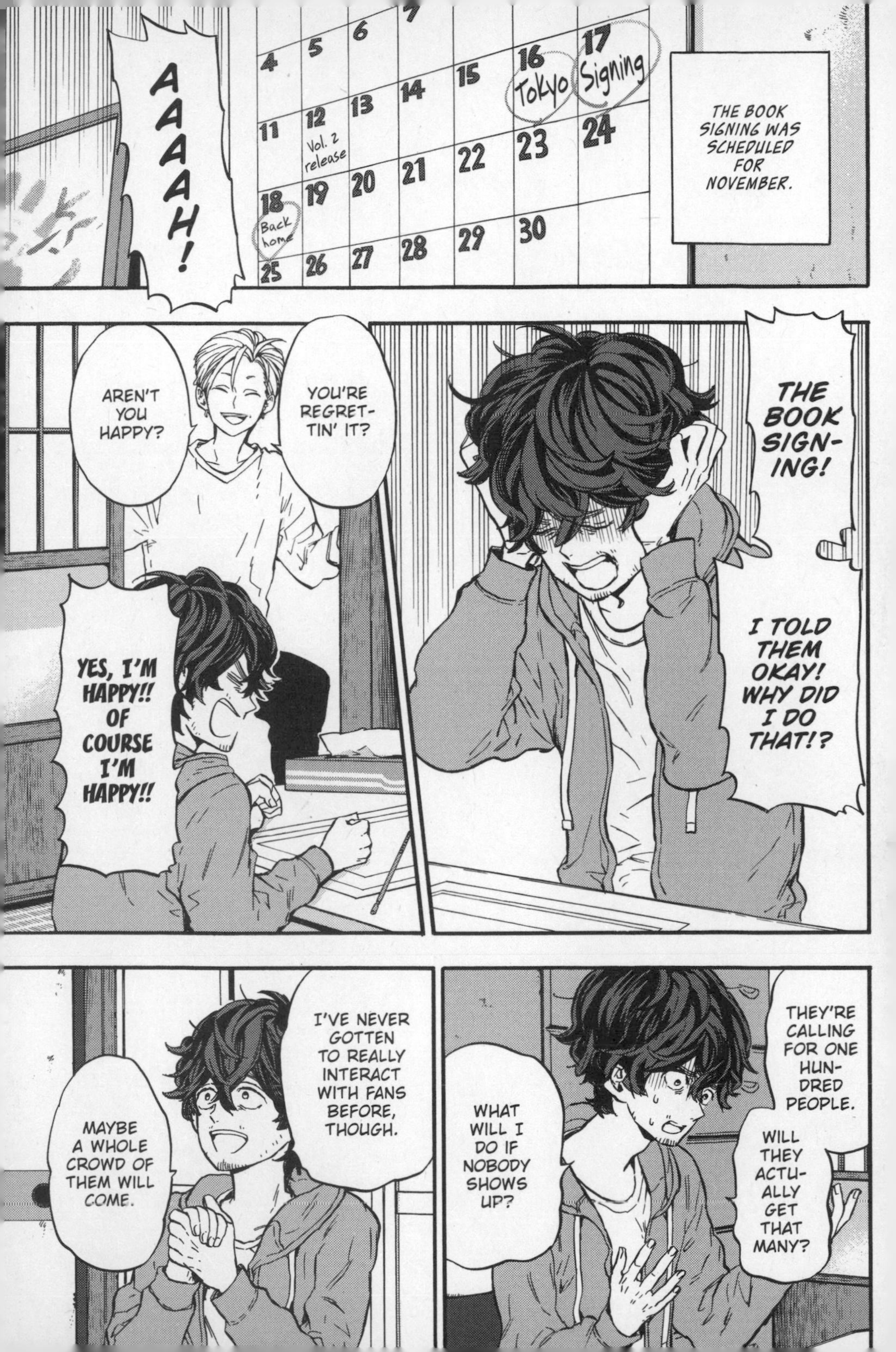
THE BOOK SIGNING WAS SCHEDULED FOR NOVEMBER.
Signing
Tokyo
Vol. 2 release
Back home
AAAAH!
THE BOOK SIGNING!
I TOLD THEM OKAY! WHY DID I DO THAT!?
YOU'RE REGRETTIN' IT?
AREN'T YOU HAPPY?
YES, I'M HAPPY!! OF COURSE I'M HAPPY!!
THEY'RE CALLING FOR ONE HUNDRED PEOPLE.
WILL THEY ACTUALLY GET THAT MANY?
WHAT WILL I DO IF NOBODY SHOWS UP?
I'VE NEVER GOTTEN TO REALLY INTERACT WITH FANS BEFORE, THOUGH.
MAYBE A WHOLE CROWD OF THEM WILL COME.

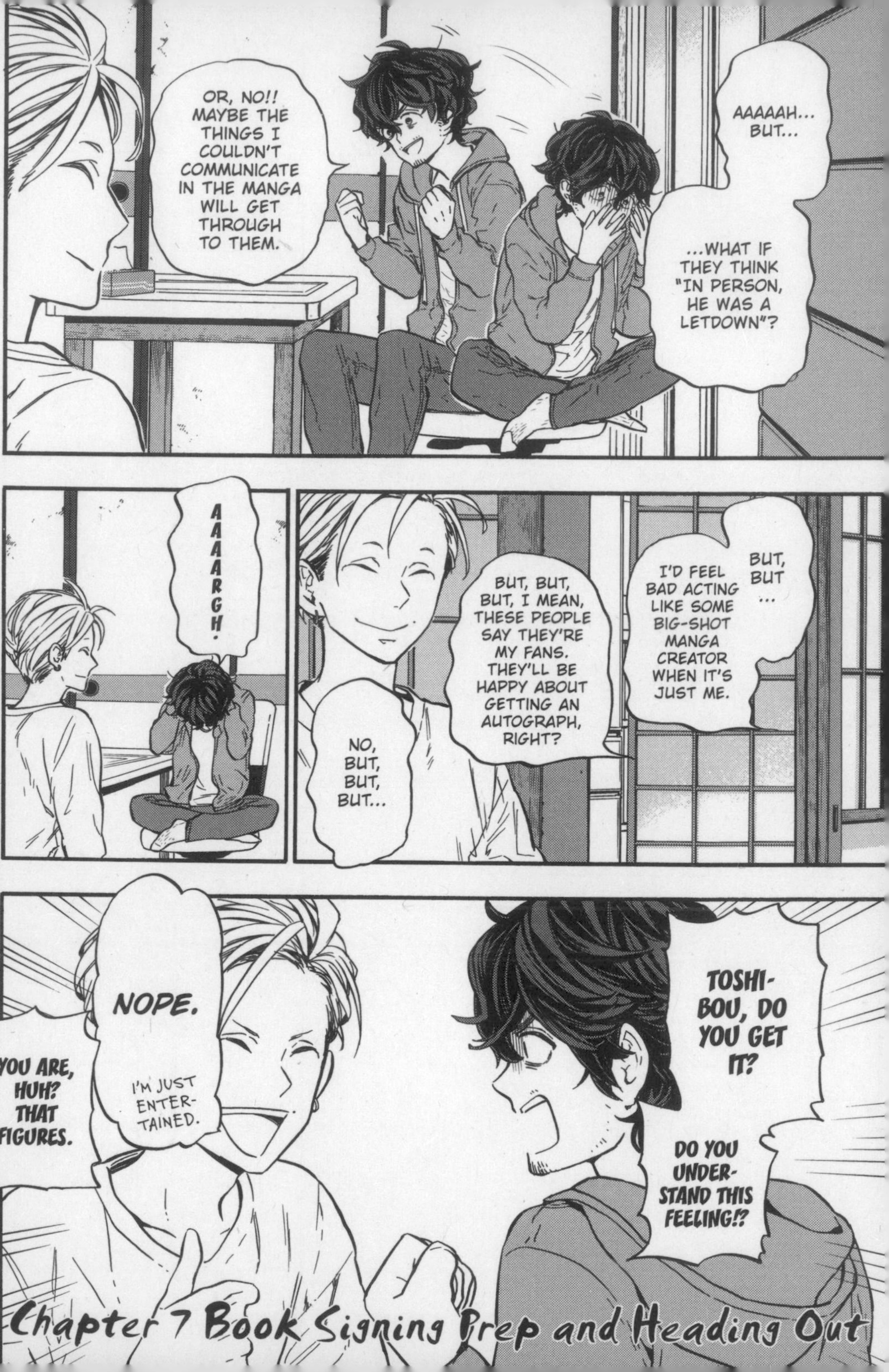
AAAAAH... BUT...
...WHAT IF THEY THINK "IN PERSON, HE WAS A LETDOWN"?
OR, NO!! MAYBE THE THINGS I COULDN'T COMMUNICATE IN THE MANGA WILL GET THROUGH TO THEM.
BUT, BUT ...
I'D FEEL BAD ACTING LIKE SOME BIG-SHOT MANGA CREATOR WHEN IT'S JUST ME.
BUT, BUT, BUT, I MEAN, THESE PEOPLE SAY THEY'RE MY FANS. THEY'LL BE HAPPY ABOUT GETTING AN AUTOGRAPH, RIGHT?
NO, BUT, BUT, BUT...
AAAAARGH!
TOSHI-BOU, DO YOU GET IT?
DO YOU UNDER-STAND THIS FEELING!?
NOPE.
I'M JUST ENTER-TAINED.
YOU ARE, HUH? THAT FIGURES.

Chapter 7 Book Signing Prep and Heading Out

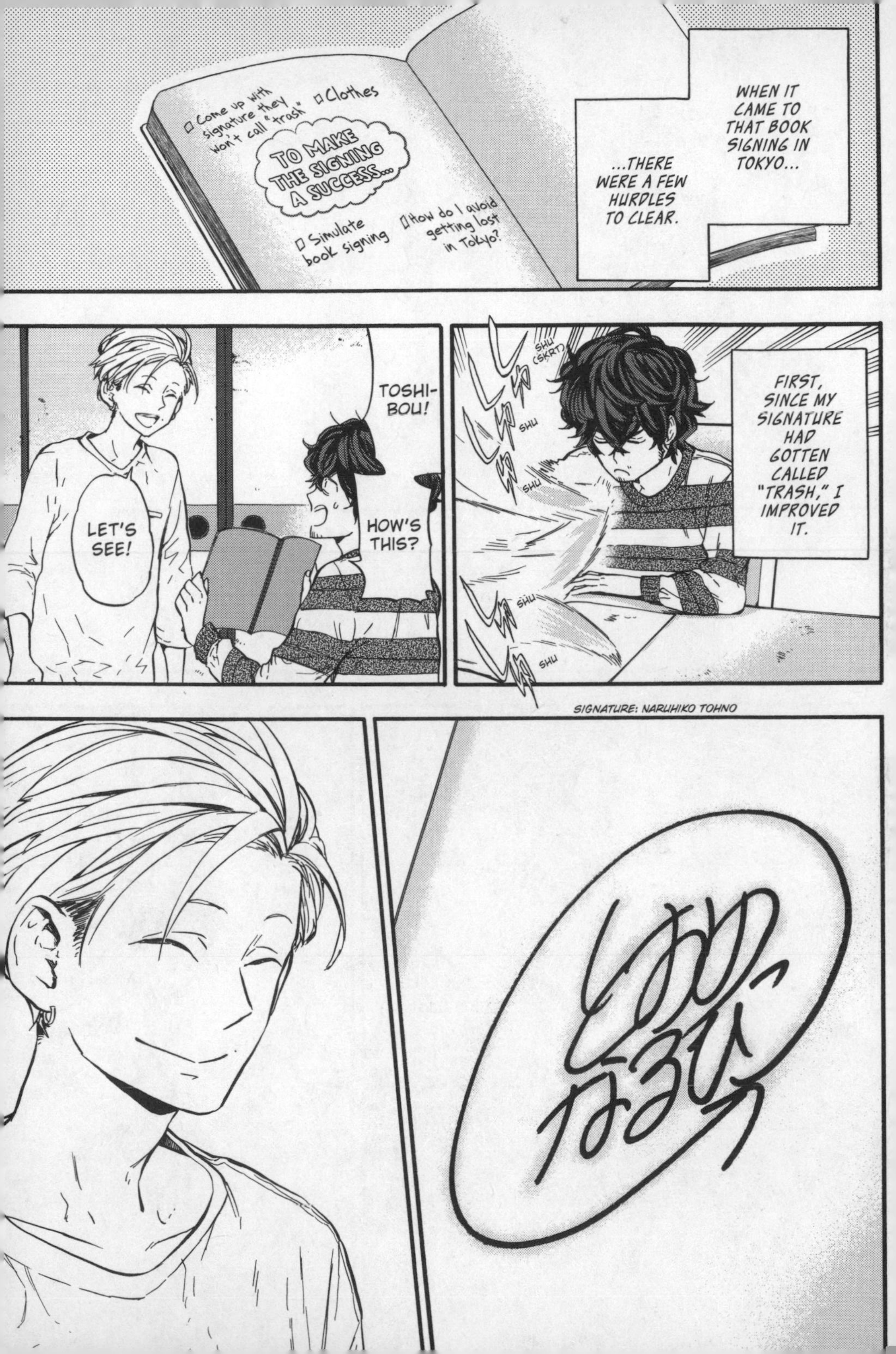
WHEN IT CAME TO THAT BOOK SIGNING IN TOKYO...
...THERE WERE A FEW HURDLES TO CLEAR.
☐ Come up with signature they won't call "trash"
☐ Clothes
TO MAKE THE SIGNING A SUCCESS...
☐ How do I avoid getting lost in Tokyo?
☐ Simulate book signing
FIRST, SINCE MY SIGNATURE HAD GOTTEN CALLED "TRASH," I IMPROVED IT.
SHU (SKRT)
SHU
SHU
SHU
SHU
TOSHI-BOU!
HOW'S THIS?
LET'S SEE!
SIGNATURE: NARUHIKO TOHNO

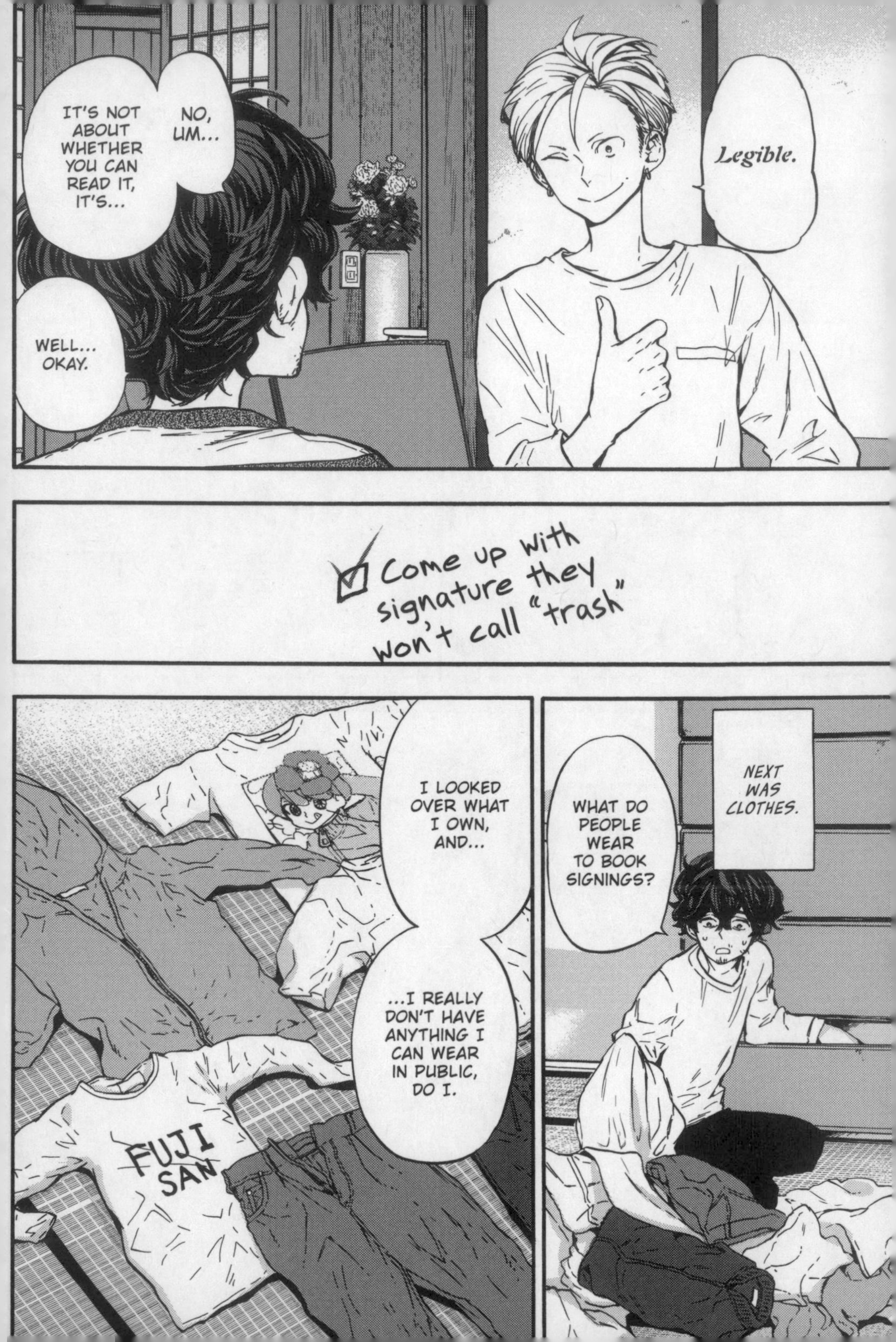
Legible.
NO, UM...
IT'S NOT ABOUT WHETHER YOU CAN READ IT, IT'S...
WELL... OKAY.
☑ Come up with signature they won't call "trash"
NEXT WAS CLOTHES.
WHAT DO PEOPLE WEAR TO BOOK SIGNINGS?
I LOOKED OVER WHAT I OWN, AND...
...I REALLY DON'T HAVE ANYTHING I CAN WEAR IN PUBLIC, DO I.
FUJI SAN

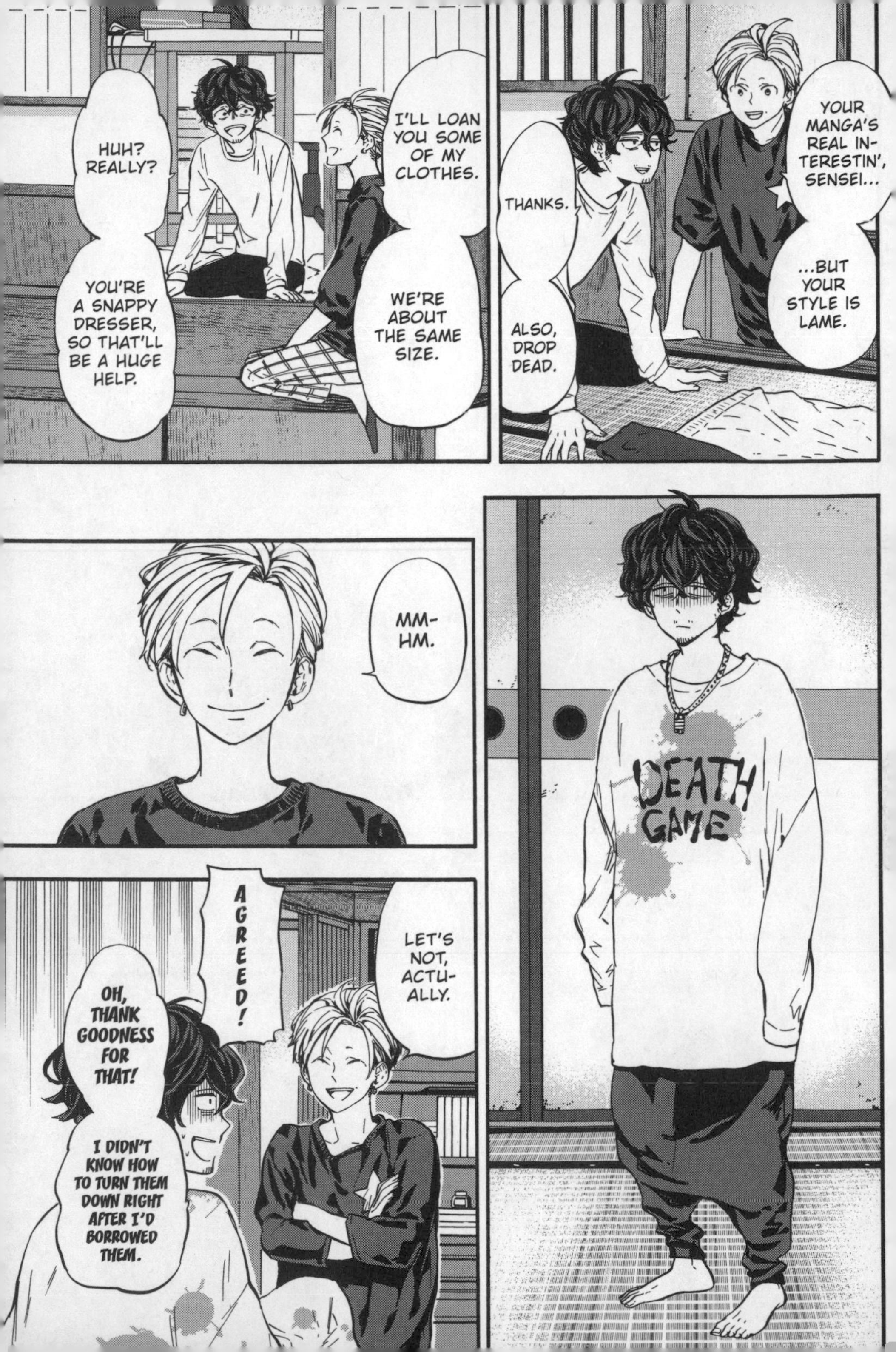
YOUR MANGA'S REAL IN-TERESTIN', SENSEI...
...BUT YOUR STYLE IS LAME.
THANKS.
ALSO, DROP DEAD.
I'LL LOAN YOU SOME OF MY CLOTHES.
WE'RE ABOUT THE SAME SIZE.
HUH? REALLY?
YOU'RE A SNAPPY DRESSER, SO THAT'LL BE A HUGE HELP.
DEATH GAME
MM-HM.
LET'S NOT, ACTUALLY.
AGREED!
OH, THANK GOODNESS FOR THAT!
I DIDN'T KNOW HOW TO TURN THEM DOWN RIGHT AFTER I'D BORROWED THEM.

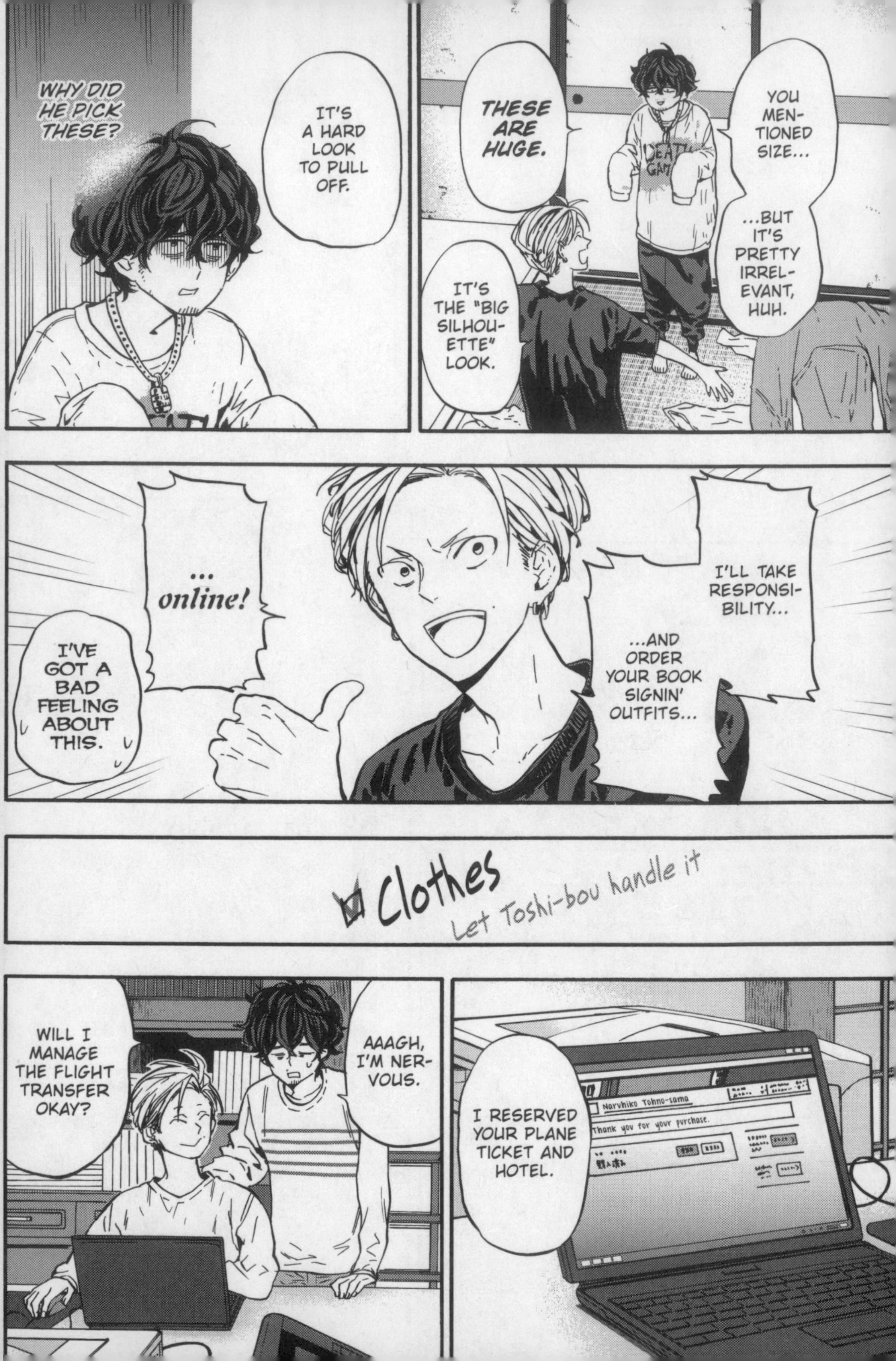
YOU MENTIONED SIZE...
...BUT IT'S PRETTY IRRELEVANT, HUH.
THESE ARE HUGE.
IT'S THE "BIG SILHOUETTE" LOOK.
IT'S A HARD LOOK TO PULL OFF.
WHY DID HE PICK THESE?
I'LL TAKE RESPONSIBILITY...
...AND ORDER YOUR BOOK SIGNIN' OUTFITS...
... online!
I'VE GOT A BAD FEELING ABOUT THIS.
Clothes
Let Toshi-bou handle it
I RESERVED YOUR PLANE TICKET AND HOTEL.
Naruhiko Tohno-sama
Thank you for your purchase.
AAAGH, I'M NERVOUS.
WILL I MANAGE THE FLIGHT TRANSFER OKAY?

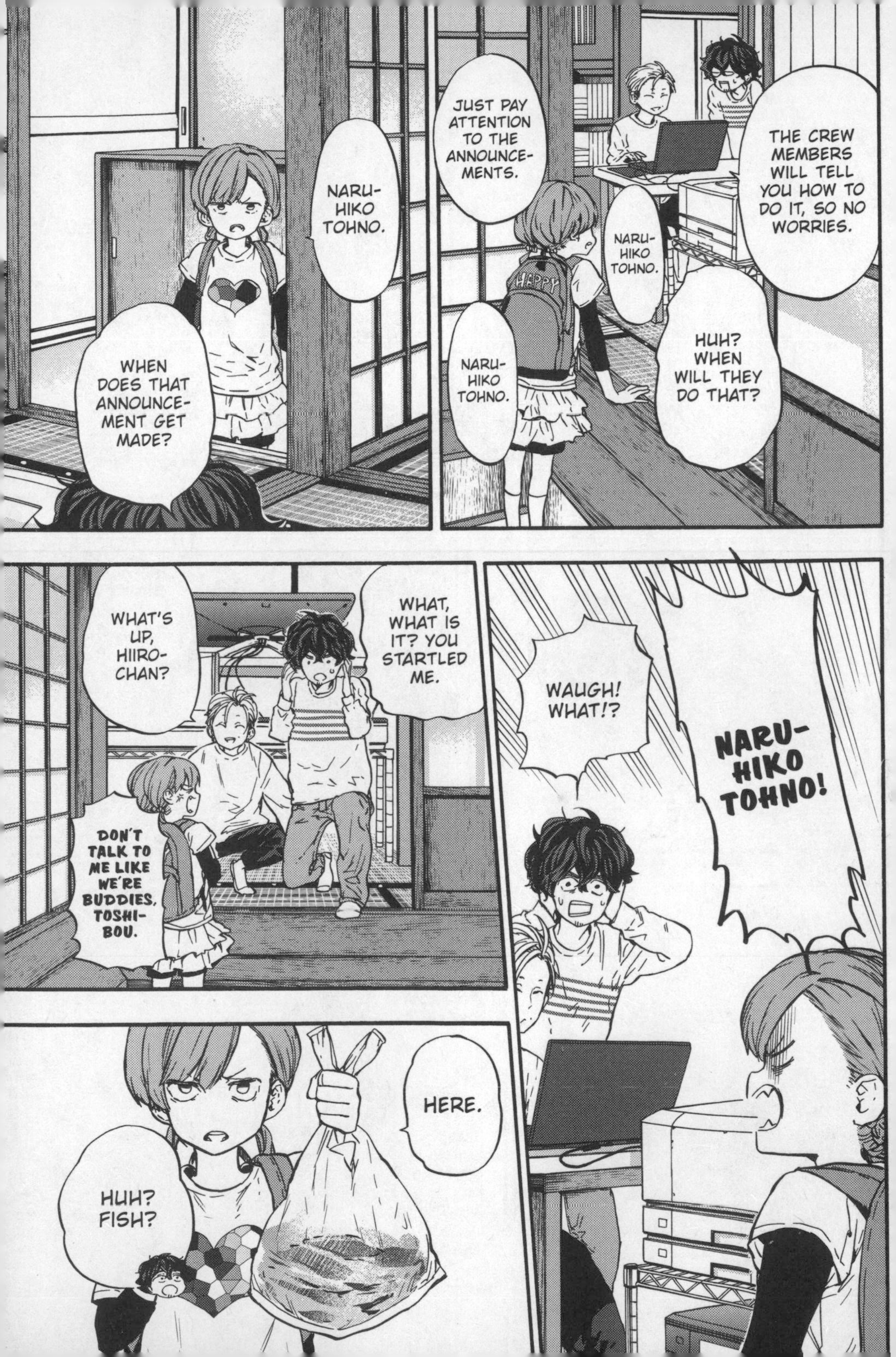
THE CREW MEMBERS WILL TELL YOU HOW TO DO IT, SO NO WORRIES.
JUST PAY ATTENTION TO THE ANNOUNCEMENTS.
NARU-HIKO TOHNO.
HUH? WHEN WILL THEY DO THAT?
NARU-HIKO TOHNO.
NARU-HIKO TOHNO.
WHEN DOES THAT ANNOUNCEMENT GET MADE?
NARU-HIKO TOHNO!
WAUGH! WHAT!?
WHAT, WHAT IS IT? YOU STARTLED ME.
WHAT'S UP, HIIRO-CHAN?
DON'T TALK TO ME LIKE WE'RE BUDDIES, TOSHI-BOU.
HERE.
HUH? FISH?

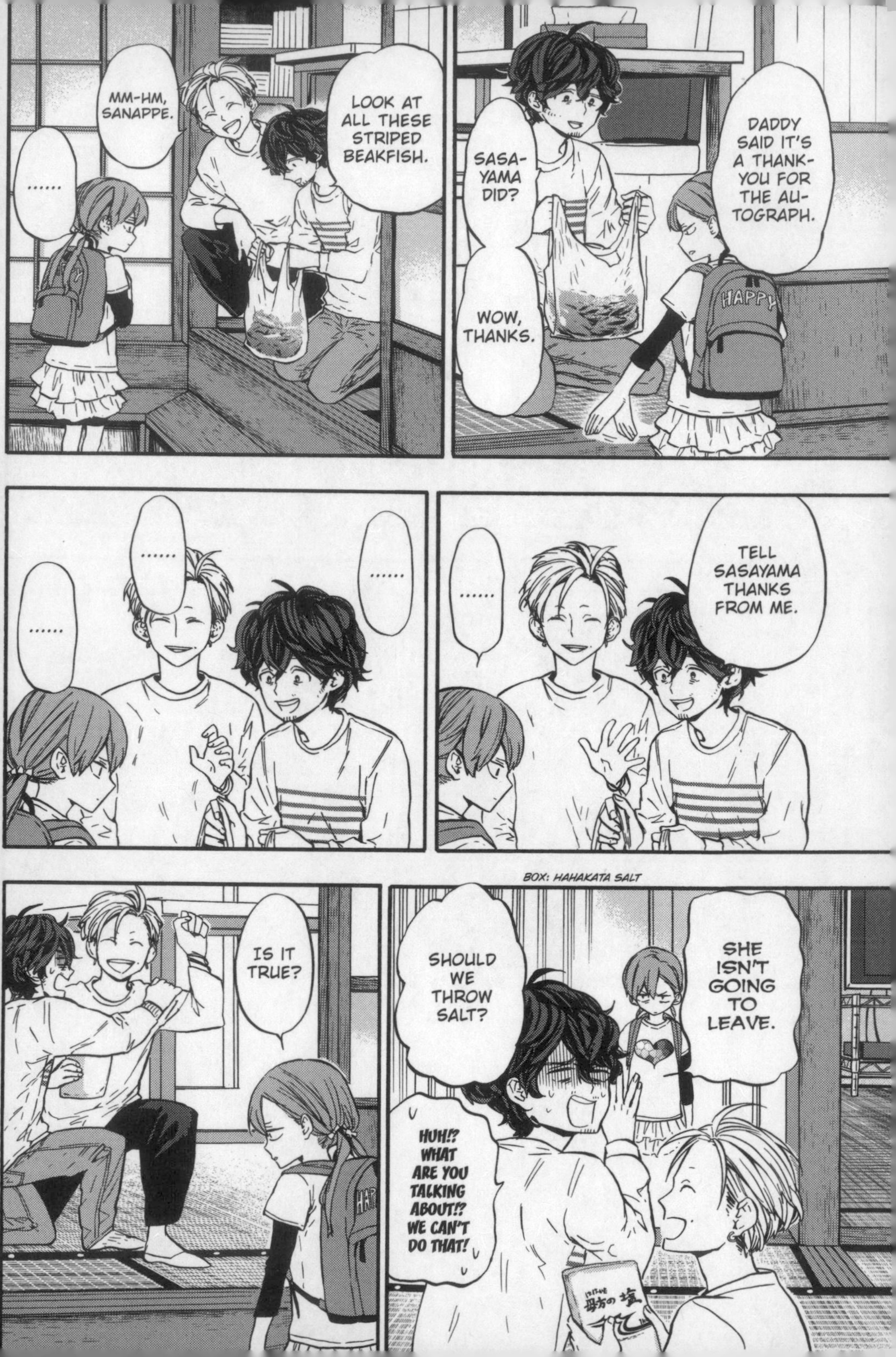
DADDY SAID IT'S A THANK-YOU FOR THE AUTOGRAPH.
SASAYAMA DID?
WOW, THANKS.
LOOK AT ALL THESE STRIPED BEAKFISH.
MM-HM, SANAPPE.
......
TELL SASAYAMA THANKS FROM ME.
......
......
......
......
BOX: HAHAKATA SALT
SHE ISN'T GOING TO LEAVE.
SHOULD WE THROW SALT?
HUH!? WHAT ARE YOU TALKING ABOUT!? WE CAN'T DO THAT!
母方の塩
IS IT TRUE?

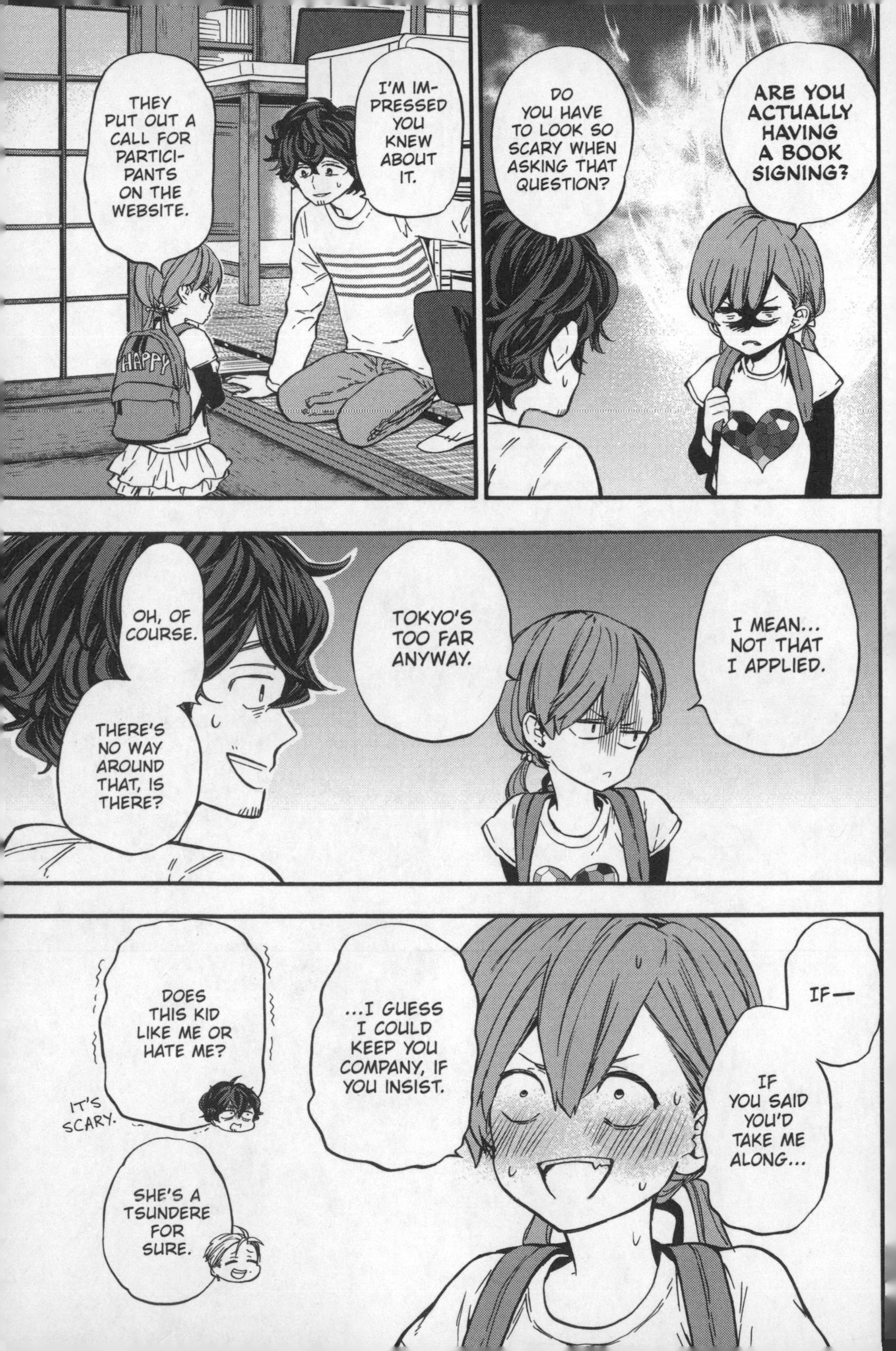

ARE YOU ACTUALLY HAVING A BOOK SIGNING?
DO YOU HAVE TO LOOK SO SCARY WHEN ASKING THAT QUESTION?
I'M IM-PRESSED YOU KNEW ABOUT IT.
THEY PUT OUT A CALL FOR PARTICI-PANTS ON THE WEBSITE.
I MEAN... NOT THAT I APPLIED.
TOKYO'S TOO FAR ANYWAY.
OH, OF COURSE.
THERE'S NO WAY AROUND THAT, IS THERE?
IF—
IF YOU SAID YOU'D TAKE ME ALONG...
...I GUESS I COULD KEEP YOU COMPANY, IF YOU INSIST.
DOES THIS KID LIKE ME OR HATE ME?
IT'S SCARY.
SHE'S A TSUNDERE FOR SURE.

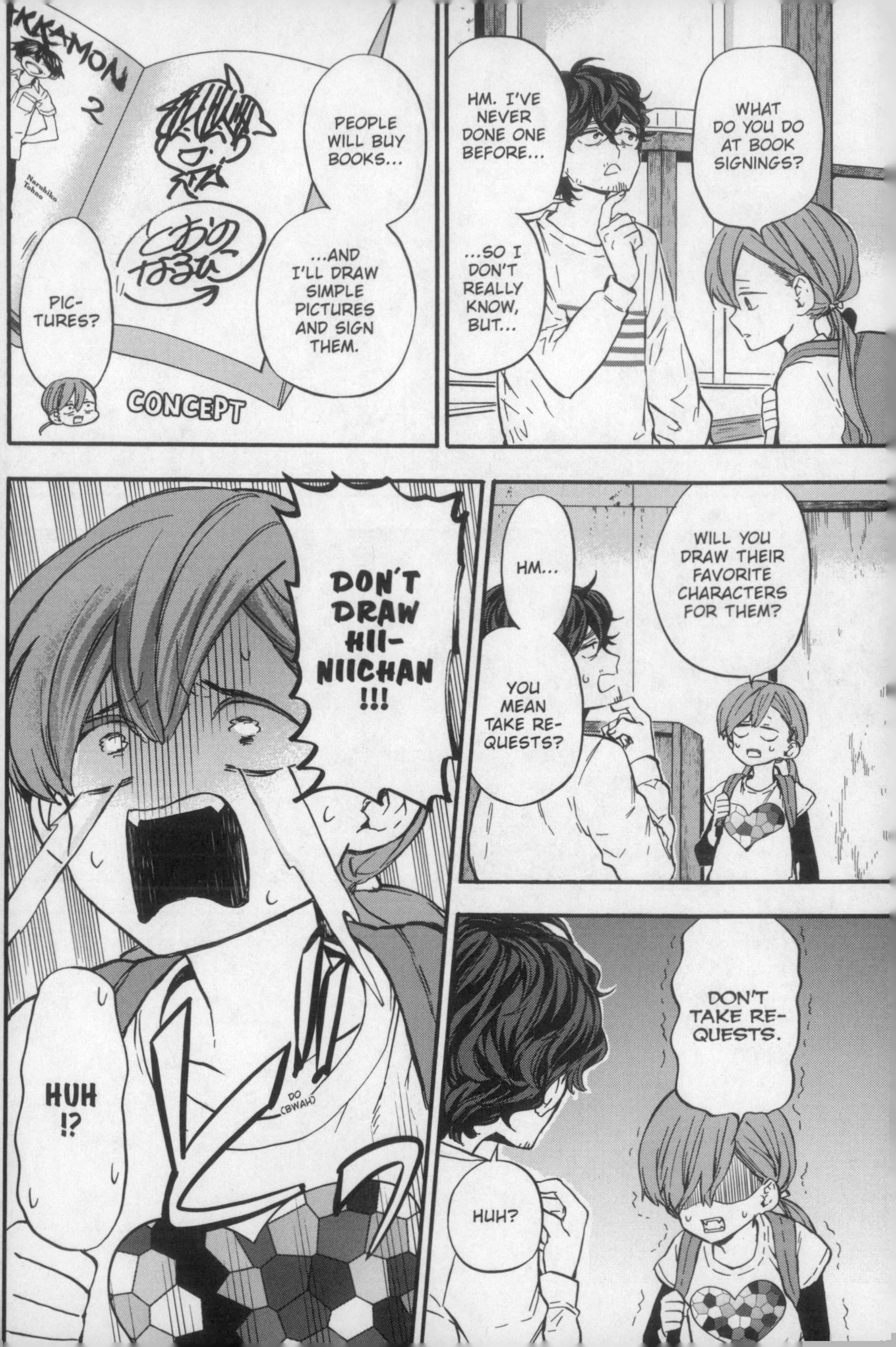
WHAT DO YOU DO AT BOOK SIGNINGS?
HM. I'VE NEVER DONE ONE BEFORE...
...SO I DON'T REALLY KNOW, BUT...
KKAMON 2
Naruhiko Tohno
とおの なるひ
PEOPLE WILL BUY BOOKS...
...AND I'LL DRAW SIMPLE PICTURES AND SIGN THEM.
PIC-TURES?
CONCEPT
WILL YOU DRAW THEIR FAVORITE CHARACTERS FOR THEM?
HM...
YOU MEAN TAKE RE-QUESTS?
DON'T TAKE RE-QUESTS.
HUH?
DON'T DRAW HII-NIICHAN!!!
DO (BWAH)
HUH!?

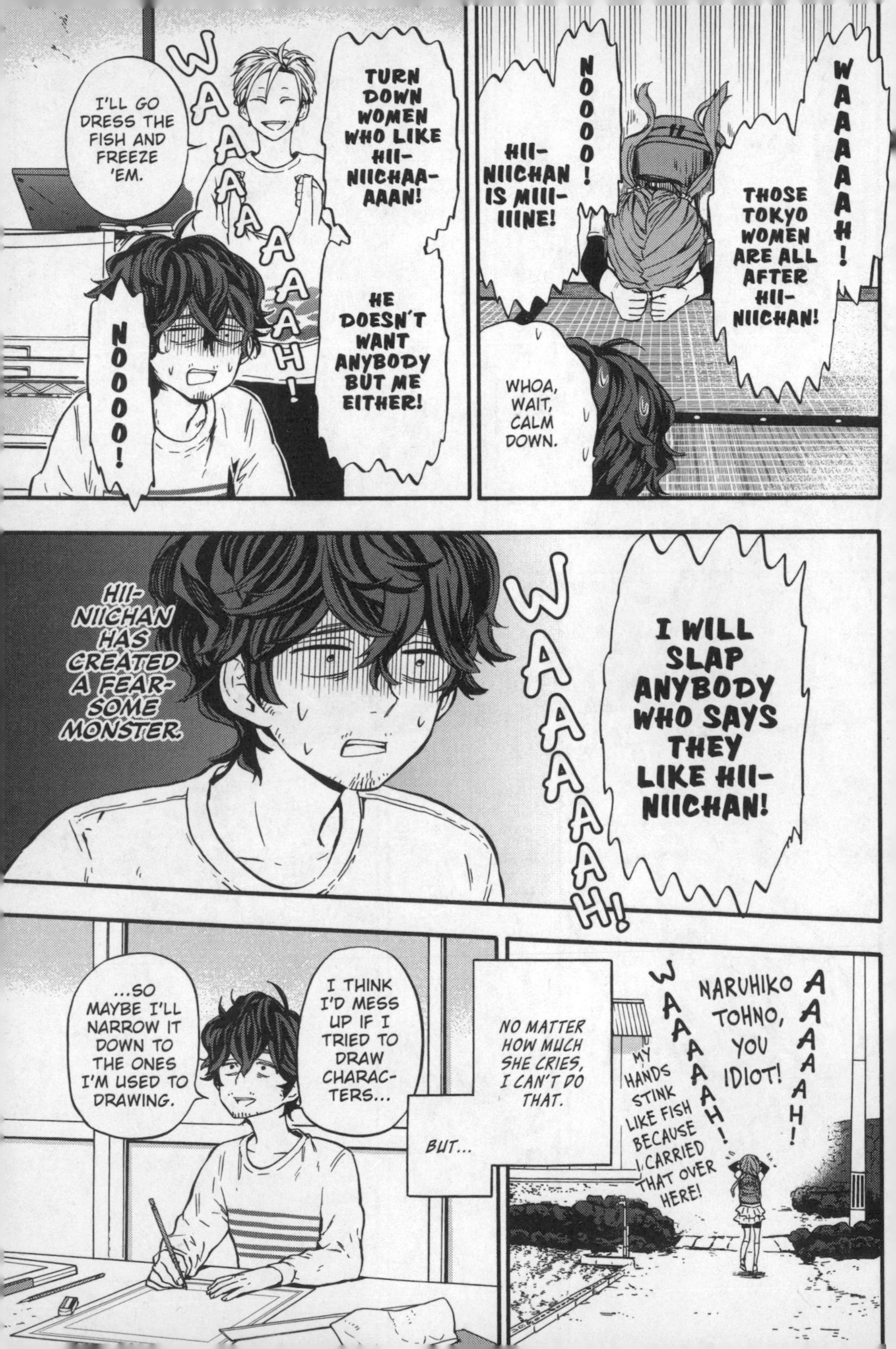
WAAAAAAH!
THOSE TOKYO WOMEN ARE ALL AFTER HII-NIICHAN!
NOOOOO!
HII-NIICHAN IS MIIIIIINE!
WHOA, WAIT, CALM DOWN.
TURN DOWN WOMEN WHO LIKE HII-NIICHAA-AAAN!
HE DOESN'T WANT ANYBODY BUT ME EITHER!
WAAAAAAAH!
I'LL GO DRESS THE FISH AND FREEZE 'EM.
NOOOOO!
WAAAAAAH!
I WILL SLAP ANYBODY WHO SAYS THEY LIKE HII-NIICHAN!
HII-NIICHAN HAS CREATED A FEAR-SOME MONSTER.
AAAAAAH!
NARUHIKO TOHNO, YOU IDIOT!
WAAAAAAH!
MY HANDS STINK LIKE FISH BECAUSE I CARRIED THAT OVER HERE!
NO MATTER HOW MUCH SHE CRIES, I CAN'T DO THAT.
BUT...
I THINK I'D MESS UP IF I TRIED TO DRAW CHARAC-TERS...
...SO MAYBE I'LL NARROW IT DOWN TO THE ONES I'M USED TO DRAWING.

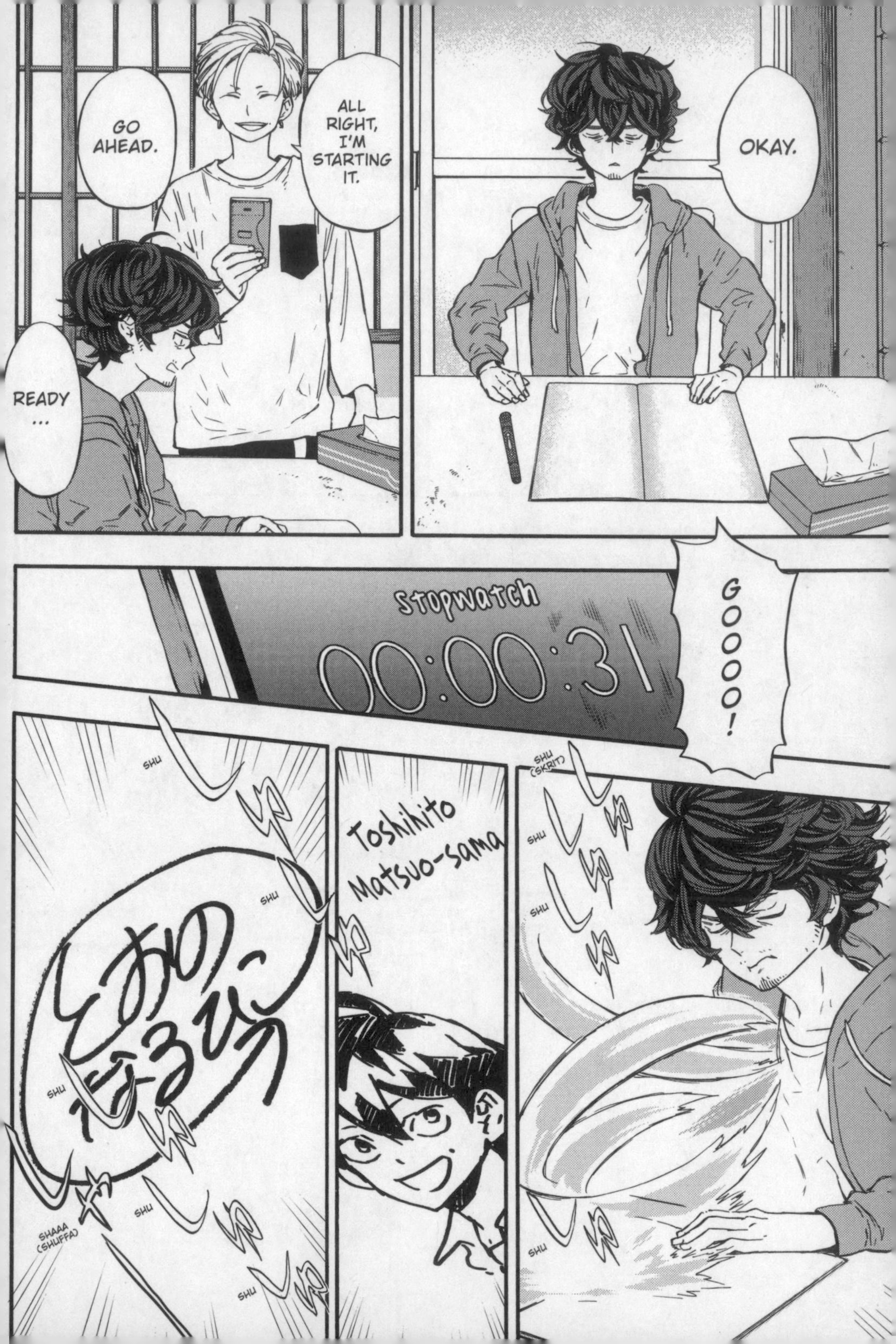
OKAY.
ALL RIGHT, I'M STARTING IT.
GO AHEAD.
READY ...
GOOOOO!
Stopwatch
00:00:31
SHU (SKRIT)
SHU
SHU
SHU
Toshihito Matsuo-sama
SHU
SHU
SHU
SHAAA (SHUFFA)
SHU

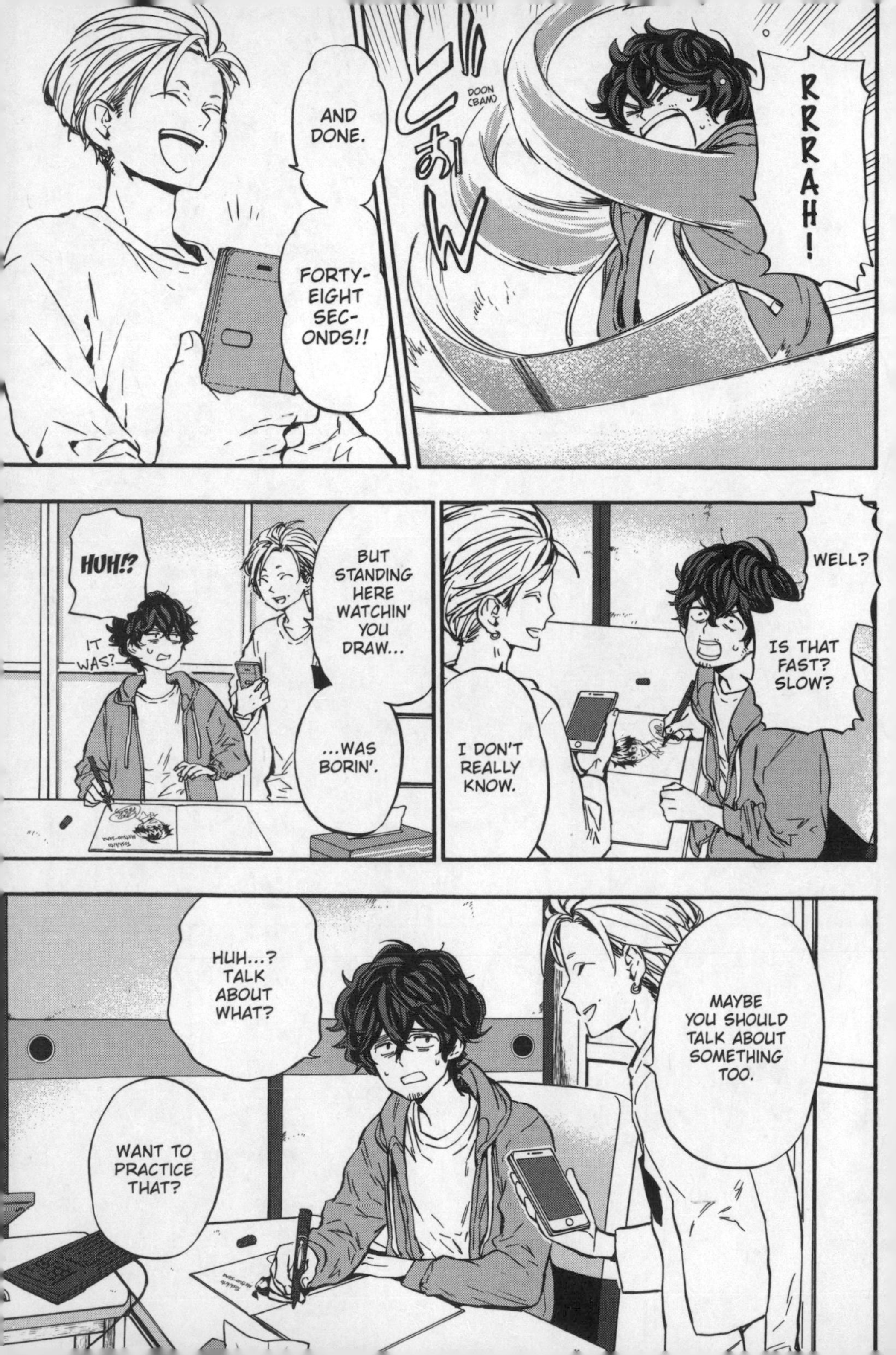
RRRAH!
DOON (BAM)
AND DONE.
FORTY-EIGHT SECONDS!!
WELL?
IS THAT FAST? SLOW?
I DON'T REALLY KNOW.
BUT STANDING HERE WATCHIN' YOU DRAW...
...WAS BORIN'.
HUH!?
IT WAS?
MAYBE YOU SHOULD TALK ABOUT SOMETHING TOO.
HUH...? TALK ABOUT WHAT?
WANT TO PRACTICE THAT?

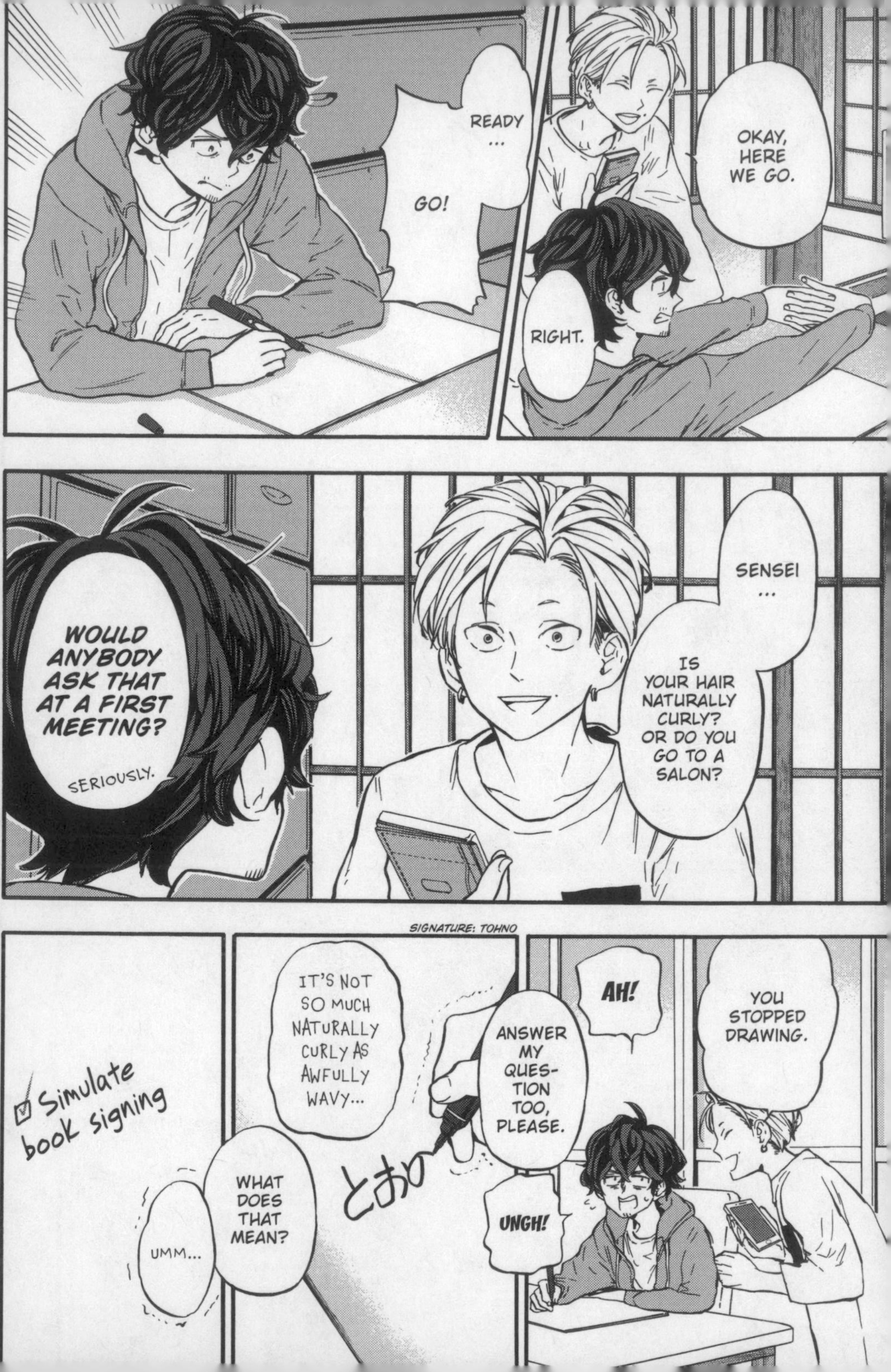
OKAY, HERE WE GO.
RIGHT.
READY ...
GO!
SENSEI ...
IS YOUR HAIR NATURALLY CURLY? OR DO YOU GO TO A SALON?
WOULD ANYBODY ASK THAT AT A FIRST MEETING?
SERIOUSLY.
SIGNATURE: TOHNO
YOU STOPPED DRAWING.
AH!
ANSWER MY QUES-TION TOO, PLEASE.
UNGH!
IT'S NOT SO MUCH NATURALLY CURLY AS AWFULLY WAVY...
とおの
WHAT DOES THAT MEAN?
UMM...
☑ Simulate book signing

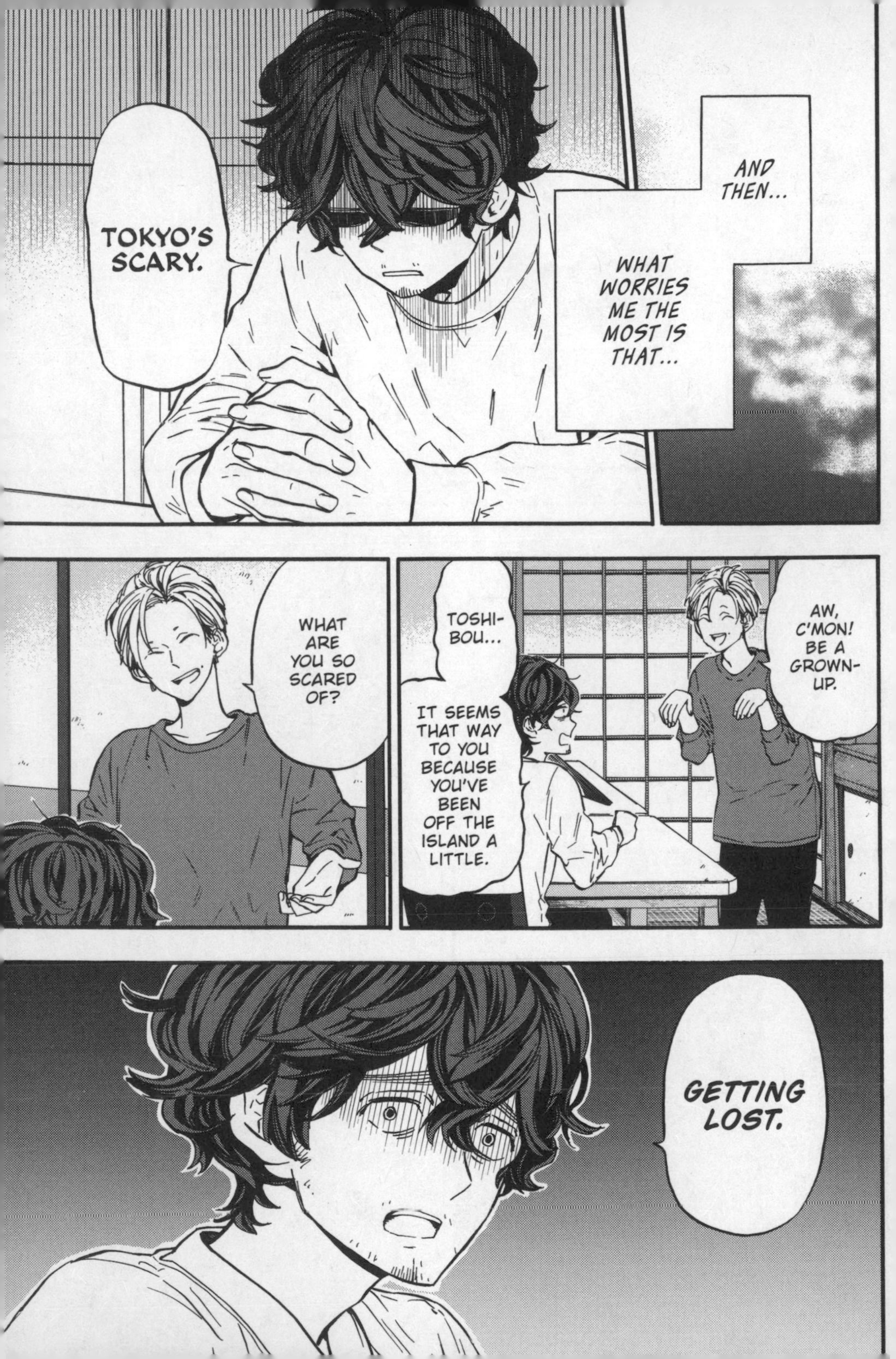
AND THEN... WHAT WORRIES ME THE MOST IS THAT...
TOKYO'S SCARY.
AW, C'MON! BE A GROWN-UP.
TOSHIBOU...
IT SEEMS THAT WAY TO YOU BECAUSE YOU'VE BEEN OFF THE ISLAND A LITTLE.
WHAT ARE YOU SO SCARED OF?
GETTING LOST.

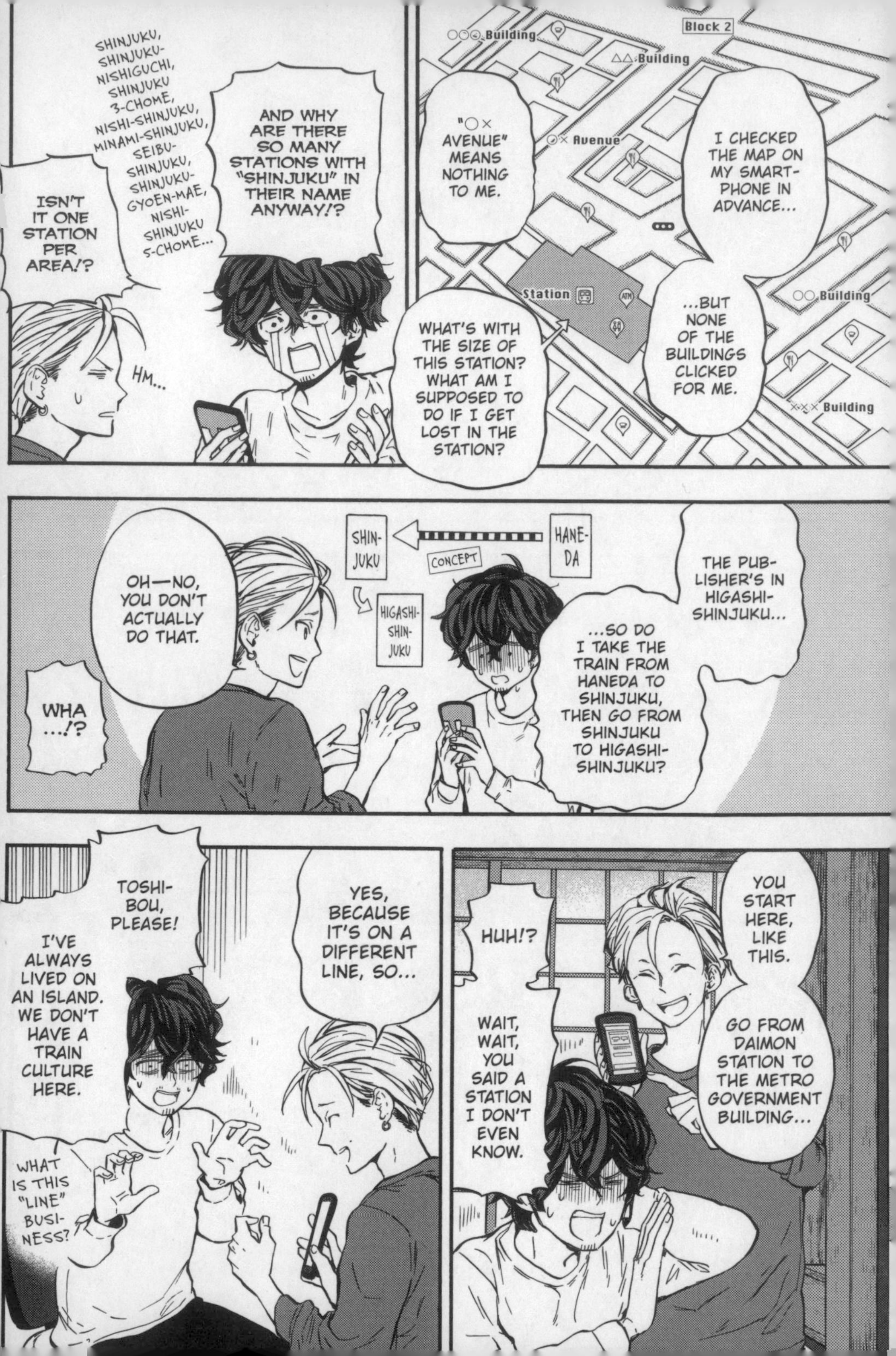

I CHECKED THE MAP ON MY SMART-PHONE IN ADVANCE...
...BUT NONE OF THE BUILDINGS CLICKED FOR ME.
"○× AVENUE" MEANS NOTHING TO ME.
WHAT'S WITH THE SIZE OF THIS STATION? WHAT AM I SUPPOSED TO DO IF I GET LOST IN THE STATION?
Block 2
○○ Building
△△ Building
○× Avenue
Station
○○ Building
×× Building
AND WHY ARE THERE SO MANY STATIONS WITH "SHINJUKU" IN THEIR NAME ANYWAY!?
SHINJUKU, SHINJUKU-NISHIGUCHI, SHINJUKU 3-CHOME, NISHI-SHINJUKU, MINAMI-SHINJUKU, SEIBU-SHINJUKU, SHINJUKU-GYOEN-MAE, NISHI-SHINJUKU 5-CHOME...
ISN'T IT ONE STATION PER AREA!?
HM...
THE PUBLISHER'S IN HIGASHI-SHINJUKU...
...SO DO I TAKE THE TRAIN FROM HANEDA TO SHINJUKU, THEN GO FROM SHINJUKU TO HIGASHI-SHINJUKU?
HANE-DA
SHIN-JUKU
CONCEPT
HIGASHI-SHIN-JUKU
OH—NO, YOU DON'T ACTUALLY DO THAT.
WHA...!?
YOU START HERE, LIKE THIS.
GO FROM DAIMON STATION TO THE METRO GOVERNMENT BUILDING...
HUH!?
WAIT, WAIT, YOU SAID A STATION I DON'T EVEN KNOW.
YES, BECAUSE IT'S ON A DIFFERENT LINE, SO...
TOSHI-BOU, PLEASE!
I'VE ALWAYS LIVED ON AN ISLAND. WE DON'T HAVE A TRAIN CULTURE HERE.
WHAT IS THIS "LINE" BUSI-NESS?

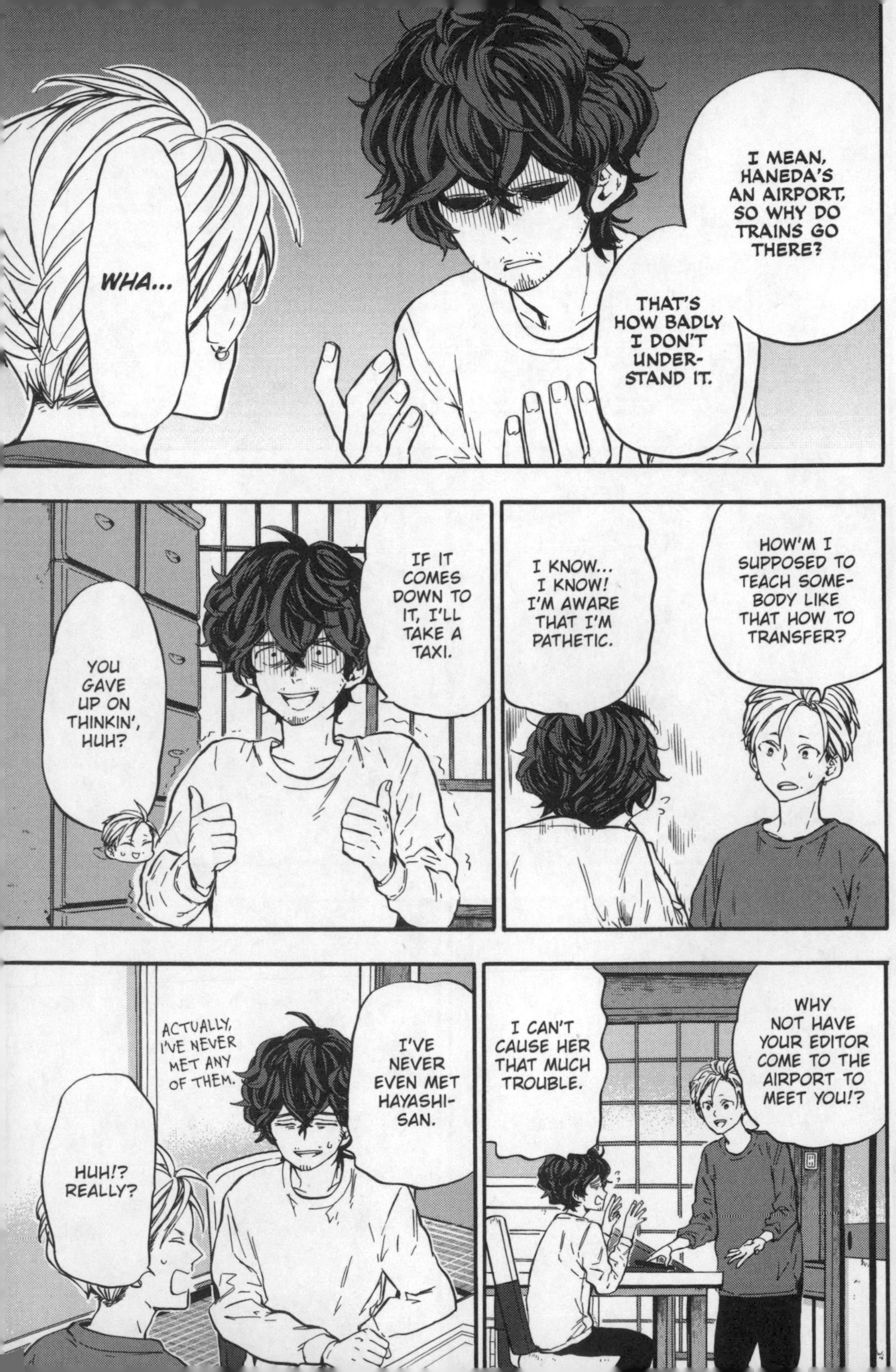
I MEAN, HANEDA'S AN AIRPORT, SO WHY DO TRAINS GO THERE?
THAT'S HOW BADLY I DON'T UNDERSTAND IT.
WHA...
HOW'M I SUPPOSED TO TEACH SOMEBODY LIKE THAT HOW TO TRANSFER?
I KNOW... I KNOW! I'M AWARE THAT I'M PATHETIC.
IF IT COMES DOWN TO IT, I'LL TAKE A TAXI.
YOU GAVE UP ON THINKIN', HUH?
WHY NOT HAVE YOUR EDITOR COME TO THE AIRPORT TO MEET YOU!?
I CAN'T CAUSE HER THAT MUCH TROUBLE.
I'VE NEVER EVEN MET HAYASHI-SAN.
ACTUALLY, I'VE NEVER MET ANY OF THEM.
HUH!? REALLY?

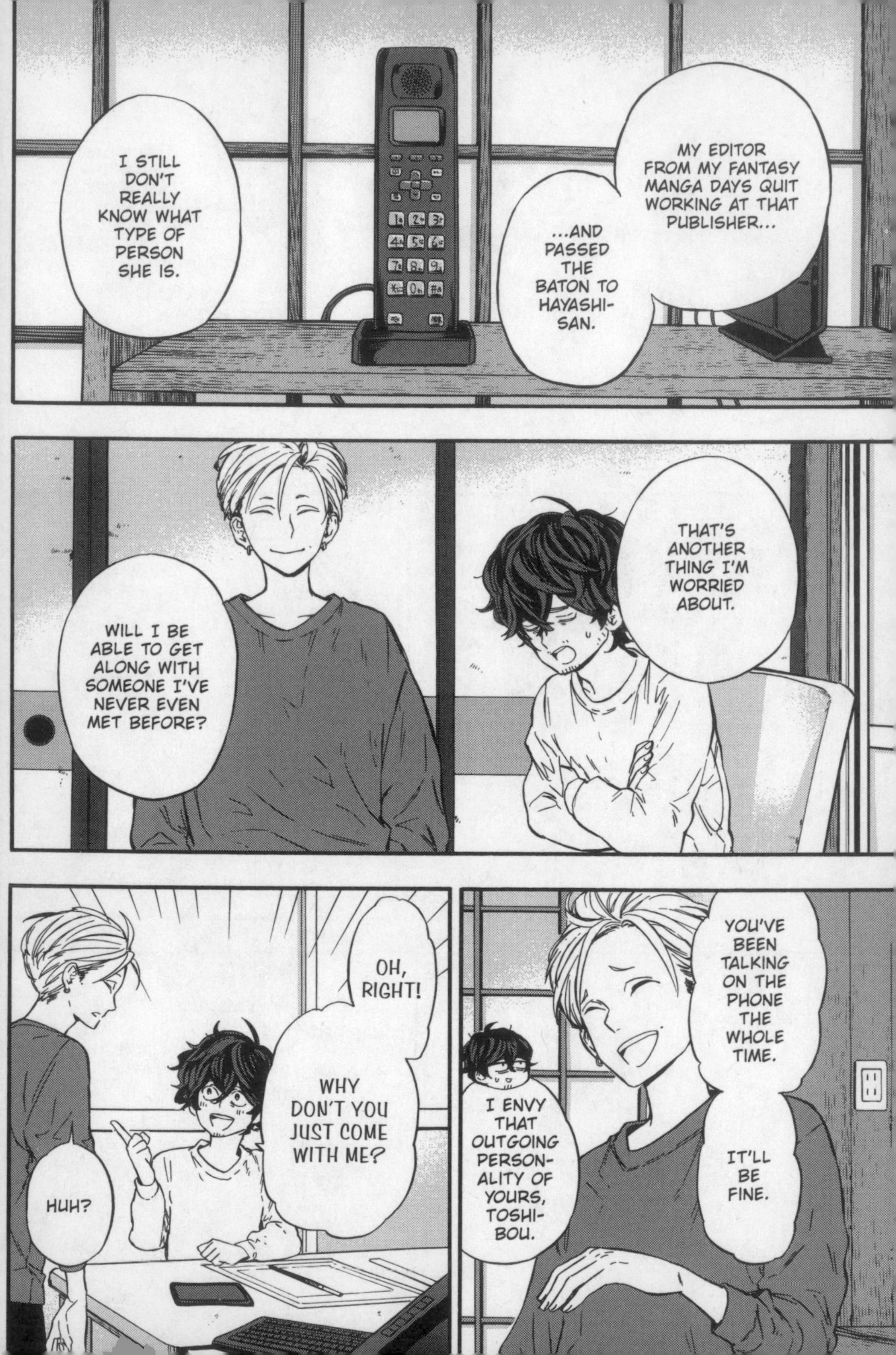
MY EDITOR FROM MY FANTASY MANGA DAYS QUIT WORKING AT THAT PUBLISHER...
...AND PASSED THE BATON TO HAYASHI-SAN.
I STILL DON'T REALLY KNOW WHAT TYPE OF PERSON SHE IS.
THAT'S ANOTHER THING I'M WORRIED ABOUT.
WILL I BE ABLE TO GET ALONG WITH SOMEONE I'VE NEVER EVEN MET BEFORE?
YOU'VE BEEN TALKING ON THE PHONE THE WHOLE TIME.
IT'LL BE FINE.
I ENVY THAT OUTGOING PERSONALITY OF YOURS, TOSHIBOU.
OH, RIGHT!
WHY DON'T YOU JUST COME WITH ME?
HUH?

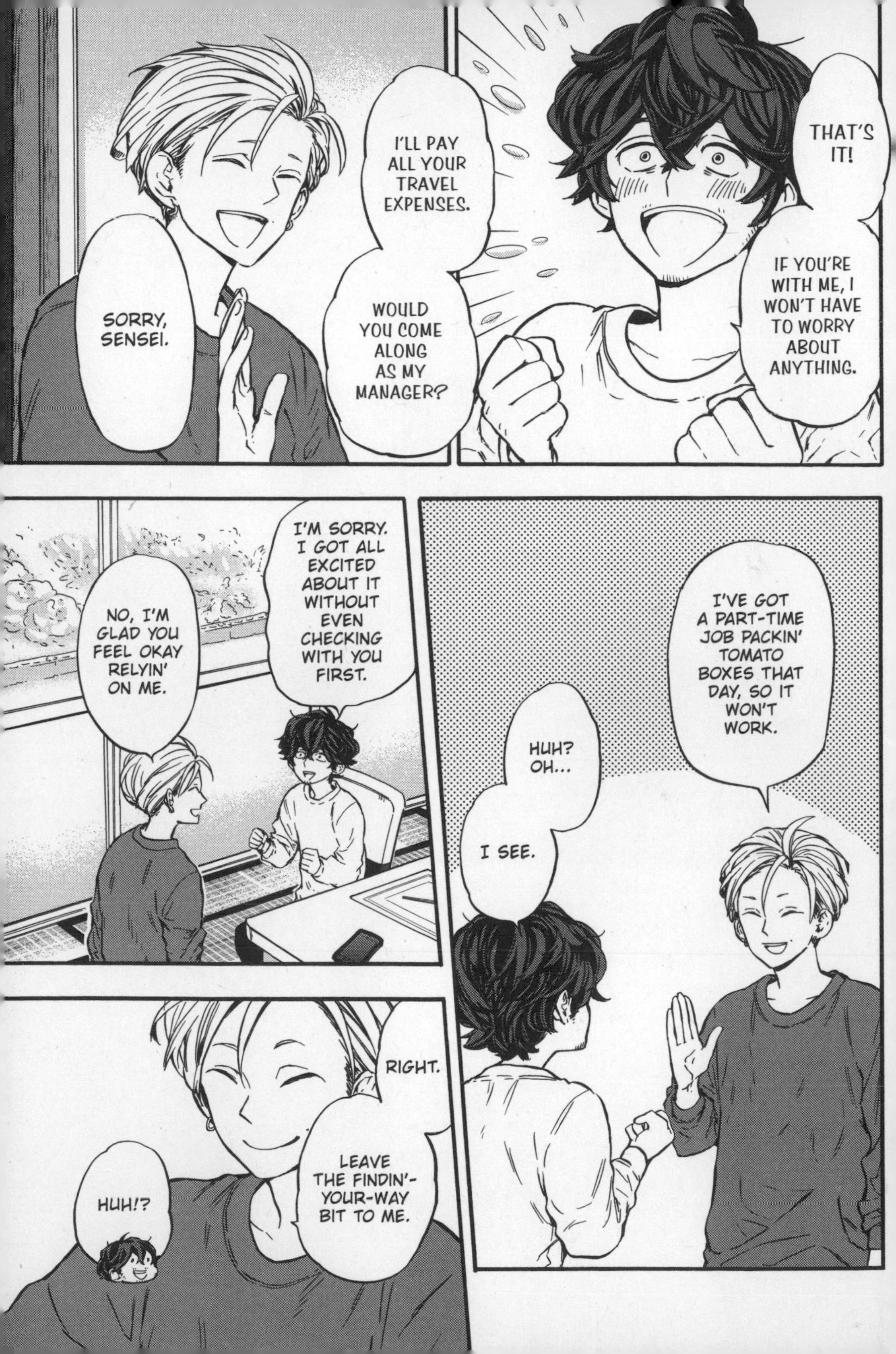
THAT'S IT!
IF YOU'RE WITH ME, I WON'T HAVE TO WORRY ABOUT ANYTHING.
I'LL PAY ALL YOUR TRAVEL EXPENSES.
WOULD YOU COME ALONG AS MY MANAGER?
SORRY, SENSEI.
I'VE GOT A PART-TIME JOB PACKIN' TOMATO BOXES THAT DAY, SO IT WON'T WORK.
HUH? OH...
I SEE.
I'M SORRY. I GOT ALL EXCITED ABOUT IT WITHOUT EVEN CHECKING WITH YOU FIRST.
NO, I'M GLAD YOU FEEL OKAY RELYIN' ON ME.
RIGHT.
LEAVE THE FINDIN'-YOUR-WAY BIT TO ME.
HUH!?

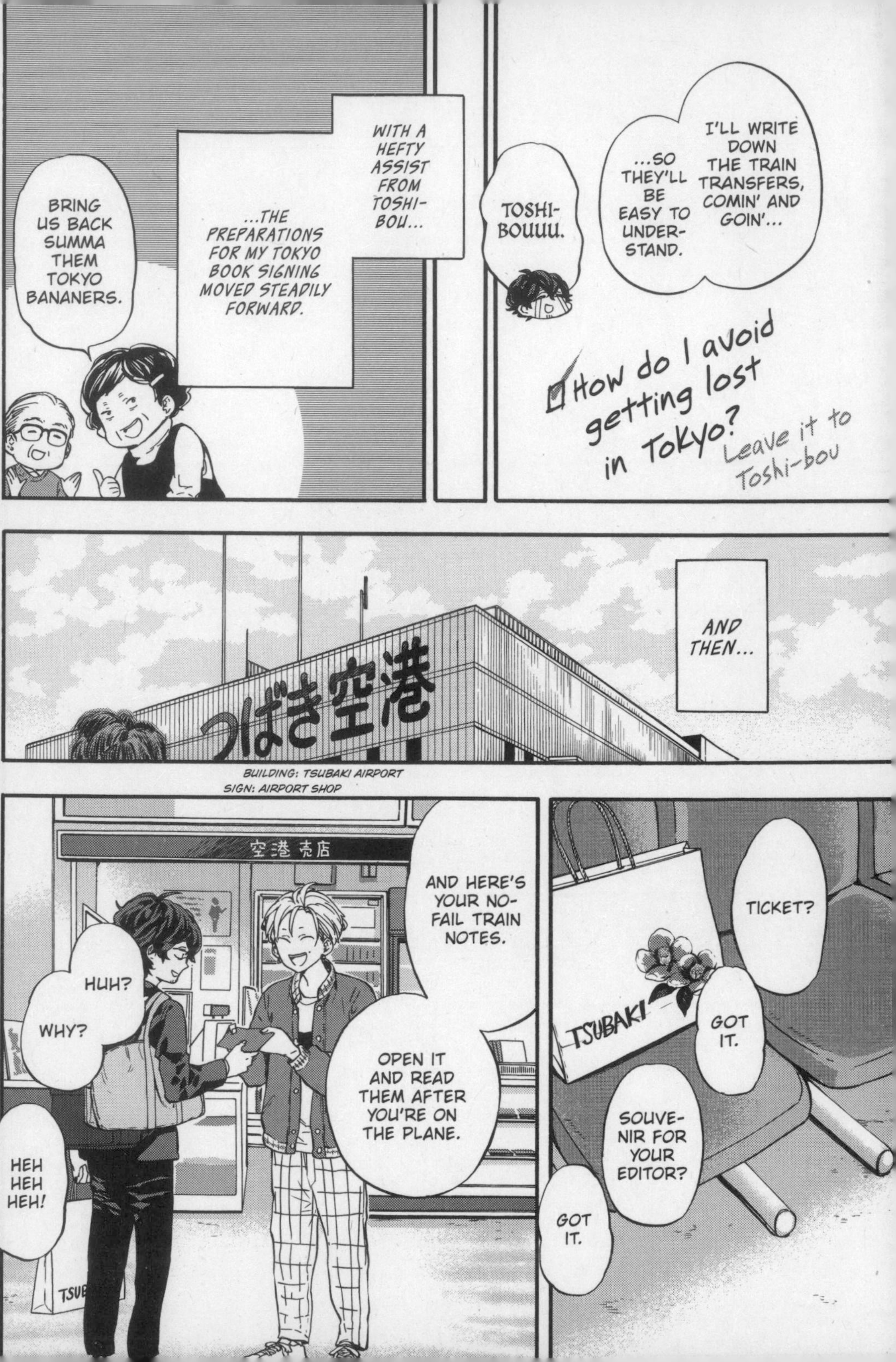
I'LL WRITE DOWN THE TRAIN TRANSFERS, COMIN' AND GOIN'...
...SO THEY'LL BE EASY TO UNDERSTAND.
TOSHI-BOUUU.
How do I avoid getting lost in Tokyo?
Leave it to Toshi-bou
WITH A HEFTY ASSIST FROM TOSHI-BOU...
...THE PREPARATIONS FOR MY TOKYO BOOK SIGNING MOVED STEADILY FORWARD.
BRING US BACK SUMMA THEM TOKYO BANANERS.
AND THEN...
つばき空港
TICKET?
GOT IT.
TSUBAKI
SOUVENIR FOR YOUR EDITOR?
GOT IT.
空港売店
AND HERE'S YOUR NO-FAIL TRAIN NOTES.
HUH?
WHY?
OPEN IT AND READ THEM AFTER YOU'RE ON THE PLANE.
HEH HEH HEH!

BUILDING: TSUBAKI AIRPORT
SIGN: AIRPORT SHOP

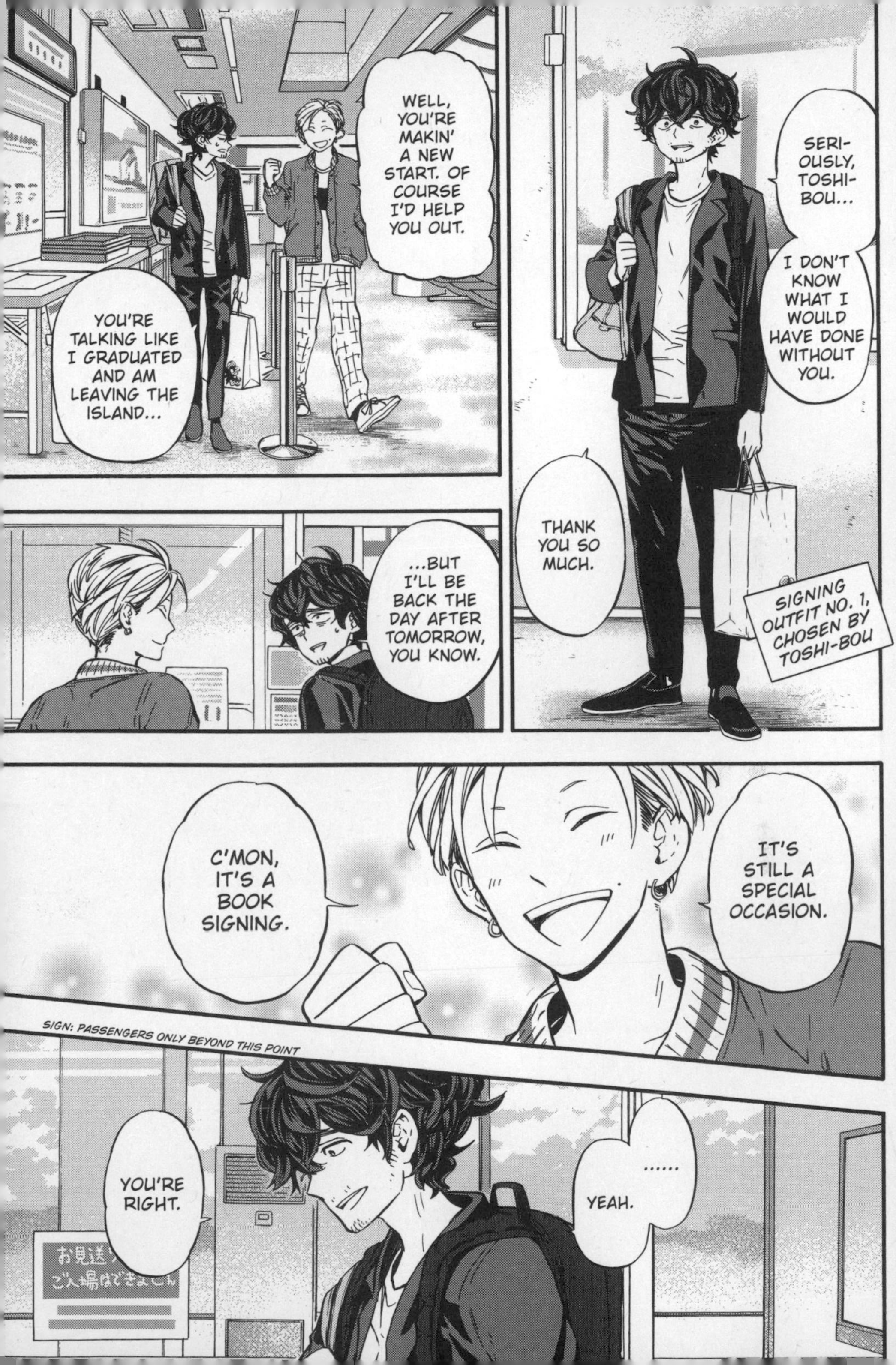
SERI-OUSLY, TOSHI-BOU...
I DON'T KNOW WHAT I WOULD HAVE DONE WITHOUT YOU.
THANK YOU SO MUCH.
SIGNING OUTFIT NO. 1, CHOSEN BY TOSHI-BOU
WELL, YOU'RE MAKIN' A NEW START. OF COURSE I'D HELP YOU OUT.
YOU'RE TALKING LIKE I GRADUATED AND AM LEAVING THE ISLAND...
...BUT I'LL BE BACK THE DAY AFTER TOMORROW, YOU KNOW.
IT'S STILL A SPECIAL OCCASION.
C'MON, IT'S A BOOK SIGNING.
SIGN: PASSENGERS ONLY BEYOND THIS POINT
......
YEAH.
YOU'RE RIGHT.

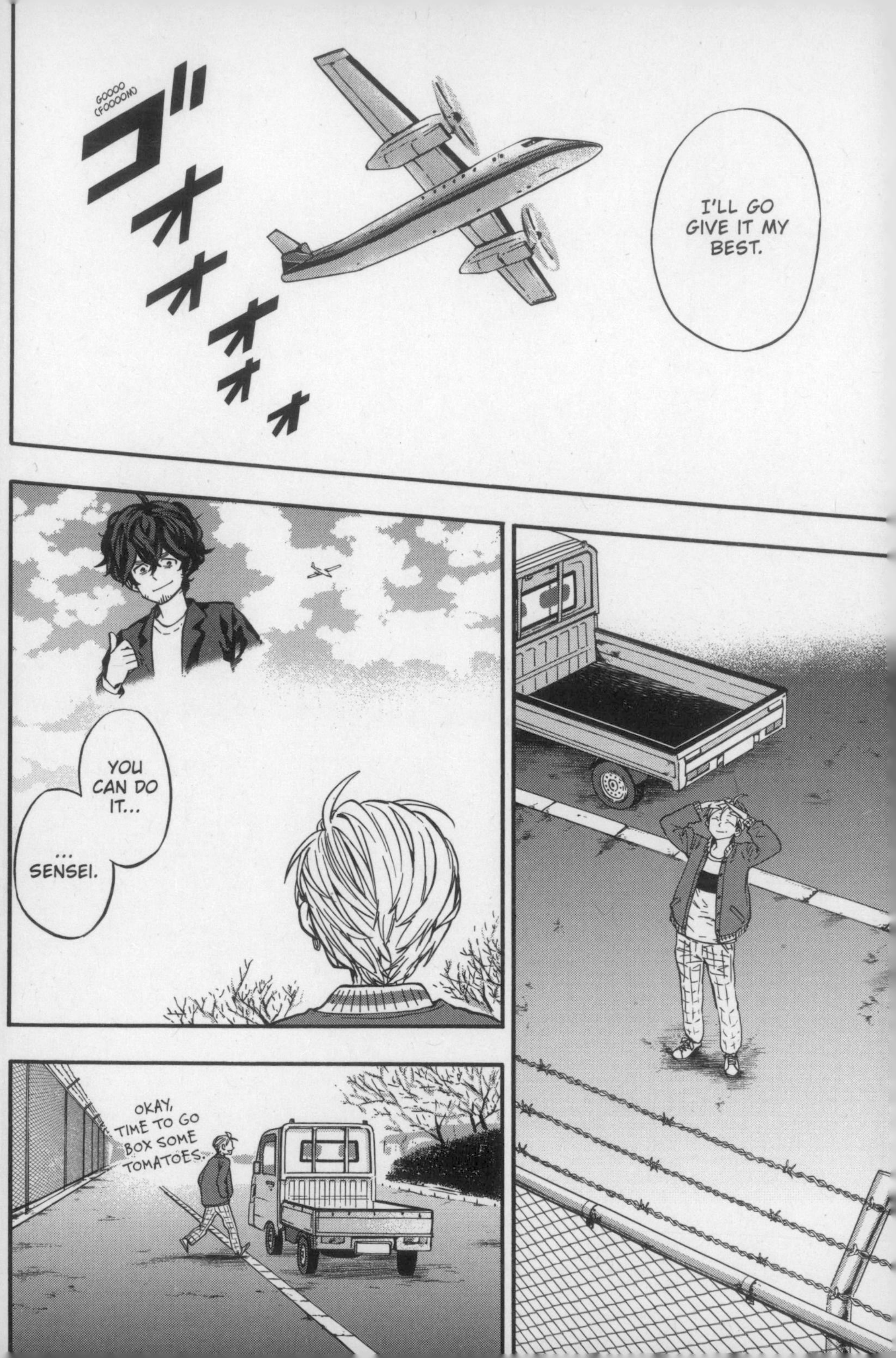
I'LL GO GIVE IT MY BEST.
GOOOO (FOOOOM)
ゴォォォォォ
YOU CAN DO IT...
... SENSEI.
OKAY, TIME TO GO BOX SOME TOMATOES.

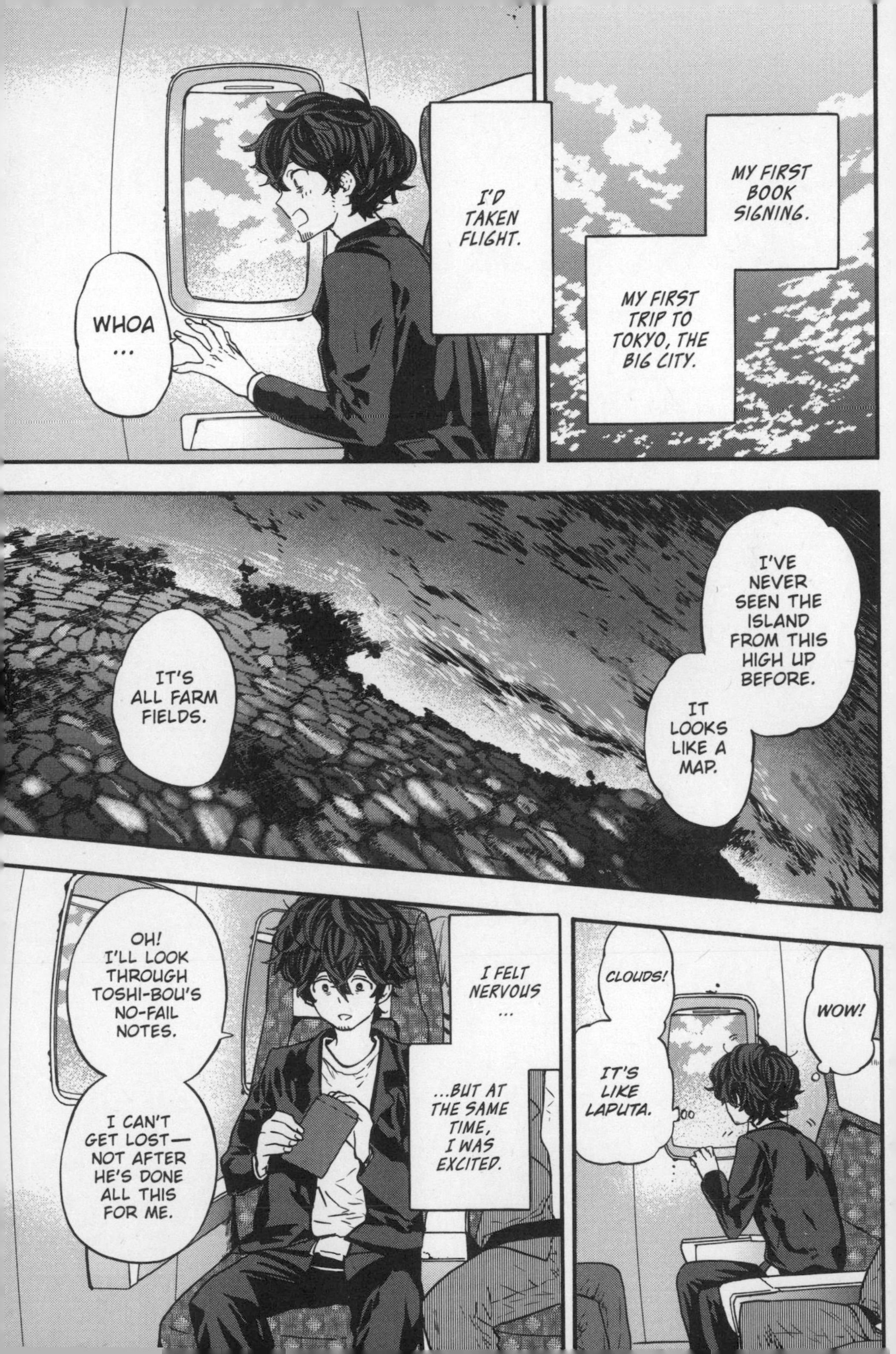
MY FIRST BOOK SIGNING.
MY FIRST TRIP TO TOKYO, THE BIG CITY.
I'D TAKEN FLIGHT.
WHOA ...
I'VE NEVER SEEN THE ISLAND FROM THIS HIGH UP BEFORE.
IT LOOKS LIKE A MAP.
IT'S ALL FARM FIELDS.
WOW!
CLOUDS!
IT'S LIKE LAPUTA.
I FELT NERVOUS ...
...BUT AT THE SAME TIME, I WAS EXCITED.
OH! I'LL LOOK THROUGH TOSHI-BOU'S NO-FAIL NOTES.
I CAN'T GET LOST—NOT AFTER HE'S DONE ALL THIS FOR ME.

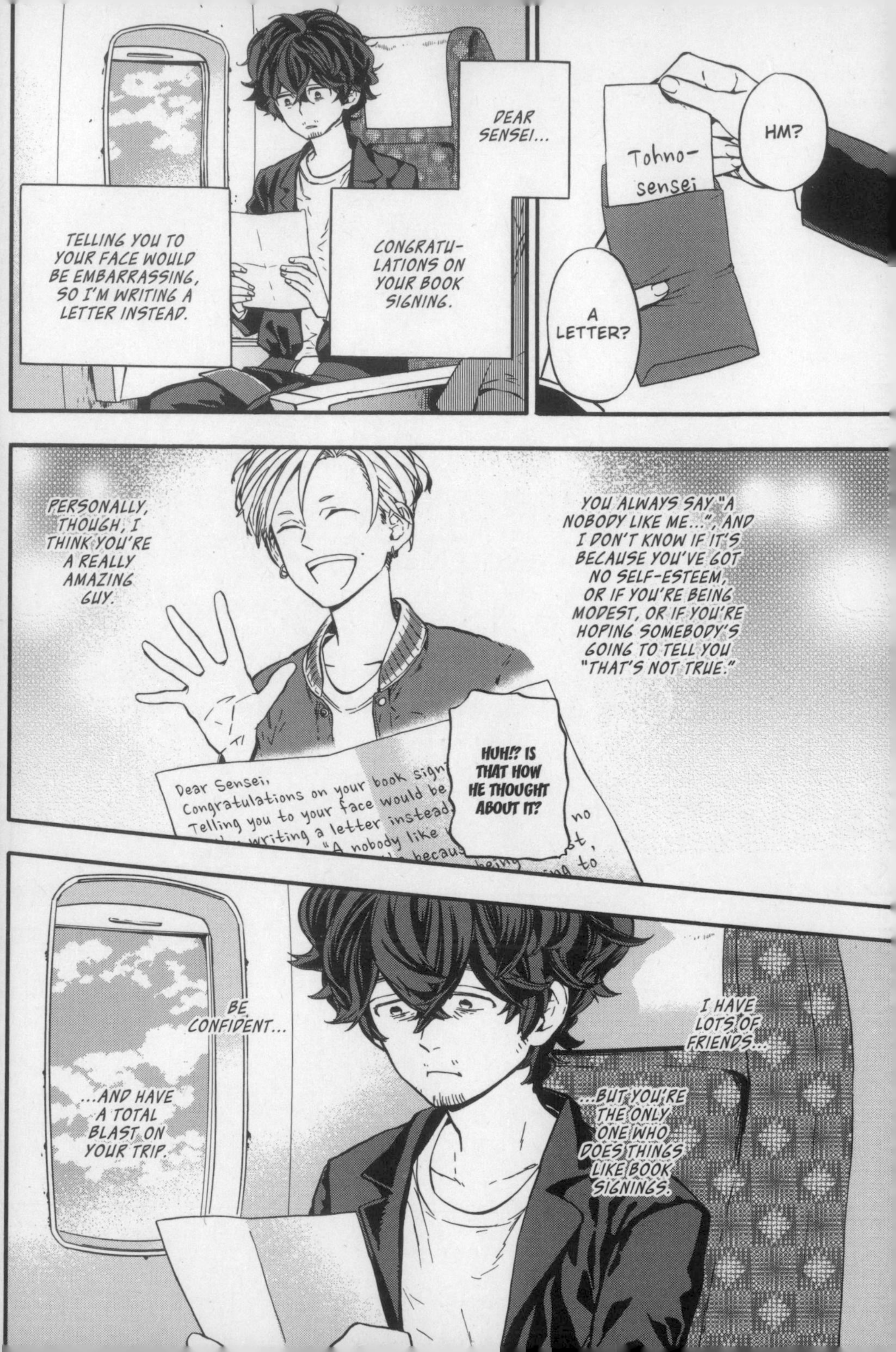
HM?
Tohno-sensei
A LETTER?
DEAR SENSEI...
CONGRATULATIONS ON YOUR BOOK SIGNING.
TELLING YOU TO YOUR FACE WOULD BE EMBARRASSING, SO I'M WRITING A LETTER INSTEAD.
YOU ALWAYS SAY "A NOBODY LIKE ME...", AND I DON'T KNOW IF IT'S BECAUSE YOU'VE GOT NO SELF-ESTEEM, OR IF YOU'RE BEING MODEST, OR IF YOU'RE HOPING SOMEBODY'S GOING TO TELL YOU "THAT'S NOT TRUE."
PERSONALLY, THOUGH, I THINK YOU'RE A REALLY AMAZING GUY.
HUH!? IS THAT HOW HE THOUGHT ABOUT IT?
Dear Sensei,
Congratulations on your book sign
Telling you to your face would be
I HAVE LOTS OF FRIENDS...
...BUT YOU'RE THE ONLY ONE WHO DOES THINGS LIKE BOOK SIGNINGS.
BE CONFIDENT...
...AND HAVE A TOTAL BLAST ON YOUR TRIP.

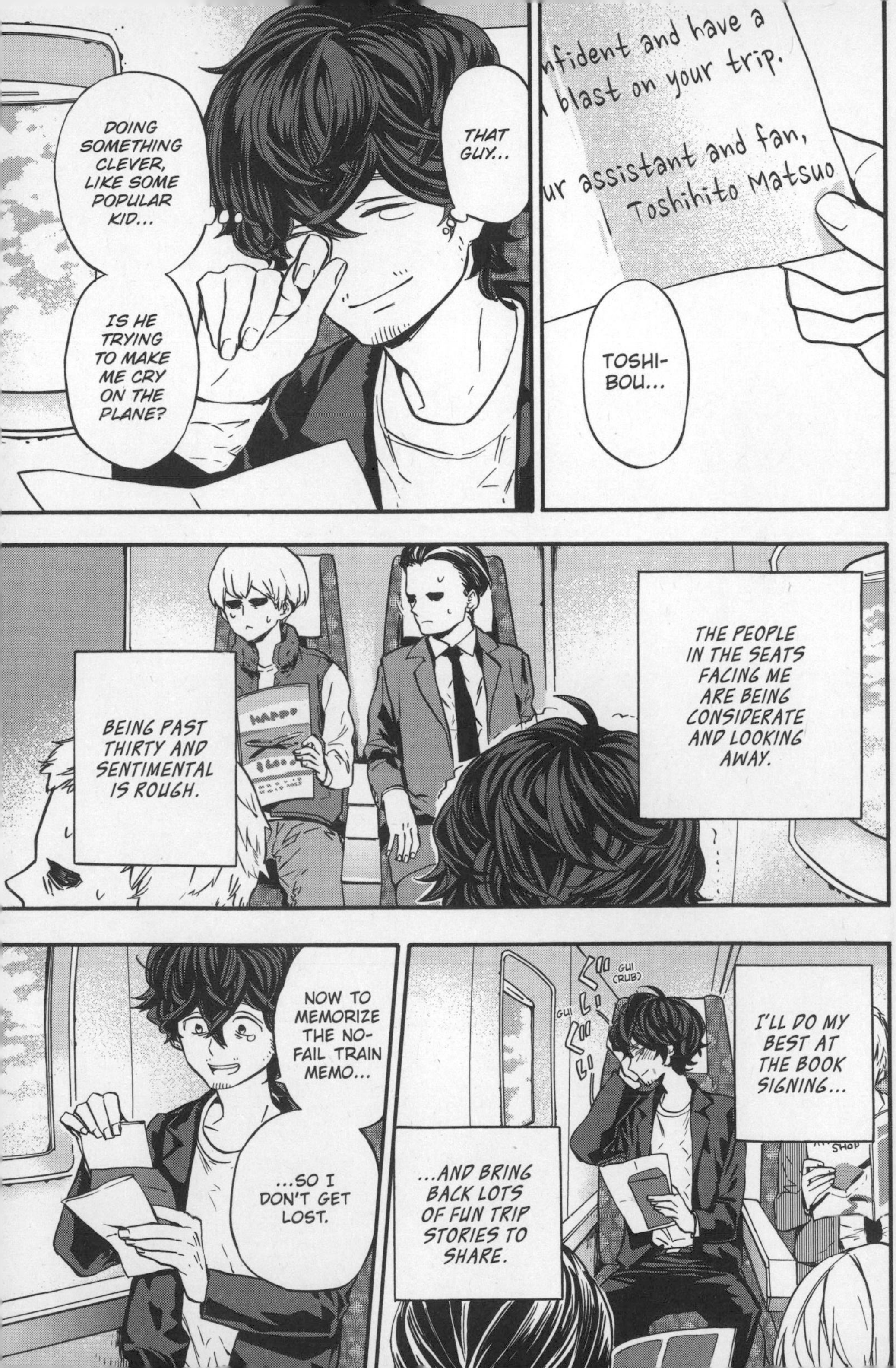
nfident and have a
blast on your trip.
ur assistant and fan,
Toshihito Matsuo
TOSHI-BOU...
THAT GUY...
DOING SOMETHING CLEVER, LIKE SOME POPULAR KID...
IS HE TRYING TO MAKE ME CRY ON THE PLANE?
THE PEOPLE IN THE SEATS FACING ME ARE BEING CONSIDERATE AND LOOKING AWAY.
BEING PAST THIRTY AND SENTIMENTAL IS ROUGH.
I'LL DO MY BEST AT THE BOOK SIGNING...
GUI (RUB)
GUI
SHOP
...AND BRING BACK LOTS OF FUN TRIP STORIES TO SHARE.
NOW TO MEMORIZE THE NO-FAIL TRAIN MEMO...
...SO I DON'T GET LOST.

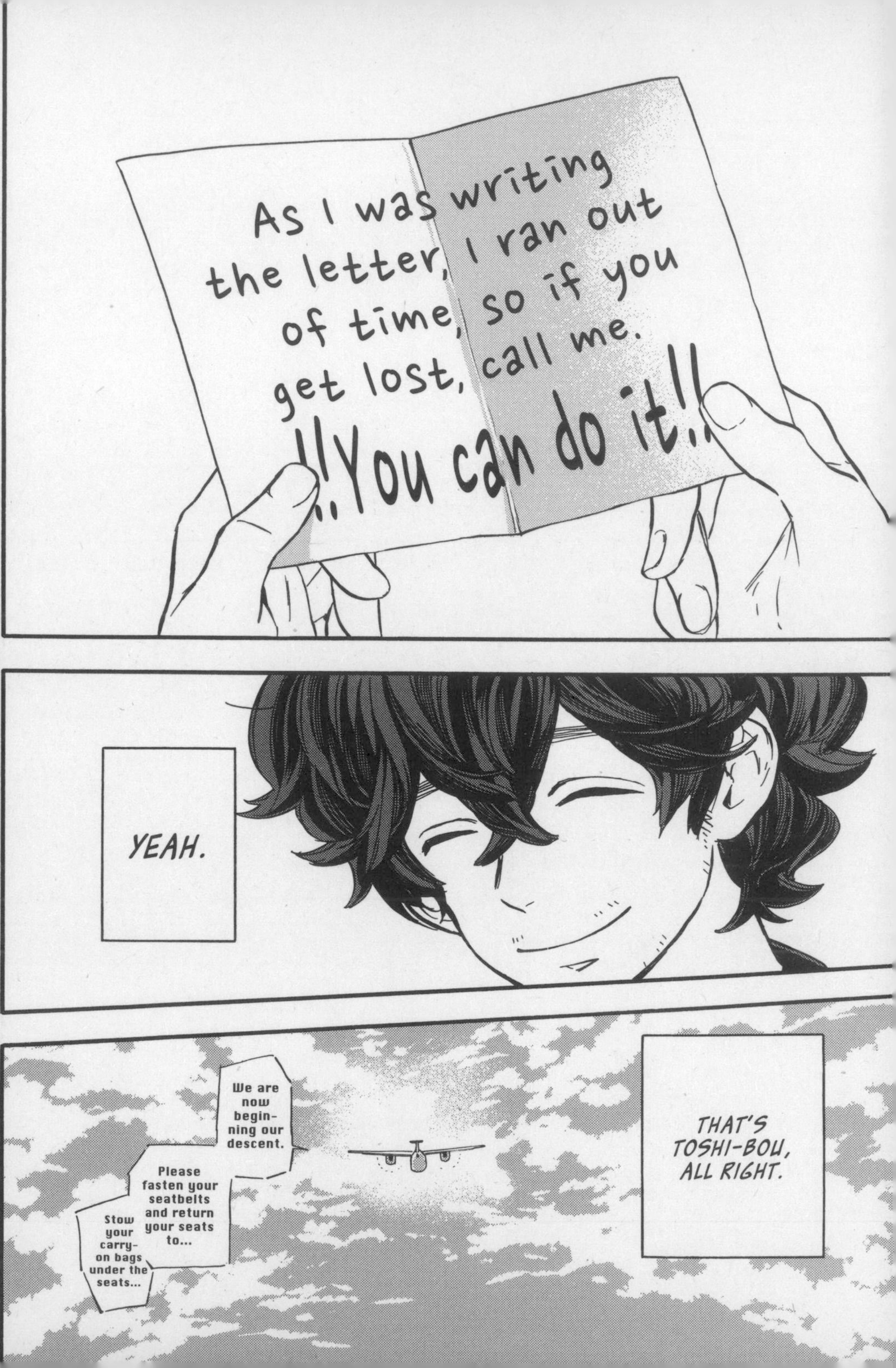
As I was writing the letter, I ran out of time, so if you get lost, call me.
!!You can do it!!
YEAH.
THAT'S TOSHI-BOU, ALL RIGHT.
We are now begin-ning our descent.
Please fasten your seatbelts and return your seats to...
Stow your carry-on bags under the seats...

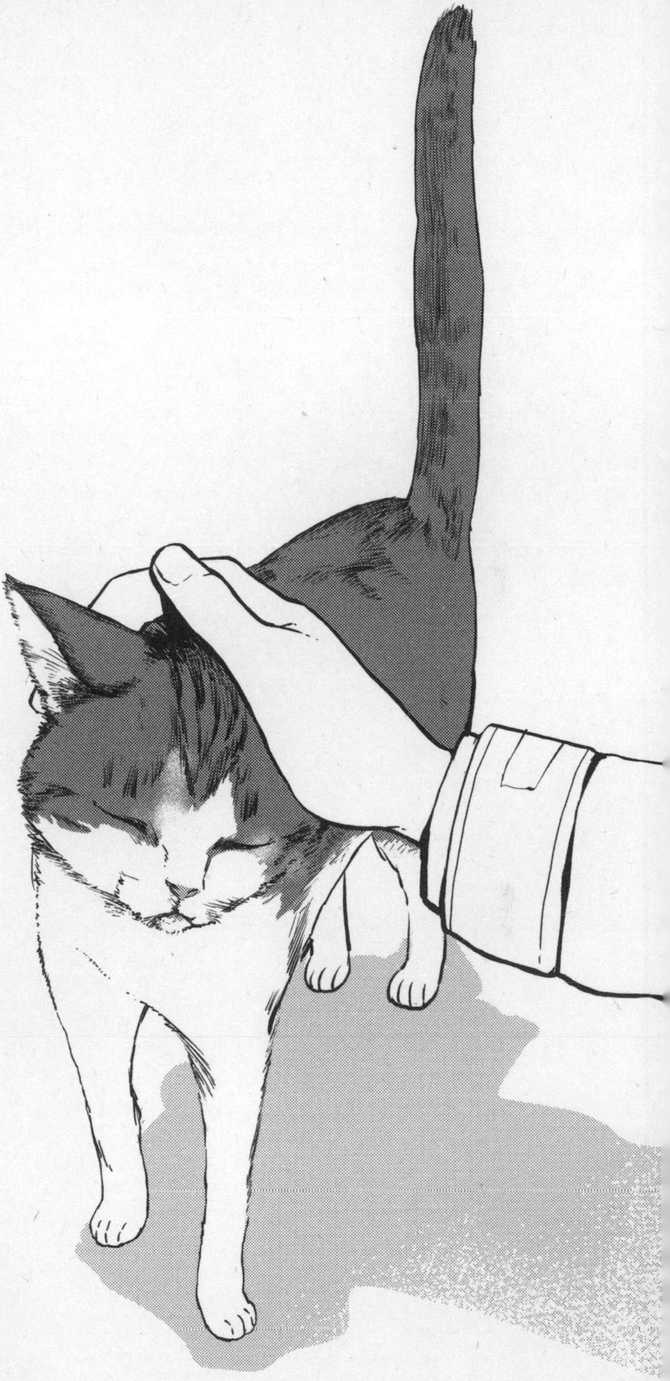

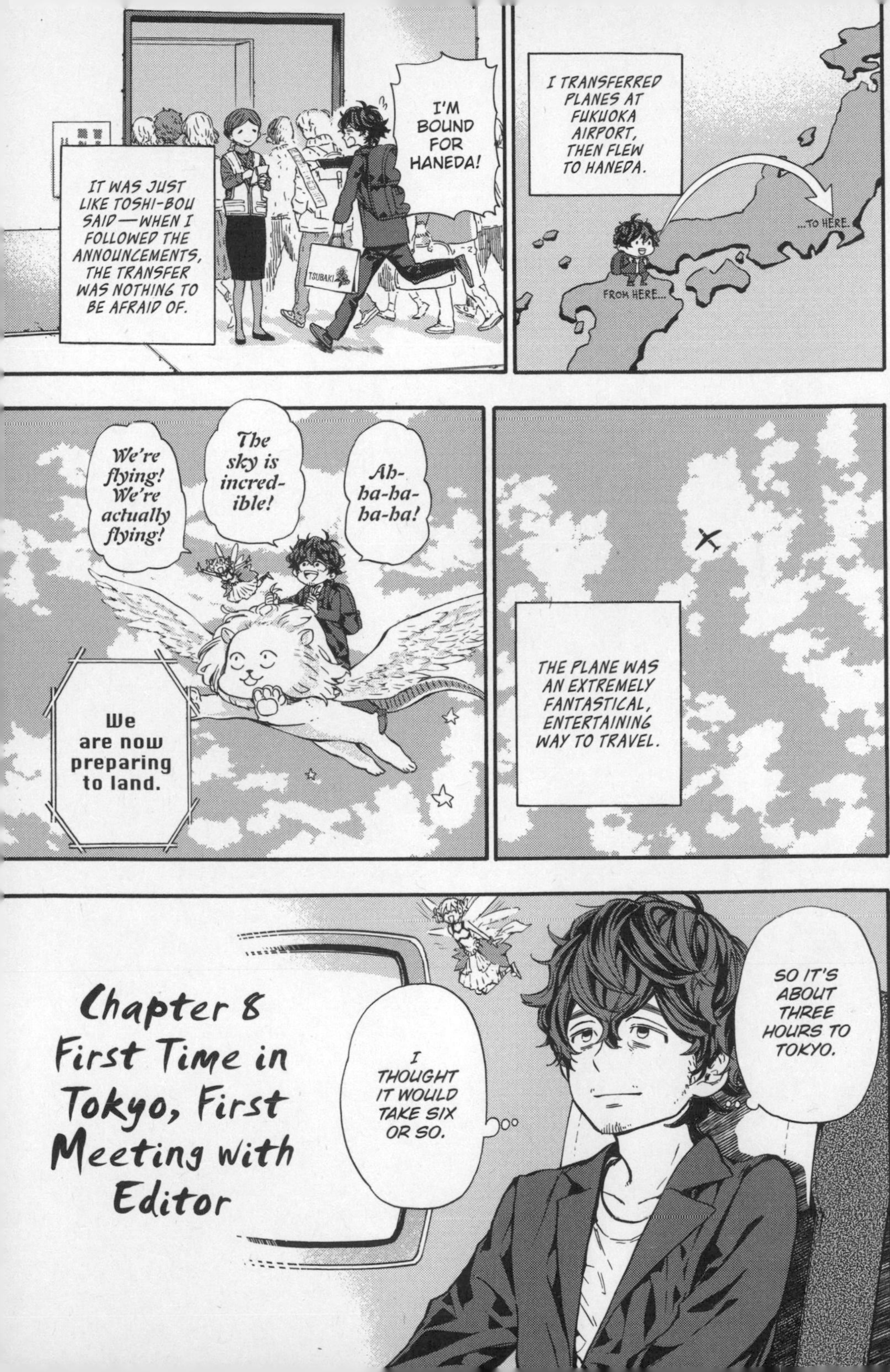
I TRANSFERRED PLANES AT FUKUOKA AIRPORT, THEN FLEW TO HANEDA.
...TO HERE.
FROM HERE...
I'M BOUND FOR HANEDA!
IT WAS JUST LIKE TOSHI-BOU SAID—WHEN I FOLLOWED THE ANNOUNCEMENTS, THE TRANSFER WAS NOTHING TO BE AFRAID OF.
TSUBAKI
THE PLANE WAS AN EXTREMELY FANTASTICAL, ENTERTAINING WAY TO TRAVEL.
Ah-ha-ha-ha-ha!
The sky is incred-ible!
We're flying! We're actually flying!
We are now preparing to land.
SO IT'S ABOUT THREE HOURS TO TOKYO.
I THOUGHT IT WOULD TAKE SIX OR SO.
Chapter 8
First Time in Tokyo, First Meeting with Editor

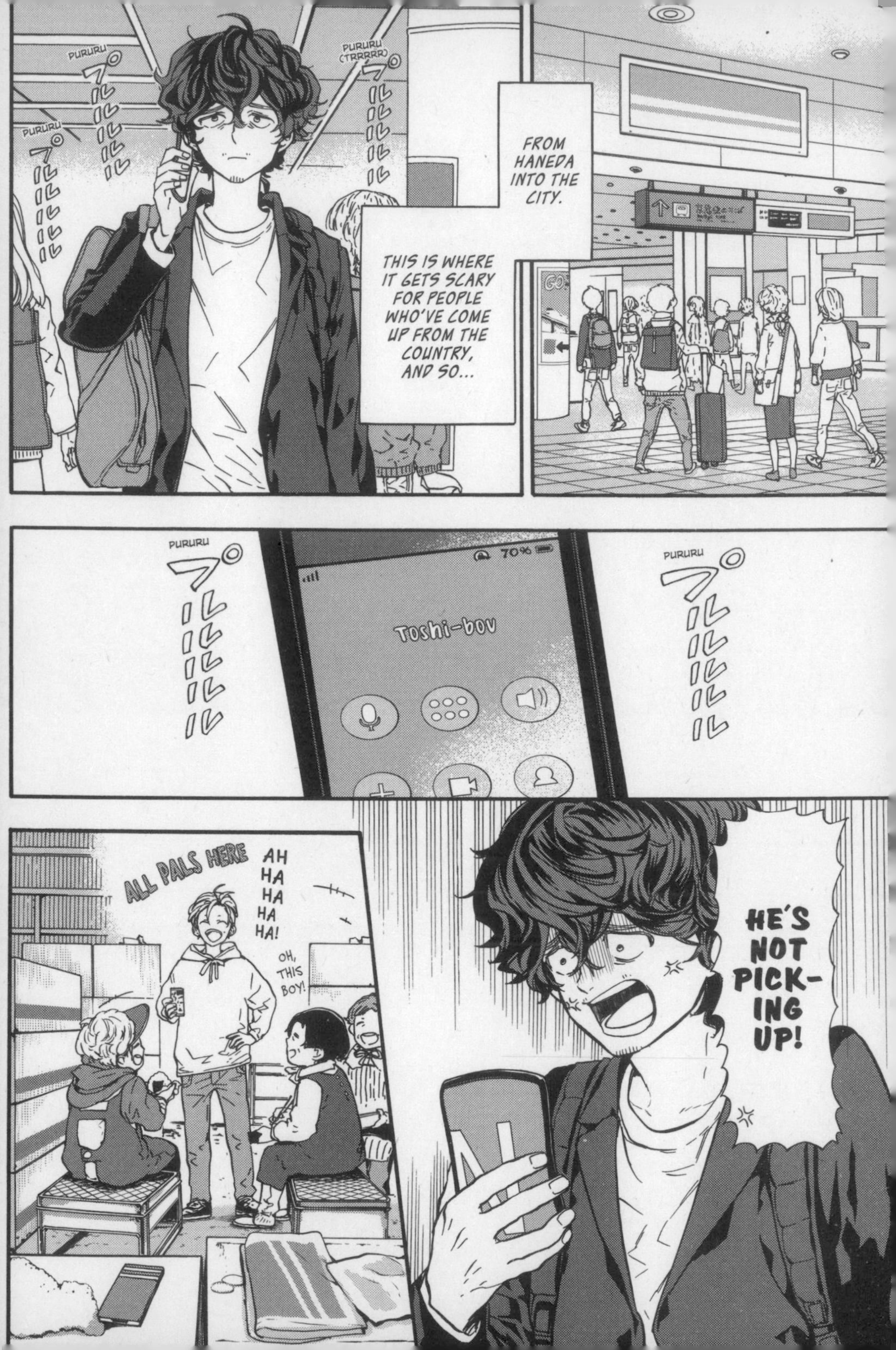

FROM HANEDA INTO THE CITY.
THIS IS WHERE IT GETS SCARY FOR PEOPLE WHO'VE COME UP FROM THE COUNTRY, AND SO...
PURURU (TRRRRR)
PURURU
PURURU
PURURU
70%
Toshi-bov
PURURU
HE'S NOT PICK-ING UP!
ALL PALS HERE
AH HA HA HA HA!
OH, THIS BOY!

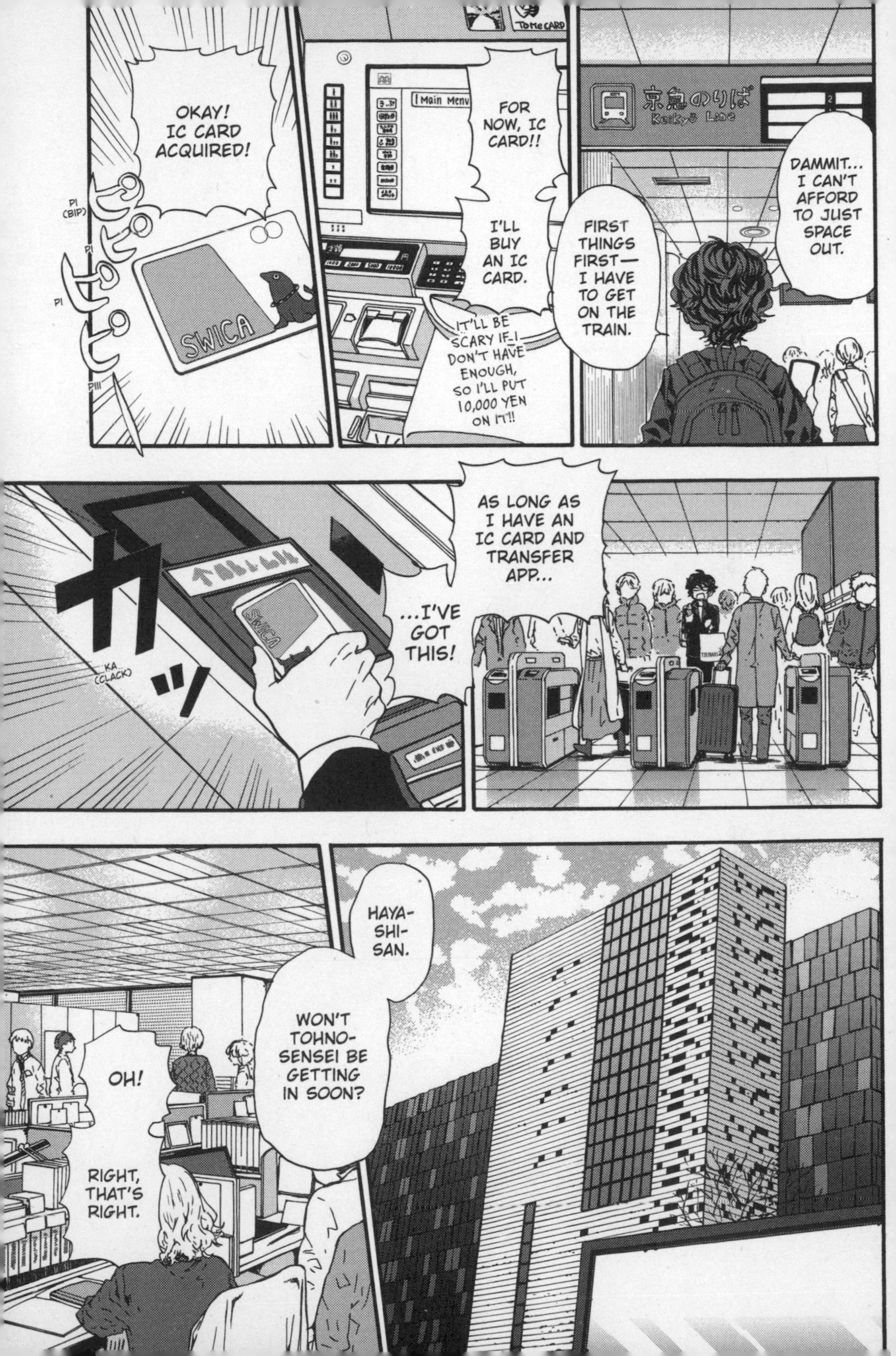
京急のりば
Keikyu Line
DAMMIT... I CAN'T AFFORD TO JUST SPACE OUT.
FIRST THINGS FIRST— I HAVE TO GET ON THE TRAIN.
FOR NOW, IC CARD!!
I'LL BUY AN IC CARD.
IT'LL BE SCARY IF I DON'T HAVE ENOUGH, SO I'LL PUT 10,000 YEN ON IT!!
OKAY! IC CARD ACQUIRED!
PI (BIP)
PI
PI
PIII
SWICA
AS LONG AS I HAVE AN IC CARD AND TRANSFER APP...
...I'VE GOT THIS!
SWICA
KA (CLACK)
HAYA-SHI-SAN.
WON'T TOHNO-SENSEI BE GETTING IN SOON?
OH!
RIGHT, THAT'S RIGHT.

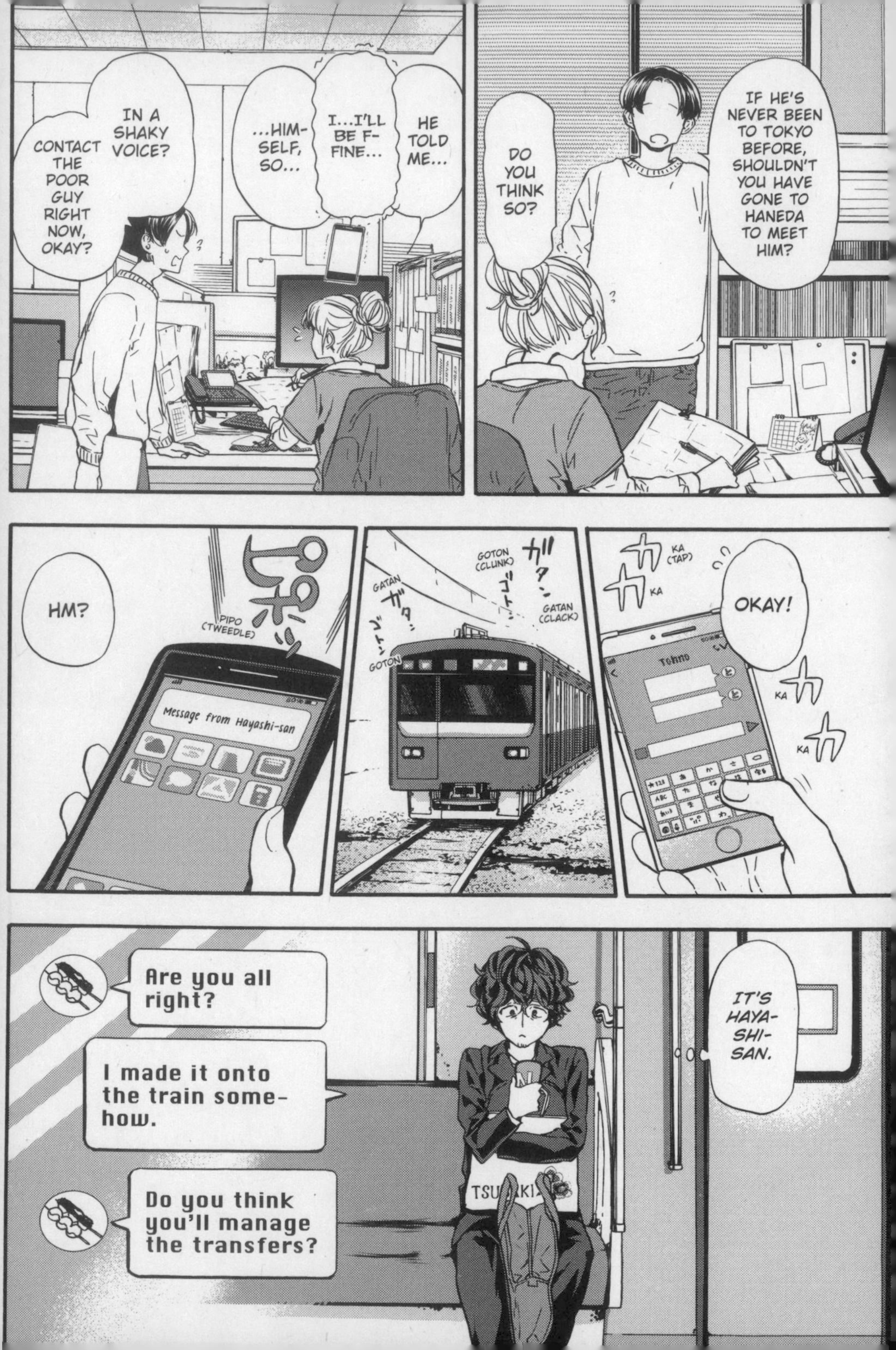
IF HE'S NEVER BEEN TO TOKYO BEFORE, SHOULDN'T YOU HAVE GONE TO HANEDA TO MEET HIM?
DO YOU THINK SO?
HE TOLD ME...
I...I'LL BE F-FINE...
...HIM-SELF, SO...
IN A SHAKY VOICE?
CONTACT THE POOR GUY RIGHT NOW, OKAY?
KA (TAP)
OKAY!
KA
KA
KA
GOTON (CLLINK)
GATAN (CLACK)
GATAN
GOTON
HM?
PIPO (TWEEDLE)
Message from Hayashi-san
IT'S HAYA-SHI-SAN.
Are you all right?
I made it onto the train some-how.
Do you think you'll manage the transfers?

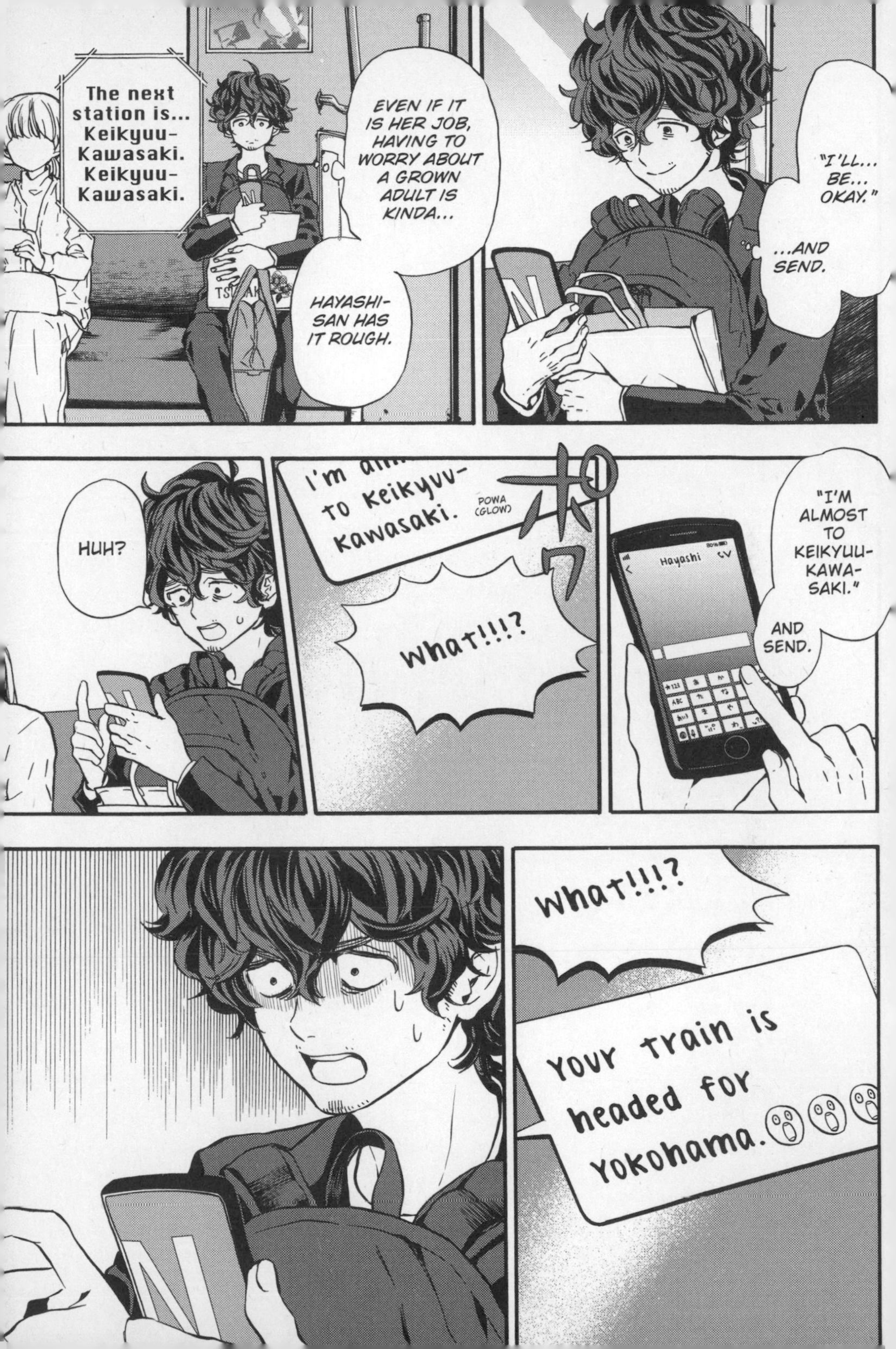

"I'LL... BE... OKAY."
...AND SEND.
EVEN IF IT IS HER JOB, HAVING TO WORRY ABOUT A GROWN ADULT IS KINDA...
The next station is... Keikyuu-Kawasaki. Keikyuu-Kawasaki.
HAYASHI-SAN HAS IT ROUGH.
"I'M ALMOST TO KEIKYUU-KAWASAKI."
Hayashi
AND SEND.
I'm alm
to Keikyuu-Kawasaki.
POWA (GLOW)
What!!!?
HUH?
What!!!?
Your train is headed for Yokohama.

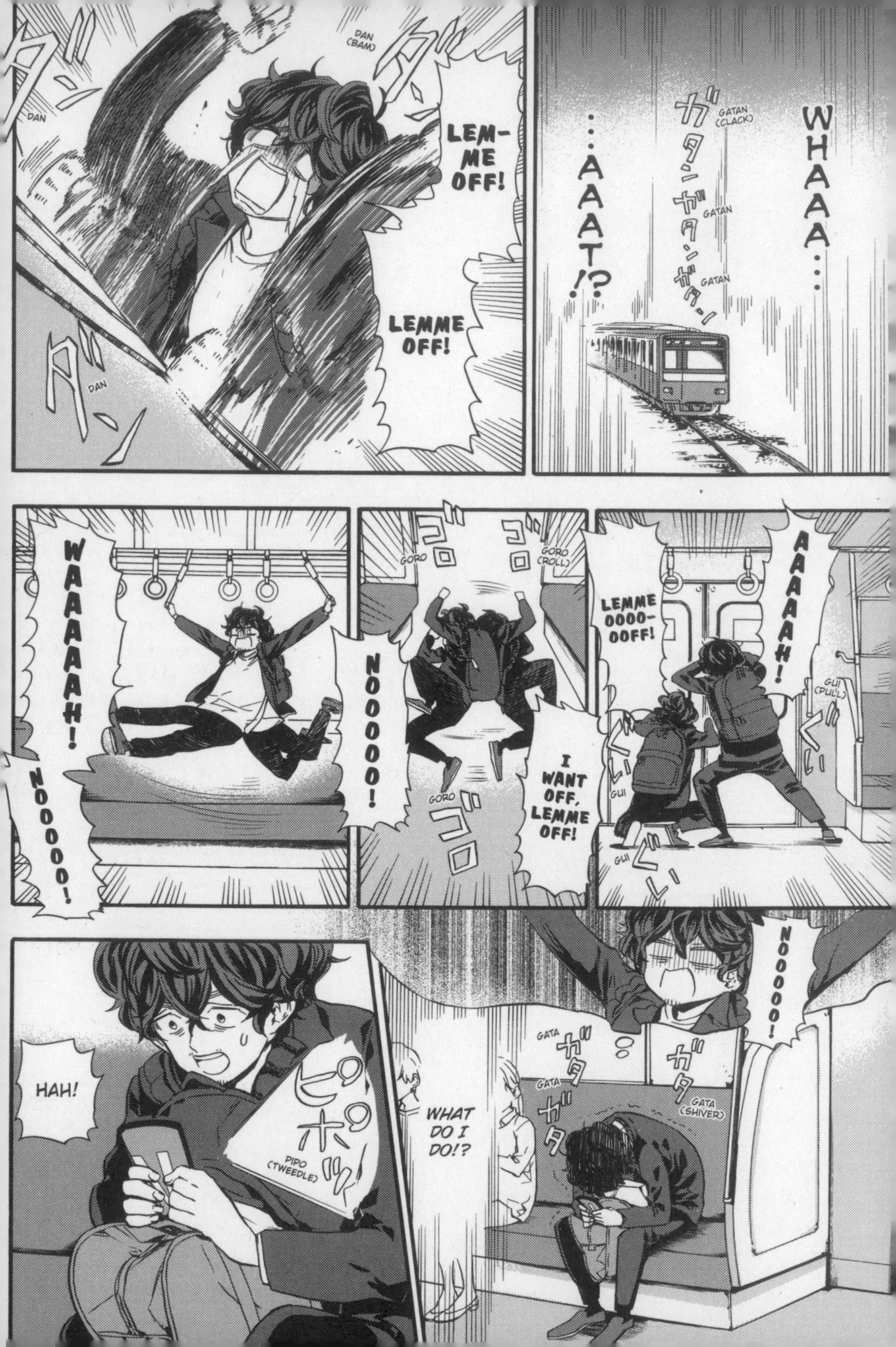
WHAAA...
GATAN (CLACK)
GATAN
GATAN
...AAAT!?
LEM-ME OFF!
DAN (BAM)
DAN
LEMME OFF!
DAN
AAAAAAH!
GUI (PULL)
LEMME OOOO-OOFF!
I WANT OFF, LEMME OFF!
GUI
GUI
GORO (ROLL)
GORO
NOOOOOO!
GORO
WAAAAAAH!
NOOOOOO!
NOOOOOO!
GATA (SHIVER)
GATA
GATA
WHAT DO I DO!?
PIPO (TWEEDLE)
HAH!

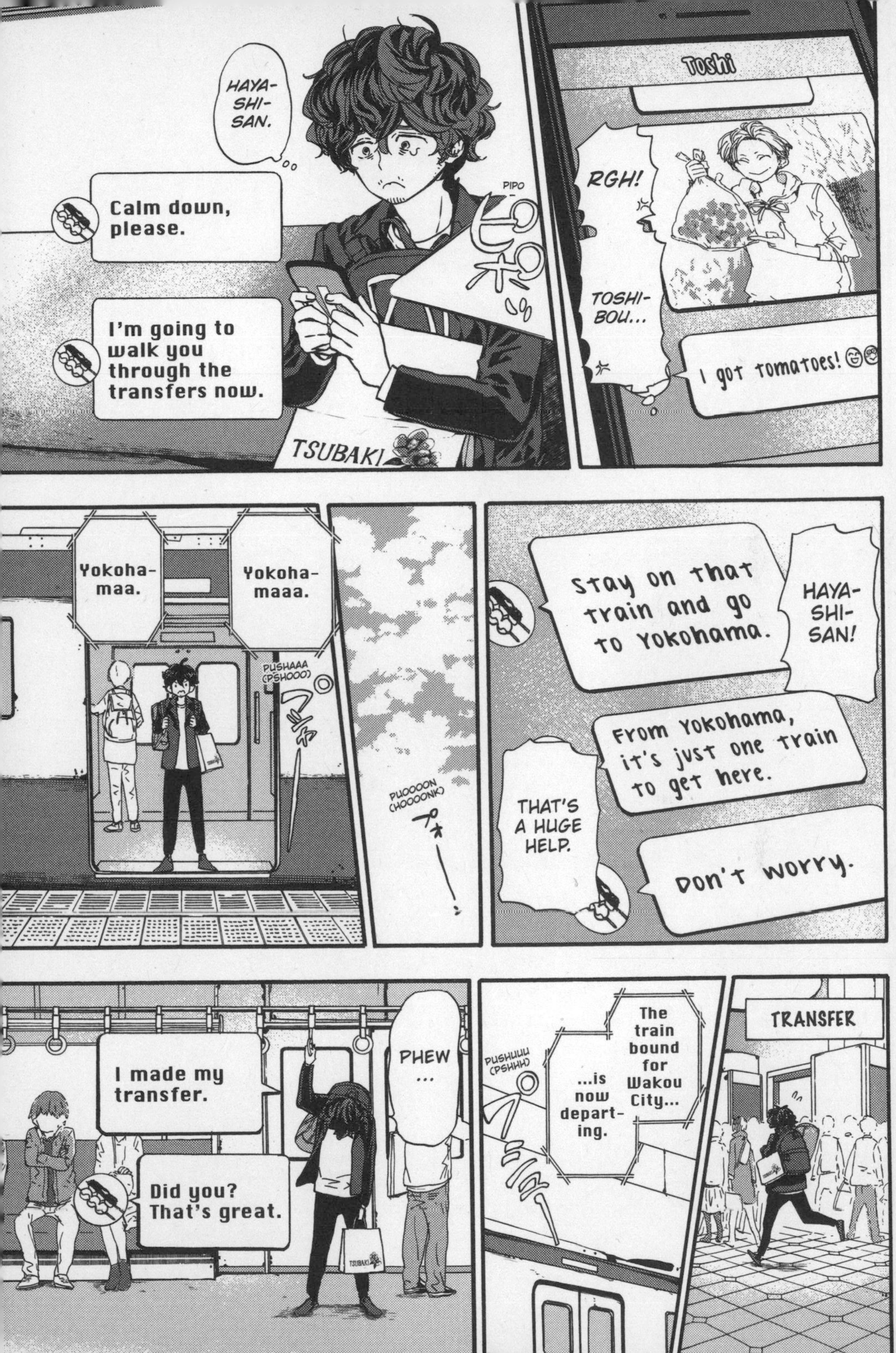

Toshi
RGH!
TOSHI-BOU...
I got tomatoes!
HAYA-SHI-SAN.
Calm down, please.
PIPO
I'm going to walk you through the transfers now.
TSUBAKI
HAYA-SHI-SAN!
Stay on that train and go to Yokohama.
From Yokohama, it's just one train to get here.
THAT'S A HUGE HELP.
Don't worry.
PUOOOON (HOOOONK)
Yokoha-maaa.
Yokoha-maa.
PUSHAAA (PSHOOO)
TRANSFER
The train bound for Wakou City...
...is now depart-ing.
PUSHUUU (PSHHH)
PHEW...
I made my transfer.
Did you? That's great.

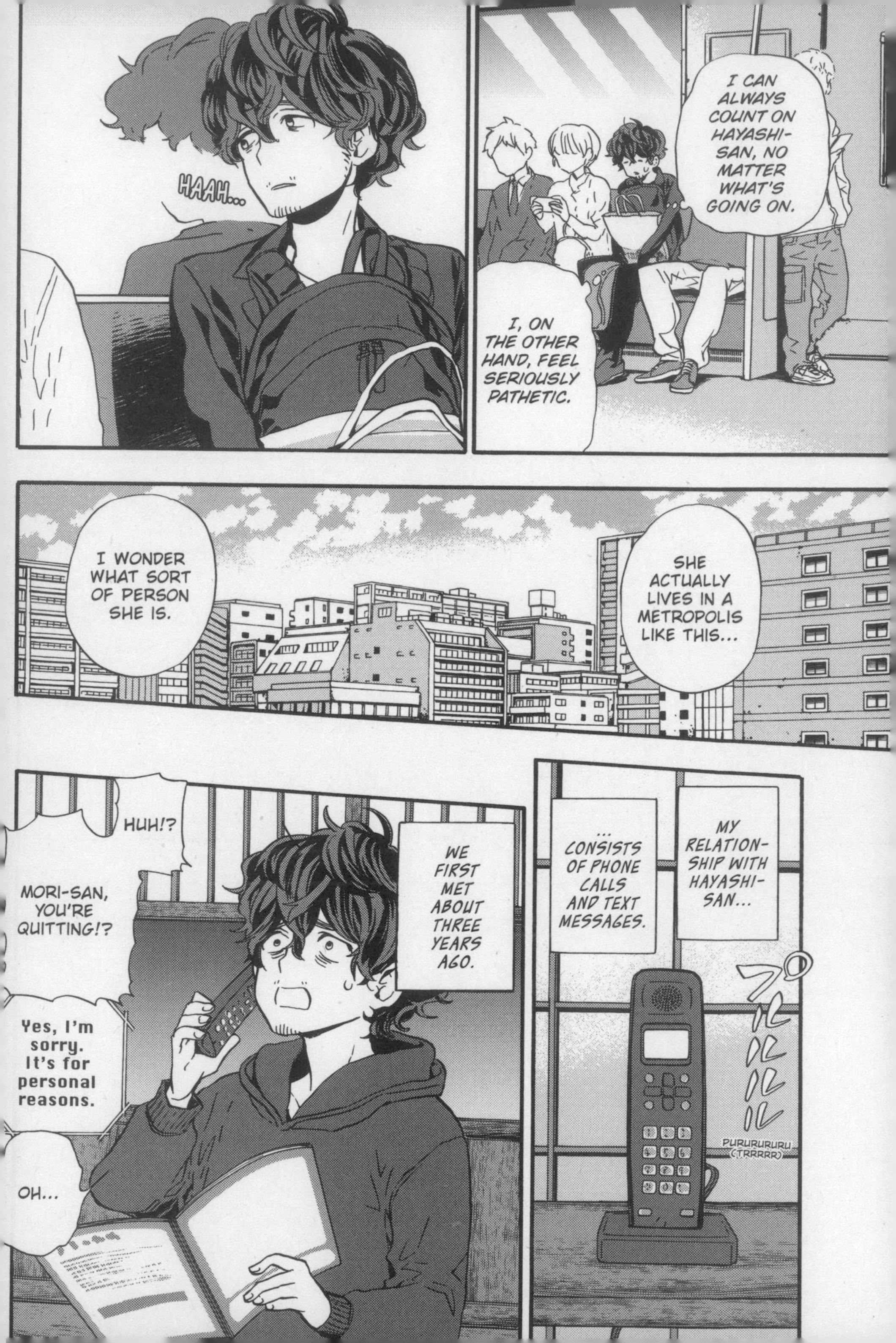
I CAN ALWAYS COUNT ON HAYASHI-SAN, NO MATTER WHAT'S GOING ON.
I, ON THE OTHER HAND, FEEL SERIOUSLY PATHETIC.
HAAH...
SHE ACTUALLY LIVES IN A METROPOLIS LIKE THIS...
I WONDER WHAT SORT OF PERSON SHE IS.
MY RELATIONSHIP WITH HAYASHI-SAN...
...CONSISTS OF PHONE CALLS AND TEXT MESSAGES.
PURURURURU (TRRRRR)
WE FIRST MET ABOUT THREE YEARS AGO.
HUH!?
MORI-SAN, YOU'RE QUITTING!?
Yes, I'm sorry. It's for personal reasons.
OH...

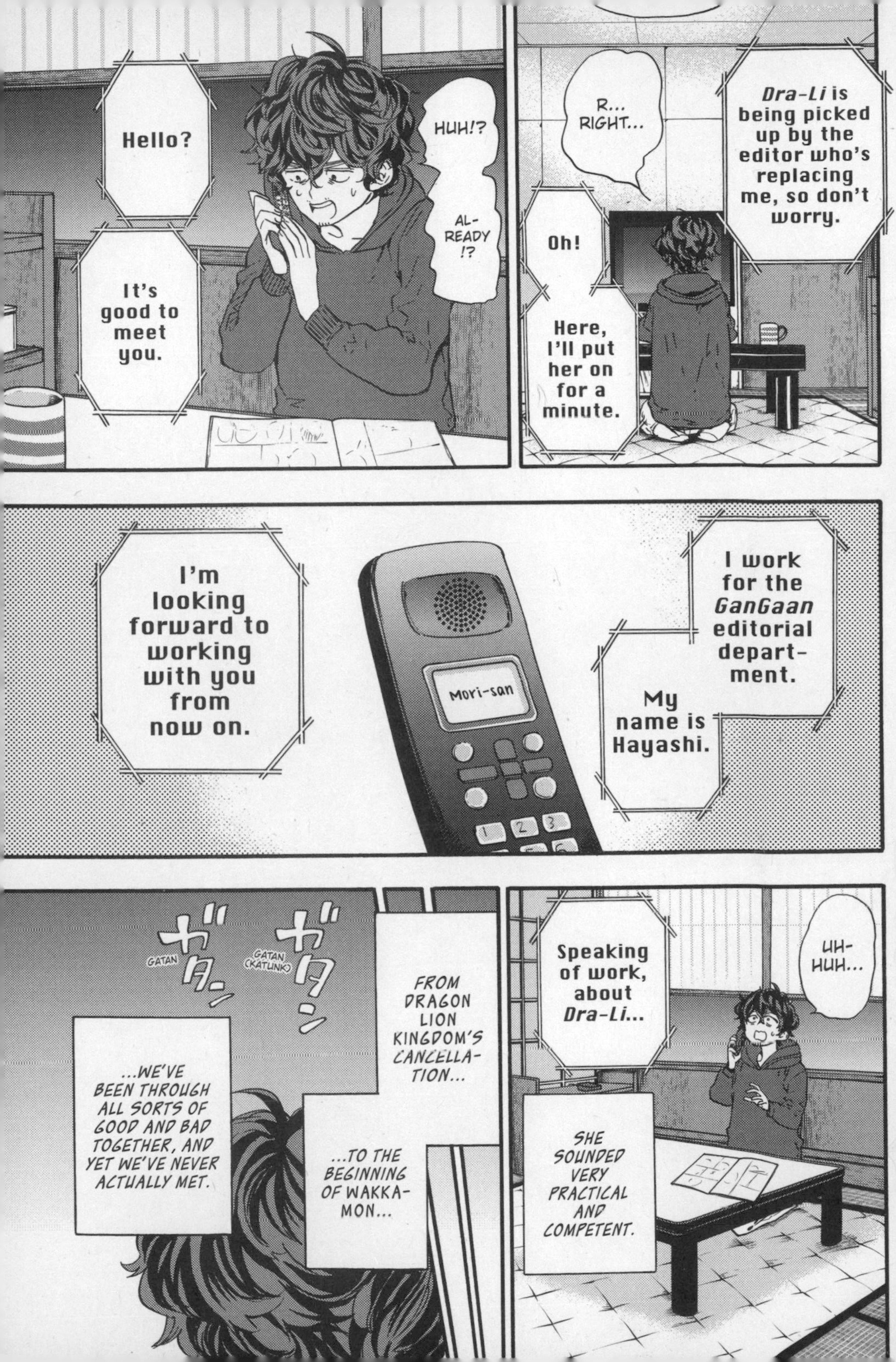

Dra-Li is being picked up by the editor who's replacing me, so don't worry.
R... RIGHT...
Oh!
Here, I'll put her on for a minute.
HUH!?
AL-READY!?
Hello?
It's good to meet you.
I work for the *GanGaan* editorial department.
My name is Hayashi.
Mori-san
I'm looking forward to working with you from now on.
UH-HUH...
Speaking of work, about *Dra-Li*...
SHE SOUNDED VERY PRACTICAL AND COMPETENT.
ガタン
GATAN (KATUNK)
ガタン
GATAN
FROM DRAGON LION KINGDOM'S CANCELLA-TION...
...TO THE BEGINNING OF WAKKA-MON...
...WE'VE BEEN THROUGH ALL SORTS OF GOOD AND BAD TOGETHER, AND YET WE'VE NEVER ACTUALLY MET.

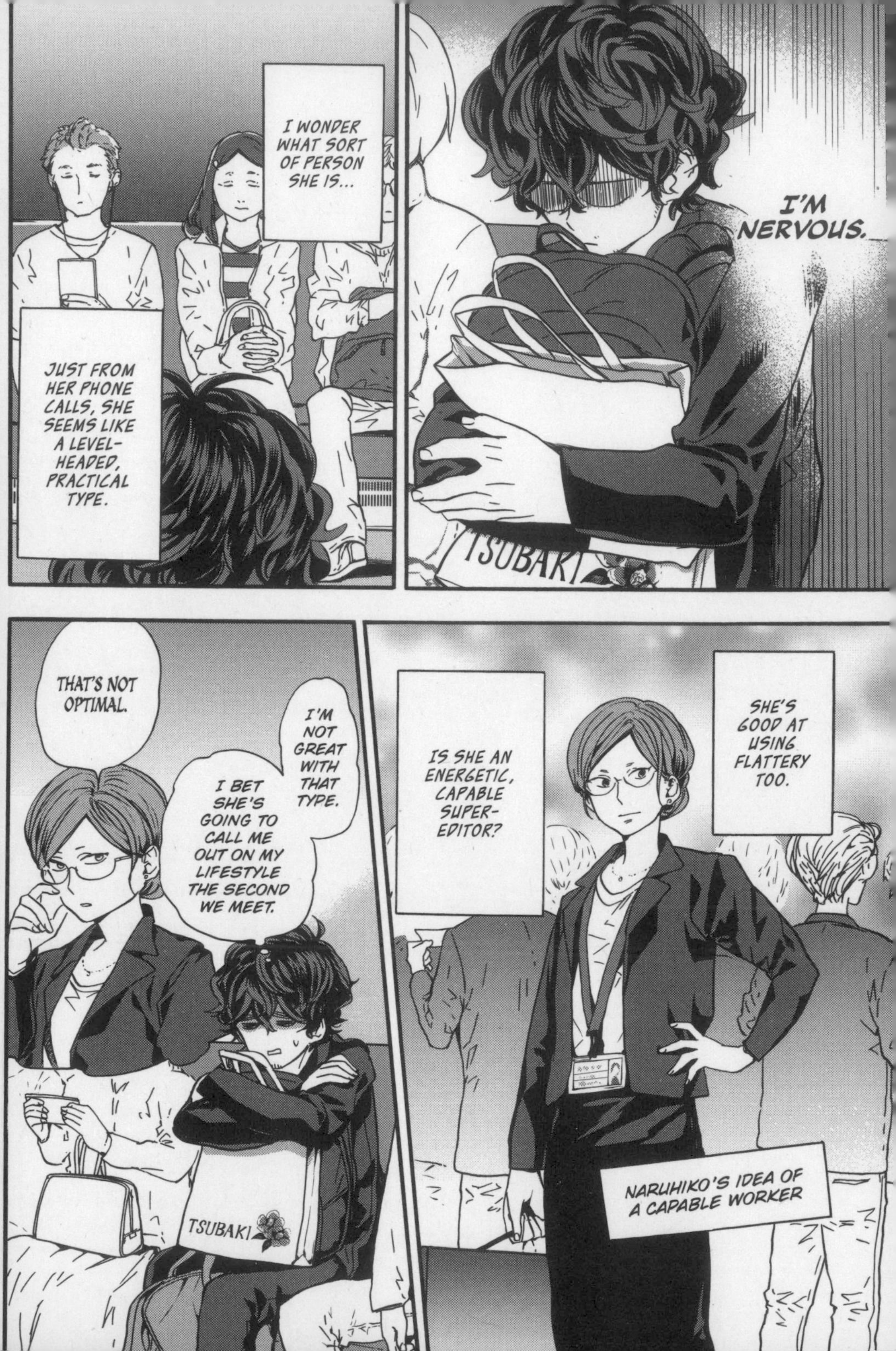
I'M NERVOUS.
TSUBAKI
I WONDER WHAT SORT OF PERSON SHE IS...
JUST FROM HER PHONE CALLS, SHE SEEMS LIKE A LEVEL-HEADED, PRACTICAL TYPE.
SHE'S GOOD AT USING FLATTERY TOO.
IS SHE AN ENERGETIC, CAPABLE SUPER-EDITOR?
NARUHIKO'S IDEA OF A CAPABLE WORKER
I'M NOT GREAT WITH THAT TYPE.
I BET SHE'S GOING TO CALL ME OUT ON MY LIFESTYLE THE SECOND WE MEET.
THAT'S NOT OPTIMAL.
TSUBAKI

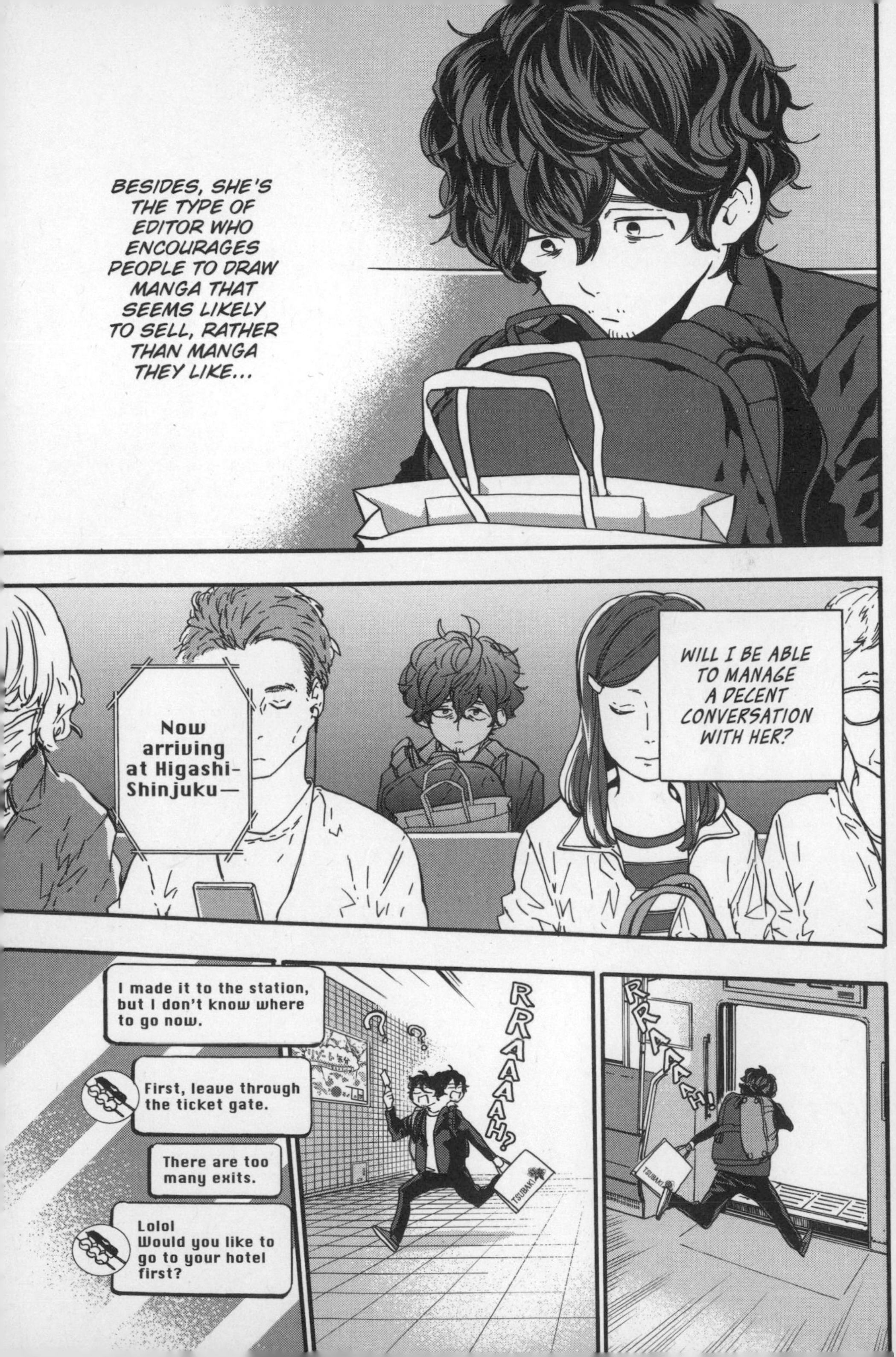
BESIDES, SHE'S THE TYPE OF EDITOR WHO ENCOURAGES PEOPLE TO DRAW MANGA THAT SEEMS LIKELY TO SELL, RATHER THAN MANGA THEY LIKE...
WILL I BE ABLE TO MANAGE A DECENT CONVERSATION WITH HER?
Now arriving at Higashi-Shinjuku—
RRAAAAH!
TSUBAKI
I made it to the station, but I don't know where to go now.
First, leave through the ticket gate.
There are too many exits.
Lolol
Would you like to go to your hotel first?
RRAAAAH?
TSUBAKI

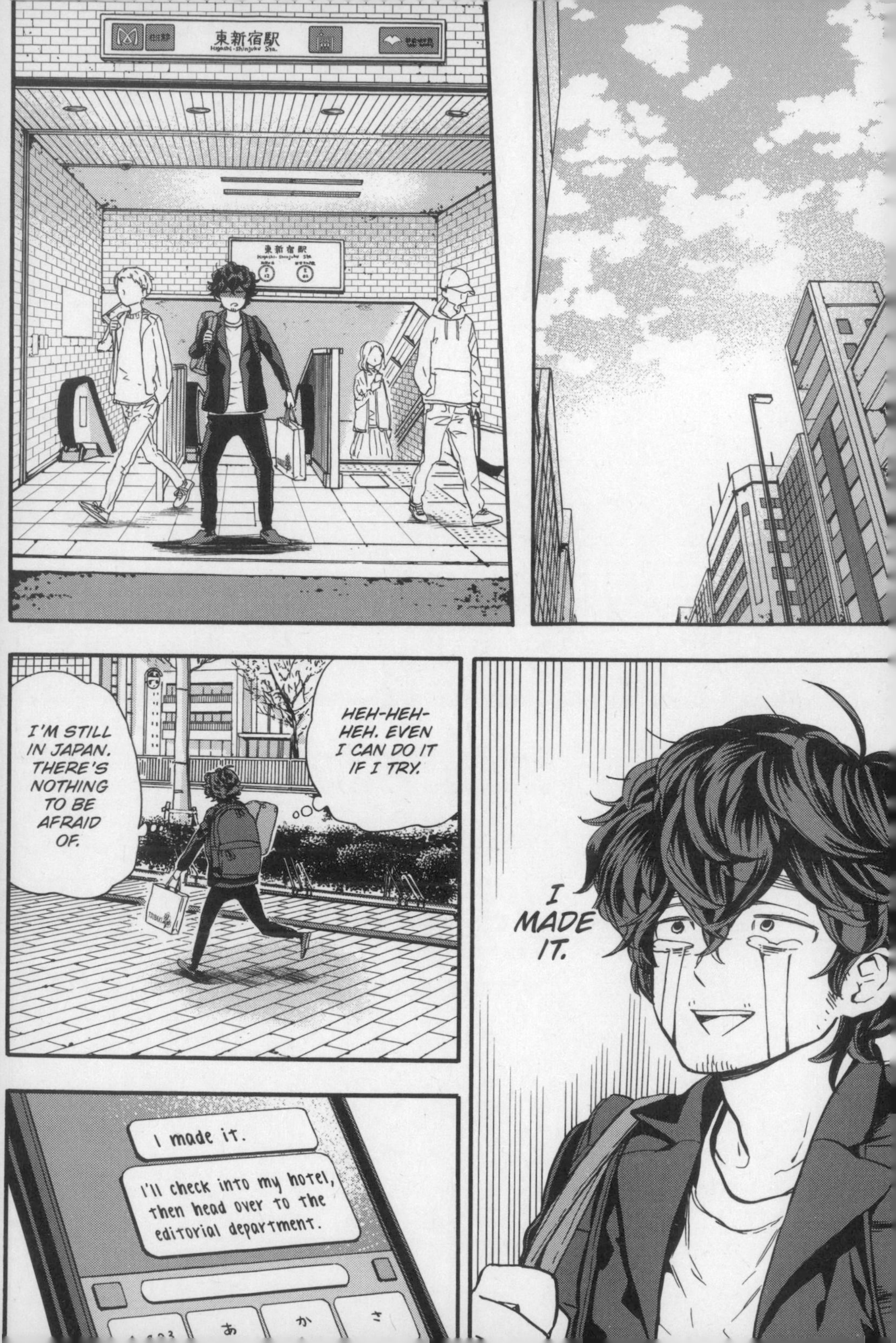
東新宿駅
Higashi-Shinjuku Sta.
東新宿駅
I MADE IT.
HEH-HEH-HEH. EVEN I CAN DO IT IF I TRY.
I'M STILL IN JAPAN. THERE'S NOTHING TO BE AFRAID OF.
I made it.
I'll check into my hotel, then head over to the editorial department.
あ
か
さ

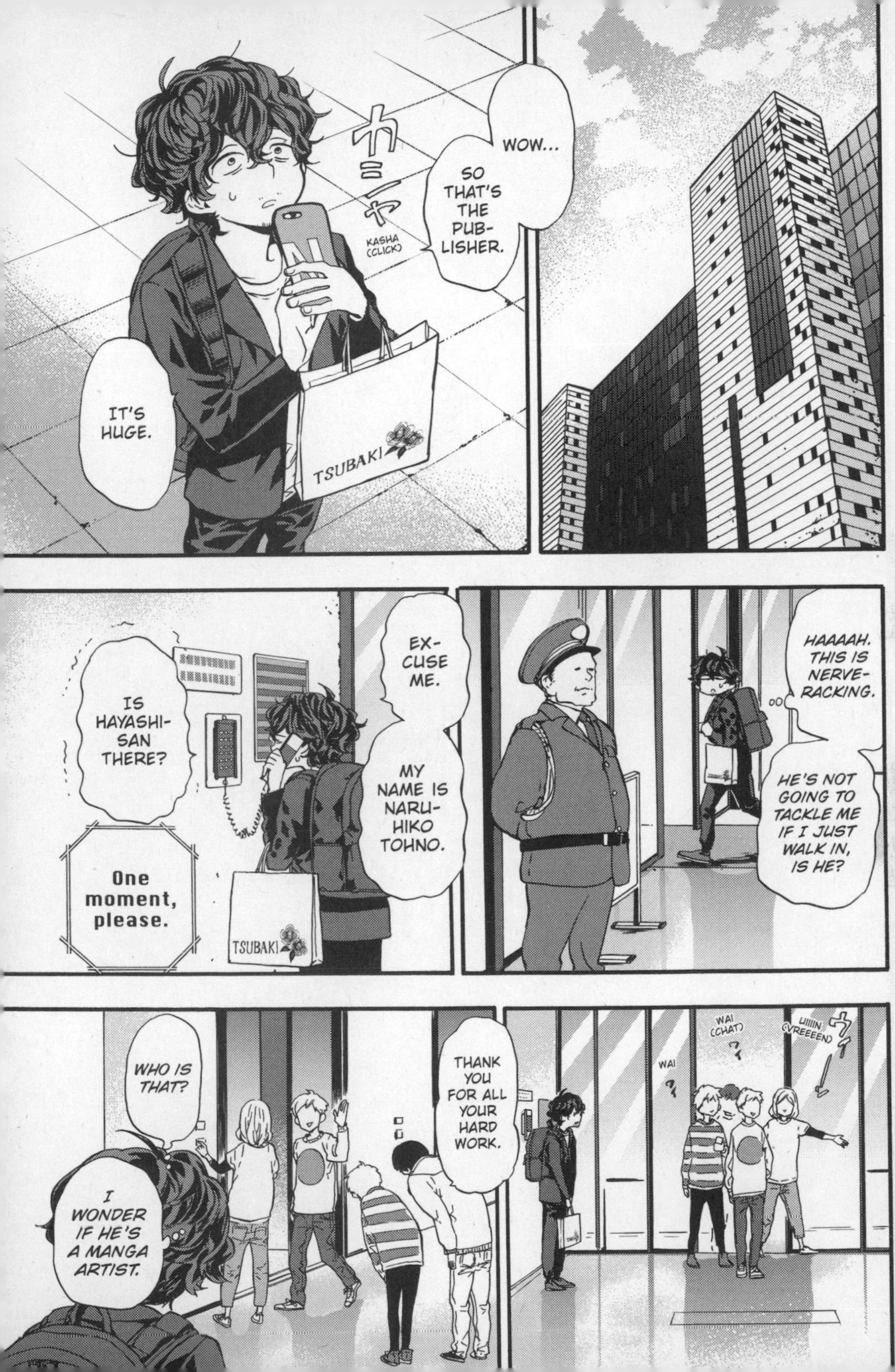
KASHA (CLICK)
WOW...
SO THAT'S THE PUB-LISHER.
IT'S HUGE.
HAAAAH. THIS IS NERVE-RACKING.
HE'S NOT GOING TO TACKLE ME IF I JUST WALK IN, IS HE?
EX-CUSE ME.
MY NAME IS NARU-HIKO TOHNO.
IS HAYASHI-SAN THERE?
One moment, please.
TSUBAKI
UIIIIN (VREEEEN)
WAI (CHAT)
WAI
THANK YOU FOR ALL YOUR HARD WORK.
WHO IS THAT?
I WONDER IF HE'S A MANGA ARTIST.

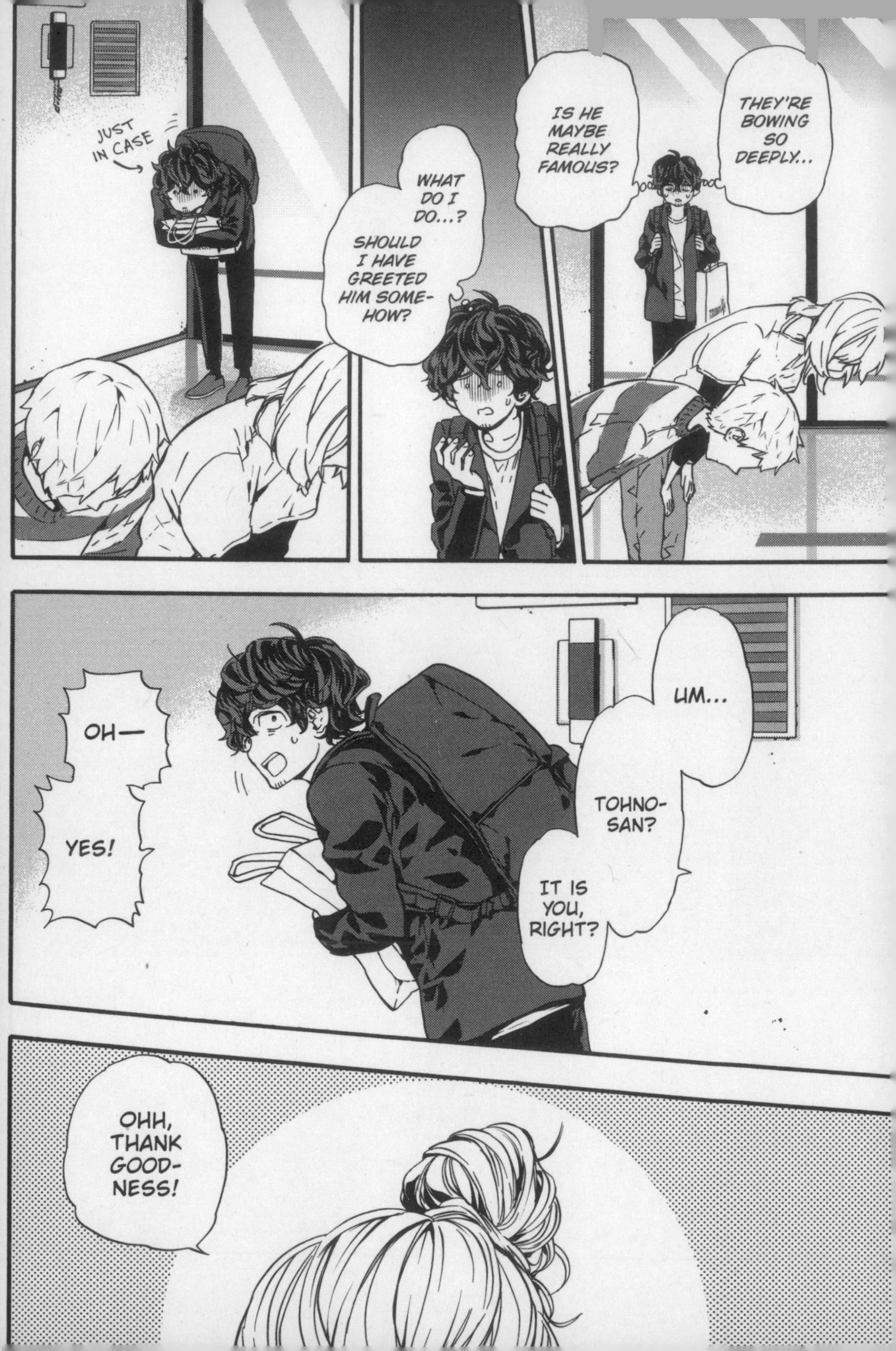
THEY'RE BOWING SO DEEPLY...
IS HE MAYBE REALLY FAMOUS?
WHAT DO I DO...?
SHOULD I HAVE GREETED HIM SOME-HOW?
JUST IN CASE
UM...
TOHNO-SAN?
IT IS YOU, RIGHT?
OH—
YES!
OHH, THANK GOOD-NESS!

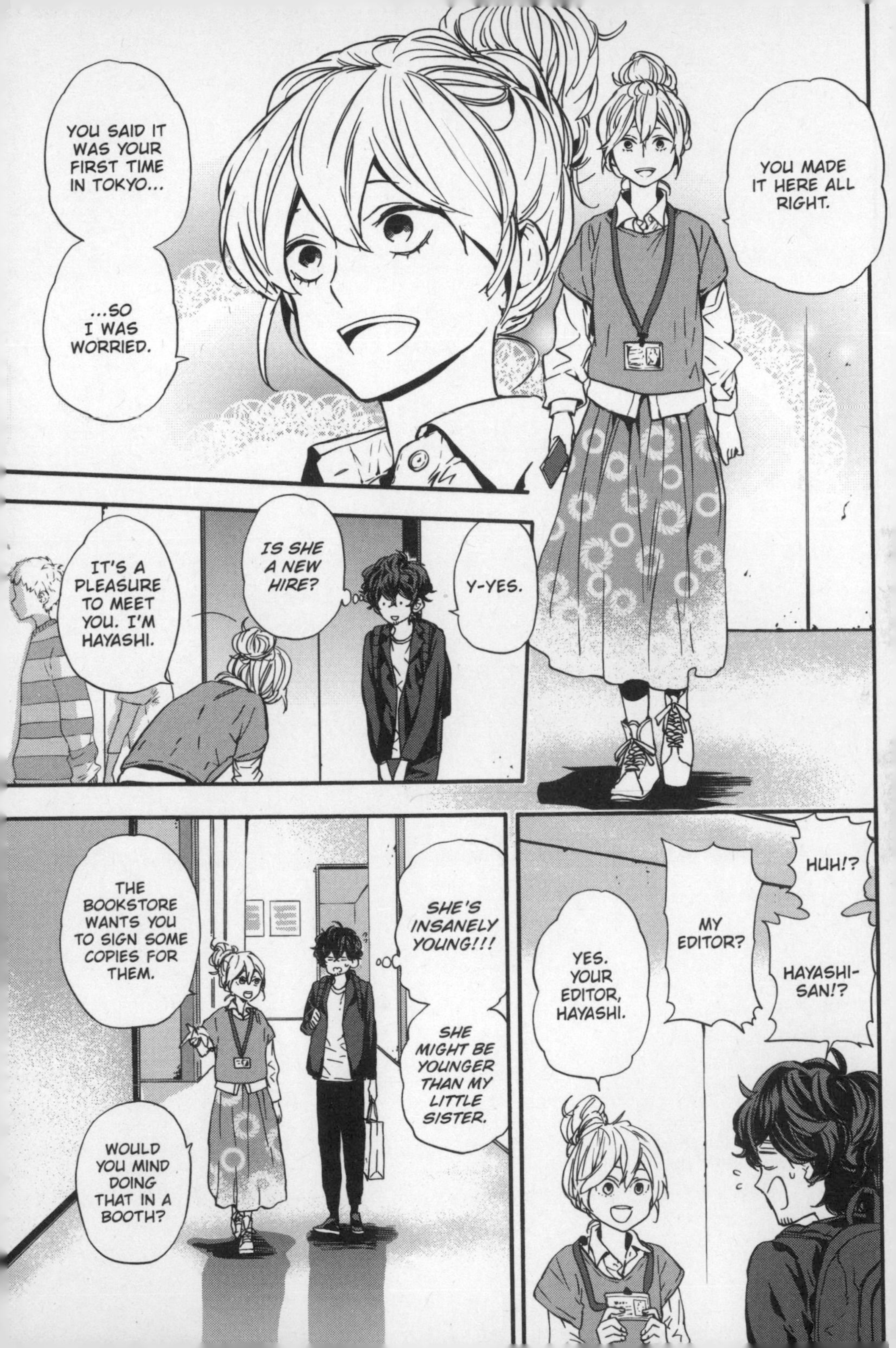
YOU MADE IT HERE ALL RIGHT.
YOU SAID IT WAS YOUR FIRST TIME IN TOKYO...
...SO I WAS WORRIED.
Y-YES.
IS SHE A NEW HIRE?
IT'S A PLEASURE TO MEET YOU. I'M HAYASHI.
HUH!?
HAYASHI-SAN!?
MY EDITOR?
YES. YOUR EDITOR, HAYASHI.
SHE'S INSANELY YOUNG!!!
SHE MIGHT BE YOUNGER THAN MY LITTLE SISTER.
THE BOOKSTORE WANTS YOU TO SIGN SOME COPIES FOR THEM.
WOULD YOU MIND DOING THAT IN A BOOTH?

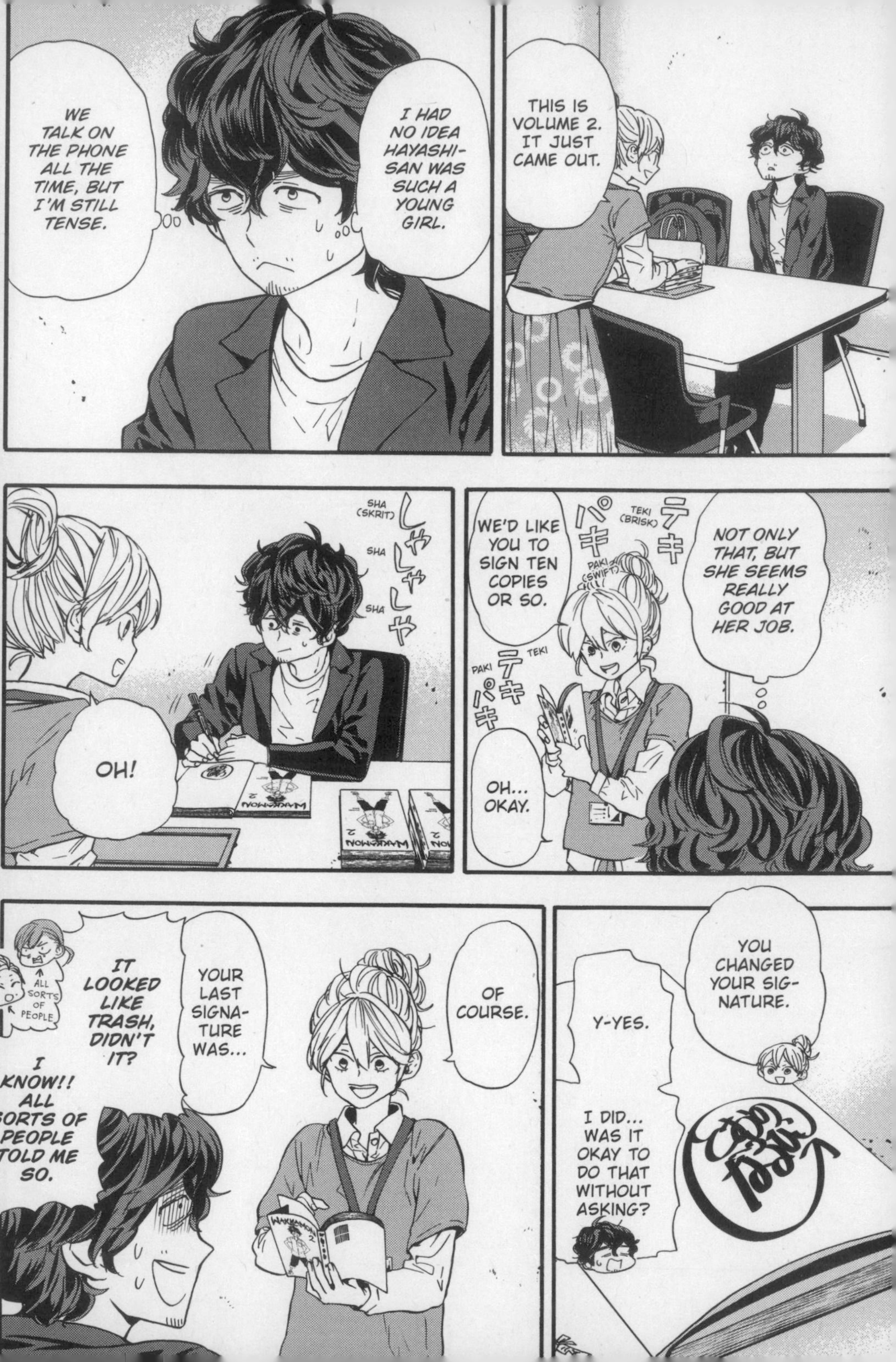
THIS IS VOLUME 2. IT JUST CAME OUT.
I HAD NO IDEA HAYASHI-SAN WAS SUCH A YOUNG GIRL.
WE TALK ON THE PHONE ALL THE TIME, BUT I'M STILL TENSE.
NOT ONLY THAT, BUT SHE SEEMS REALLY GOOD AT HER JOB.
テキ TEKI (BRISK)
パキ PAKI (SWIFT)
WE'D LIKE YOU TO SIGN TEN COPIES OR SO.
テキ TEKI
パキ PAKI
OH... OKAY.
しゃ SHA (SKRIT)
しゃ SHA
しゃ SHA
OH!
YOU CHANGED YOUR SIG-NATURE.
Y-YES.
I DID... WAS IT OKAY TO DO THAT WITHOUT ASKING?
OF COURSE.
YOUR LAST SIGNA-TURE WAS...
IT LOOKED LIKE TRASH, DIDN'T IT?
ALL SORTS OF PEOPLE
I KNOW!! ALL SORTS OF PEOPLE TOLD ME SO.

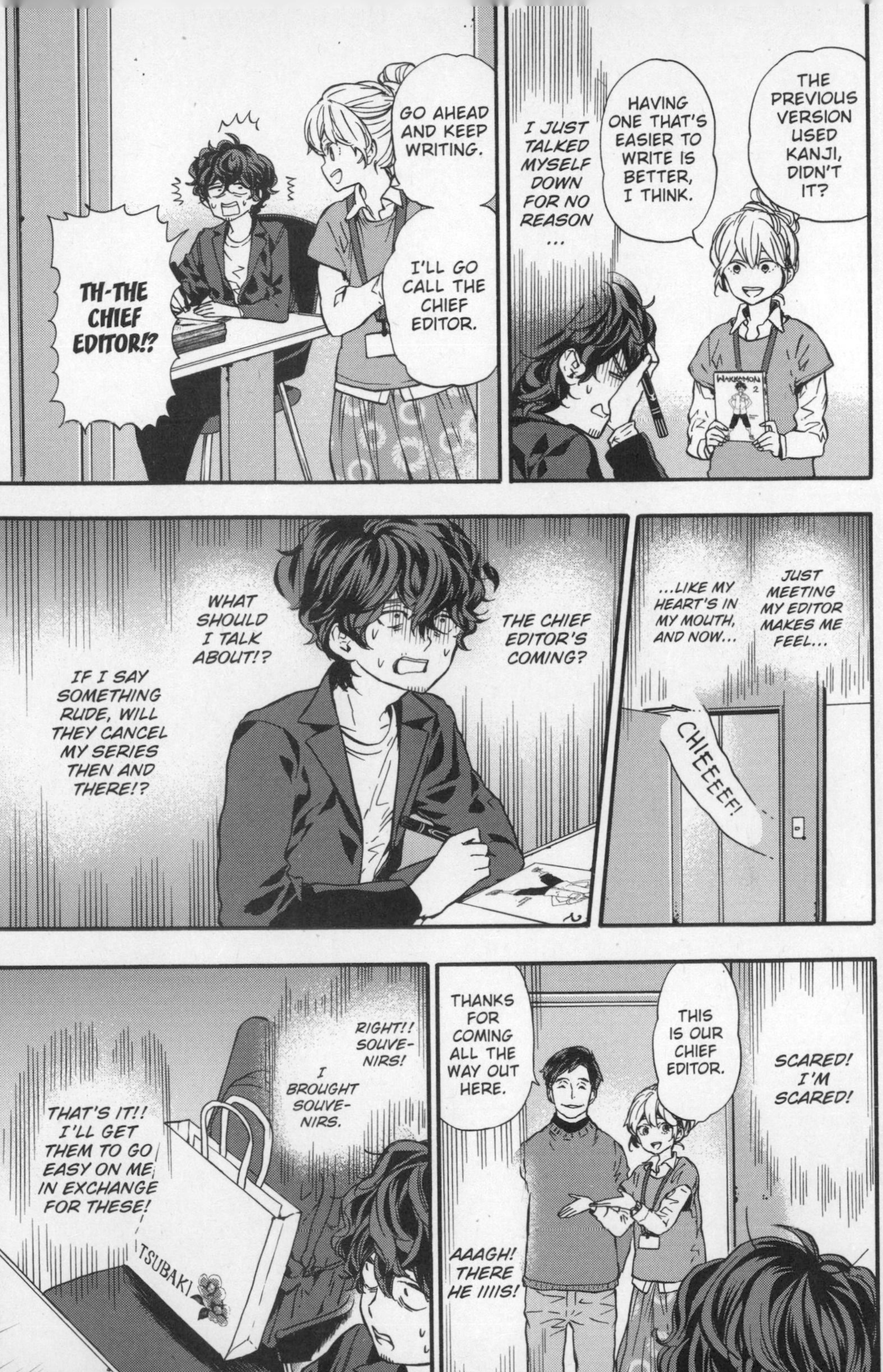
THE PREVIOUS VERSION USED KANJI, DIDN'T IT?
HAVING ONE THAT'S EASIER TO WRITE IS BETTER, I THINK.
I JUST TALKED MYSELF DOWN FOR NO REASON...
GO AHEAD AND KEEP WRITING.
I'LL GO CALL THE CHIEF EDITOR.
TH-THE CHIEF EDITOR!?
JUST MEETING MY EDITOR MAKES ME FEEL...
...LIKE MY HEART'S IN MY MOUTH, AND NOW...
CHIEEEEF!
THE CHIEF EDITOR'S COMING?
WHAT SHOULD I TALK ABOUT!?
IF I SAY SOMETHING RUDE, WILL THEY CANCEL MY SERIES THEN AND THERE!?
SCARED! I'M SCARED!
THIS IS OUR CHIEF EDITOR.
THANKS FOR COMING ALL THE WAY OUT HERE.
AAAGH! THERE HE IIIIS!
RIGHT!! SOUVENIRS!
I BROUGHT SOUVENIRS.
THAT'S IT!! I'LL GET THEM TO GO EASY ON ME IN EXCHANGE FOR THESE!
TSUBAKI

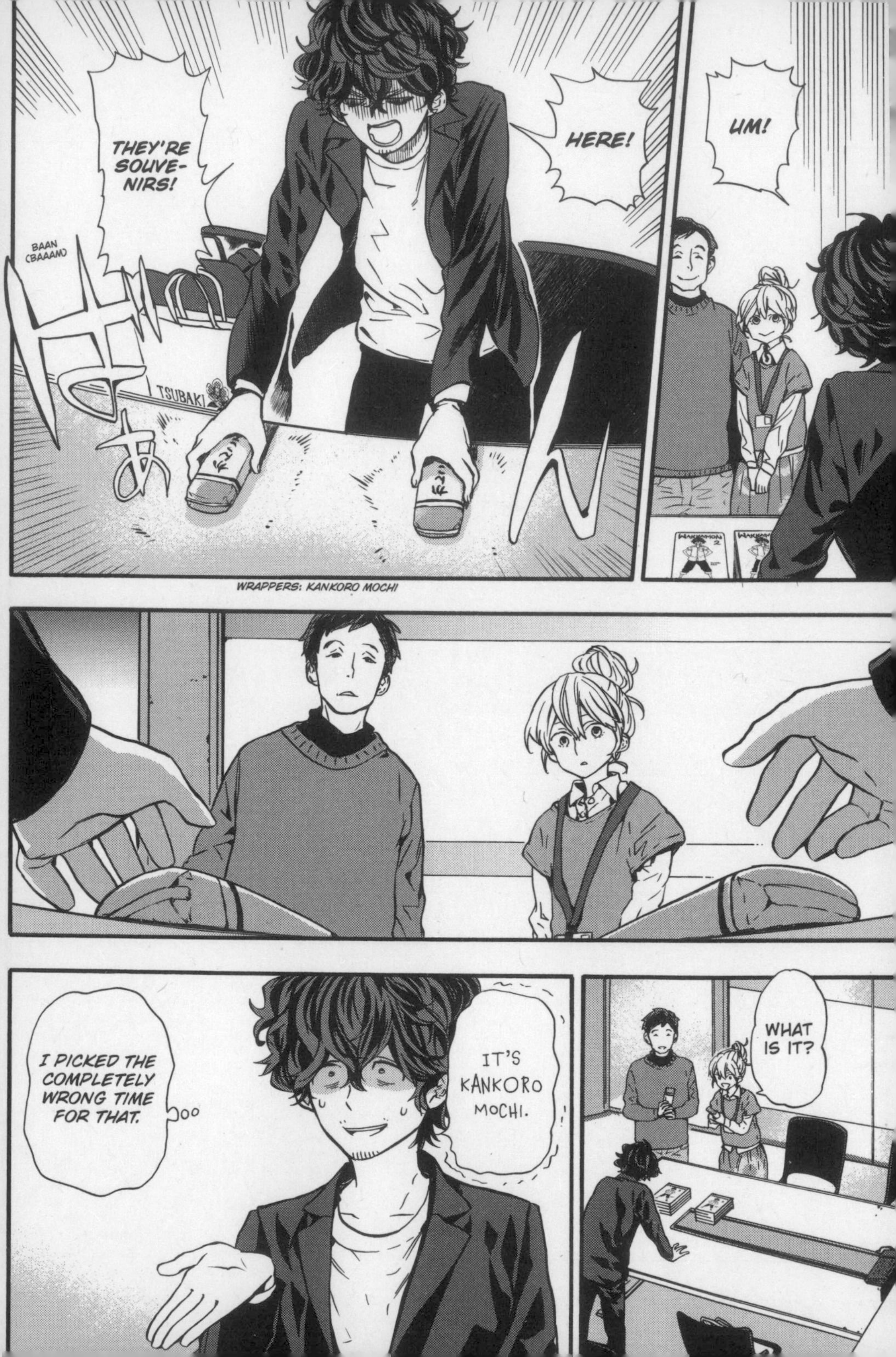
UM!
HERE!
THEY'RE SOUVE-NIRS!
BAAN (BAAAM)
TSUBAKI
WRAPPERS: KANKORO MOCHI
WHAT IS IT?
IT'S KANKORO MOCHI.
I PICKED THE COMPLETELY WRONG TIME FOR THAT.

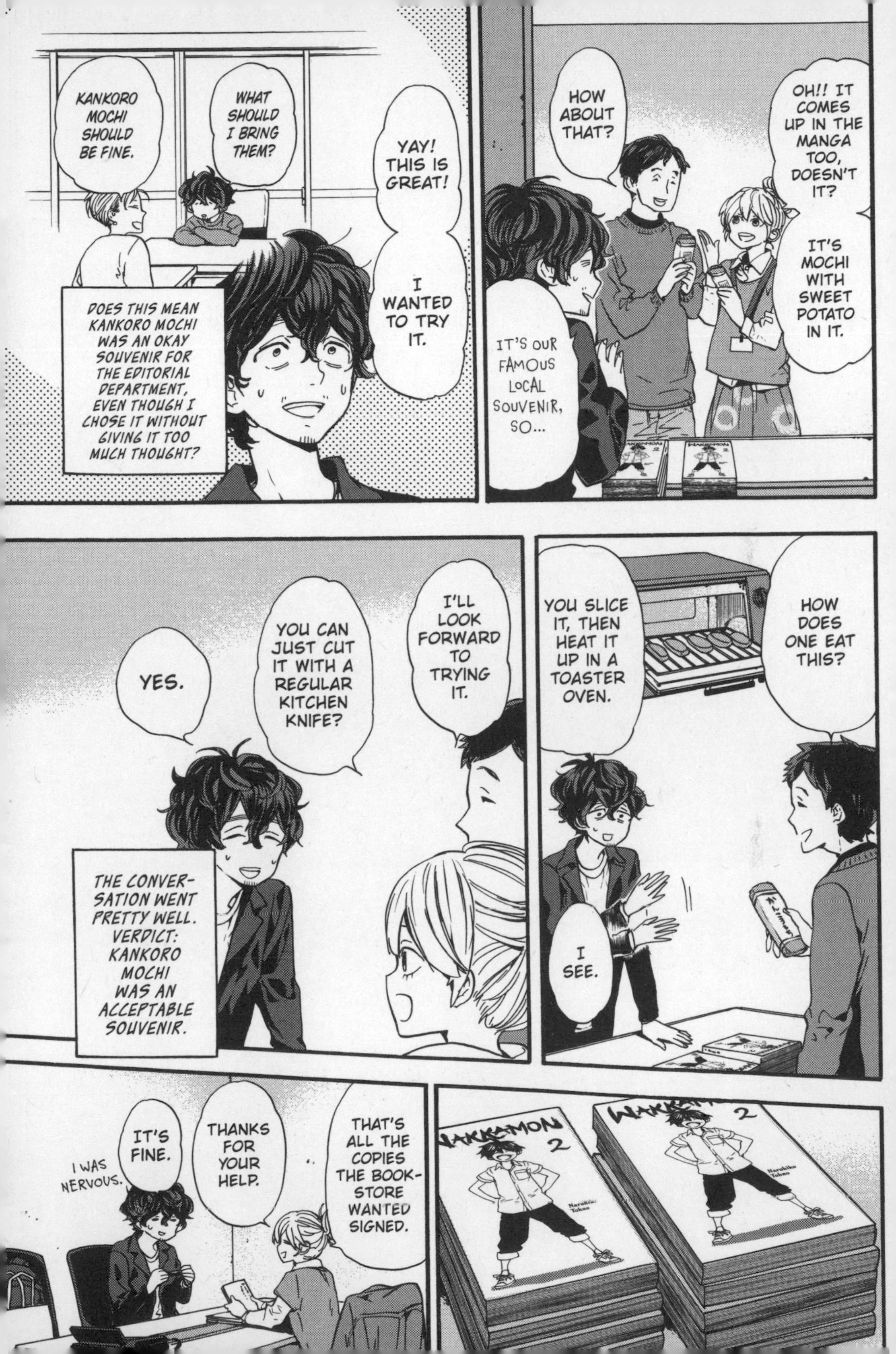
OH!! IT COMES UP IN THE MANGA TOO, DOESN'T IT?
IT'S MOCHI WITH SWEET POTATO IN IT.
HOW ABOUT THAT?
IT'S OUR FAMOUS LOCAL SOUVENIR, SO...
YAY! THIS IS GREAT!
I WANTED TO TRY IT.
WHAT SHOULD I BRING THEM?
KANKORO MOCHI SHOULD BE FINE.
DOES THIS MEAN KANKORO MOCHI WAS AN OKAY SOUVENIR FOR THE EDITORIAL DEPARTMENT, EVEN THOUGH I CHOSE IT WITHOUT GIVING IT TOO MUCH THOUGHT?
HOW DOES ONE EAT THIS?
YOU SLICE IT, THEN HEAT IT UP IN A TOASTER OVEN.
I SEE.
I'LL LOOK FORWARD TO TRYING IT.
YOU CAN JUST CUT IT WITH A REGULAR KITCHEN KNIFE?
YES.
THE CONVERSATION WENT PRETTY WELL. VERDICT: KANKORO MOCHI WAS AN ACCEPTABLE SOUVENIR.
WAKKAMON 2
WAKKAMON 2
THAT'S ALL THE COPIES THE BOOKSTORE WANTED SIGNED.
THANKS FOR YOUR HELP.
IT'S FINE.
I WAS NERVOUS.

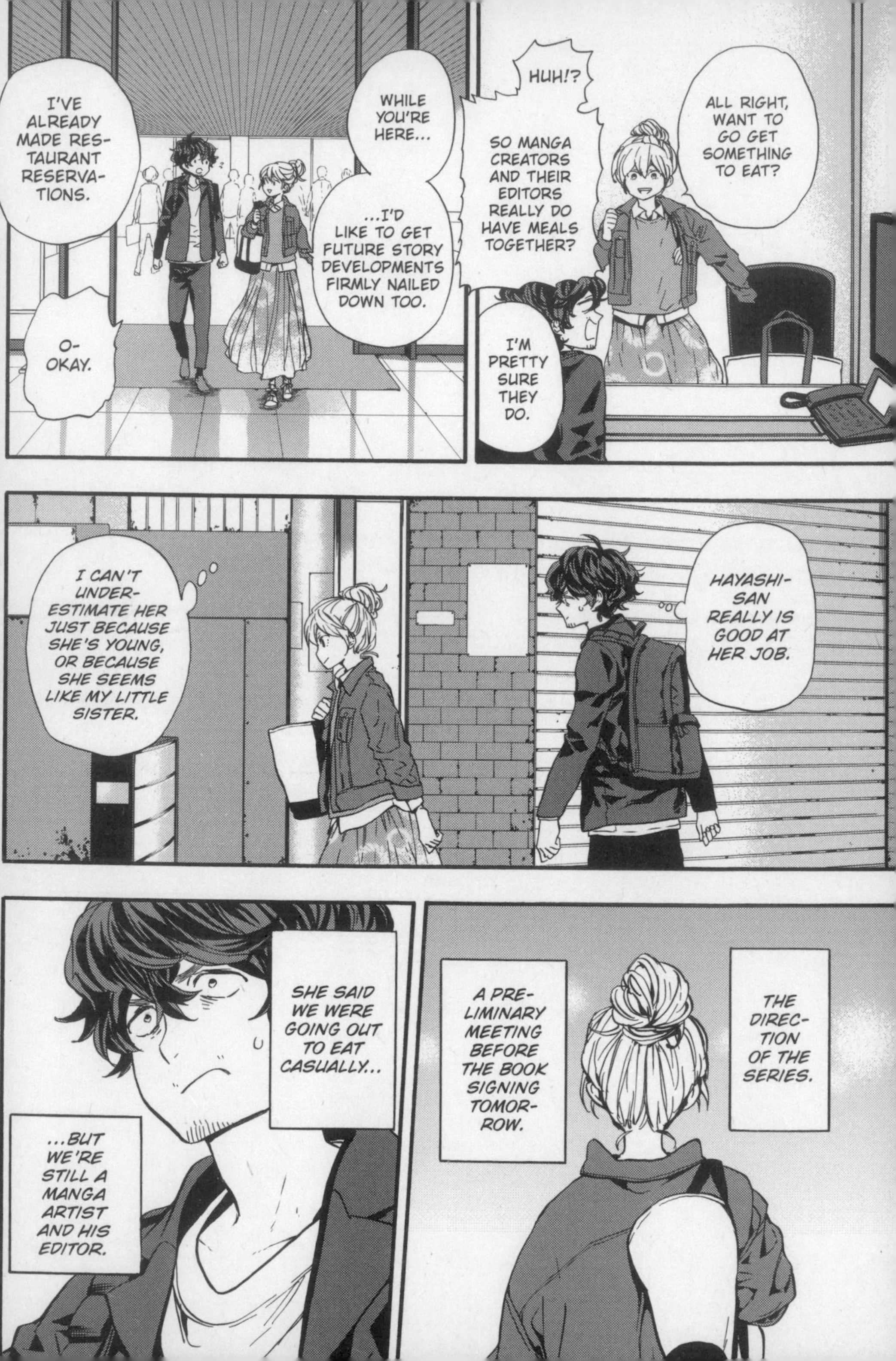
ALL RIGHT, WANT TO GO GET SOMETHING TO EAT?
HUH!?
SO MANGA CREATORS AND THEIR EDITORS REALLY DO HAVE MEALS TOGETHER?
I'M PRETTY SURE THEY DO.
WHILE YOU'RE HERE...
...I'D LIKE TO GET FUTURE STORY DEVELOPMENTS FIRMLY NAILED DOWN TOO.
I'VE ALREADY MADE RESTAURANT RESERVATIONS.
O-OKAY.
HAYASHI-SAN REALLY IS GOOD AT HER JOB.
I CAN'T UNDERESTIMATE HER JUST BECAUSE SHE'S YOUNG, OR BECAUSE SHE SEEMS LIKE MY LITTLE SISTER.
THE DIRECTION OF THE SERIES.
A PRELIMINARY MEETING BEFORE THE BOOK SIGNING TOMORROW.
SHE SAID WE WERE GOING OUT TO EAT CASUALLY...
...BUT WE'RE STILL A MANGA ARTIST AND HIS EDITOR.

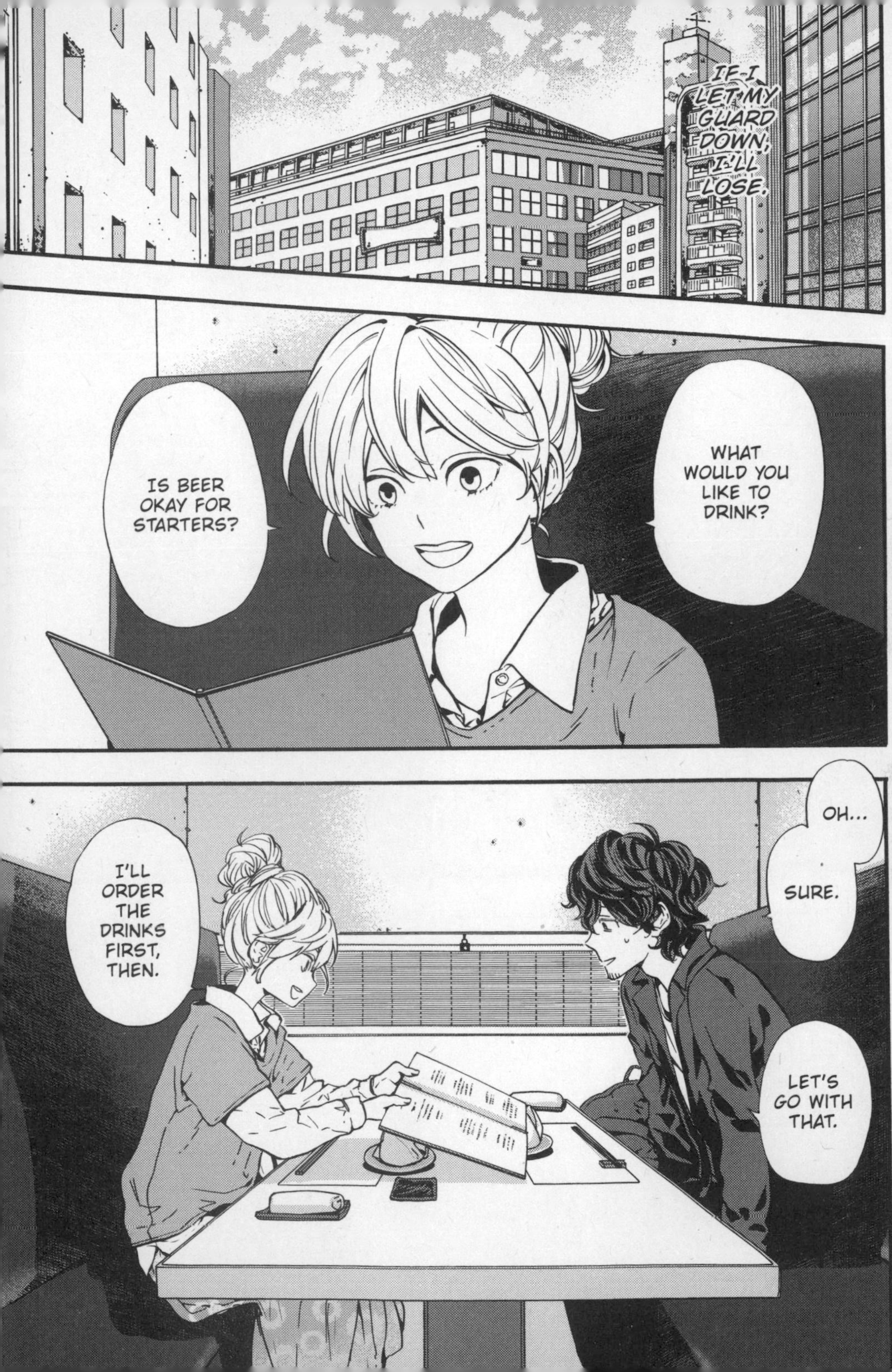
IF I LET MY GUARD DOWN, I'LL LOSE.
WHAT WOULD YOU LIKE TO DRINK?
IS BEER OKAY FOR STARTERS?
OH... SURE.
LET'S GO WITH THAT.
I'LL ORDER THE DRINKS FIRST, THEN.

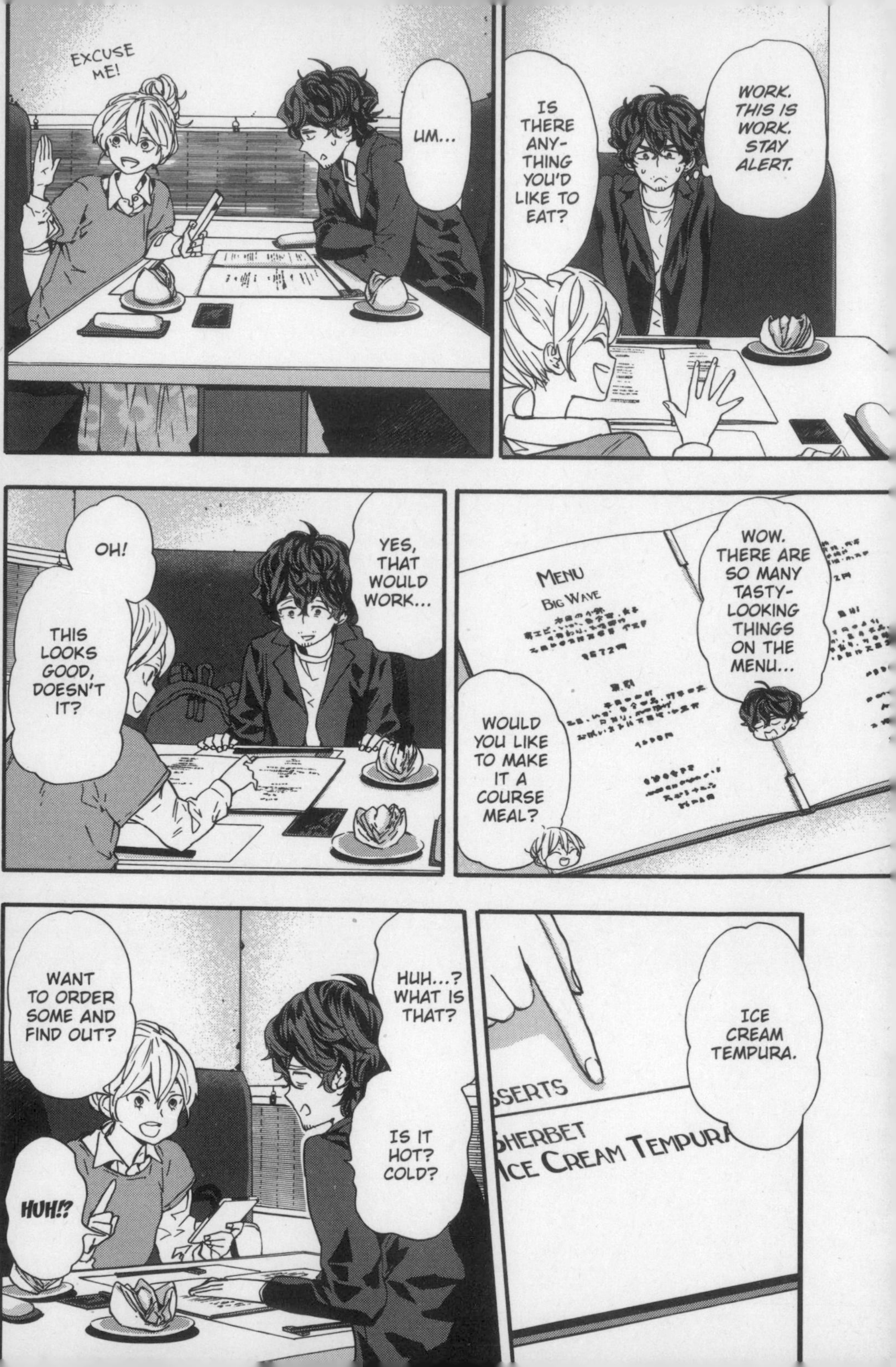
WORK. THIS IS WORK. STAY ALERT.
IS THERE ANYTHING YOU'D LIKE TO EAT?
UM...
EXCUSE ME!
WOW. THERE ARE SO MANY TASTY-LOOKING THINGS ON THE MENU...
MENU
BIG WAVE
WOULD YOU LIKE TO MAKE IT A COURSE MEAL?
YES, THAT WOULD WORK...
OH!
THIS LOOKS GOOD, DOESN'T IT?
ICE CREAM TEMPURA.
SSERTS
SHERBET
ICE CREAM TEMPURA
HUH...? WHAT IS THAT?
IS IT HOT? COLD?
WANT TO ORDER SOME AND FIND OUT?
HUH!?

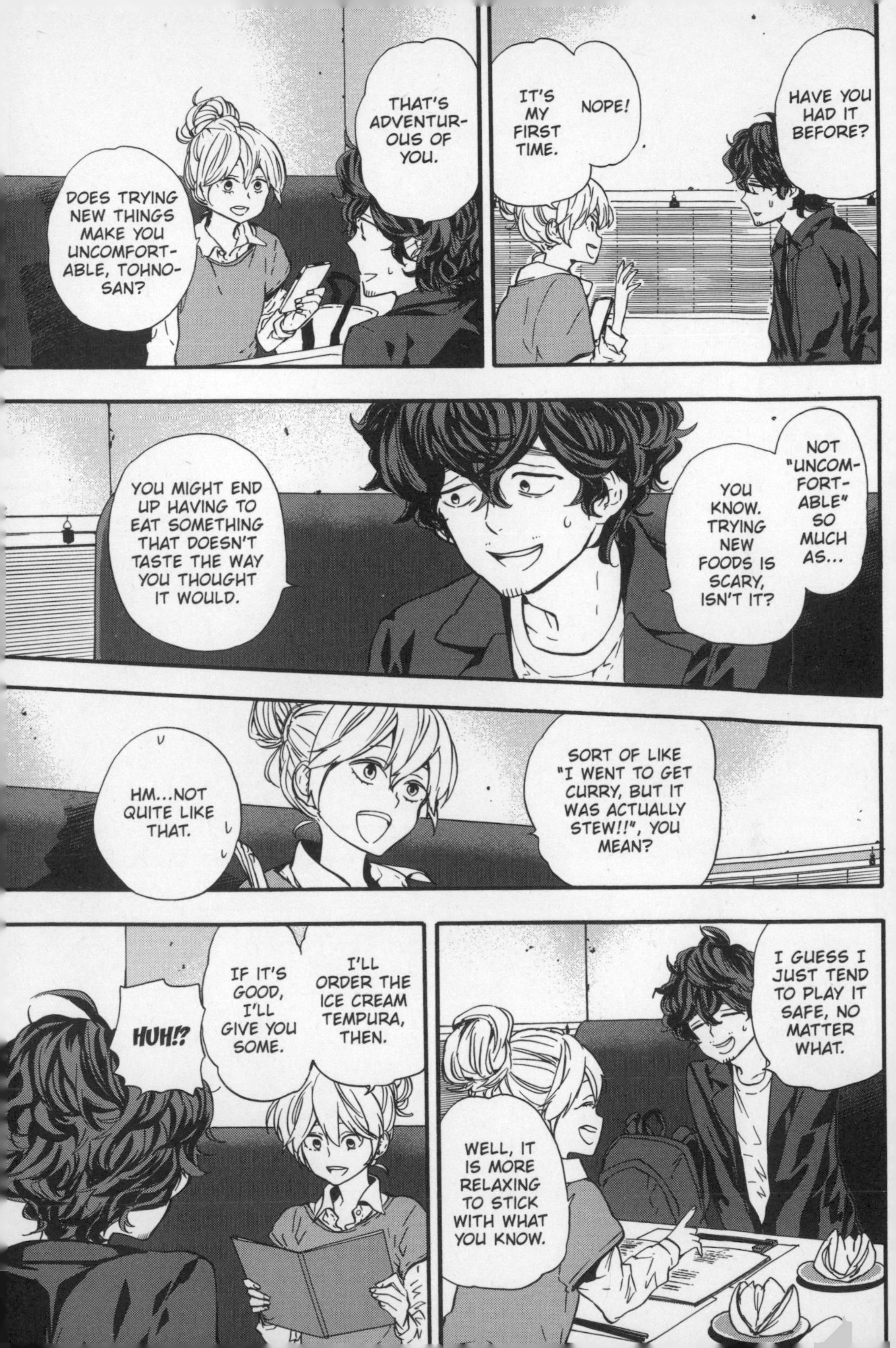
HAVE YOU HAD IT BEFORE?
NOPE!
IT'S MY FIRST TIME.
THAT'S ADVENTUROUS OF YOU.
DOES TRYING NEW THINGS MAKE YOU UNCOMFORTABLE, TOHNO-SAN?
NOT "UNCOMFORTABLE" SO MUCH AS...
YOU KNOW. TRYING NEW FOODS IS SCARY, ISN'T IT?
YOU MIGHT END UP HAVING TO EAT SOMETHING THAT DOESN'T TASTE THE WAY YOU THOUGHT IT WOULD.
SORT OF LIKE "I WENT TO GET CURRY, BUT IT WAS ACTUALLY STEW!!", YOU MEAN?
HM...NOT QUITE LIKE THAT.
I GUESS I JUST TEND TO PLAY IT SAFE, NO MATTER WHAT.
WELL, IT IS MORE RELAXING TO STICK WITH WHAT YOU KNOW.
I'LL ORDER THE ICE CREAM TEMPURA, THEN.
IF IT'S GOOD, I'LL GIVE YOU SOME.
HUH!?

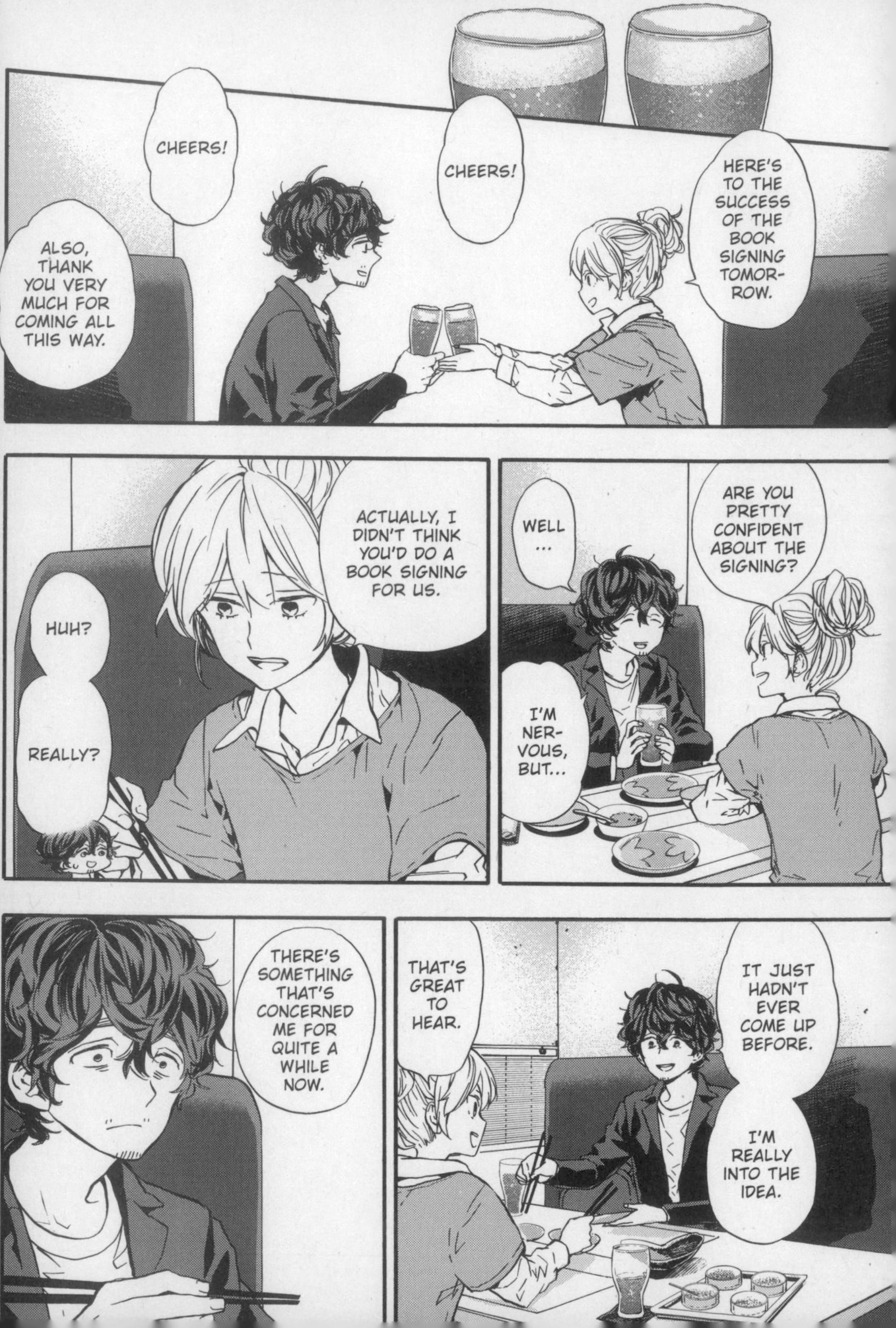
HERE'S TO THE SUCCESS OF THE BOOK SIGNING TOMORROW.
CHEERS!
CHEERS!
ALSO, THANK YOU VERY MUCH FOR COMING ALL THIS WAY.
ARE YOU PRETTY CONFIDENT ABOUT THE SIGNING?
WELL...
I'M NERVOUS, BUT...
ACTUALLY, I DIDN'T THINK YOU'D DO A BOOK SIGNING FOR US.
HUH?
REALLY?
IT JUST HADN'T EVER COME UP BEFORE.
I'M REALLY INTO THE IDEA.
THAT'S GREAT TO HEAR.
THERE'S SOMETHING THAT'S CONCERNED ME FOR QUITE A WHILE NOW.

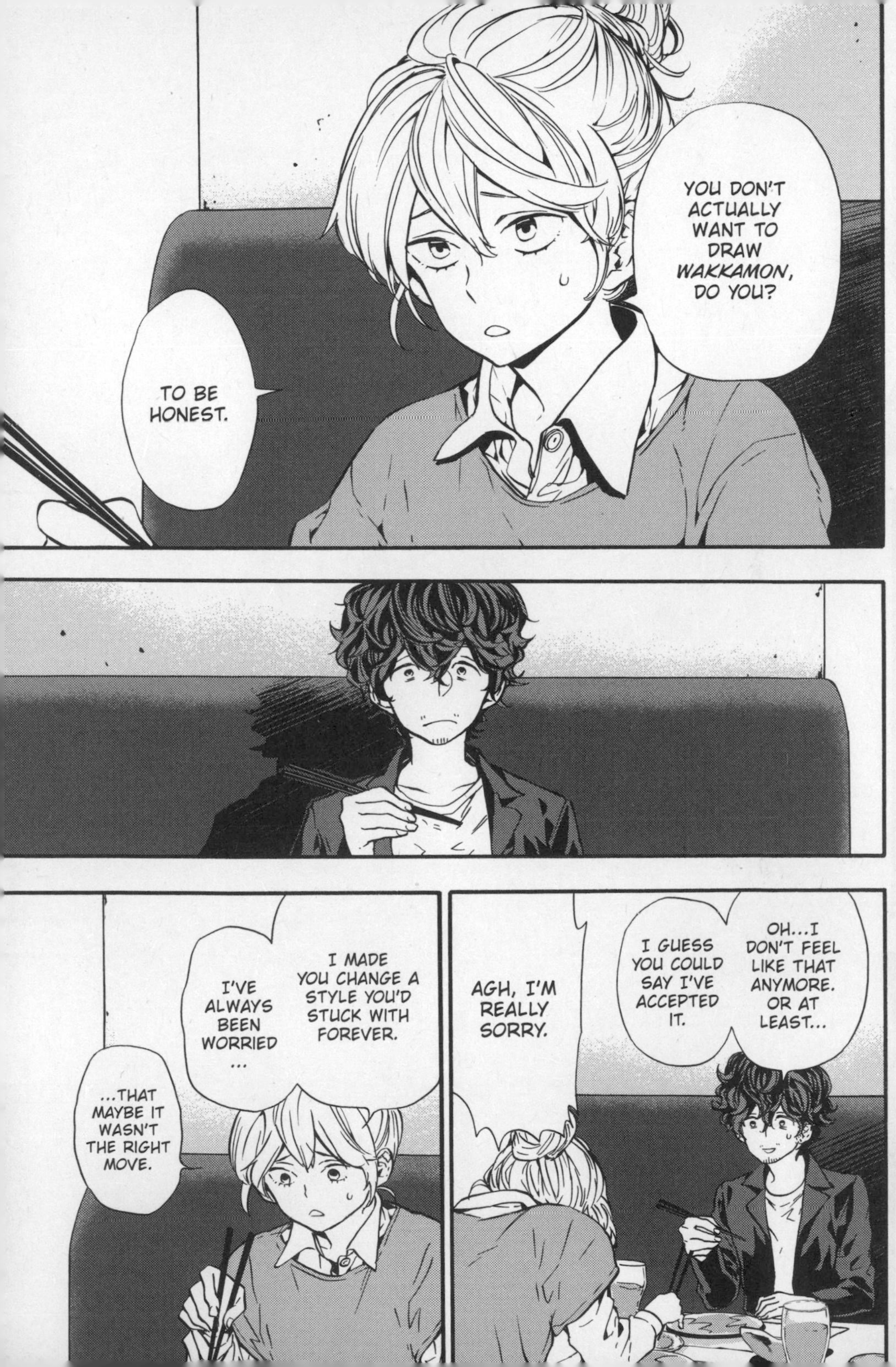
YOU DON'T ACTUALLY WANT TO DRAW *WAKKAMON*, DO YOU?
TO BE HONEST.
OH...I DON'T FEEL LIKE THAT ANYMORE. OR AT LEAST...
I GUESS YOU COULD SAY I'VE ACCEPTED IT.
AGH, I'M REALLY SORRY.
I MADE YOU CHANGE A STYLE YOU'D STUCK WITH FOREVER.
I'VE ALWAYS BEEN WORRIED...
...THAT MAYBE IT WASN'T THE RIGHT MOVE.

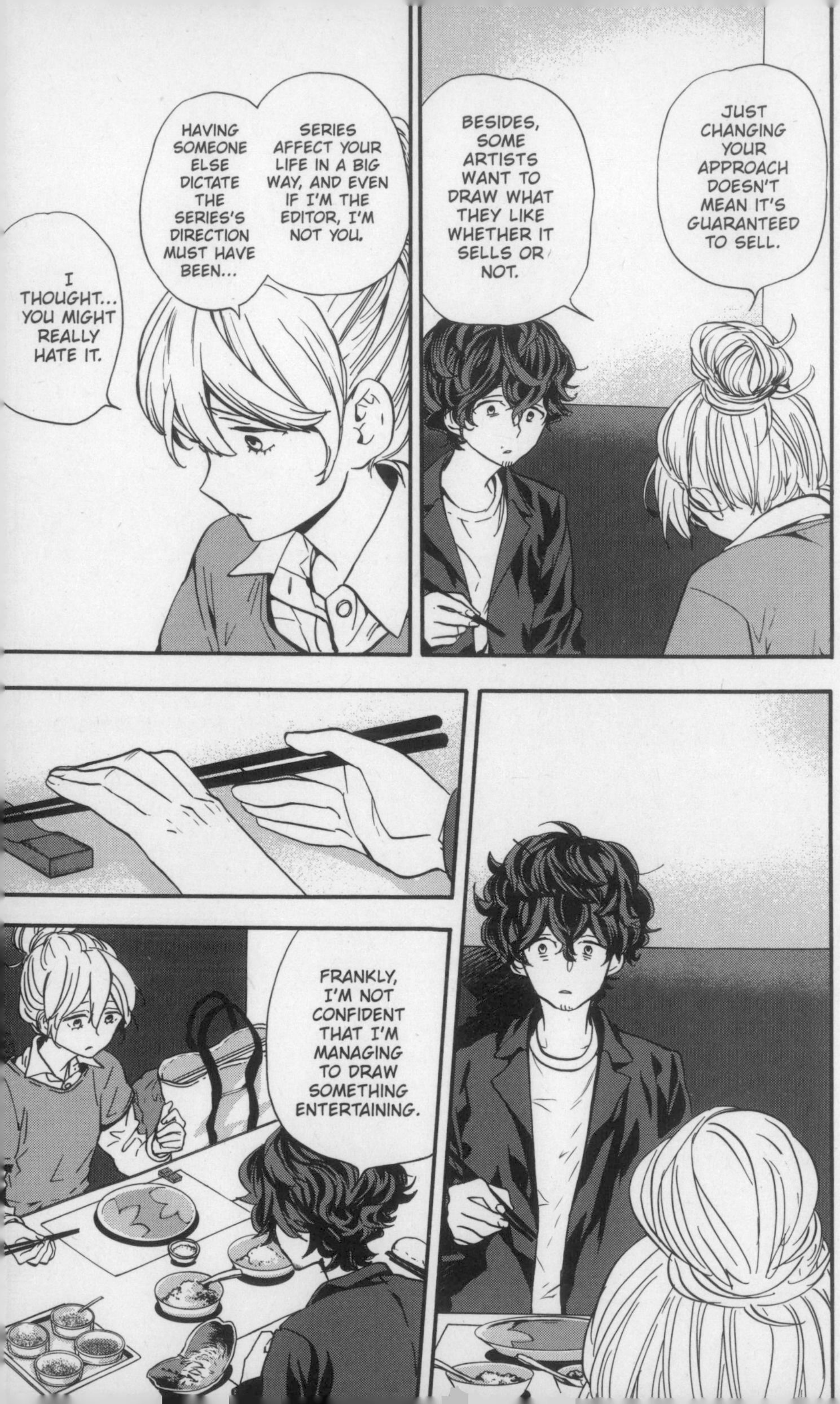
JUST CHANGING YOUR APPROACH DOESN'T MEAN IT'S GUARANTEED TO SELL.
BESIDES, SOME ARTISTS WANT TO DRAW WHAT THEY LIKE WHETHER IT SELLS OR NOT.
SERIES AFFECT YOUR LIFE IN A BIG WAY, AND EVEN IF I'M THE EDITOR, I'M NOT YOU.
HAVING SOMEONE ELSE DICTATE THE SERIES'S DIRECTION MUST HAVE BEEN...
I THOUGHT... YOU MIGHT REALLY HATE IT.
FRANKLY, I'M NOT CONFIDENT THAT I'M MANAGING TO DRAW SOMETHING ENTERTAINING.

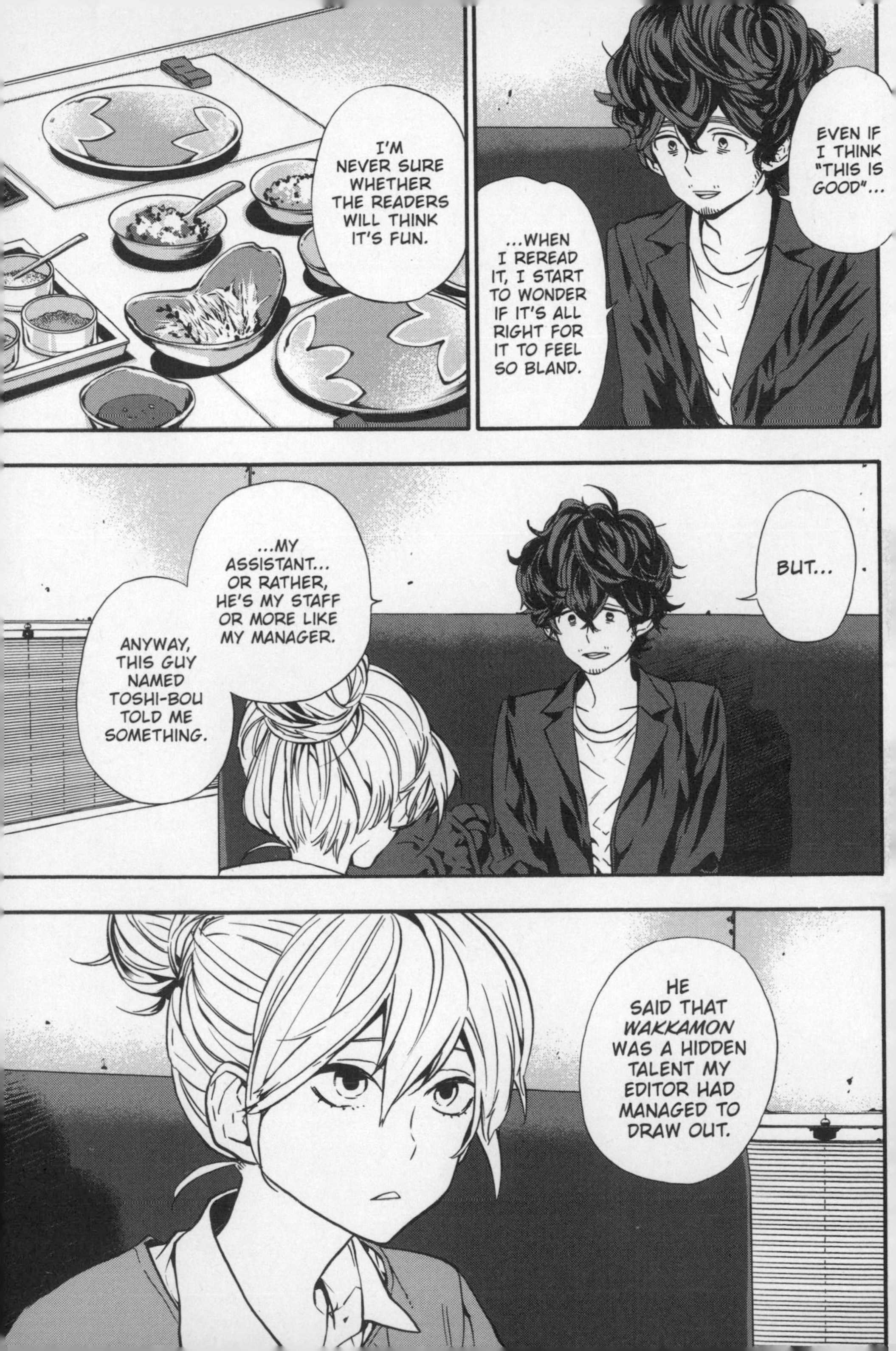
EVEN IF I THINK "THIS IS GOOD"...
...WHEN I REREAD IT, I START TO WONDER IF IT'S ALL RIGHT FOR IT TO FEEL SO BLAND.
I'M NEVER SURE WHETHER THE READERS WILL THINK IT'S FUN.
BUT...
...MY ASSISTANT... OR RATHER, HE'S MY STAFF OR MORE LIKE MY MANAGER.
ANYWAY, THIS GUY NAMED TOSHI-BOU TOLD ME SOMETHING.
HE SAID THAT *WAKKAMON* WAS A HIDDEN TALENT MY EDITOR HAD MANAGED TO DRAW OUT.

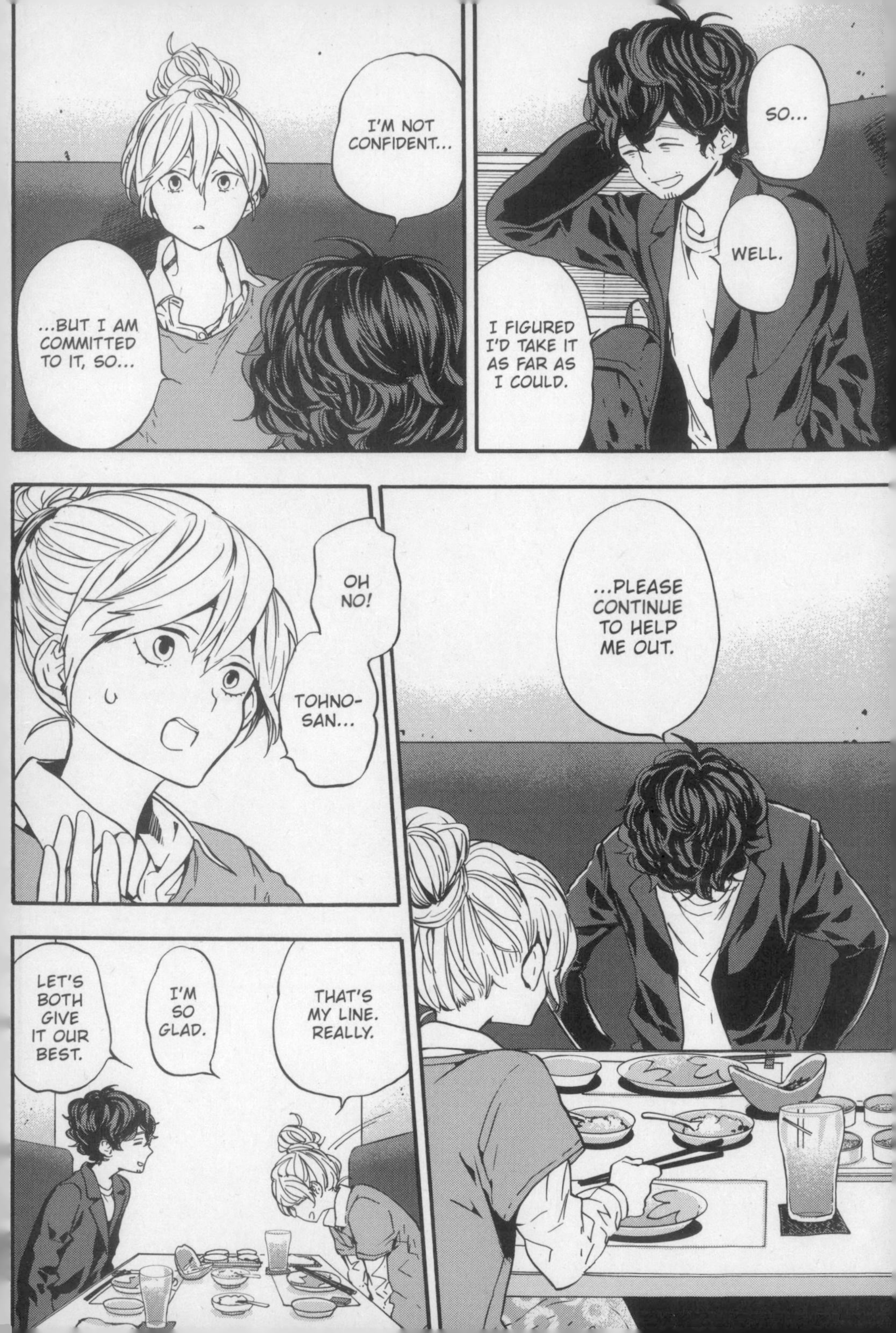
SO...
WELL.
I FIGURED I'D TAKE IT AS FAR AS I COULD.
I'M NOT CONFIDENT...
...BUT I AM COMMITTED TO IT, SO...
...PLEASE CONTINUE TO HELP ME OUT.
OH NO!
TOHNO-SAN...
THAT'S MY LINE. REALLY.
I'M SO GLAD.
LET'S BOTH GIVE IT OUR BEST.

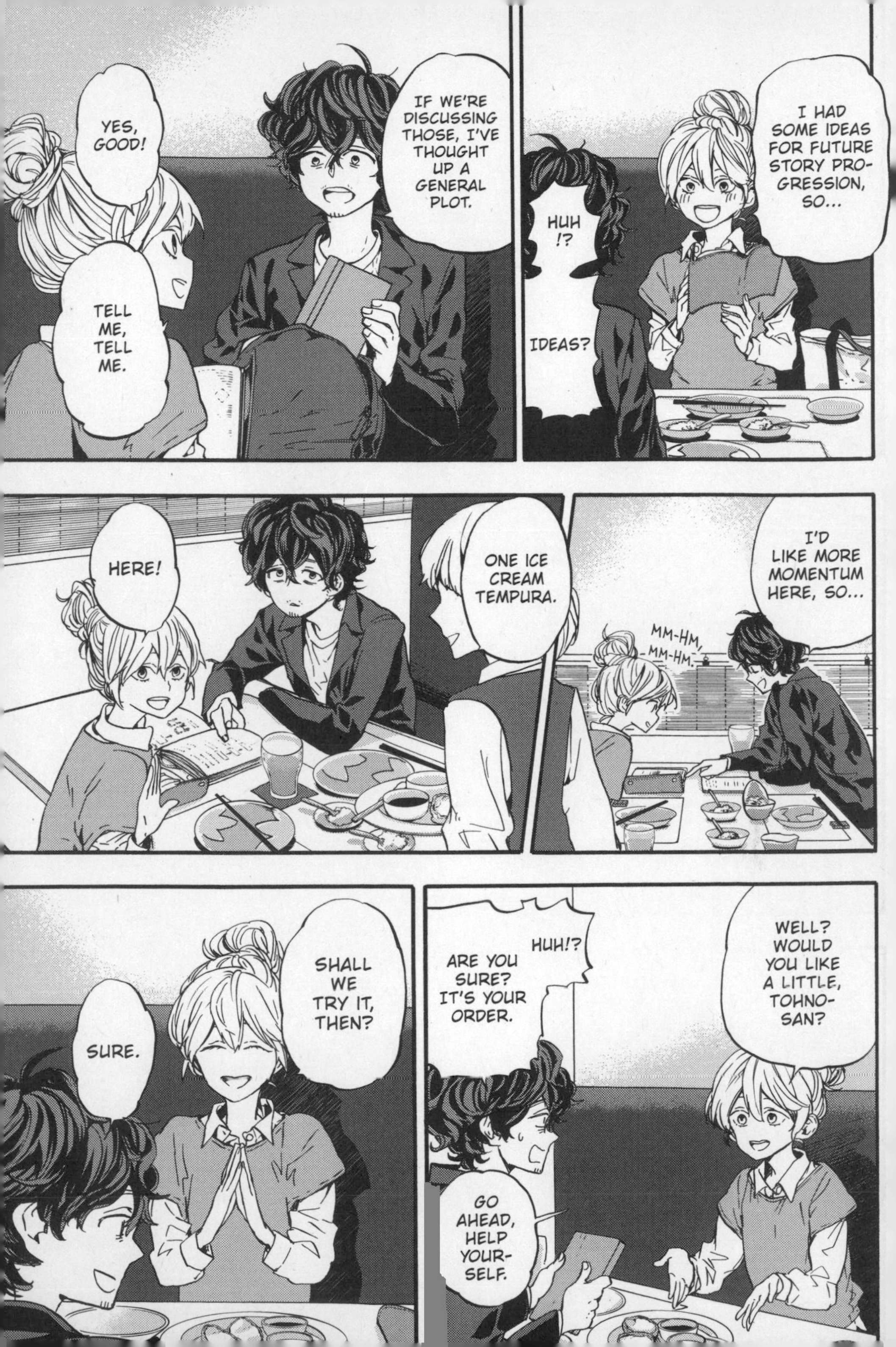
I HAD SOME IDEAS FOR FUTURE STORY PRO-GRESSION, SO...
HUH!?
IDEAS?
IF WE'RE DISCUSSING THOSE, I'VE THOUGHT UP A GENERAL PLOT.
YES, GOOD!
TELL ME, TELL ME.
I'D LIKE MORE MOMENTUM HERE, SO...
MM-HM, MM-HM.
ONE ICE CREAM TEMPURA.
HERE!
WELL? WOULD YOU LIKE A LITTLE, TOHNO-SAN?
HUH!?
ARE YOU SURE? IT'S YOUR ORDER.
GO AHEAD, HELP YOUR-SELF.
SHALL WE TRY IT, THEN?
SURE.

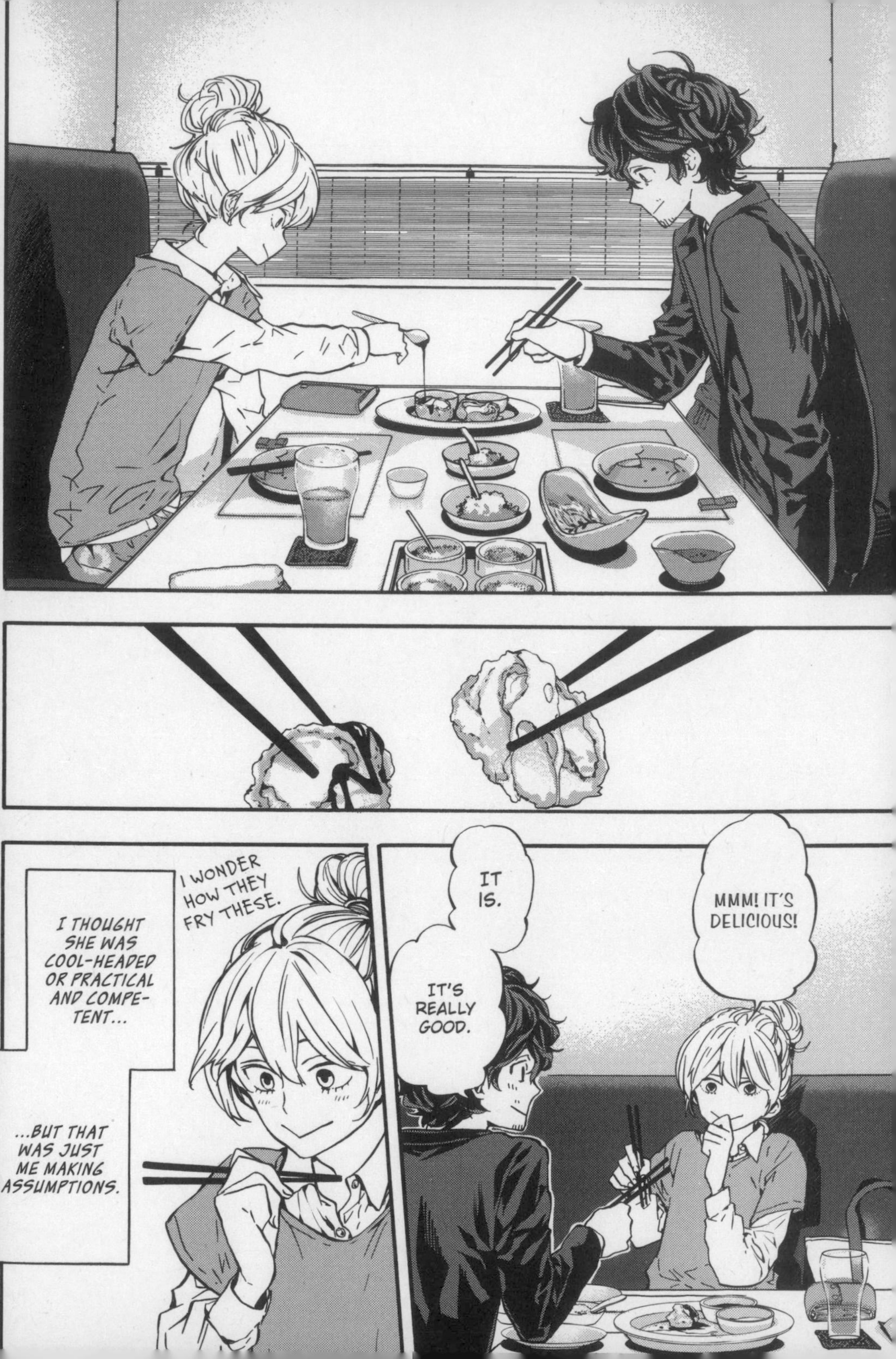
MMM! IT'S DELICIOUS!
IT IS.
IT'S REALLY GOOD.
I WONDER HOW THEY FRY THESE.
I THOUGHT SHE WAS COOL-HEADED OR PRACTICAL AND COMPE- TENT...
...BUT THAT WAS JUST ME MAKING ASSUMPTIONS.

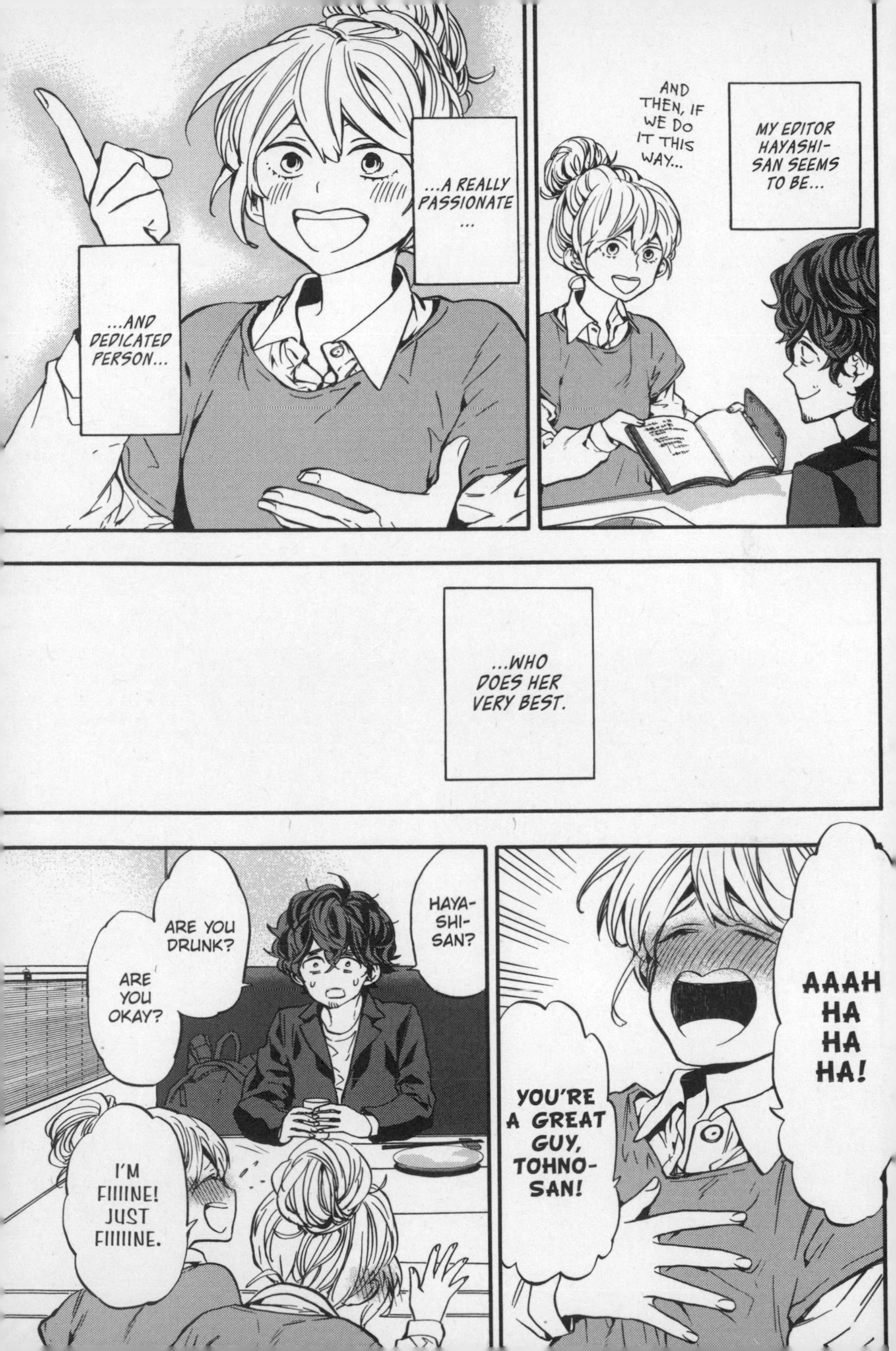
MY EDITOR HAYASHI-SAN SEEMS TO BE...
AND THEN, IF WE DO IT THIS WAY...
...A REALLY PASSIONATE ...
...AND DEDICATED PERSON...
...WHO DOES HER VERY BEST.
AAAH HA HA HA!
YOU'RE A GREAT GUY, TOHNO-SAN!
HAYA-SHI-SAN?
ARE YOU DRUNK?
ARE YOU OKAY?
I'M FIIIINE! JUST FIIIINE.

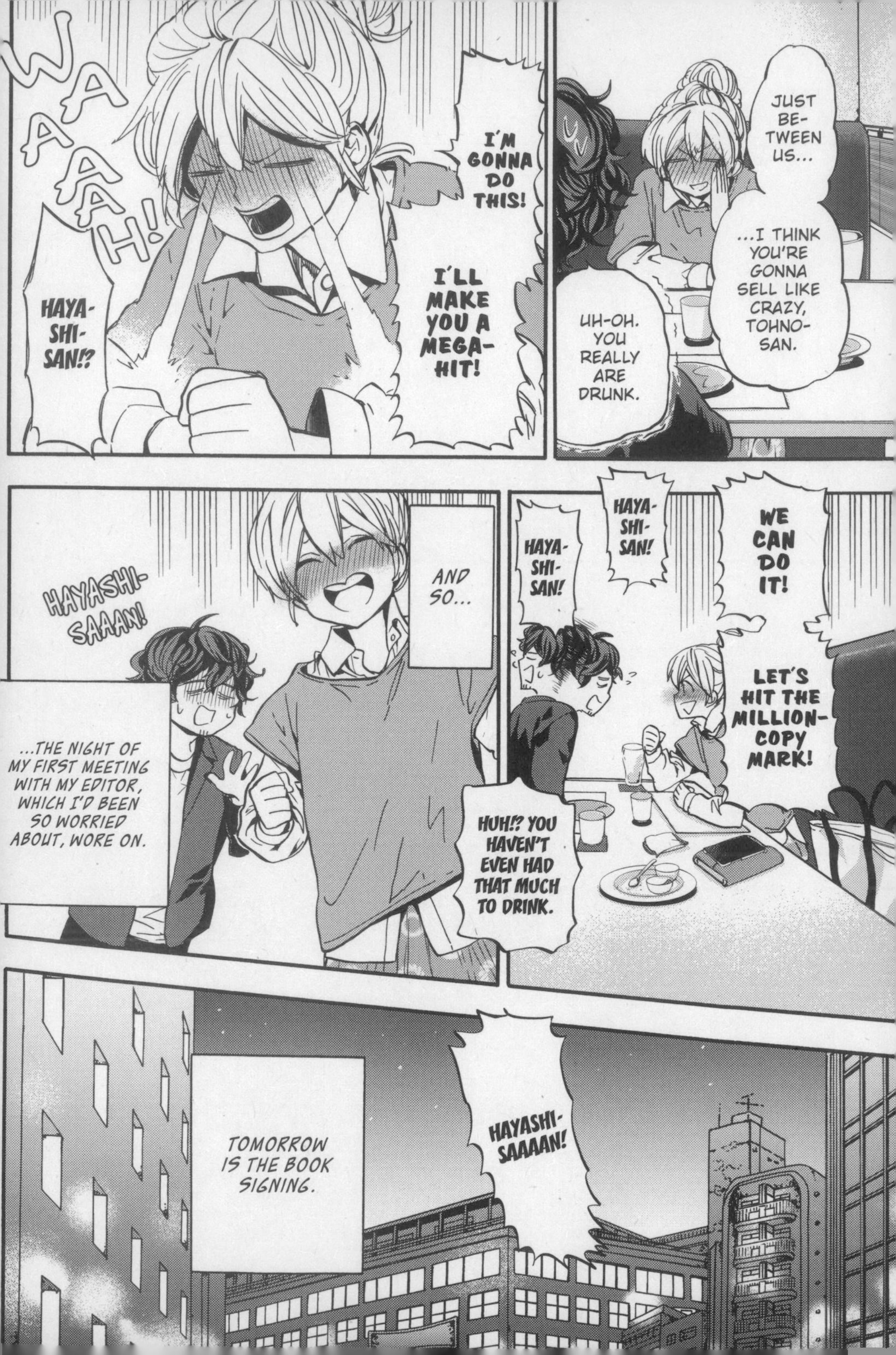
JUST BETWEEN US...
...I THINK YOU'RE GONNA SELL LIKE CRAZY, TOHNO-SAN.
UH-OH. YOU REALLY ARE DRUNK.
I'M GONNA DO THIS!
I'LL MAKE YOU A MEGA-HIT!
WAAAAH!
HAYASHI-SAN!?
WE CAN DO IT!
LET'S HIT THE MILLION-COPY MARK!
HAYASHI-SAN!
HAYASHI-SAN!
HUH!? YOU HAVEN'T EVEN HAD THAT MUCH TO DRINK.
AND SO...
HAYASHI-SAAAN!
...THE NIGHT OF MY FIRST MEETING WITH MY EDITOR, WHICH I'D BEEN SO WORRIED ABOUT, WORE ON.
HAYASHI-SAAAAN!
TOMORROW IS THE BOOK SIGNING.

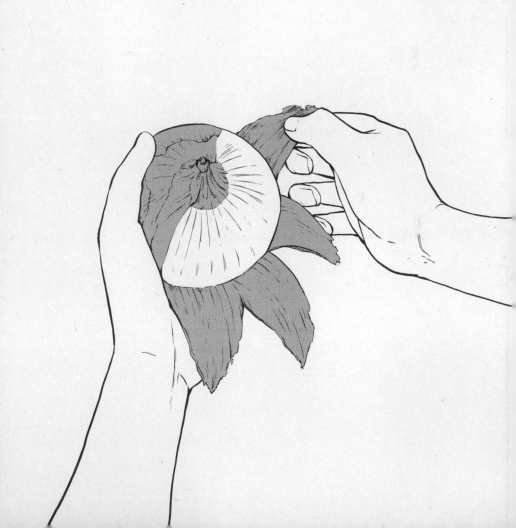

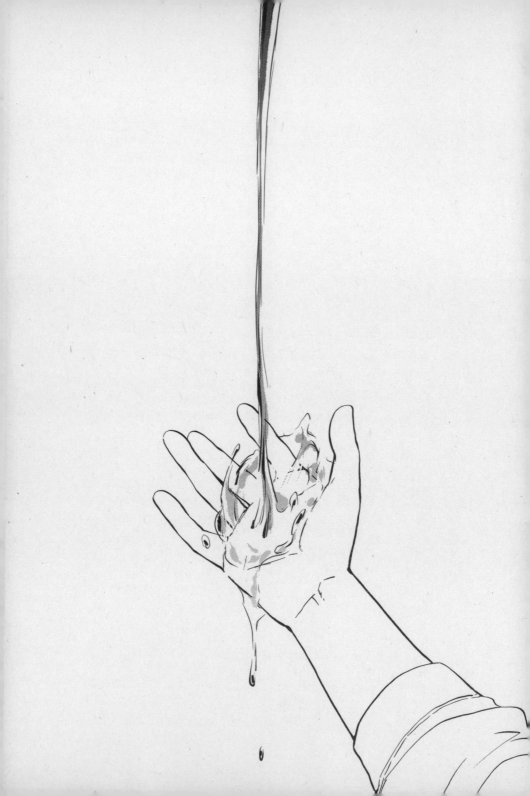

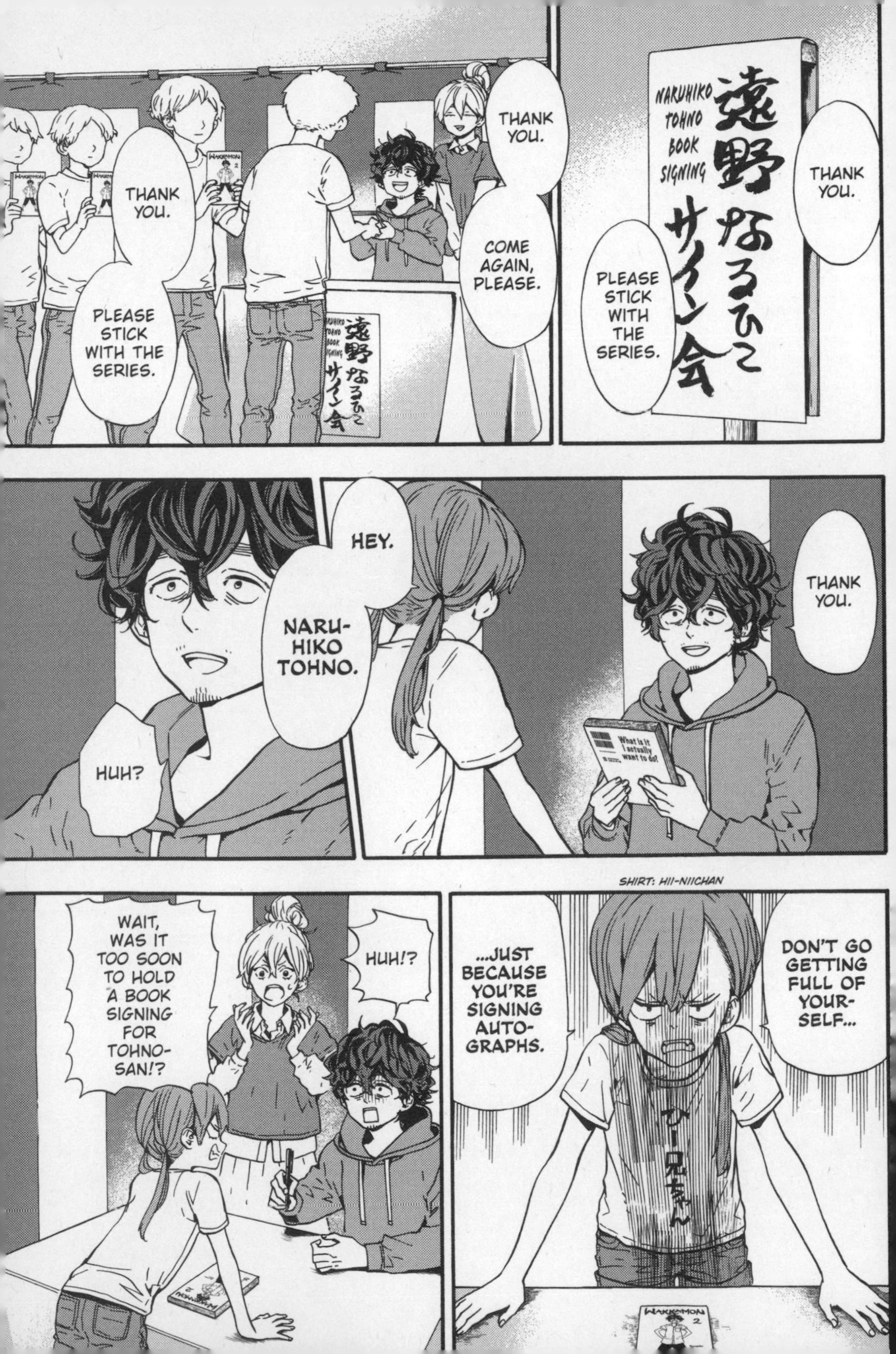
NARUHIKO TOHNO BOOK SIGNING
遠野なるひこサイン会
THANK YOU.
PLEASE STICK WITH THE SERIES.
THANK YOU.
COME AGAIN, PLEASE.
THANK YOU.
PLEASE STICK WITH THE SERIES.
THANK YOU.
What is it I actually want to do?
HEY.
NARUHIKO TOHNO.
HUH?
SHIRT: HII-NIICHAN
ひー兄ちゃん
DON'T GO GETTING FULL OF YOURSELF...
...JUST BECAUSE YOU'RE SIGNING AUTOGRAPHS.
HUH!?
WAIT, WAS IT TOO SOON TO HOLD A BOOK SIGNING FOR TOHNO-SAN!?
WAKKAMON 2

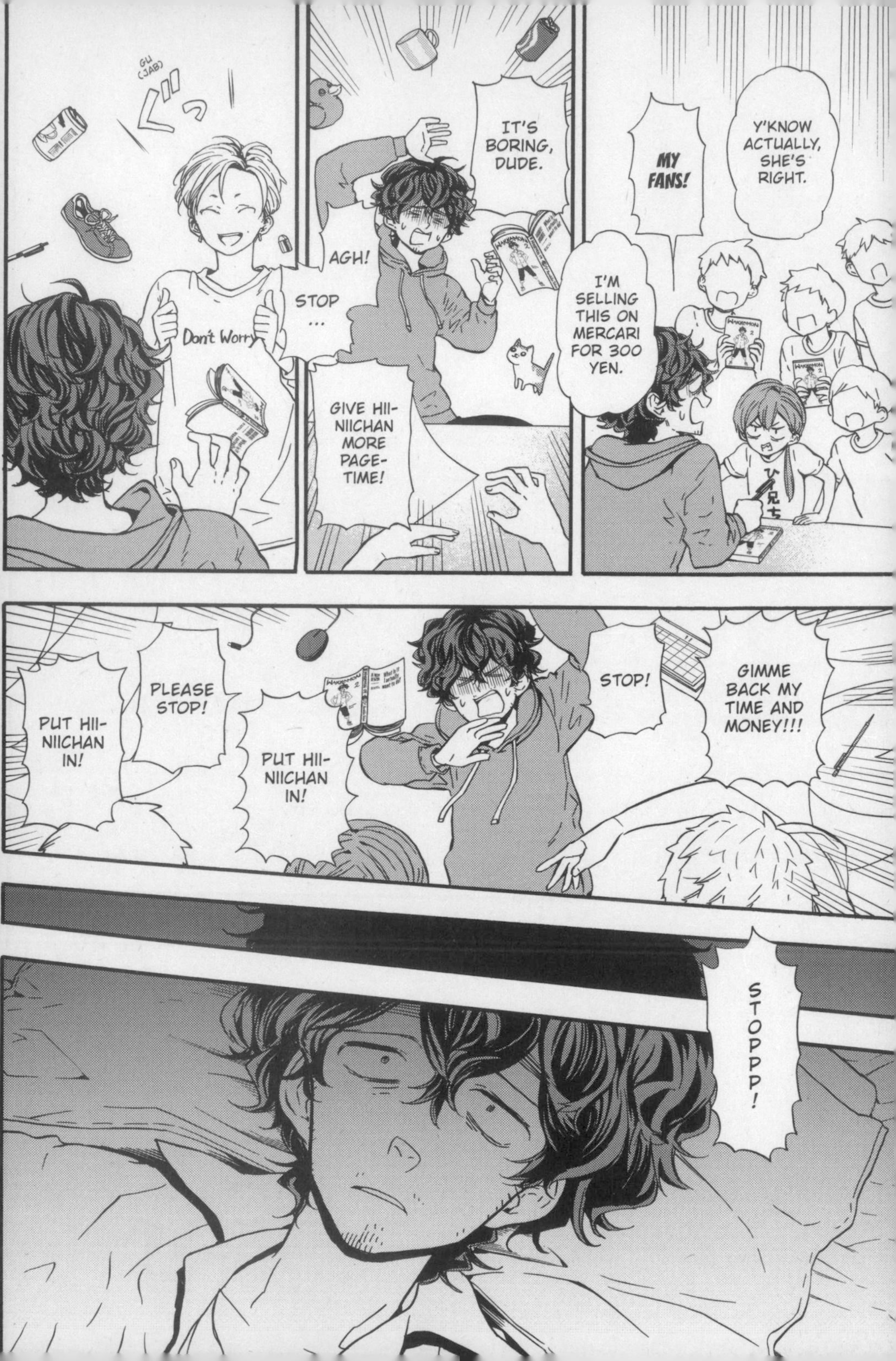
Y'KNOW ACTUALLY, SHE'S RIGHT.
MY FANS!
I'M SELLING THIS ON MERCARI FOR 300 YEN.
IT'S BORING, DUDE.
AGH!
STOP ...
GIVE HII-NIICHAN MORE PAGE-TIME!
GU (JAB)
Don't Worry
GIMME BACK MY TIME AND MONEY!!!
STOP!
PUT HII-NIICHAN IN!
PLEASE STOP!
PUT HII-NIICHAN IN!
STOPPP!

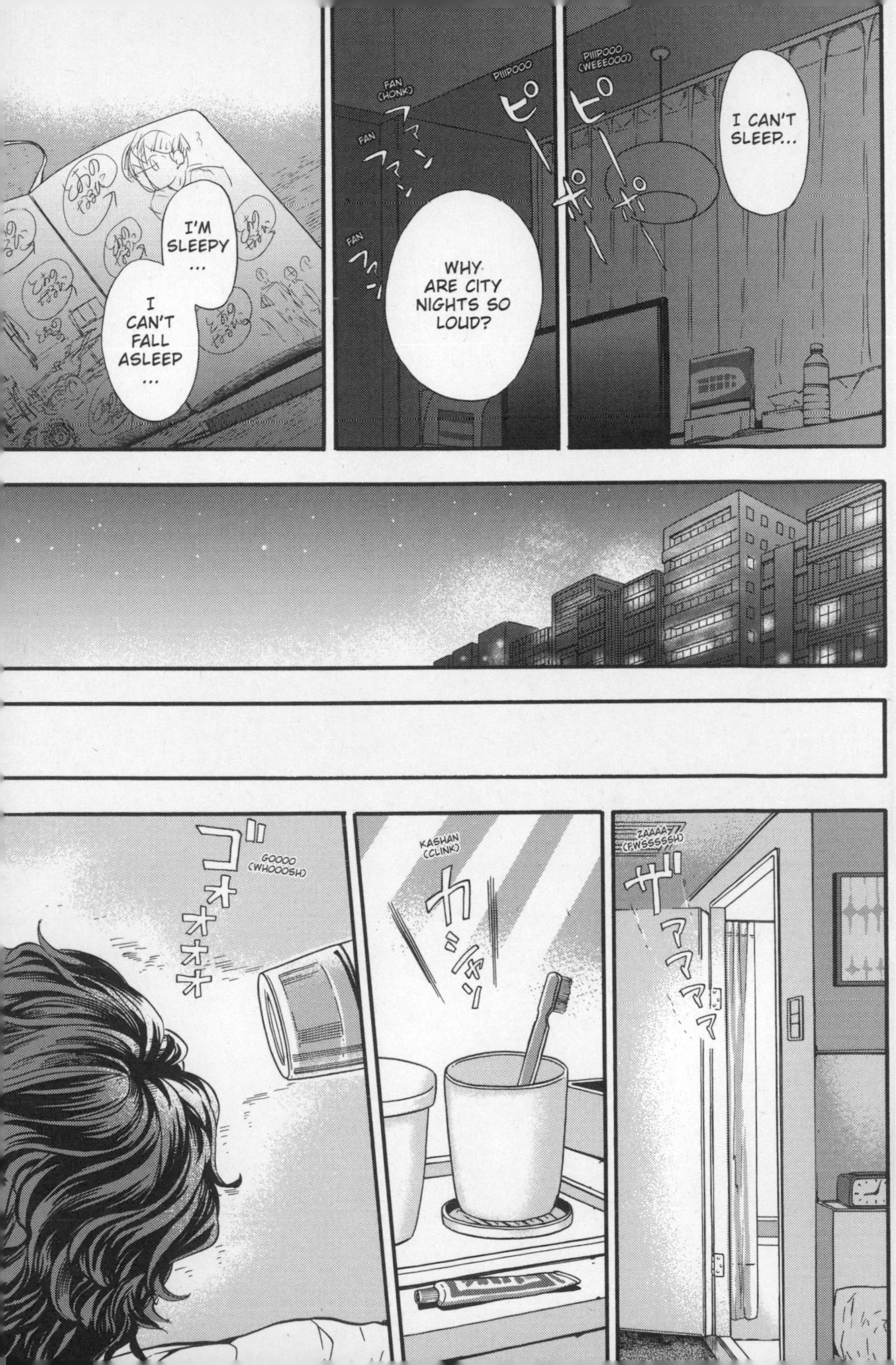
PIIIPOOO (WEEEOOO)
I CAN'T SLEEP...
FAN (HONK)
PIIIPOOO
FAN
FAN
WHY ARE CITY NIGHTS SO LOUD?
I'M SLEEPY ...
I CAN'T FALL ASLEEP ...
ZAAAA (F.WSSSSSH)
KASHAN (CLINK)
GOOOO (WHOOOSH)

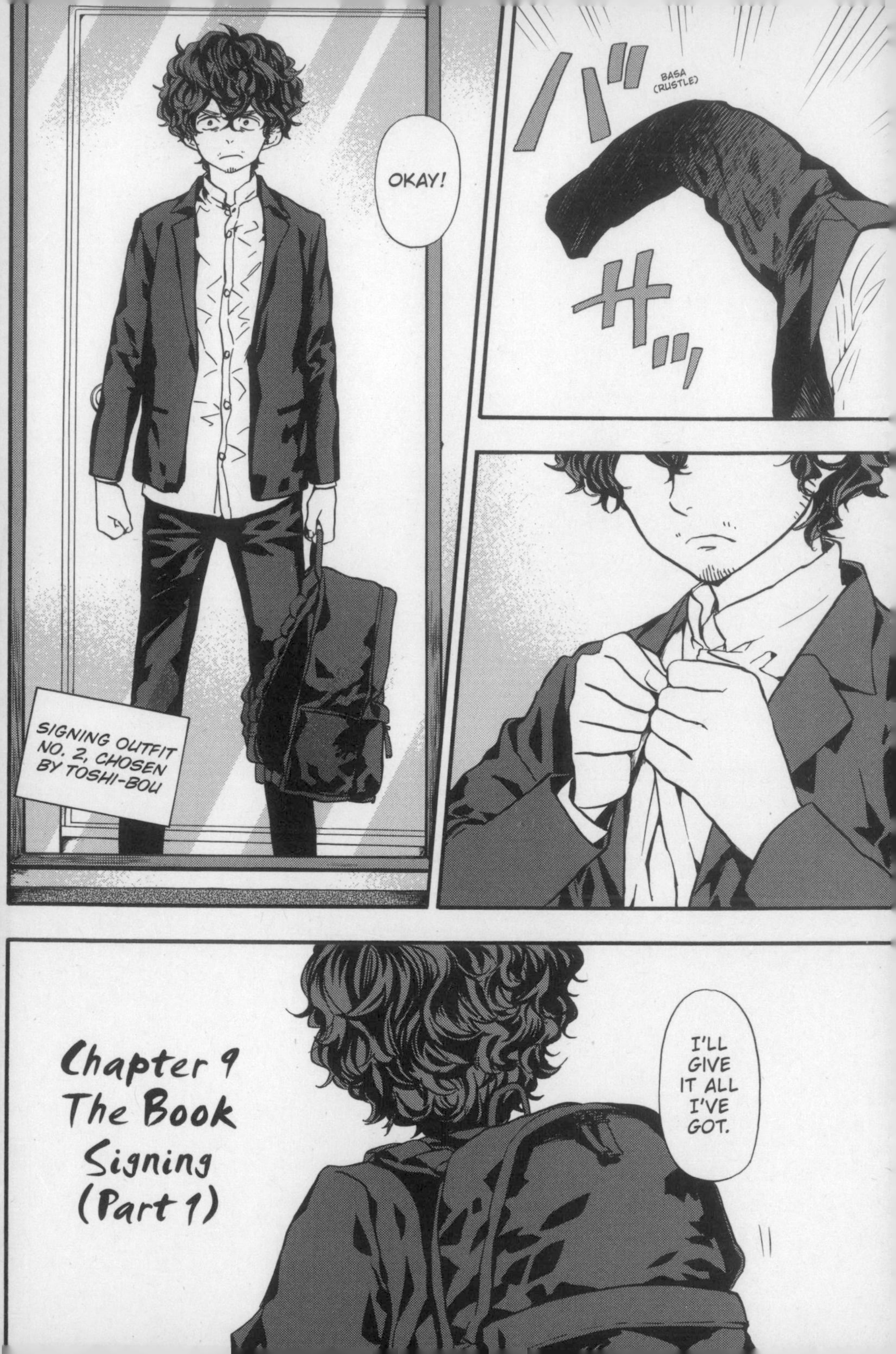
BASA (RUSTLE)
OKAY!
SIGNING OUTFIT NO. 2, CHOSEN BY TOSHI-BOU
I'LL GIVE IT ALL I'VE GOT.
Chapter 9 The Book Signing (Part 1)

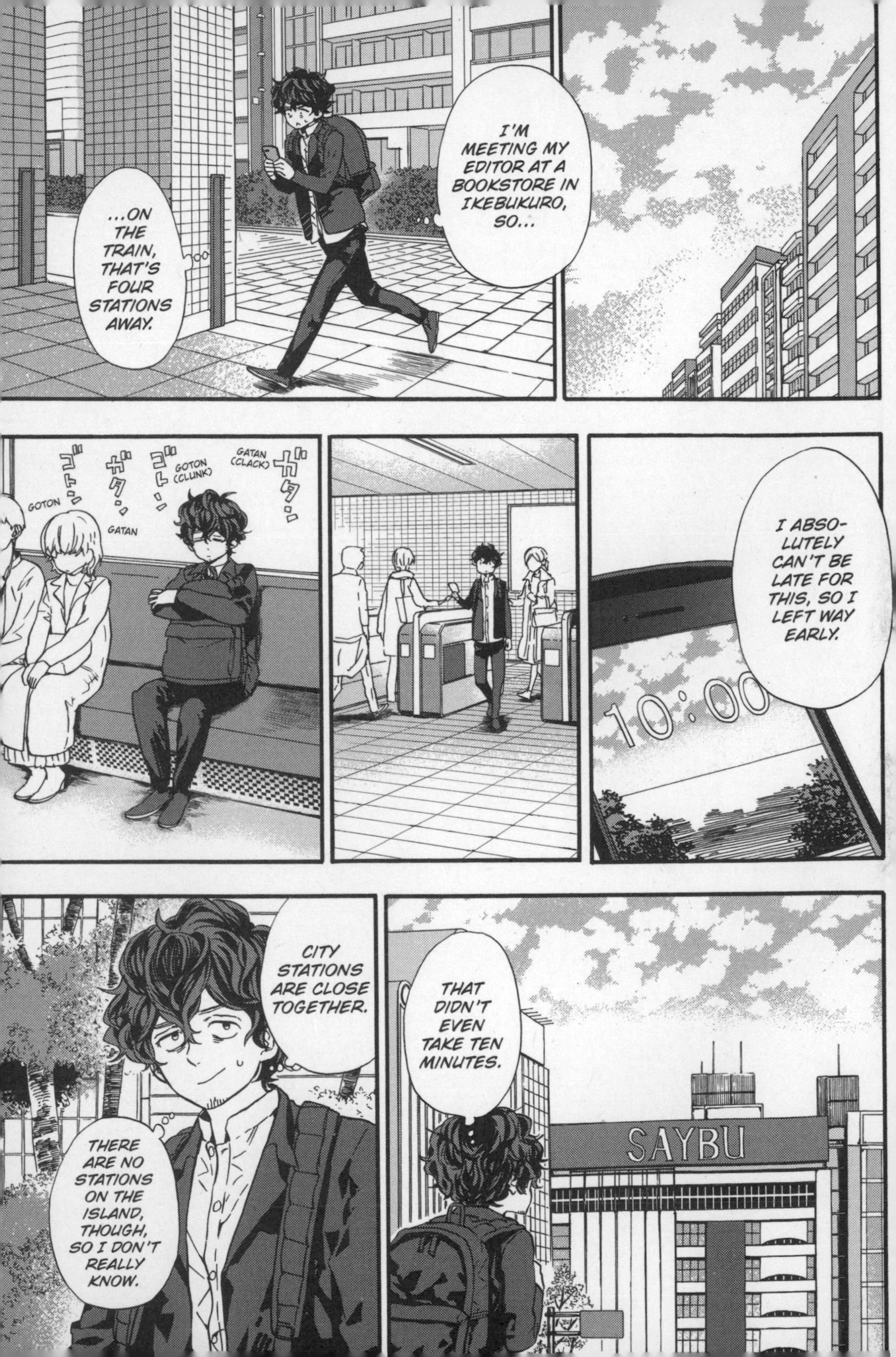
I'M MEETING MY EDITOR AT A BOOKSTORE IN IKEBUKURO, SO...
...ON THE TRAIN, THAT'S FOUR STATIONS AWAY.
I ABSO-LUTELY CAN'T BE LATE FOR THIS, SO I LEFT WAY EARLY.
10:00
GATAN (CLACK)
GOTON (CLUNK)
GATAN
GOTON
THAT DIDN'T EVEN TAKE TEN MINUTES.
SAYBU
CITY STATIONS ARE CLOSE TOGETHER.
THERE ARE NO STATIONS ON THE ISLAND, THOUGH, SO I DON'T REALLY KNOW.

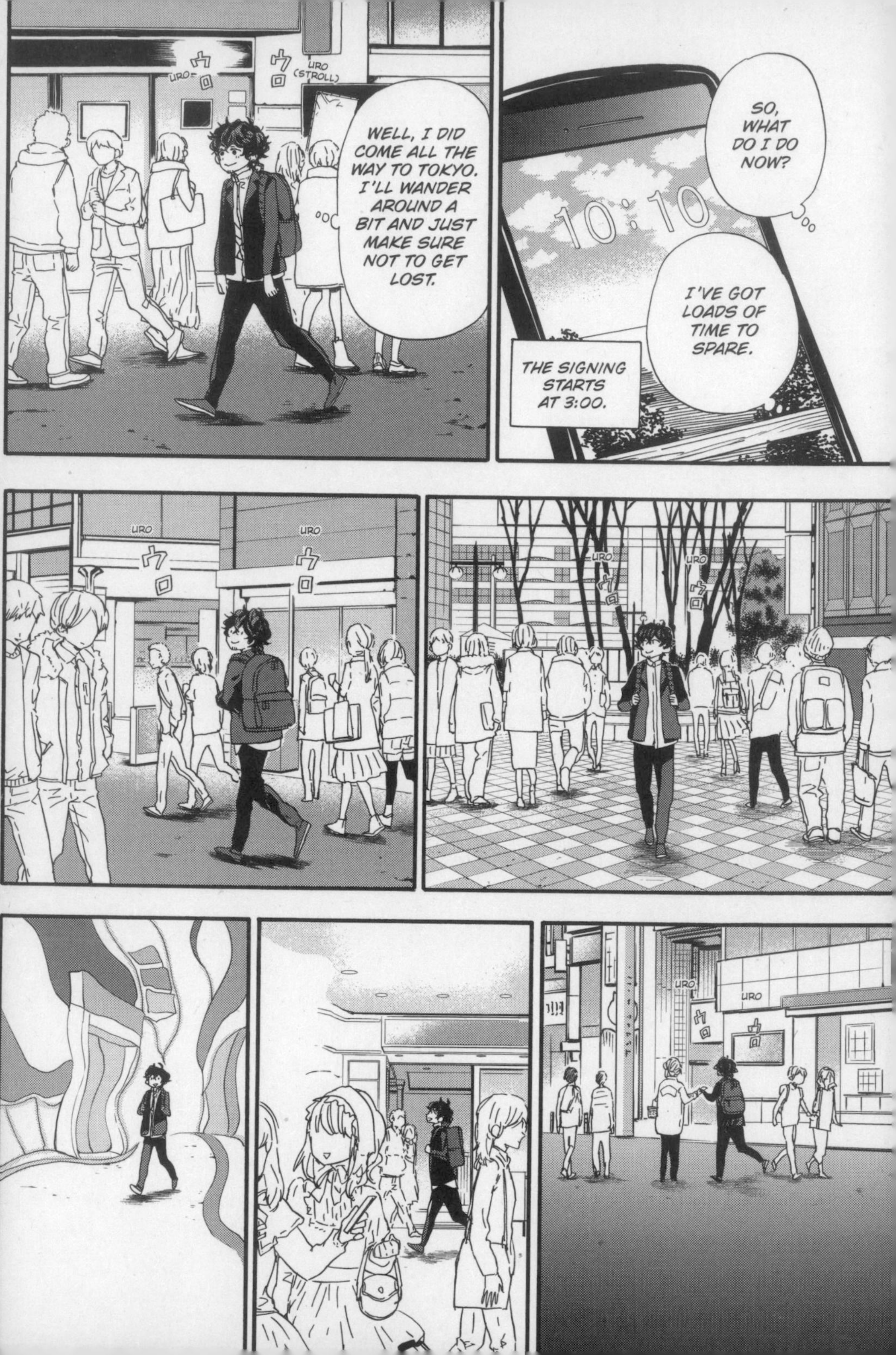
SO, WHAT DO I DO NOW?
I'VE GOT LOADS OF TIME TO SPARE.
THE SIGNING STARTS AT 3:00.
URO (STROLL)
URO
WELL, I DID COME ALL THE WAY TO TOKYO. I'LL WANDER AROUND A BIT AND JUST MAKE SURE NOT TO GET LOST.
URO
URO
URO
URO
URO
URO

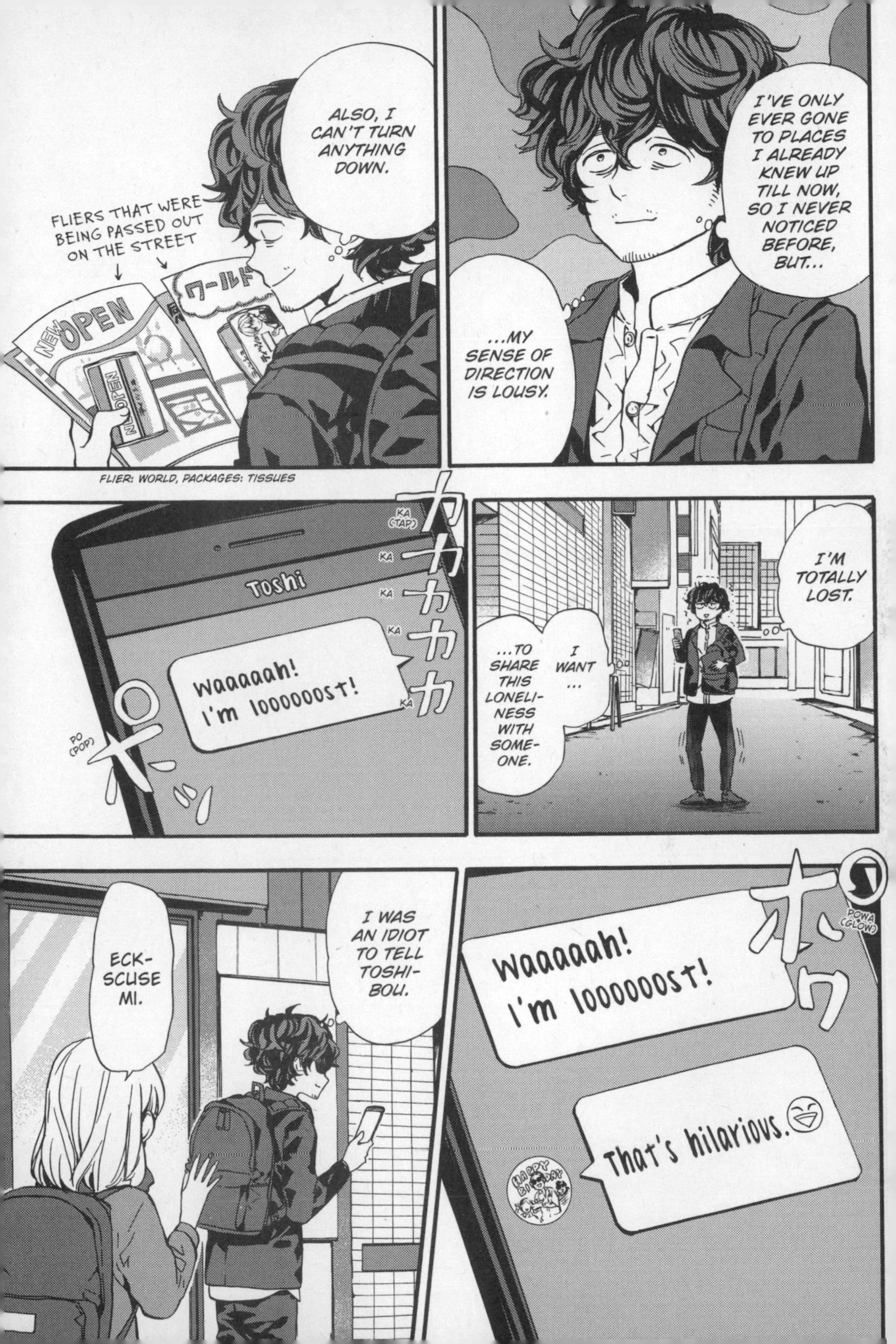
I'VE ONLY EVER GONE TO PLACES I ALREADY KNEW UP TILL NOW, SO I NEVER NOTICED BEFORE, BUT...
...MY SENSE OF DIRECTION IS LOUSY.
ALSO, I CAN'T TURN ANYTHING DOWN.
FLIERS THAT WERE BEING PASSED OUT ON THE STREET
NEW OPEN
ワールド
FLIER: WORLD, PACKAGES: TISSUES
I'M TOTALLY LOST.
I WANT...
...TO SHARE THIS LONELINESS WITH SOMEONE.
KA (TAP)
KA
KA
KA
KA
Toshi
Waaaaah! I'm looooost!
PO (POP)
POWA (GLOW)
Waaaaah! I'm looooost!
That's hilarious.
I WAS AN IDIOT TO TELL TOSHIBOU.
ECK-SCUSE MI.

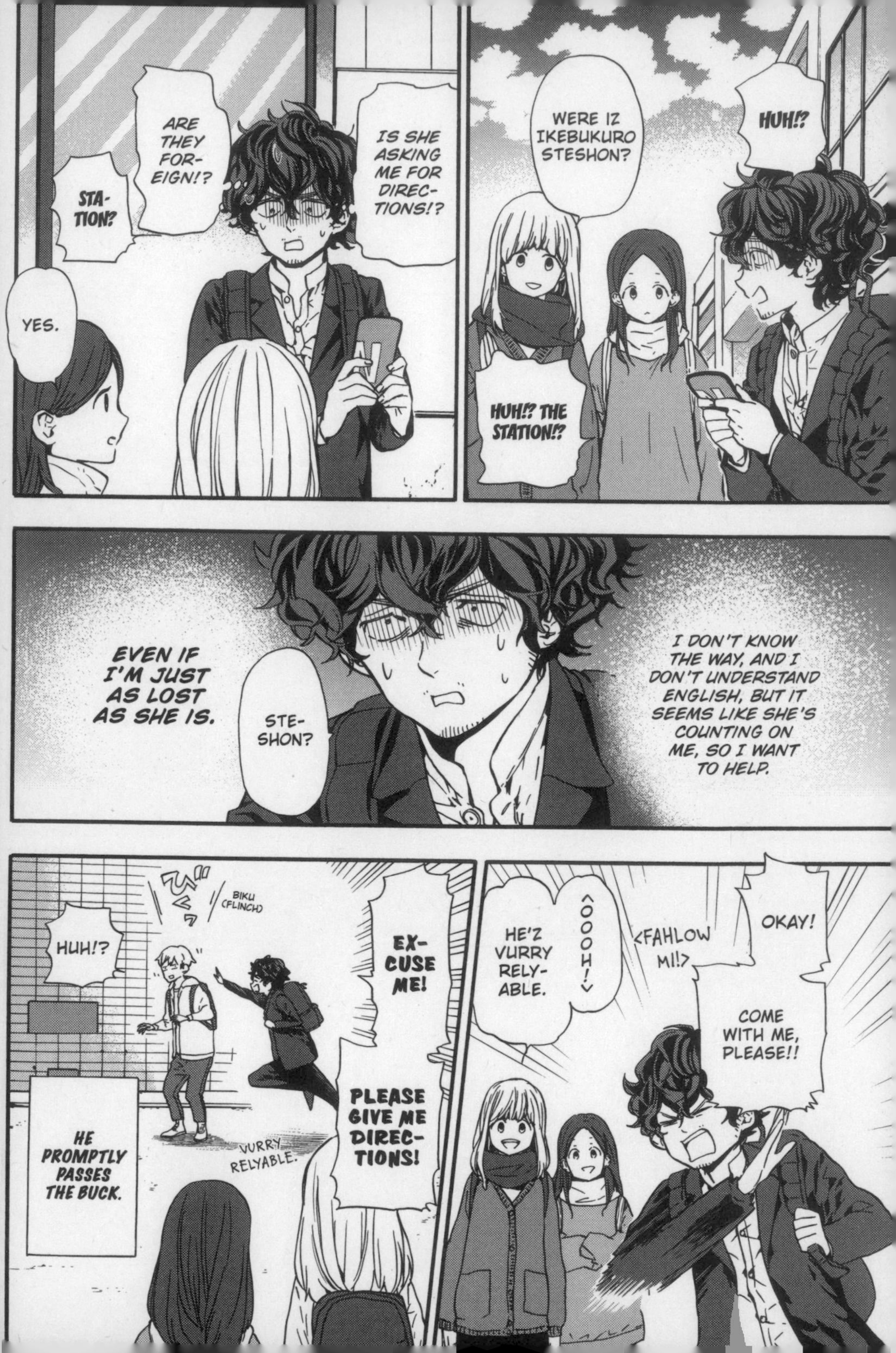
HUH!?
WERE IZ IKEBUKURO STESHON?
HUH!? THE STATION!?
IS SHE ASKING ME FOR DIREC-TIONS!?
ARE THEY FOR-EIGN!?
STA-TION?
YES.
I DON'T KNOW THE WAY, AND I DON'T UNDERSTAND ENGLISH, BUT IT SEEMS LIKE SHE'S COUNTING ON ME, SO I WANT TO HELP.
STE-SHON?
EVEN IF I'M JUST AS LOST AS SHE IS.
OKAY!
<FAHLOW MI!>
COME WITH ME, PLEASE!!
<OOOH!>
HE'Z VURRY RELY-ABLE.
EX-CUSE ME!
PLEASE GIVE ME DIREC-TIONS!
BIKU (FLINCH)
HUH!?
VURRY RELYABLE.
HE PROMPTLY PASSES THE BUCK.

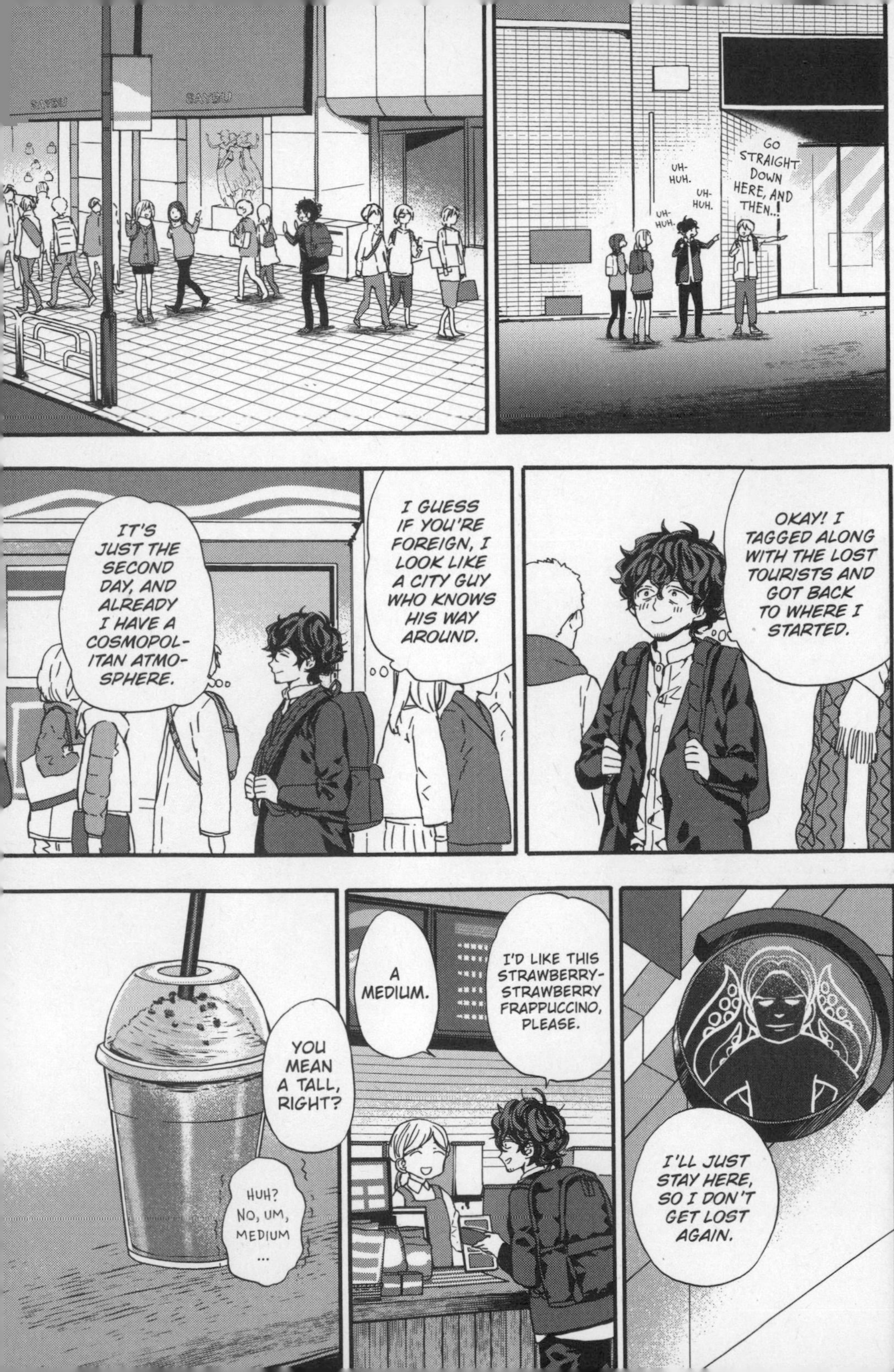

SAYBU
SAYBU
GO STRAIGHT DOWN HERE, AND THEN...!
UH-HUH.
UH-HUH.
UH-HUH.
IT'S JUST THE SECOND DAY, AND ALREADY I HAVE A COSMOPOLITAN ATMOSPHERE.
I GUESS IF YOU'RE FOREIGN, I LOOK LIKE A CITY GUY WHO KNOWS HIS WAY AROUND.
OKAY! I TAGGED ALONG WITH THE LOST TOURISTS AND GOT BACK TO WHERE I STARTED.
I'D LIKE THIS STRAWBERRY-STRAWBERRY FRAPPUCCINO, PLEASE.
A MEDIUM.
YOU MEAN A TALL, RIGHT?
HUH? NO, UM, MEDIUM ...
I'LL JUST STAY HERE, SO I DON'T GET LOST AGAIN.

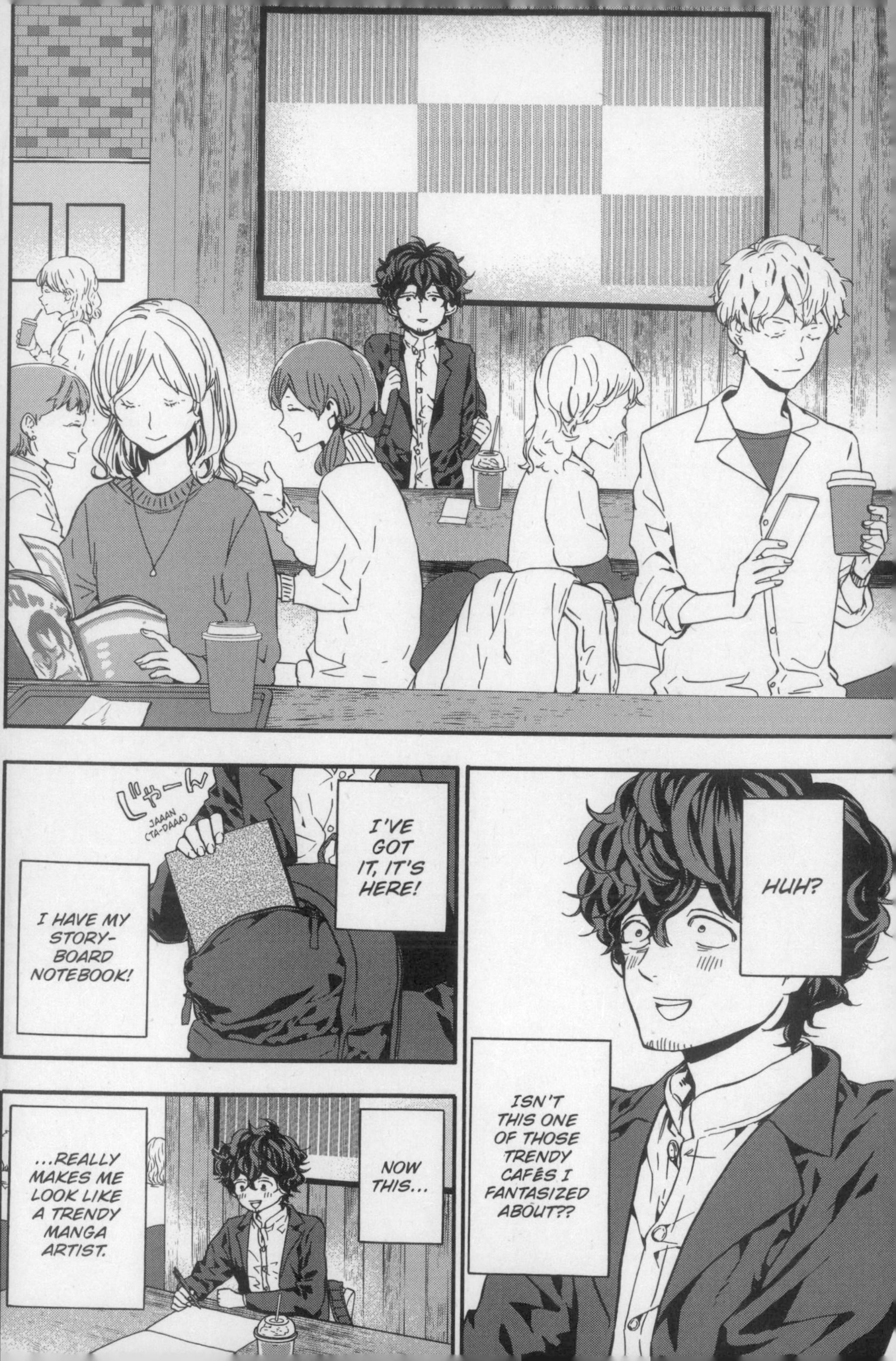
HUH?
ISN'T THIS ONE OF THOSE TRENDY CAFÉS I FANTASIZED ABOUT??
じゃーん
JAAAN (TA-DAAA)
I'VE GOT IT, IT'S HERE!
I HAVE MY STORY-BOARD NOTEBOOK!
NOW THIS...
...REALLY MAKES ME LOOK LIKE A TRENDY MANGA ARTIST.

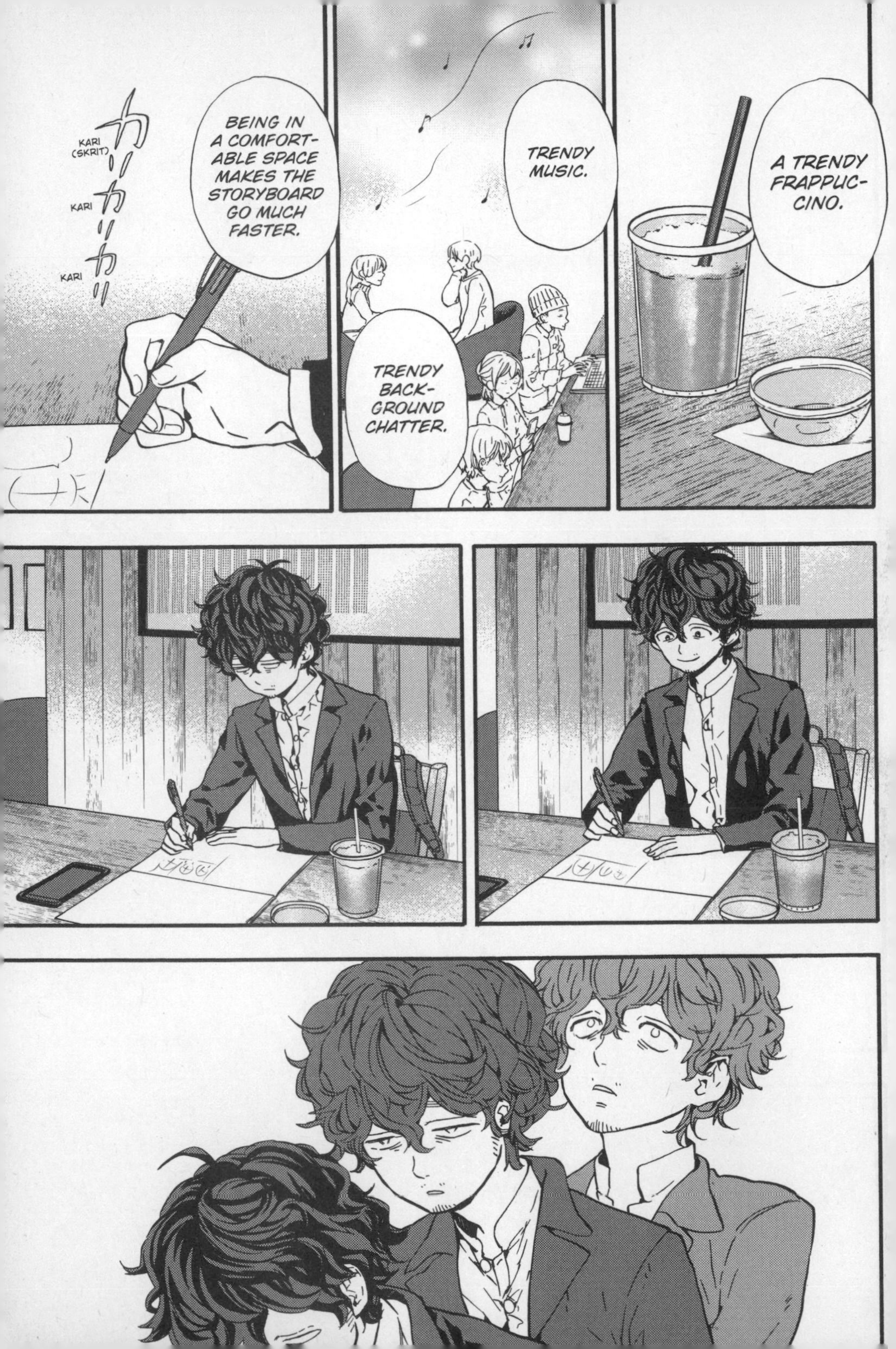
A TRENDY FRAPPUC-CINO.
TRENDY MUSIC.
TRENDY BACK-GROUND CHATTER.
BEING IN A COMFORT-ABLE SPACE MAKES THE STORYBOARD GO MUCH FASTER.
KARI (SKRIT)
KARI
KARI

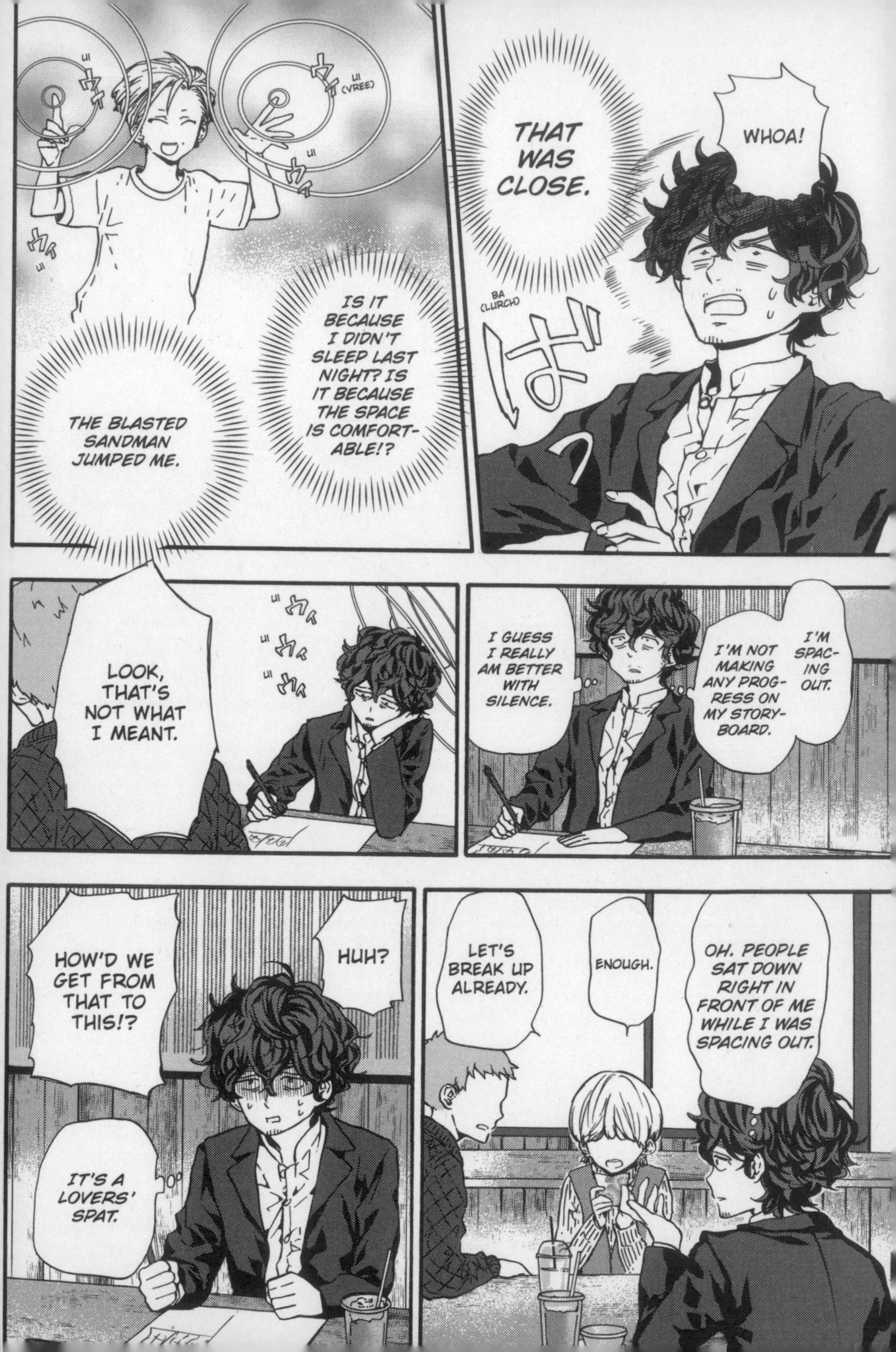
WHOA!
THAT WAS CLOSE.
BA (LURCH)
UI (VREE)
UI
UI
UI
IS IT BECAUSE I DIDN'T SLEEP LAST NIGHT? IS IT BECAUSE THE SPACE IS COMFORTABLE!?
THE BLASTED SANDMAN JUMPED ME.
I'M SPACING OUT.
I'M NOT MAKING ANY PROGRESS ON MY STORYBOARD.
I GUESS I REALLY AM BETTER WITH SILENCE.
UI
UI
UI
LOOK, THAT'S NOT WHAT I MEANT.
OH. PEOPLE SAT DOWN RIGHT IN FRONT OF ME WHILE I WAS SPACING OUT.
ENOUGH.
LET'S BREAK UP ALREADY.
HUH?
HOW'D WE GET FROM THAT TO THIS!?
IT'S A LOVERS' SPAT.

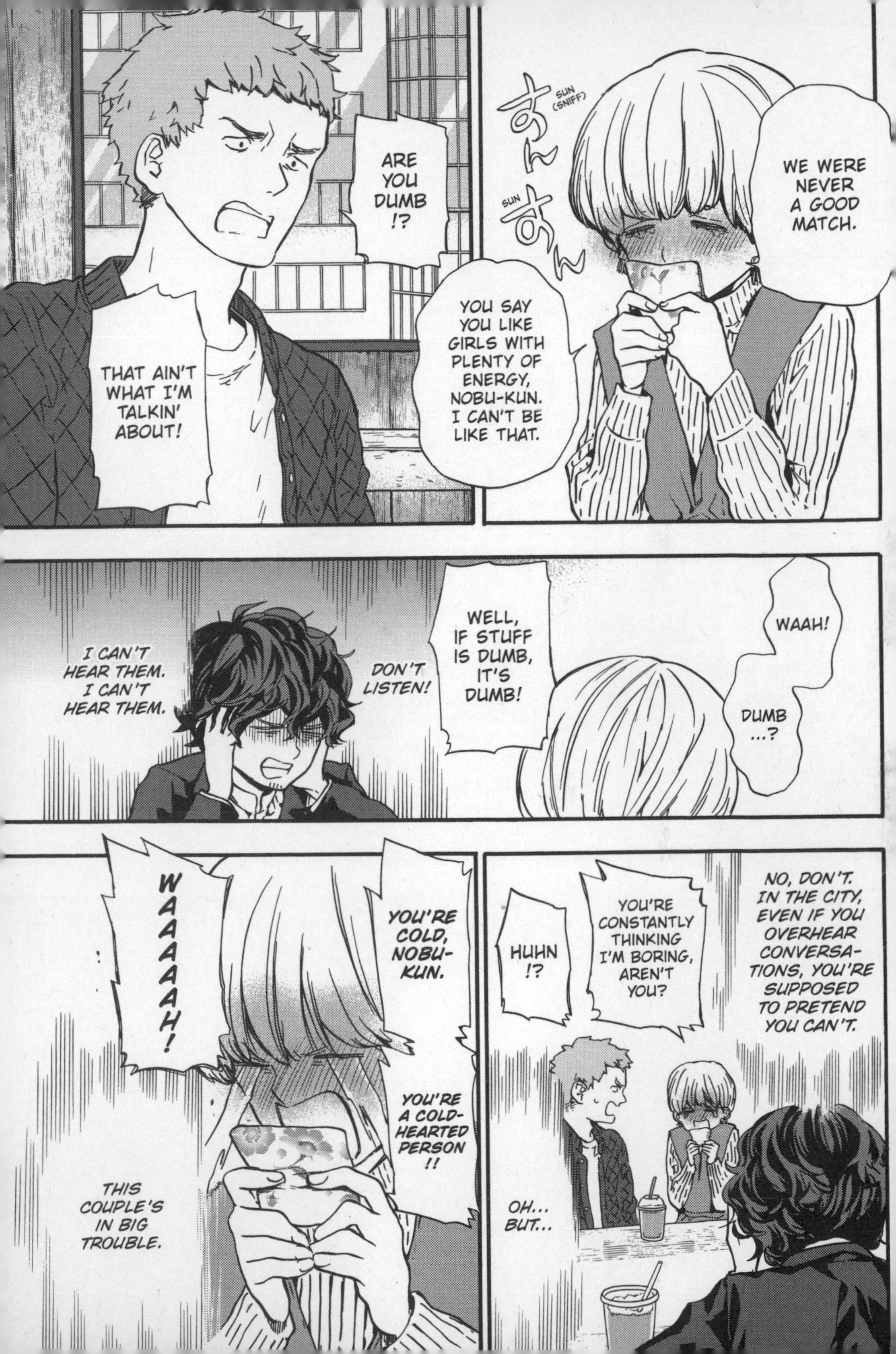
WE WERE NEVER A GOOD MATCH.
すん SUN (SNIFF)
すん SUN
YOU SAY YOU LIKE GIRLS WITH PLENTY OF ENERGY, NOBU-KUN. I CAN'T BE LIKE THAT.
ARE YOU DUMB !?
THAT AIN'T WHAT I'M TALKIN' ABOUT!
WAAH!
DUMB ...?
WELL, IF STUFF IS DUMB, IT'S DUMB!
DON'T LISTEN!
I CAN'T HEAR THEM. I CAN'T HEAR THEM.
NO, DON'T. IN THE CITY, EVEN IF YOU OVERHEAR CONVERSATIONS, YOU'RE SUPPOSED TO PRETEND YOU CAN'T.
YOU'RE CONSTANTLY THINKING I'M BORING, AREN'T YOU?
HUHN !?
OH... BUT...
YOU'RE COLD, NOBU-KUN.
WAAAAAAH!
YOU'RE A COLD-HEARTED PERSON !!
THIS COUPLE'S IN BIG TROUBLE.

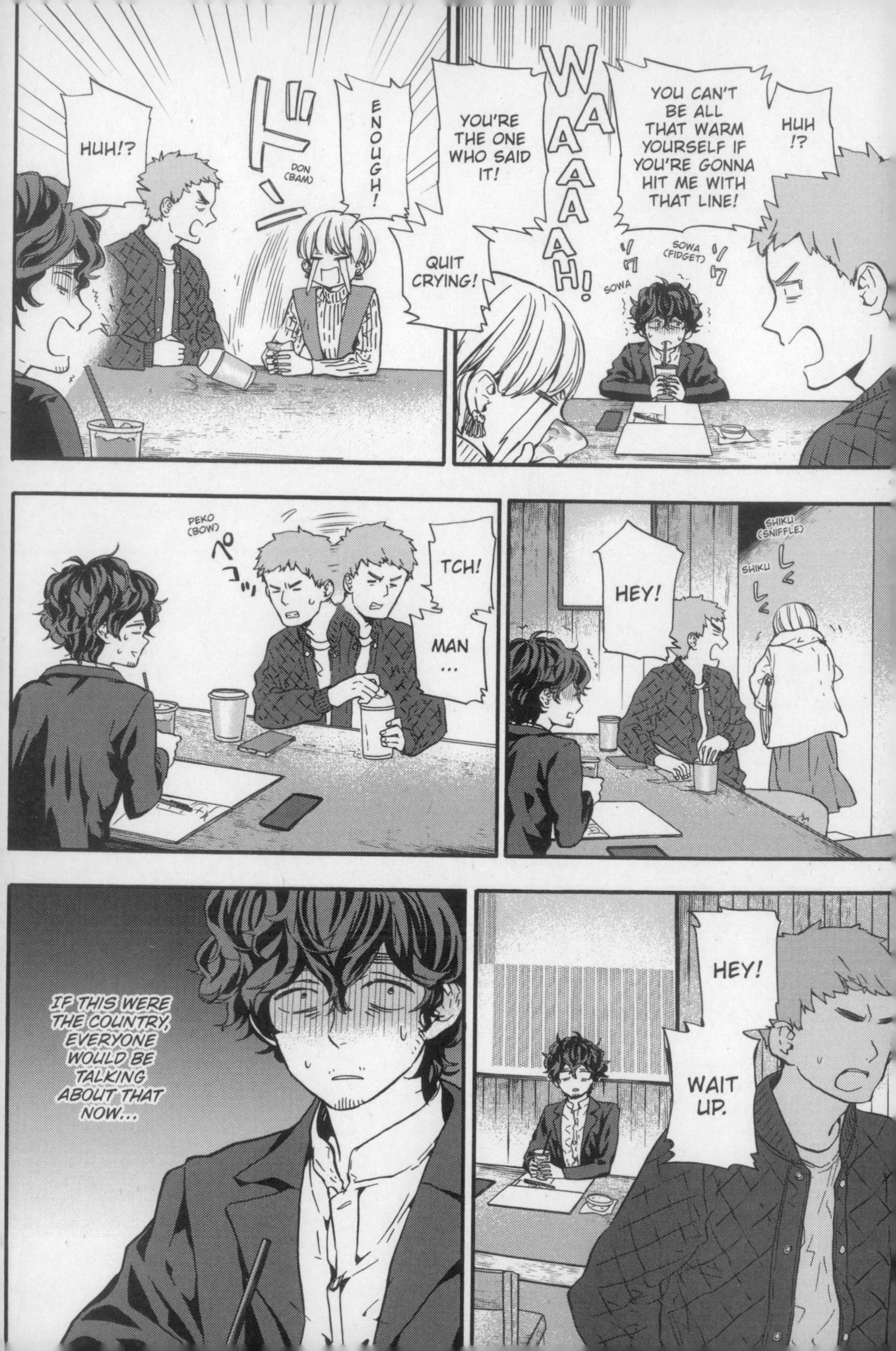
HUH!?
YOU CAN'T BE ALL THAT WARM YOURSELF IF YOU'RE GONNA HIT ME WITH THAT LINE!
WAAAAAAH!
SOWA (FIDGET)
SOWA
YOU'RE THE ONE WHO SAID IT!
QUIT CRYING!
ENOUGH!
DON (BAM)
HUH!?
SHIKU (SNIFFLE)
SHIKU
HEY!
TCH!
MAN ...
PEKO (BOW)
HEY!
WAIT UP.
IF THIS WERE THE COUNTRY, EVERYONE WOULD BE TALKING ABOUT THAT NOW...

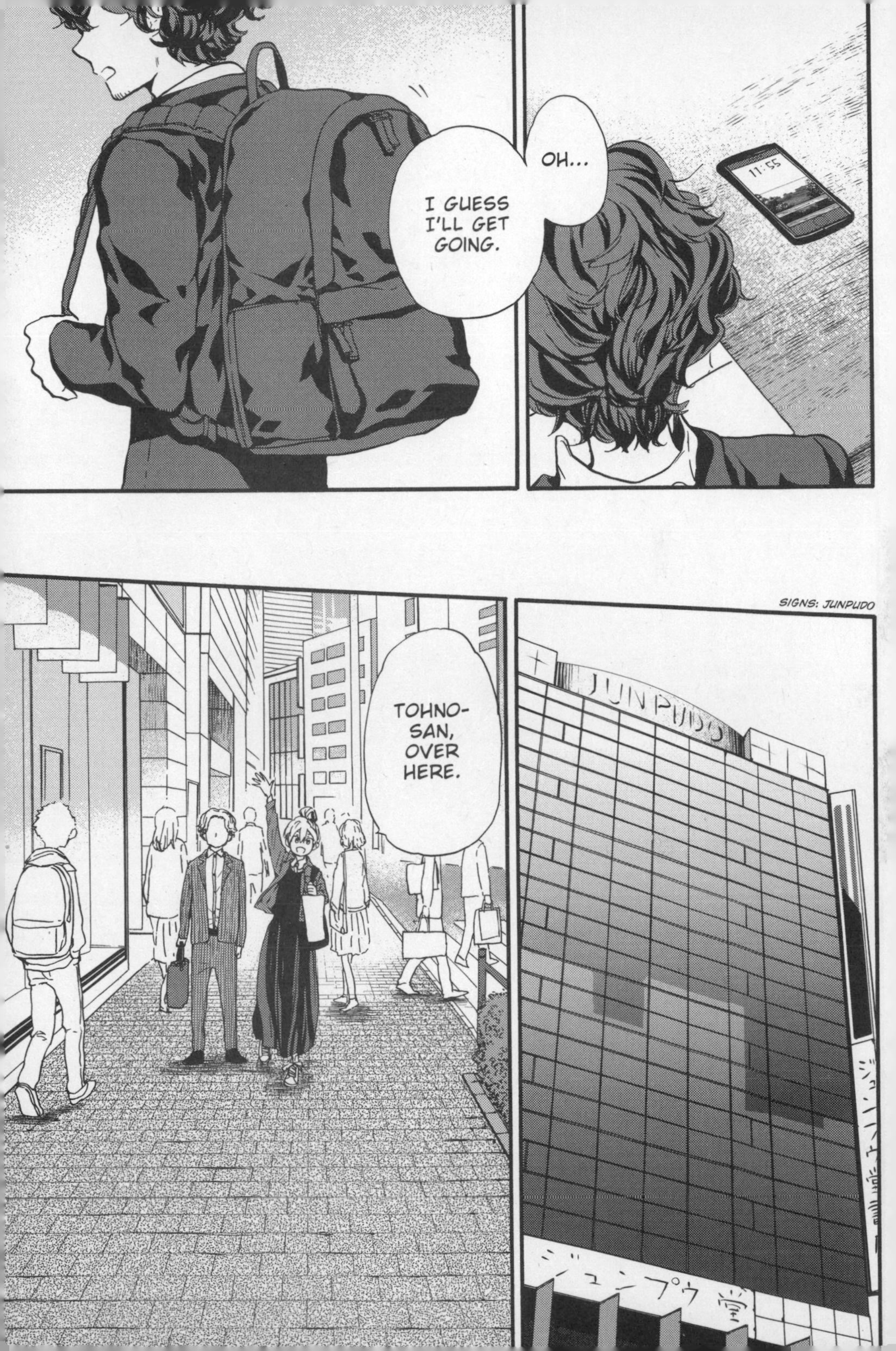
11:55
OH...
I GUESS I'LL GET GOING.
SIGNS: JUNPUDO
JUNPUDO
ジュンプウ堂
TOHNO-SAN, OVER HERE.

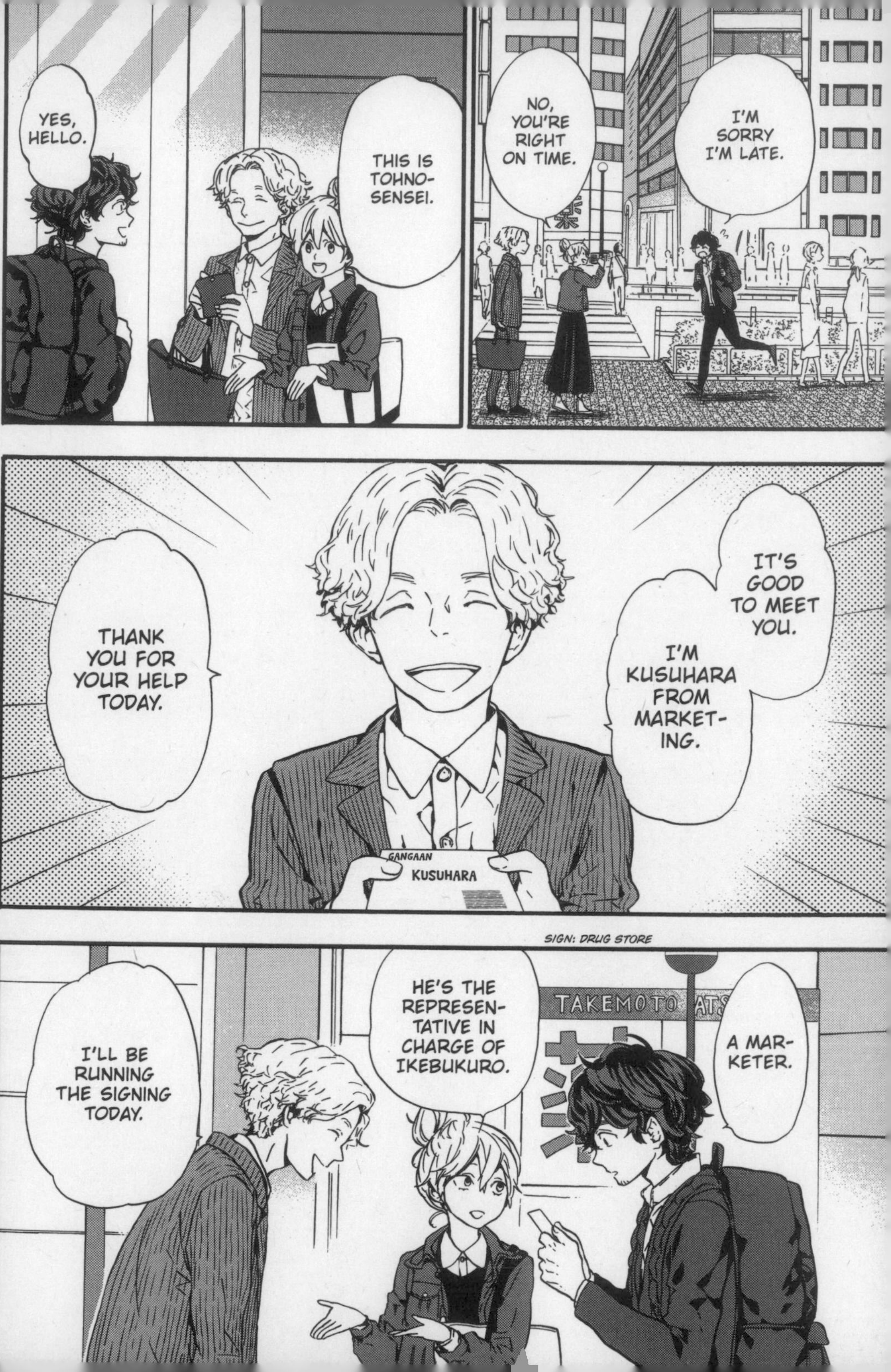
I'M SORRY I'M LATE.
NO, YOU'RE RIGHT ON TIME.
THIS IS TOHNO-SENSEI.
YES, HELLO.
IT'S GOOD TO MEET YOU.
I'M KUSUHARA FROM MARKETING.
GANGAAN
KUSUHARA
THANK YOU FOR YOUR HELP TODAY.
SIGN: DRUG STORE
TAKEMOTO
A MARKETER.
HE'S THE REPRESENTATIVE IN CHARGE OF IKEBUKURO.
I'LL BE RUNNING THE SIGNING TODAY.

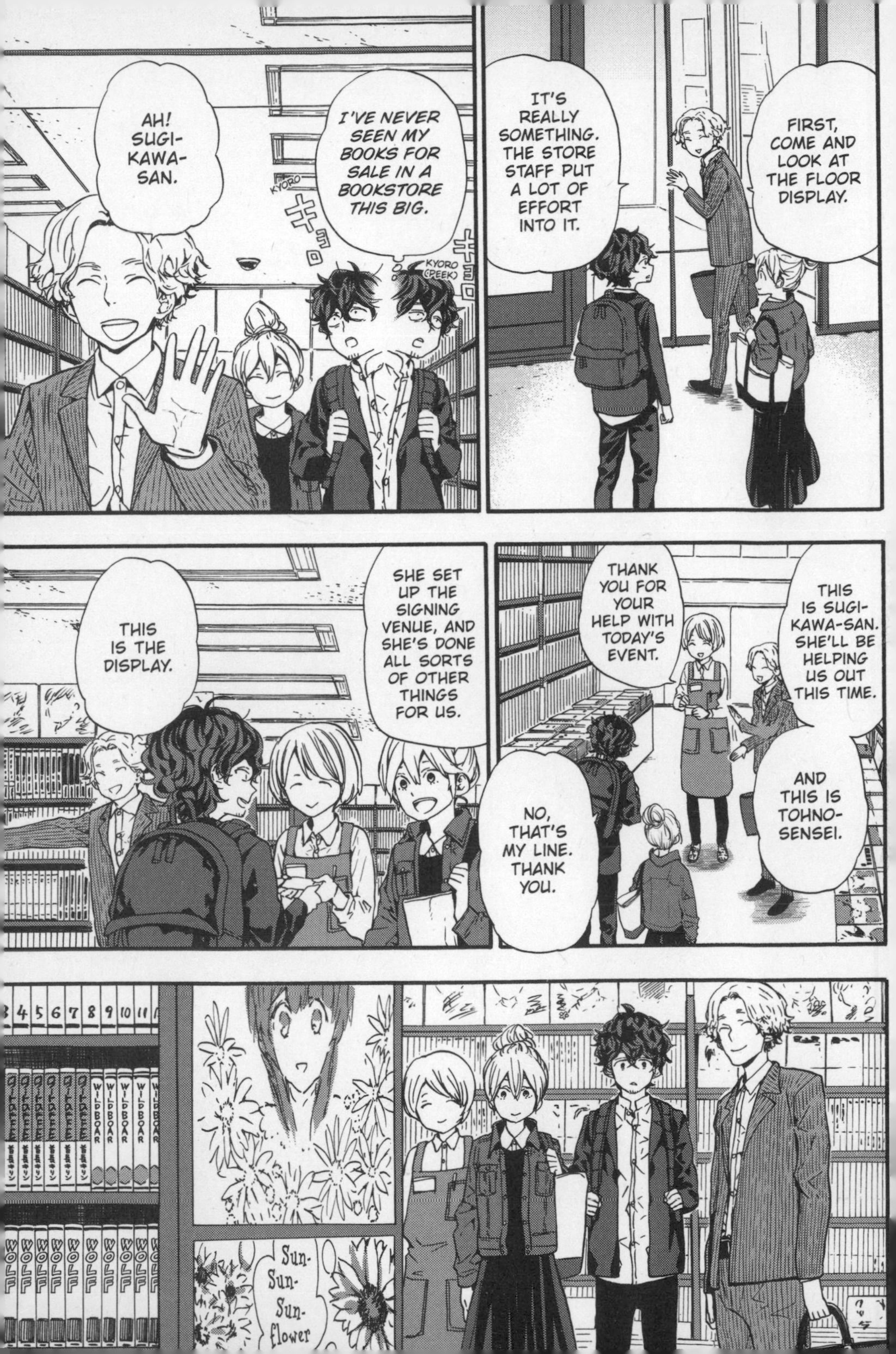
FIRST, COME AND LOOK AT THE FLOOR DISPLAY.
IT'S REALLY SOMETHING. THE STORE STAFF PUT A LOT OF EFFORT INTO IT.
KYORO (PEEK)
I'VE NEVER SEEN MY BOOKS FOR SALE IN A BOOKSTORE THIS BIG.
KYORO
AH! SUGI-KAWA-SAN.
THIS IS SUGI-KAWA-SAN. SHE'LL BE HELPING US OUT THIS TIME.
THANK YOU FOR YOUR HELP WITH TODAY'S EVENT.
AND THIS IS TOHNO-SENSEI.
NO, THAT'S MY LINE. THANK YOU.
SHE SET UP THE SIGNING VENUE, AND SHE'S DONE ALL SORTS OF OTHER THINGS FOR US.
THIS IS THE DISPLAY.
Sun-Sun-Sun-flower

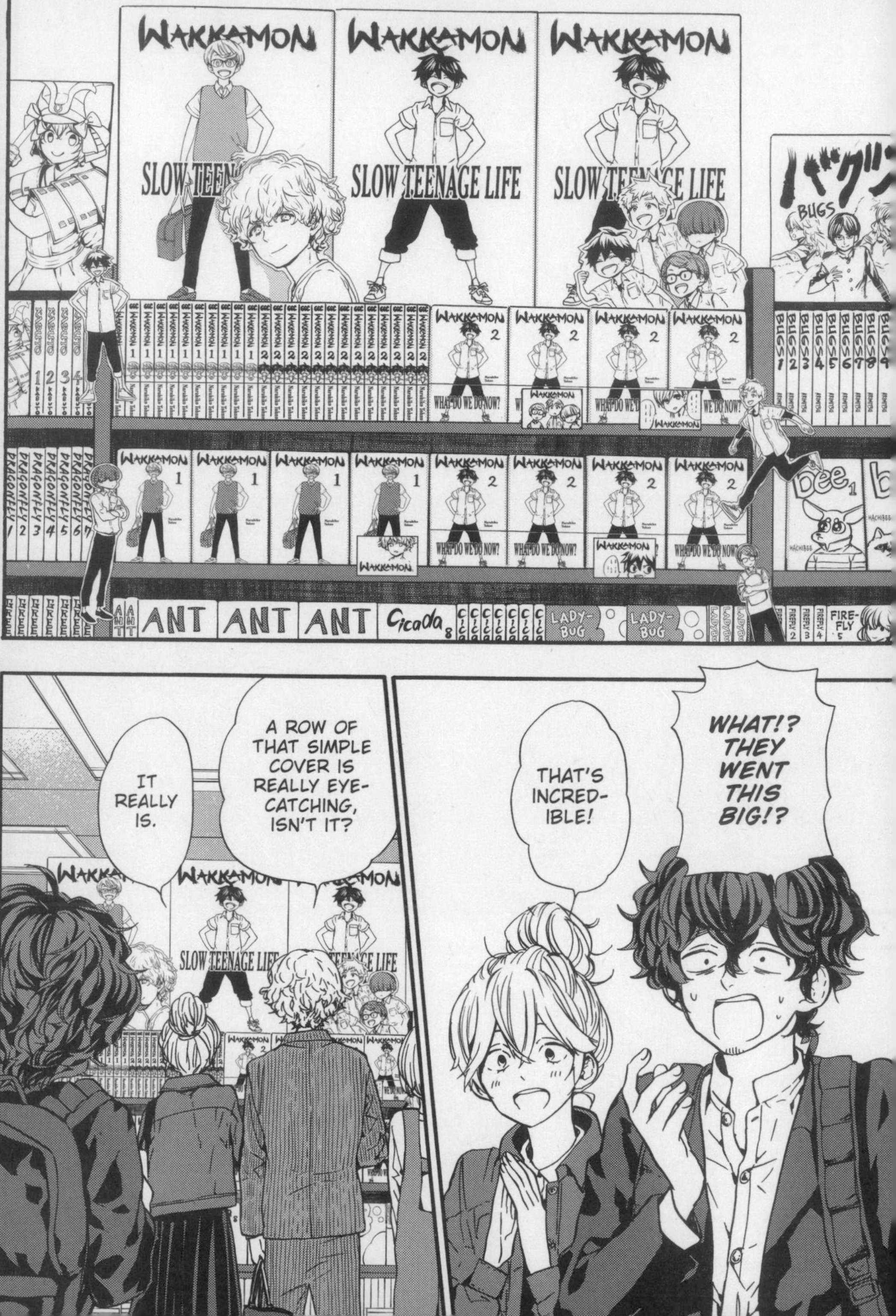
WAKKAMON
SLOW TEEN
WAKKAMON
SLOW TEENAGE LIFE
WAKKAMON
SLOW TEENAGE LIFE
BUGS
WAKKAMON 2
WHAT DO WE DO NOW?
WAKKAMON 1
ANT
ANT
ANT
Cicada 8
LADY-BUG
LADY-BUG
FIRE-FLY 5
WHAT!? THEY WENT THIS BIG!?
THAT'S INCREDIBLE!
A ROW OF THAT SIMPLE COVER IS REALLY EYE-CATCHING, ISN'T IT?
IT REALLY IS.

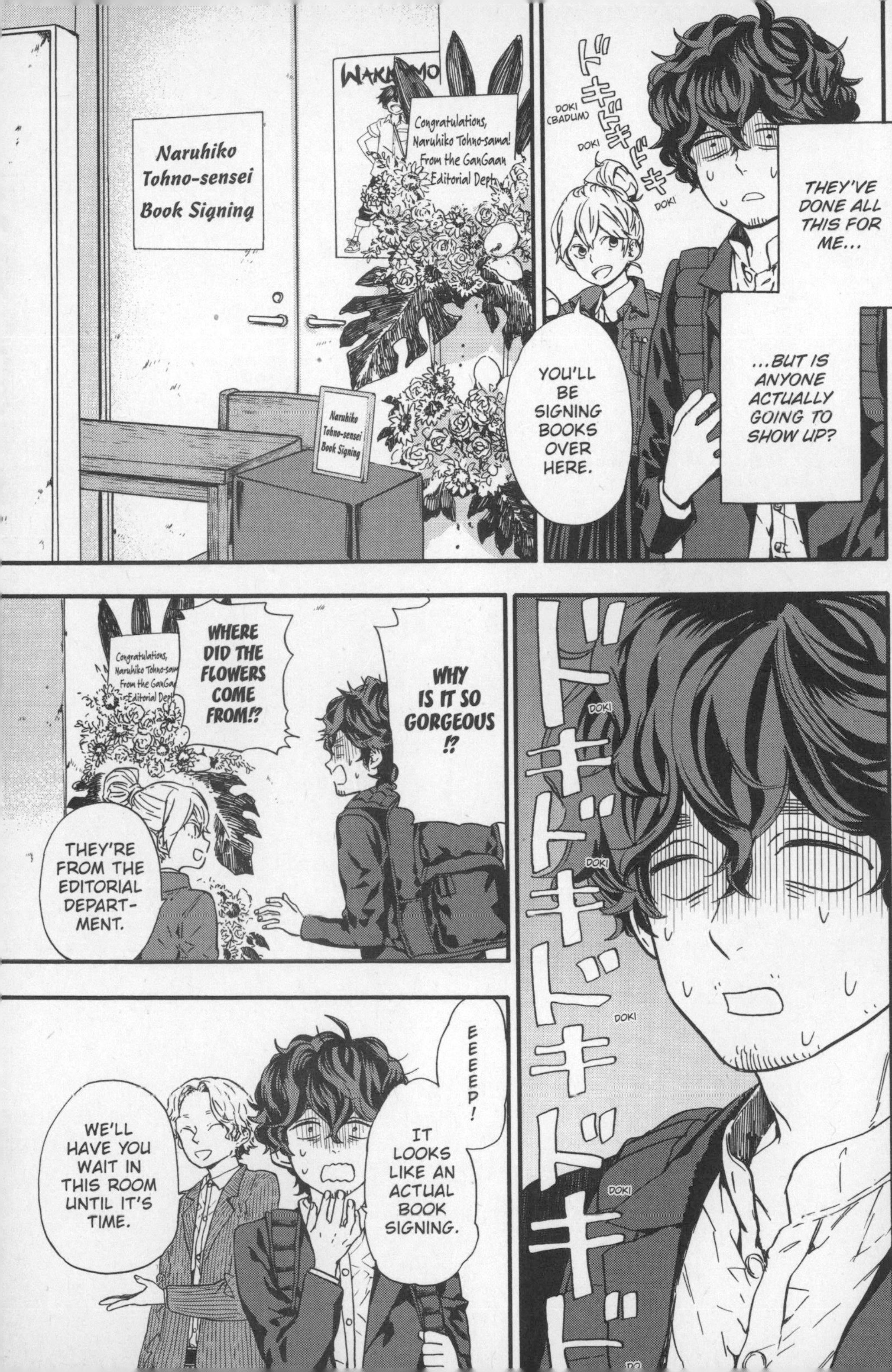
THEY'VE DONE ALL THIS FOR ME...
...BUT IS ANYONE ACTUALLY GOING TO SHOW UP?
ドキドキドキ
DOKI (BADUM)
DOKI
DOKI
YOU'LL BE SIGNING BOOKS OVER HERE.
Congratulations, Naruhiko Tohno-sama! From the GanGaan Editorial Dept.
Naruhiko Tohno-sensei Book Signing
Naruhiko Tohno-sensei Book Signing
ドキドキドキドキ
DOKI
DOKI
DOKI
DOKI
WHY IS IT SO GORGEOUS!?
WHERE DID THE FLOWERS COME FROM!?
THEY'RE FROM THE EDITORIAL DEPARTMENT.
EEEEP!
IT LOOKS LIKE AN ACTUAL BOOK SIGNING.
WE'LL HAVE YOU WAIT IN THIS ROOM UNTIL IT'S TIME.

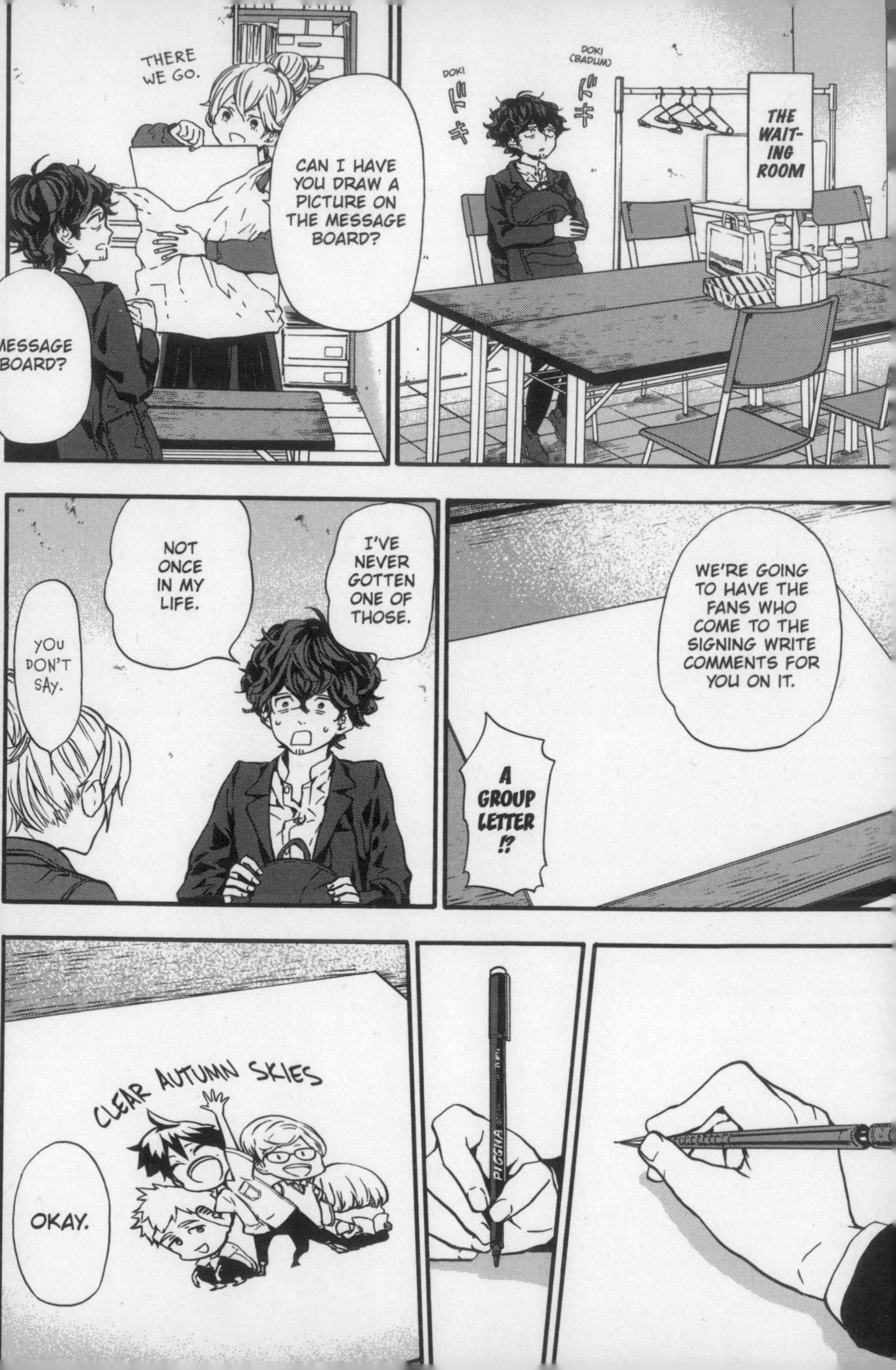
DOKI (BADUM)
DOKI
THE WAITING ROOM
THERE WE GO.
CAN I HAVE YOU DRAW A PICTURE ON THE MESSAGE BOARD?
MESSAGE BOARD?
WE'RE GOING TO HAVE THE FANS WHO COME TO THE SIGNING WRITE COMMENTS FOR YOU ON IT.
A GROUP LETTER!?
I'VE NEVER GOTTEN ONE OF THOSE.
NOT ONCE IN MY LIFE.
YOU DON'T SAY.
PIGGMA
CLEAR AUTUMN SKIES
OKAY.

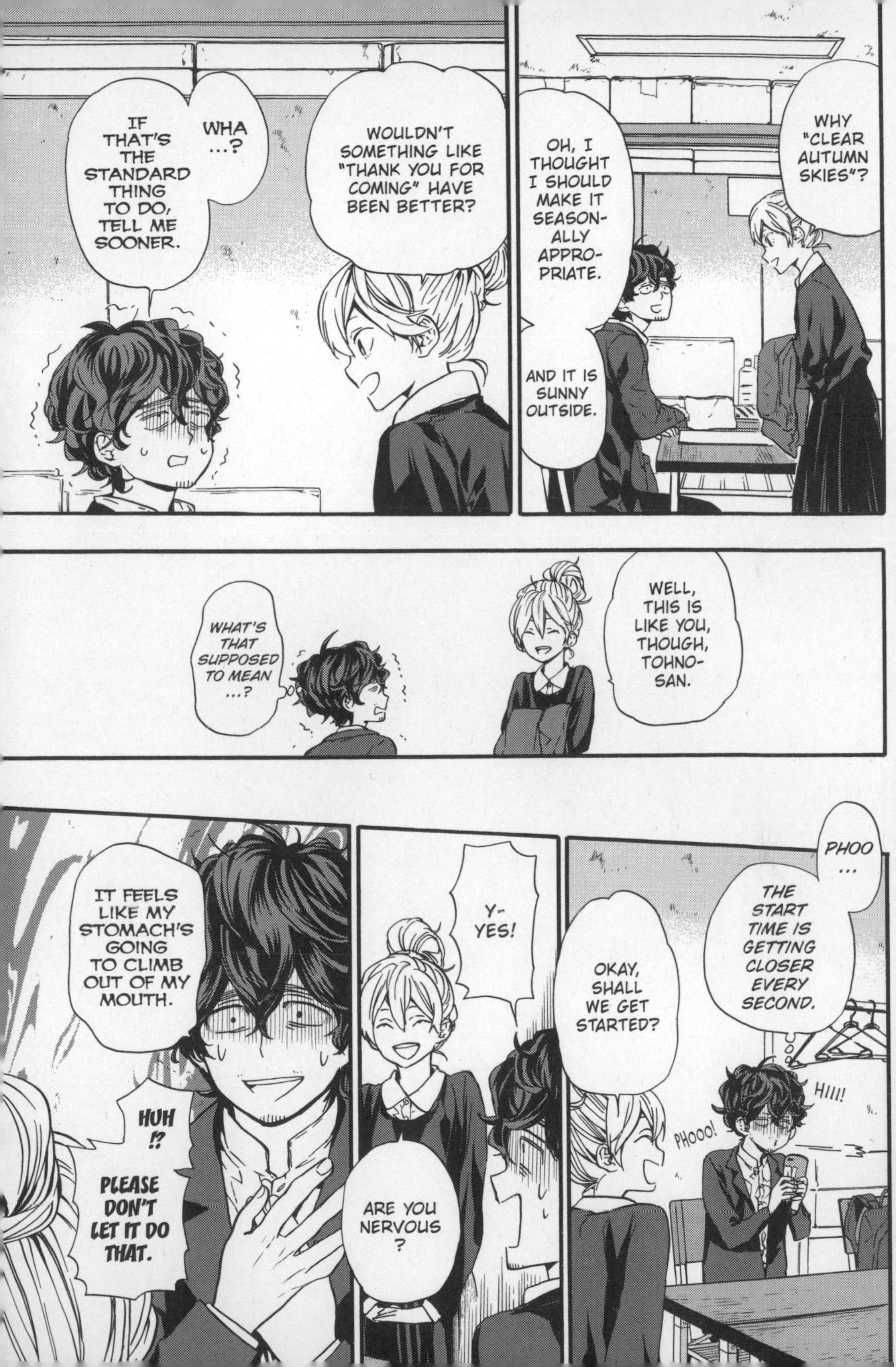
WHY "CLEAR AUTUMN SKIES"?
OH, I THOUGHT I SHOULD MAKE IT SEASON-ALLY APPRO-PRIATE.
AND IT IS SUNNY OUTSIDE.
WOULDN'T SOMETHING LIKE "THANK YOU FOR COMING" HAVE BEEN BETTER?
WHA ...?
IF THAT'S THE STANDARD THING TO DO, TELL ME SOONER.
WELL, THIS IS LIKE YOU, THOUGH, TOHNO-SAN.
WHAT'S THAT SUPPOSED TO MEAN ...?
PHOO ...
THE START TIME IS GETTING CLOSER EVERY SECOND.
OKAY, SHALL WE GET STARTED?
HIII!
PHOOO!
Y-YES!
ARE YOU NERVOUS ?
IT FEELS LIKE MY STOMACH'S GOING TO CLIMB OUT OF MY MOUTH.
HUH !?
PLEASE DON'T LET IT DO THAT.

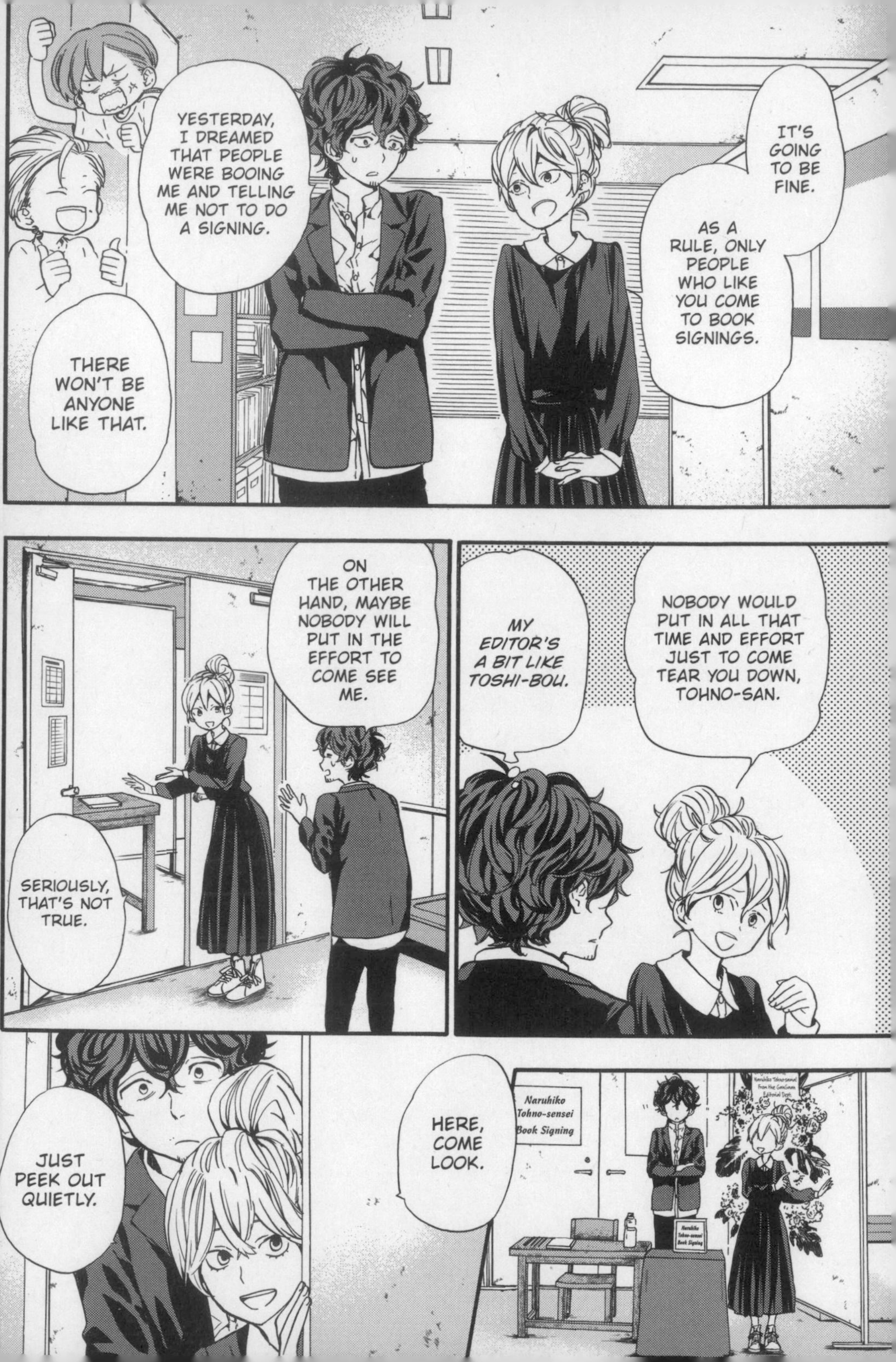
IT'S GOING TO BE FINE.
AS A RULE, ONLY PEOPLE WHO LIKE YOU COME TO BOOK SIGNINGS.
YESTERDAY, I DREAMED THAT PEOPLE WERE BOOING ME AND TELLING ME NOT TO DO A SIGNING.
THERE WON'T BE ANYONE LIKE THAT.
NOBODY WOULD PUT IN ALL THAT TIME AND EFFORT JUST TO COME TEAR YOU DOWN, TOHNO-SAN.
MY EDITOR'S A BIT LIKE TOSHI-BOU.
ON THE OTHER HAND, MAYBE NOBODY WILL PUT IN THE EFFORT TO COME SEE ME.
SERIOUSLY, THAT'S NOT TRUE.
HERE, COME LOOK.
Naruhiko Tohno-sensei Book Signing
JUST PEEK OUT QUIETLY.

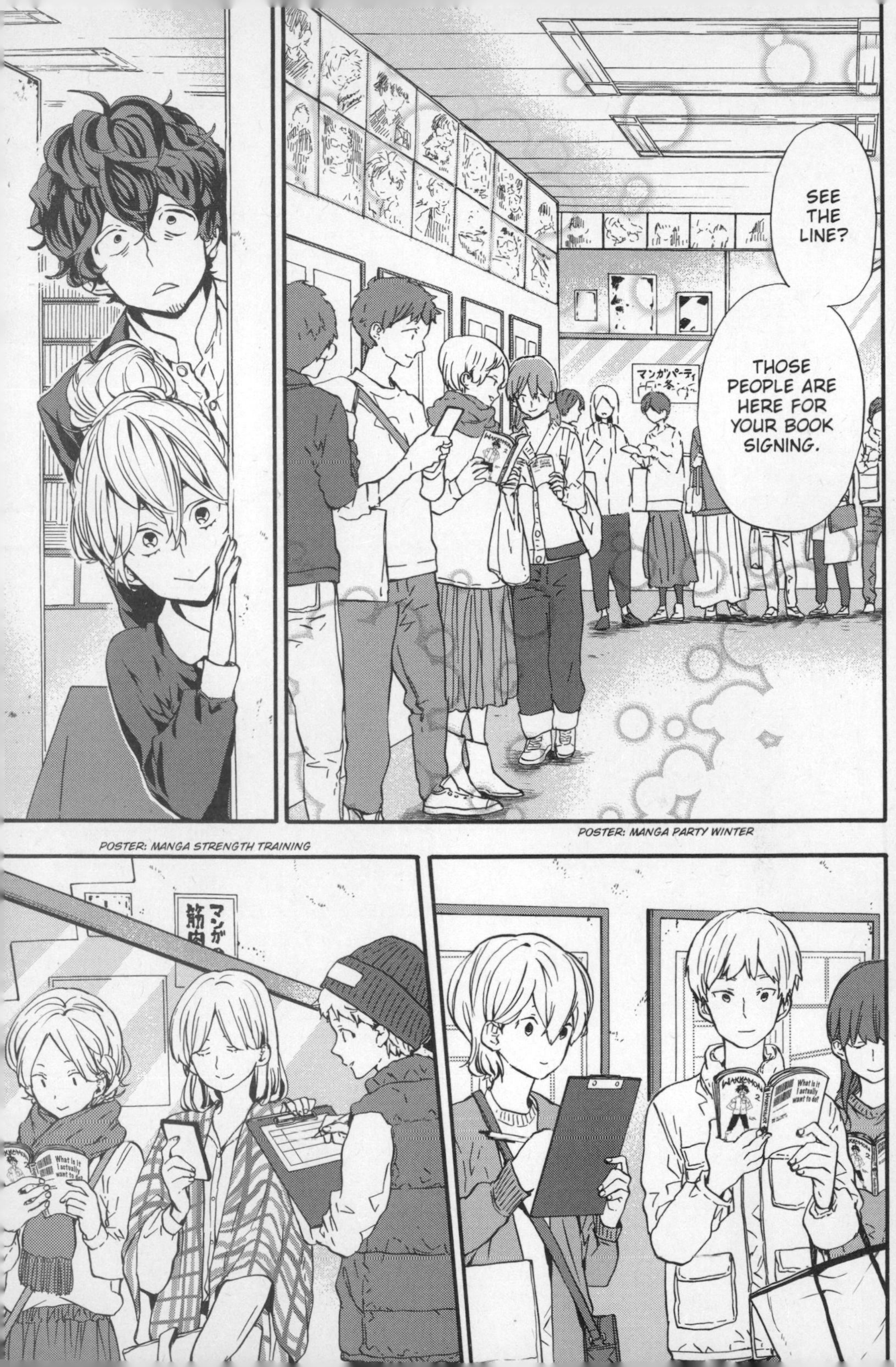
SEE THE LINE?
THOSE PEOPLE ARE HERE FOR YOUR BOOK SIGNING.
マンガパーティ
WAKKAMON 2
What is it I actually want to do?
POSTER: MANGA PARTY WINTER

POSTER: MANGA STRENGTH TRAINING

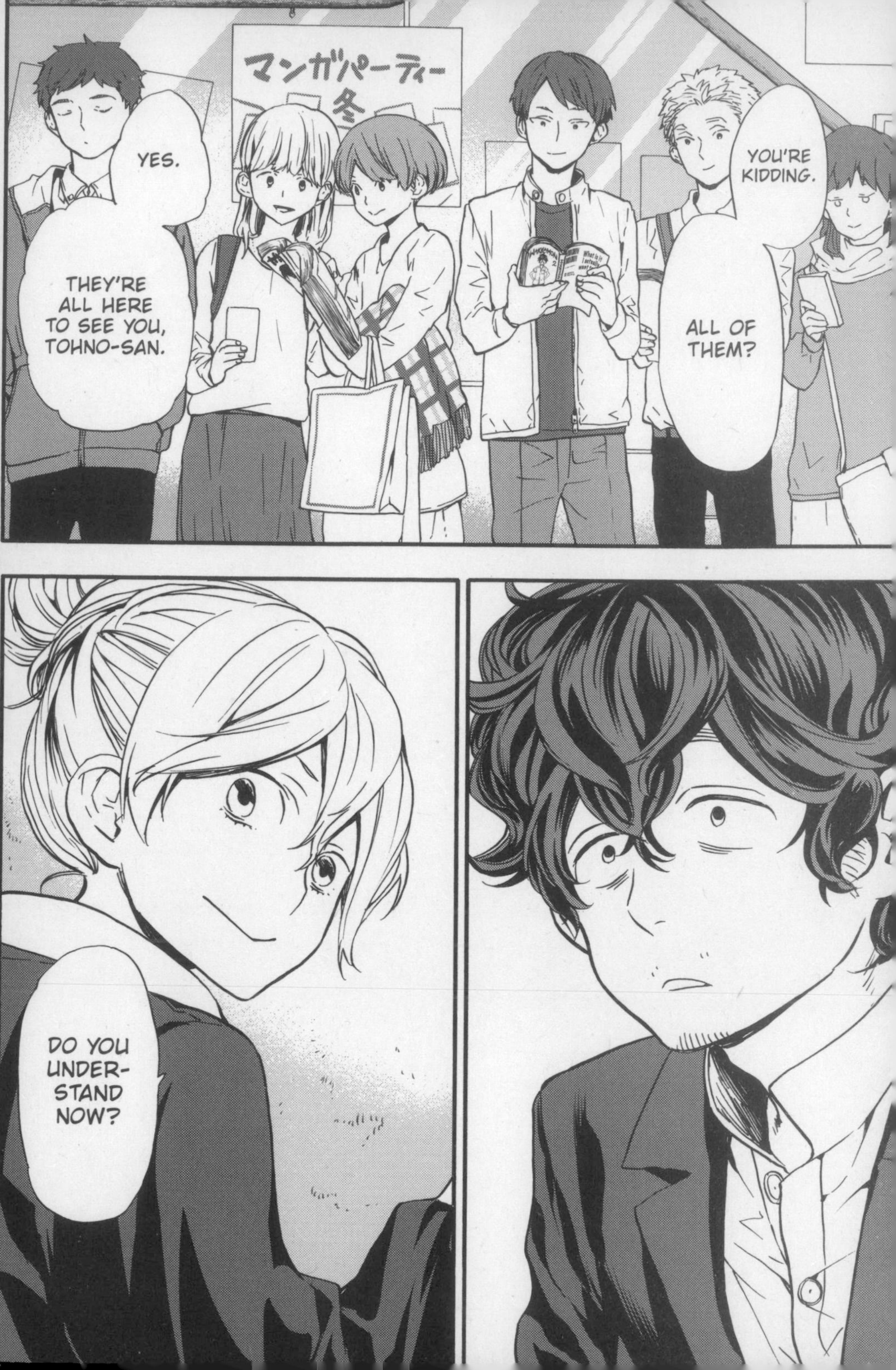
マンガパーティー
冬
YOU'RE KIDDING.
ALL OF THEM?
YES.
THEY'RE ALL HERE TO SEE YOU, TOHNO-SAN.
DO YOU UNDER-STAND NOW?

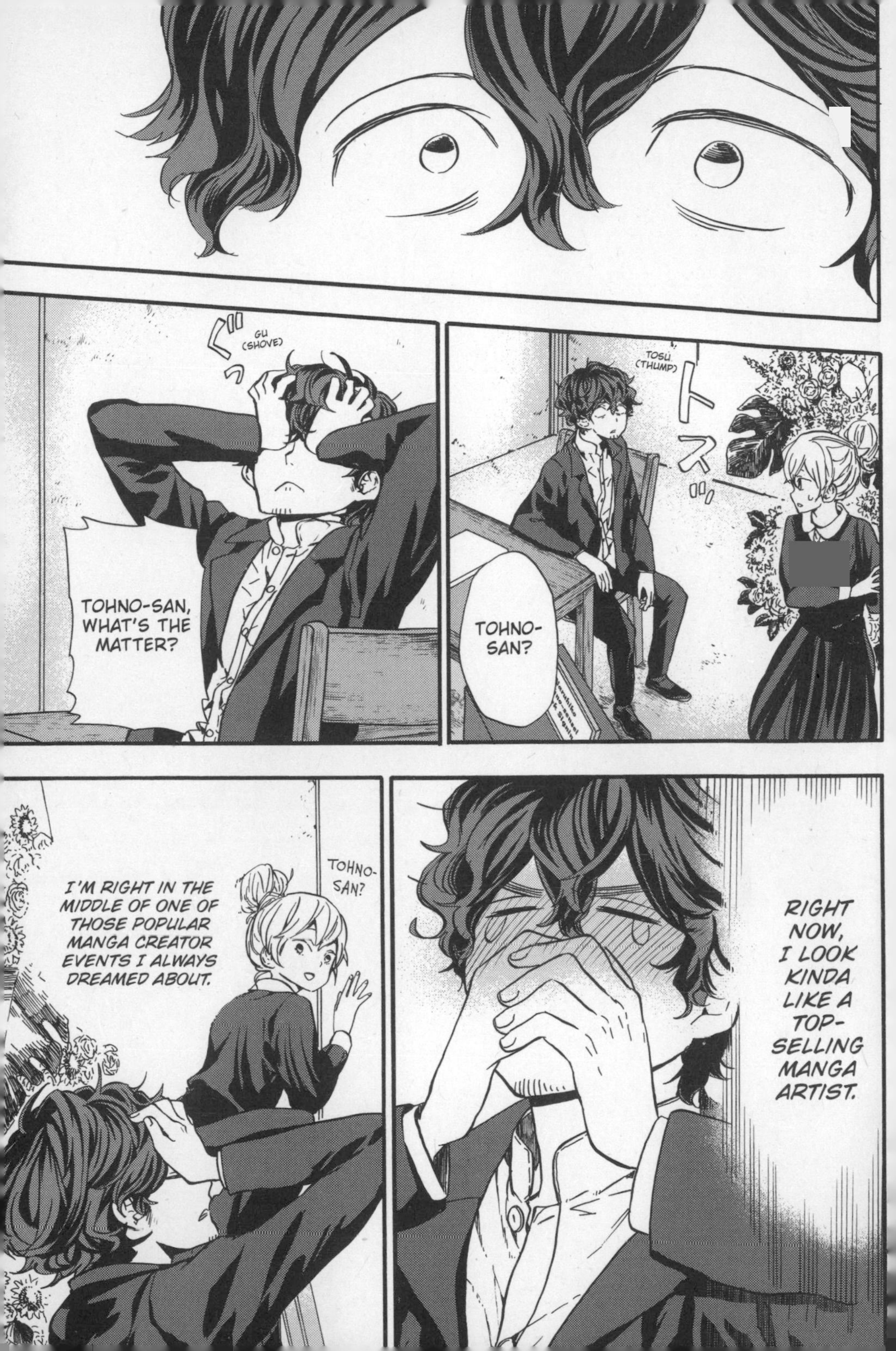
トスッ
TOSU (THUMP)
TOHNO-SAN?
ぐっ
GU (SHOVE)
TOHNO-SAN, WHAT'S THE MATTER?
RIGHT NOW, I LOOK KINDA LIKE A TOP-SELLING MANGA ARTIST.
TOHNO-SAN?
I'M RIGHT IN THE MIDDLE OF ONE OF THOSE POPULAR MANGA CREATOR EVENTS I ALWAYS DREAMED ABOUT.

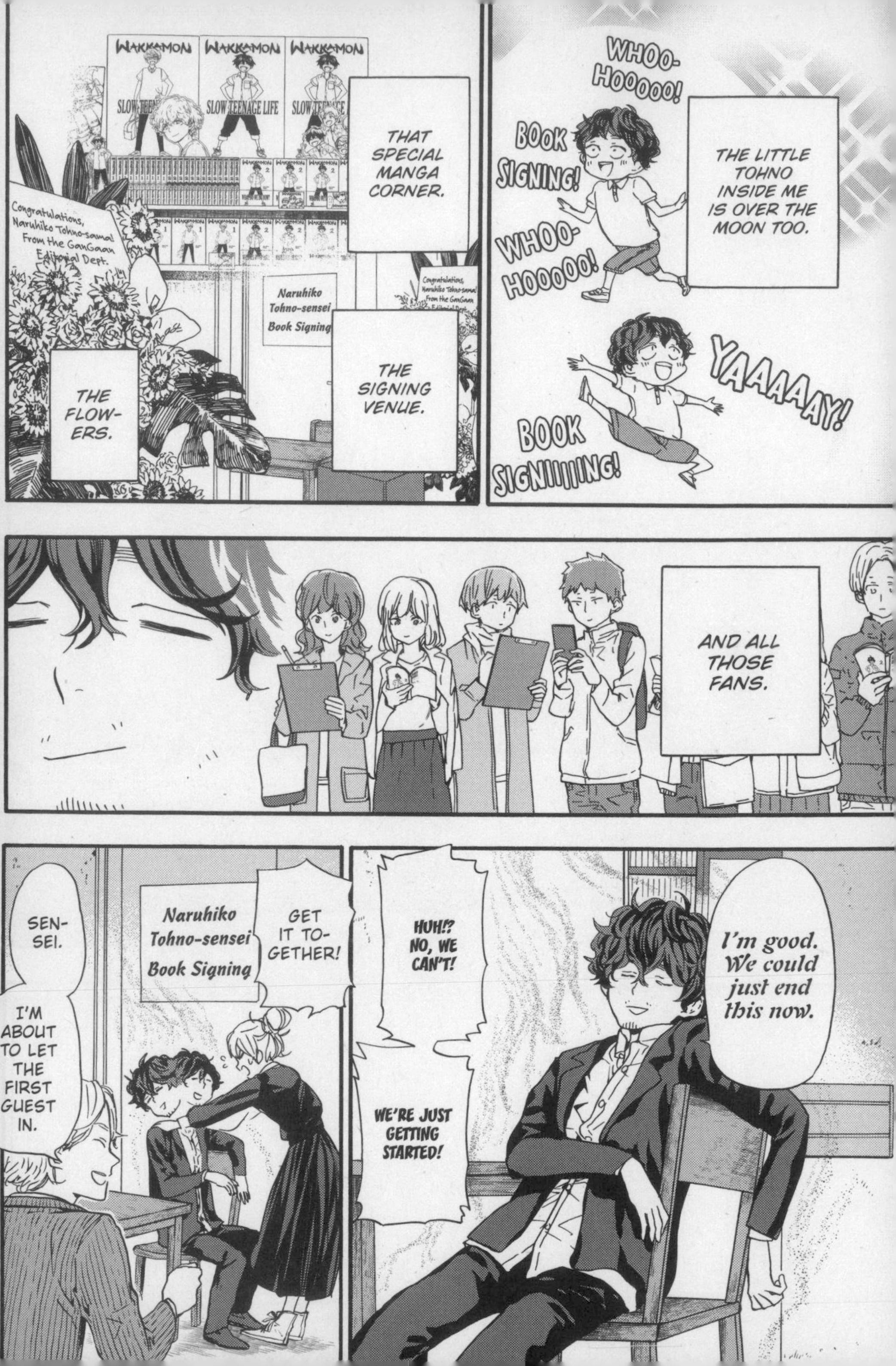
WHOO-HOOOOO!
BOOK SIGNING!
THE LITTLE TOHNO INSIDE ME IS OVER THE MOON TOO.
WHOO-HOOOOO!
YAAAAAY!
BOOK SIGNIIIIING!
WAKKAMON
SLOW TEENAGE LIFE
THAT SPECIAL MANGA CORNER.
Congratulations, Naruhiko Tohno-sama! From the GanGaan Editorial Dept.
Naruhiko Tohno-sensei Book Signing
THE SIGNING VENUE.
THE FLOWERS.
AND ALL THOSE FANS.
I'm good. We could just end this now.
HUH!? NO, WE CAN'T!
WE'RE JUST GETTING STARTED!
GET IT TOGETHER!
Naruhiko Tohno-sensei Book Signing
SENSEI.
I'M ABOUT TO LET THE FIRST GUEST IN.

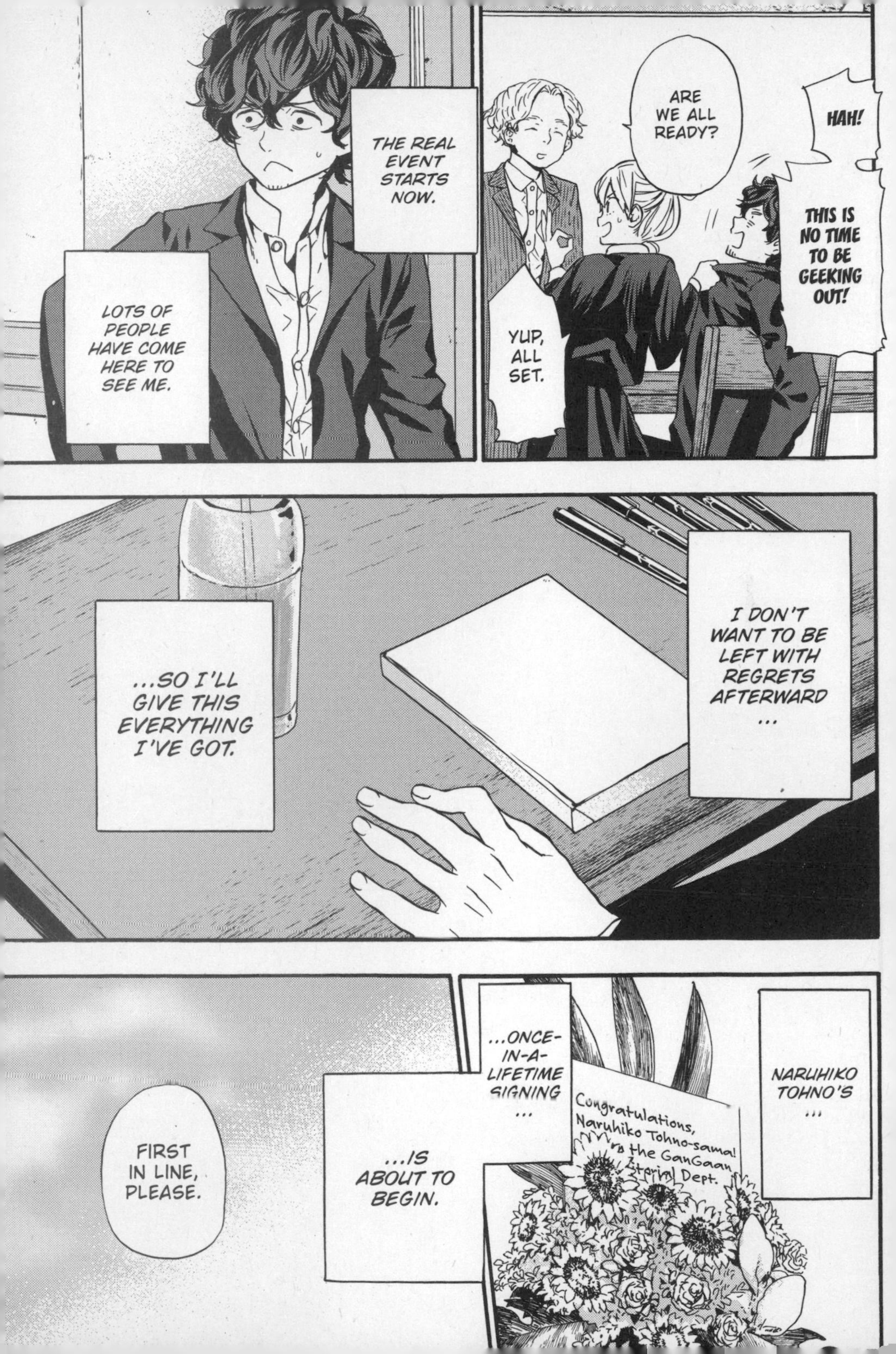
HAH!
ARE WE ALL READY?
THIS IS NO TIME TO BE GEEKING OUT!
YUP, ALL SET.
THE REAL EVENT STARTS NOW.
LOTS OF PEOPLE HAVE COME HERE TO SEE ME.
I DON'T WANT TO BE LEFT WITH REGRETS AFTERWARD...
...SO I'LL GIVE THIS EVERYTHING I'VE GOT.
NARUHIKO TOHNO'S...
...ONCE-IN-A-LIFETIME SIGNING...
Congratulations, Naruhiko Tohno-sama!
...IS ABOUT TO BEGIN.
FIRST IN LINE, PLEASE.

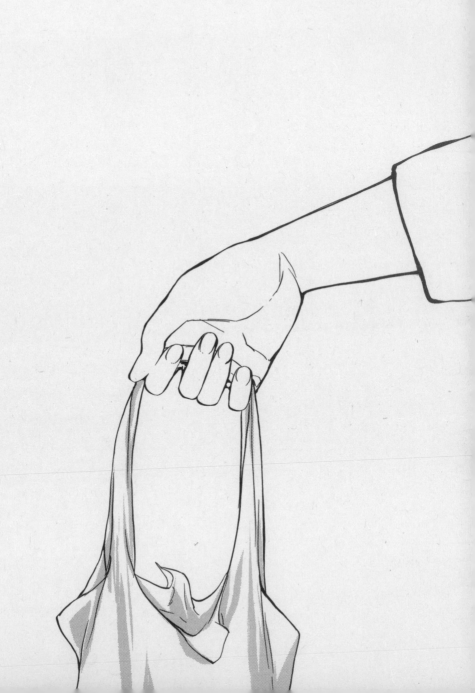

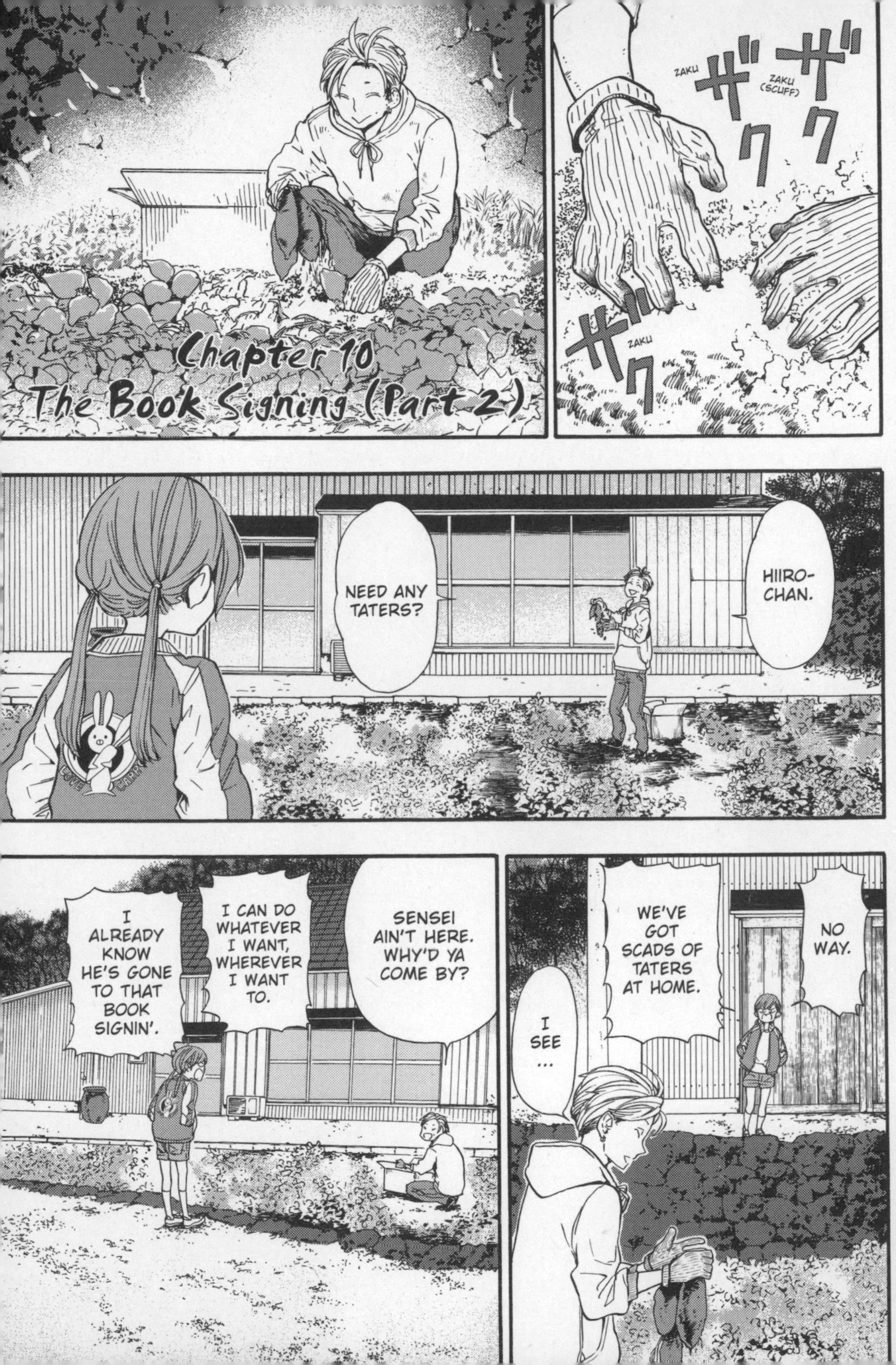

ザク
ZAKU (SCUFF)
ザク
ZAKU
ザク
ZAKU
Chapter 10
The Book Signing (Part 2)
HIIRO-CHAN.
NEED ANY TATERS?
NO WAY.
WE'VE GOT SCADS OF TATERS AT HOME.
I SEE ...
SENSEI AIN'T HERE. WHY'D YA COME BY?
I CAN DO WHATEVER I WANT, WHEREVER I WANT TO.
I ALREADY KNOW HE'S GONE TO THAT BOOK SIGNIN'.

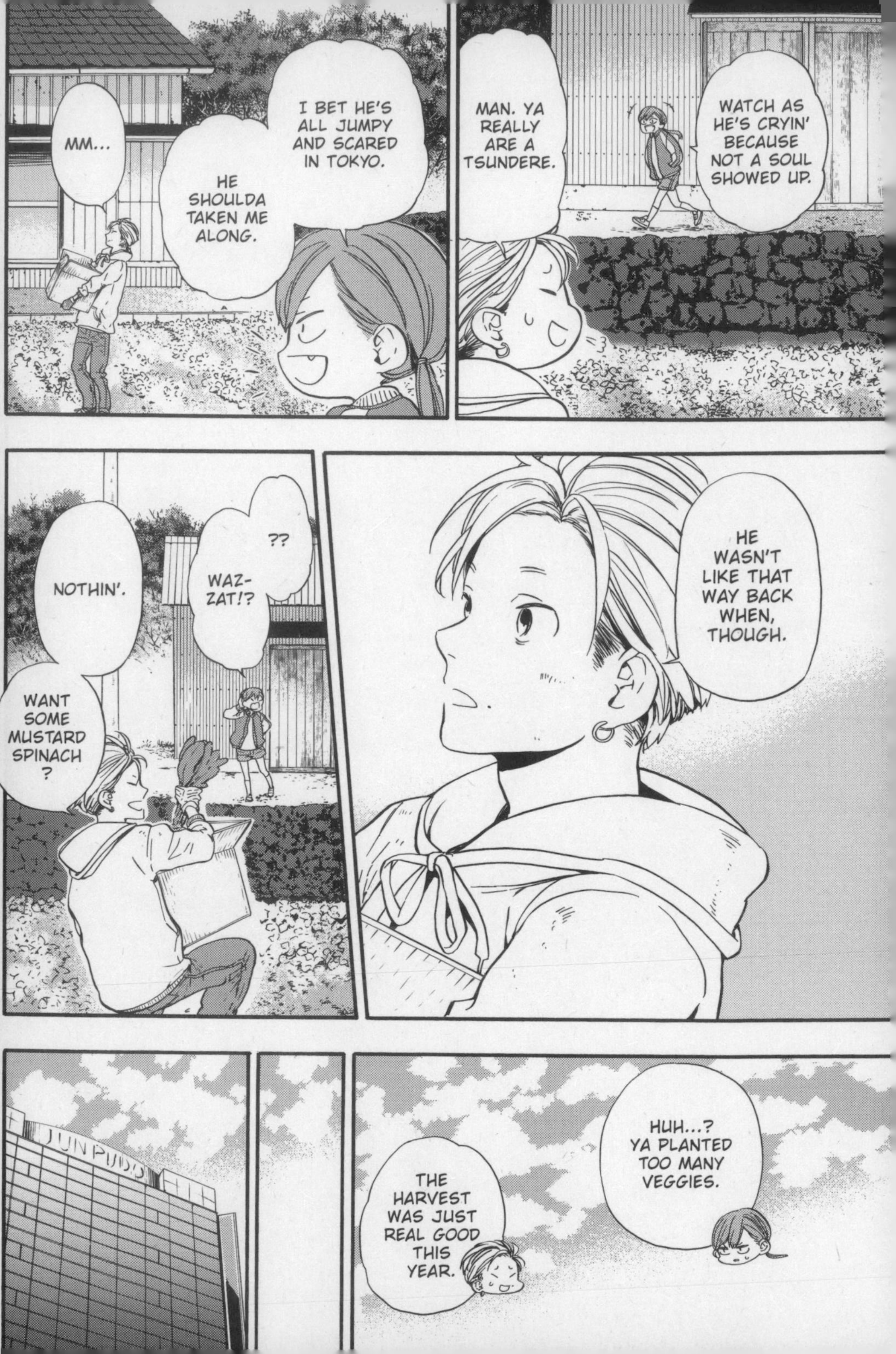

WATCH AS HE'S CRYIN' BECAUSE NOT A SOUL SHOWED UP.
MAN. YA REALLY ARE A TSUNDERE.
I BET HE'S ALL JUMPY AND SCARED IN TOKYO.
HE SHOULDA TAKEN ME ALONG.
MM...
HE WASN'T LIKE THAT WAY BACK WHEN, THOUGH.
??
WAZ-ZAT!?
NOTHIN'.
WANT SOME MUSTARD SPINACH?
HUH...? YA PLANTED TOO MANY VEGGIES.
THE HARVEST WAS JUST REAL GOOD THIS YEAR.

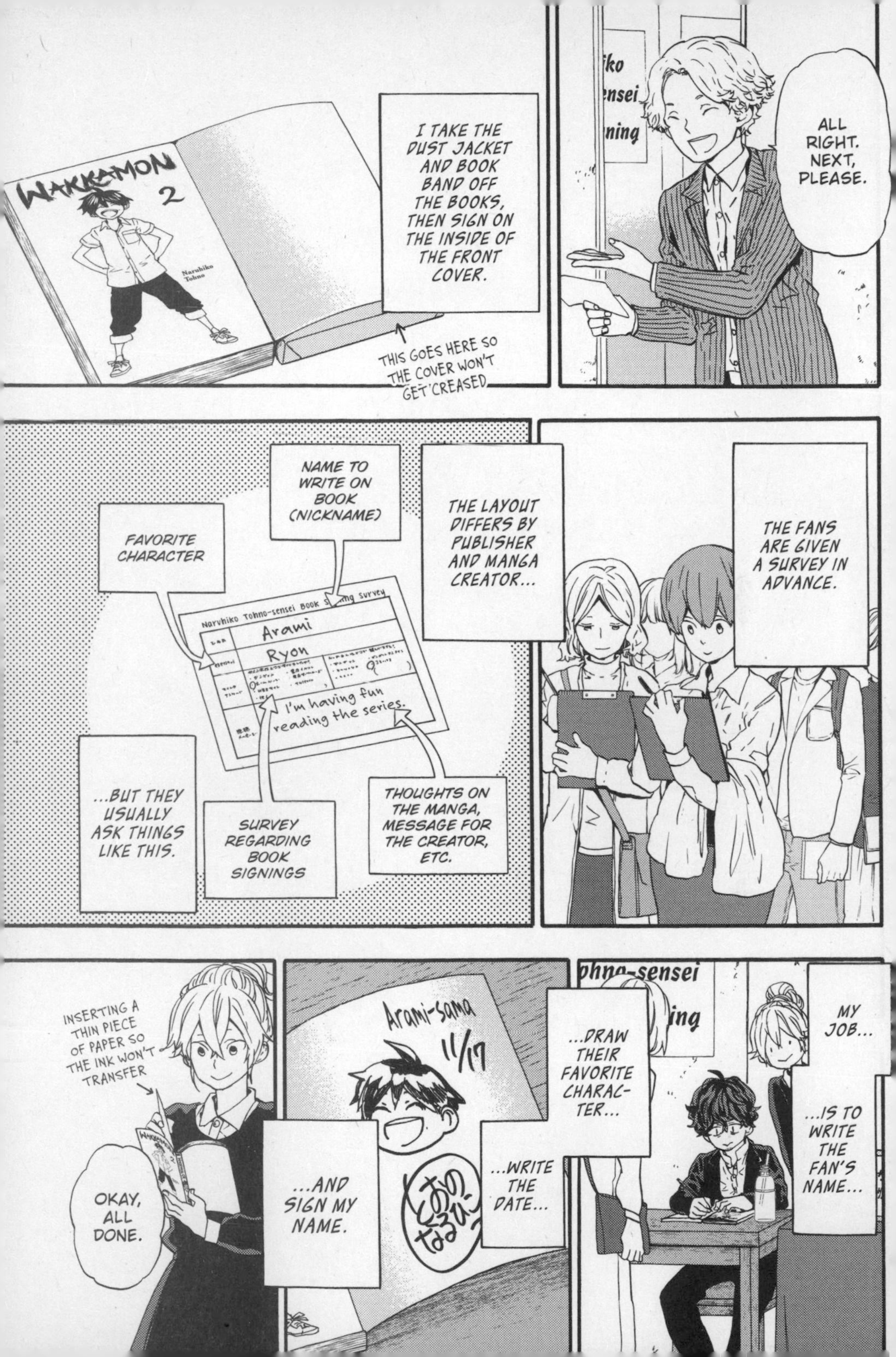
ALL RIGHT. NEXT, PLEASE.
I TAKE THE DUST JACKET AND BOOK BAND OFF THE BOOKS, THEN SIGN ON THE INSIDE OF THE FRONT COVER.
WAKKAMON 2
Naruhiko Tohno
THIS GOES HERE SO THE COVER WON'T GET CREASED
THE FANS ARE GIVEN A SURVEY IN ADVANCE.
THE LAYOUT DIFFERS BY PUBLISHER AND MANGA CREATOR...
NAME TO WRITE ON BOOK (NICKNAME)
FAVORITE CHARACTER
Naruhiko Tohno-sensei Book Signing Survey
Arami
Ryon
I'm having fun reading the series.
THOUGHTS ON THE MANGA, MESSAGE FOR THE CREATOR, ETC.
SURVEY REGARDING BOOK SIGNINGS
...BUT THEY USUALLY ASK THINGS LIKE THIS.
MY JOB...
...IS TO WRITE THE FAN'S NAME...
...DRAW THEIR FAVORITE CHARAC-TER...
...WRITE THE DATE...
Arami-sama
11/17
...AND SIGN MY NAME.
INSERTING A THIN PIECE OF PAPER SO THE INK WON'T TRANSFER
OKAY, ALL DONE.

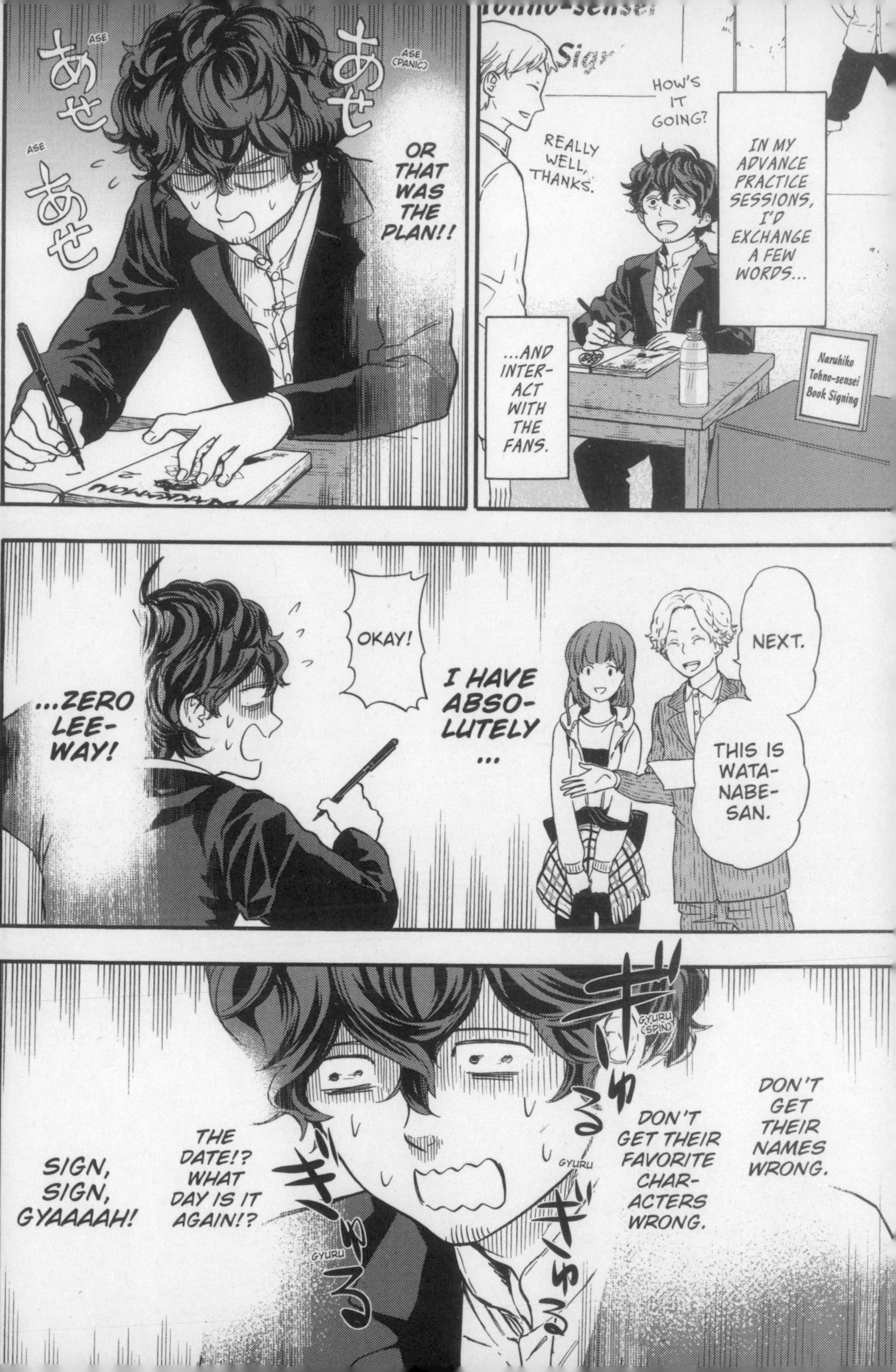
HOW'S IT GOING?
REALLY WELL, THANKS.
IN MY ADVANCE PRACTICE SESSIONS, I'D EXCHANGE A FEW WORDS...
...AND INTERACT WITH THE FANS.
Naruhiko Tohno-sensei Book Signing
あせ
ASE (PANIC)
あせ
ASE
あせ
ASE
OR THAT WAS THE PLAN!!
NEXT.
THIS IS WATANABE-SAN.
OKAY!
I HAVE ABSOLUTELY...
...ZERO LEEWAY!
ぎゅる
GYURU (SPIN)
DON'T GET THEIR NAMES WRONG.
DON'T GET THEIR FAVORITE CHARACTERS WRONG.
GYURU
THE DATE!? WHAT DAY IS IT AGAIN!?
SIGN, SIGN, GYAAAAH!
GYURU

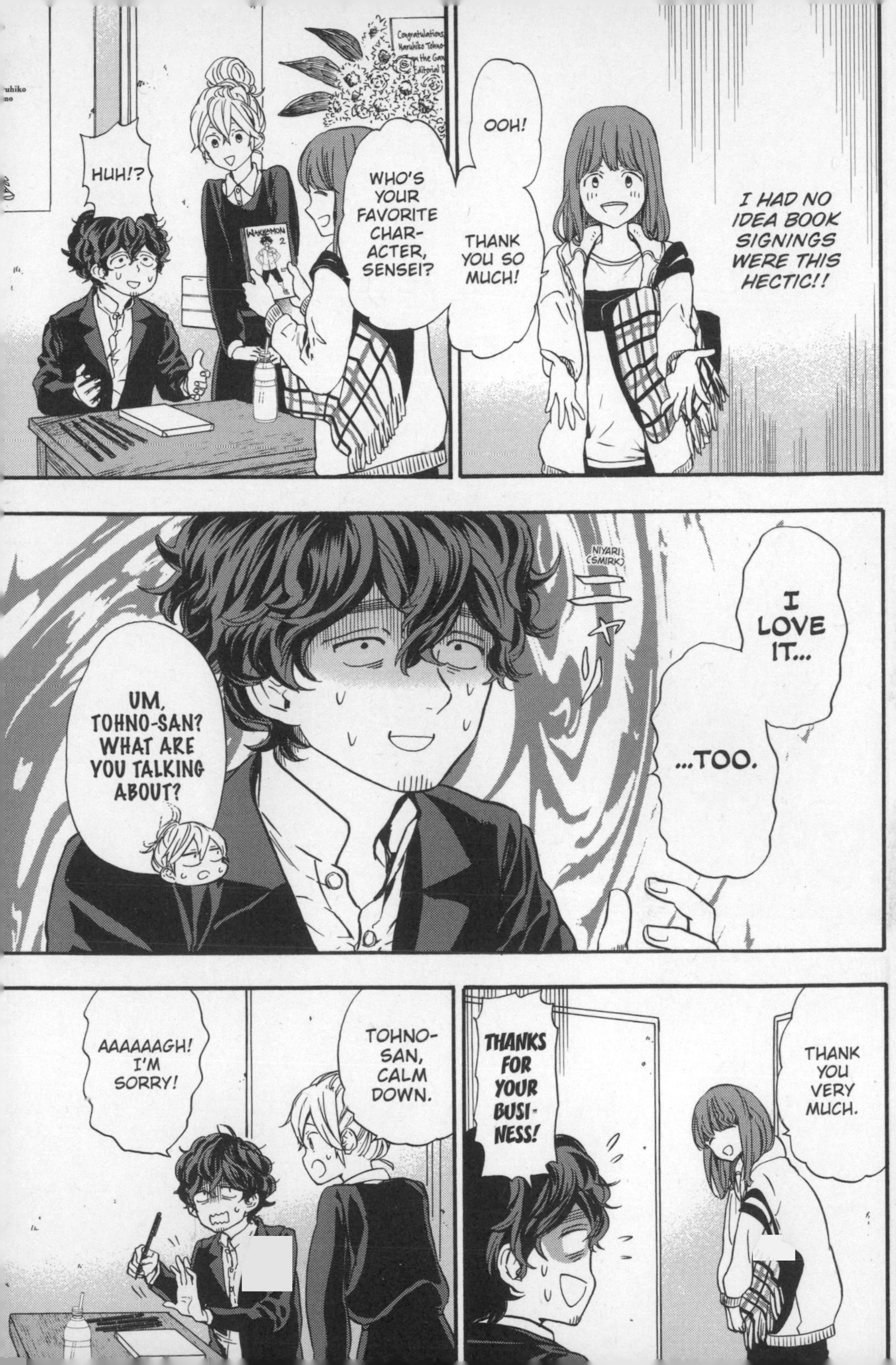
I HAD NO IDEA BOOK SIGNINGS WERE THIS HECTIC!!
OOH!
THANK YOU SO MUCH!
WHO'S YOUR FAVORITE CHARACTER, SENSEI?
HUH!?
I LOVE IT...
...TOO.
NIYARI (SMIRK)
UM, TOHNO-SAN? WHAT ARE YOU TALKING ABOUT?
THANK YOU VERY MUCH.
THANKS FOR YOUR BUSINESS!
TOHNO-SAN, CALM DOWN.
AAAAAAGH! I'M SORRY!

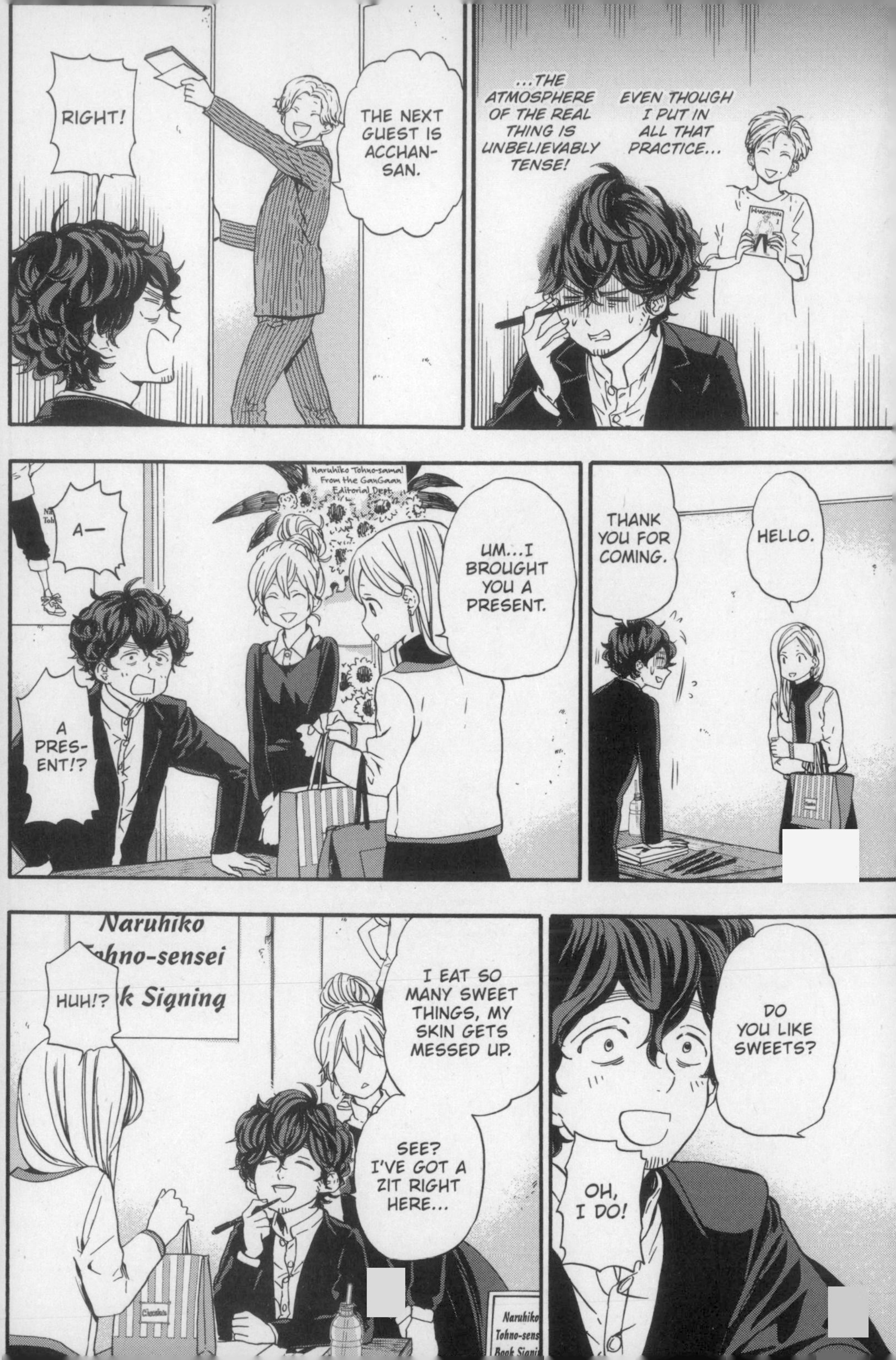
EVEN THOUGH I PUT IN ALL THAT PRACTICE...
...THE ATMOSPHERE OF THE REAL THING IS UNBELIEVABLY TENSE!
THE NEXT GUEST IS ACCHAN-SAN.
RIGHT!
HELLO.
THANK YOU FOR COMING.
Naruhiko Tohno-sama! From the GanGaan Editorial Dept.
UM...I BROUGHT YOU A PRESENT.
A—
A PRESENT!?
DO YOU LIKE SWEETS?
OH, I DO!
I EAT SO MANY SWEET THINGS, MY SKIN GETS MESSED UP.
SEE? I'VE GOT A ZIT RIGHT HERE...
HUH!?

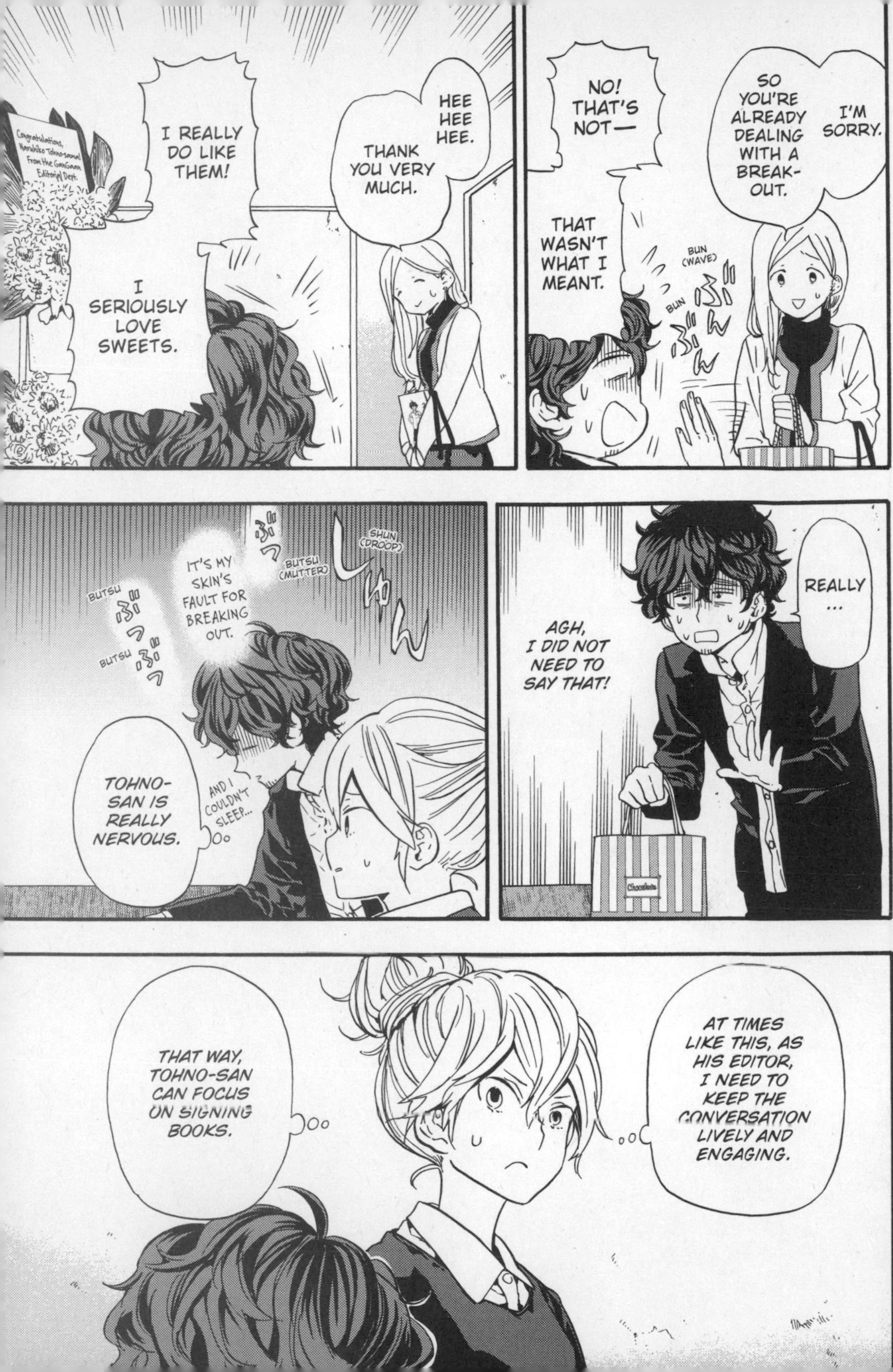
I'M SORRY.
SO YOU'RE ALREADY DEALING WITH A BREAK-OUT.
NO! THAT'S NOT—
THAT WASN'T WHAT I MEANT.
BUN (WAVE)
BUN
HEE HEE HEE.
THANK YOU VERY MUCH.
I REALLY DO LIKE THEM!
I SERIOUSLY LOVE SWEETS.
REALLY ...
AGH, I DID NOT NEED TO SAY THAT!
SHUN (DROOP)
BUTSU (MUTTER)
IT'S MY SKIN'S FAULT FOR BREAKING OUT.
BUTSU
BUTSU
AND I COULDN'T SLEEP...
TOHNO-SAN IS REALLY NERVOUS.
AT TIMES LIKE THIS, AS HIS EDITOR, I NEED TO KEEP THE CONVERSATION LIVELY AND ENGAGING.
THAT WAY, TOHNO-SAN CAN FOCUS ON SIGNING BOOKS.

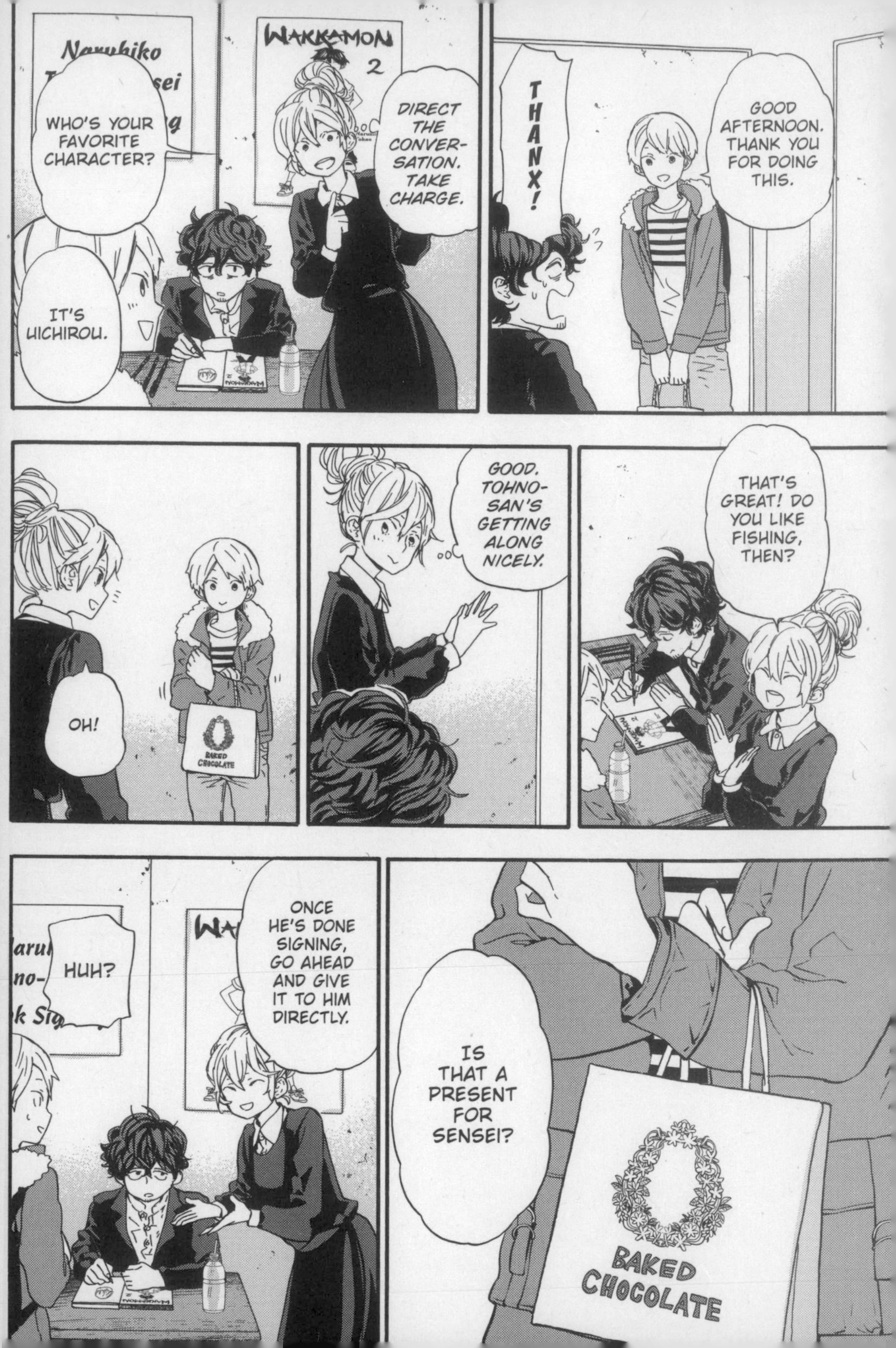
GOOD AFTERNOON. THANK YOU FOR DOING THIS.
THANX!
WAKKAMON
2
DIRECT THE CONVERSATION. TAKE CHARGE.
WHO'S YOUR FAVORITE CHARACTER?
IT'S UICHIROU.
THAT'S GREAT! DO YOU LIKE FISHING, THEN?
GOOD. TOHNO-SAN'S GETTING ALONG NICELY.
OH!
BAKED CHOCOLATE
IS THAT A PRESENT FOR SENSEI?
BAKED CHOCOLATE
ONCE HE'S DONE SIGNING, GO AHEAD AND GIVE IT TO HIM DIRECTLY.
HUH?

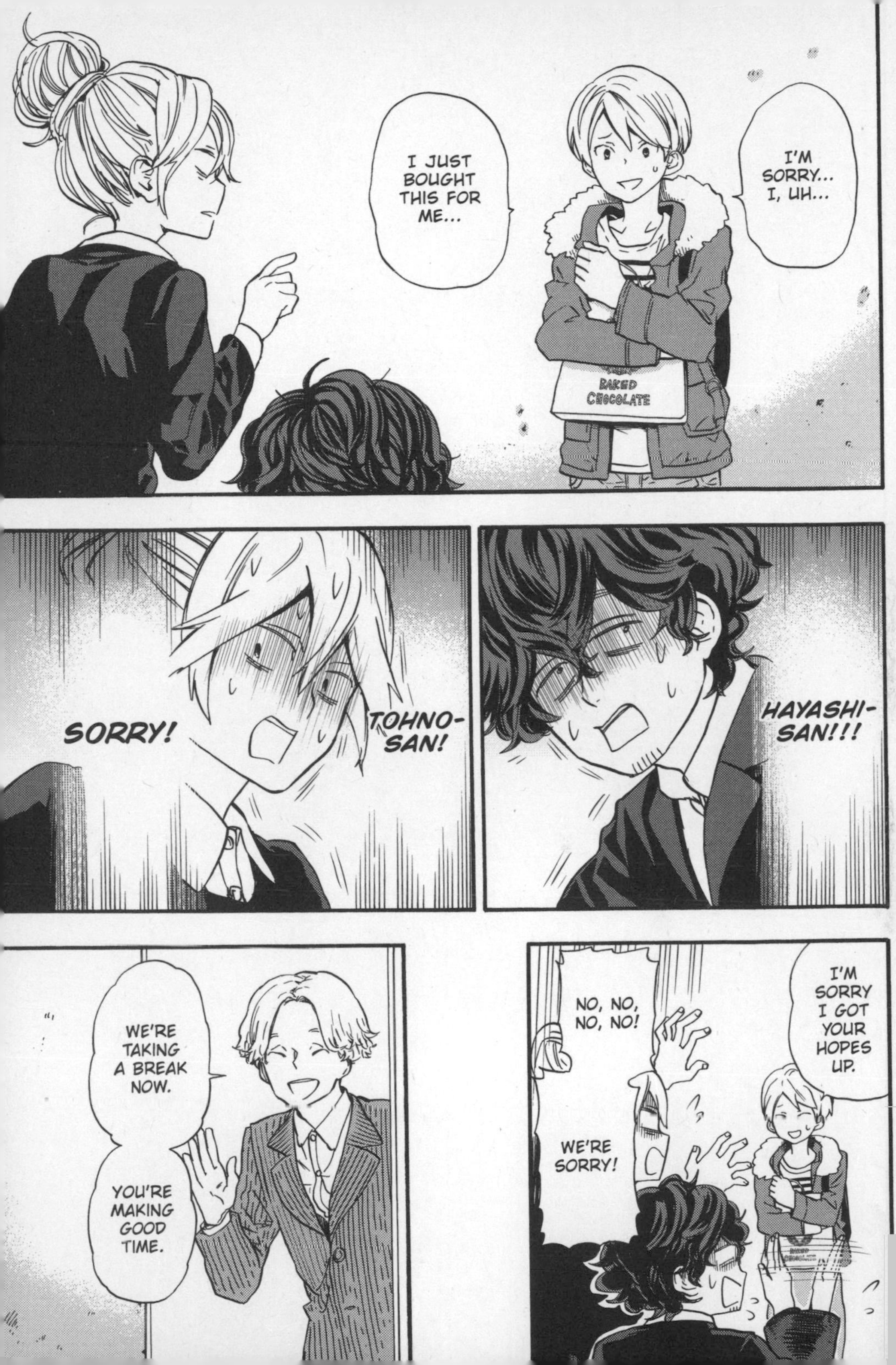
I'M SORRY... I, UH...
I JUST BOUGHT THIS FOR ME...
BAKED CHOCOLATE
HAYASHI-SAN!!!
TOHNO-SAN!
SORRY!
I'M SORRY I GOT YOUR HOPES UP.
NO, NO, NO, NO!
WE'RE SORRY!
WE'RE TAKING A BREAK NOW.
YOU'RE MAKING GOOD TIME.

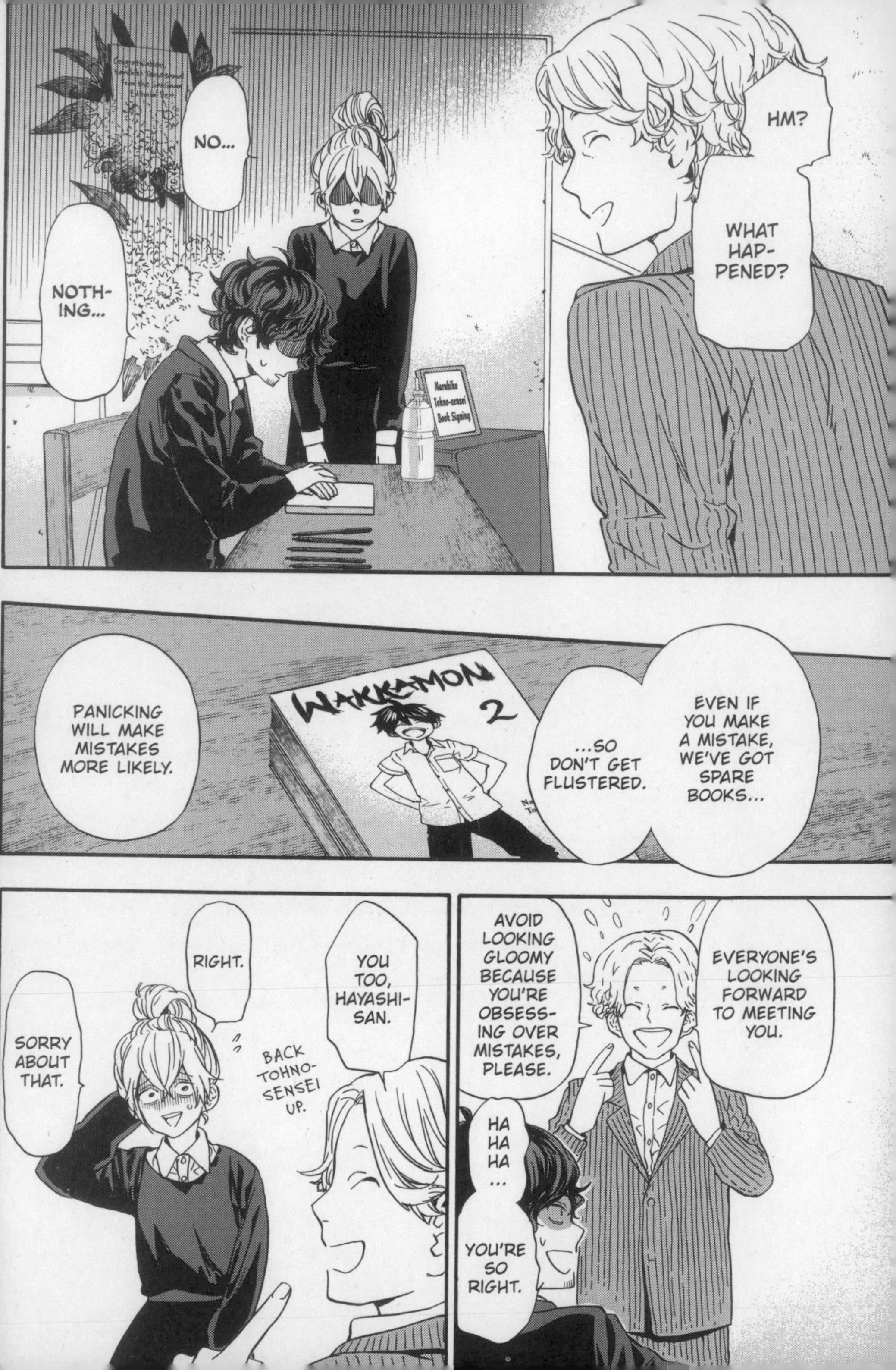
HM?
WHAT HAPPENED?
NO...
NOTHING...
Naruhiko Tohno-sensei Book Signing
EVEN IF YOU MAKE A MISTAKE, WE'VE GOT SPARE BOOKS...
...SO DON'T GET FLUSTERED.
WAKKAMON 2
PANICKING WILL MAKE MISTAKES MORE LIKELY.
EVERYONE'S LOOKING FORWARD TO MEETING YOU.
AVOID LOOKING GLOOMY BECAUSE YOU'RE OBSESSING OVER MISTAKES, PLEASE.
HA HA HA...
YOU'RE SO RIGHT.
YOU TOO, HAYASHI-SAN.
BACK TOHNO-SENSEI UP.
RIGHT.
SORRY ABOUT THAT.

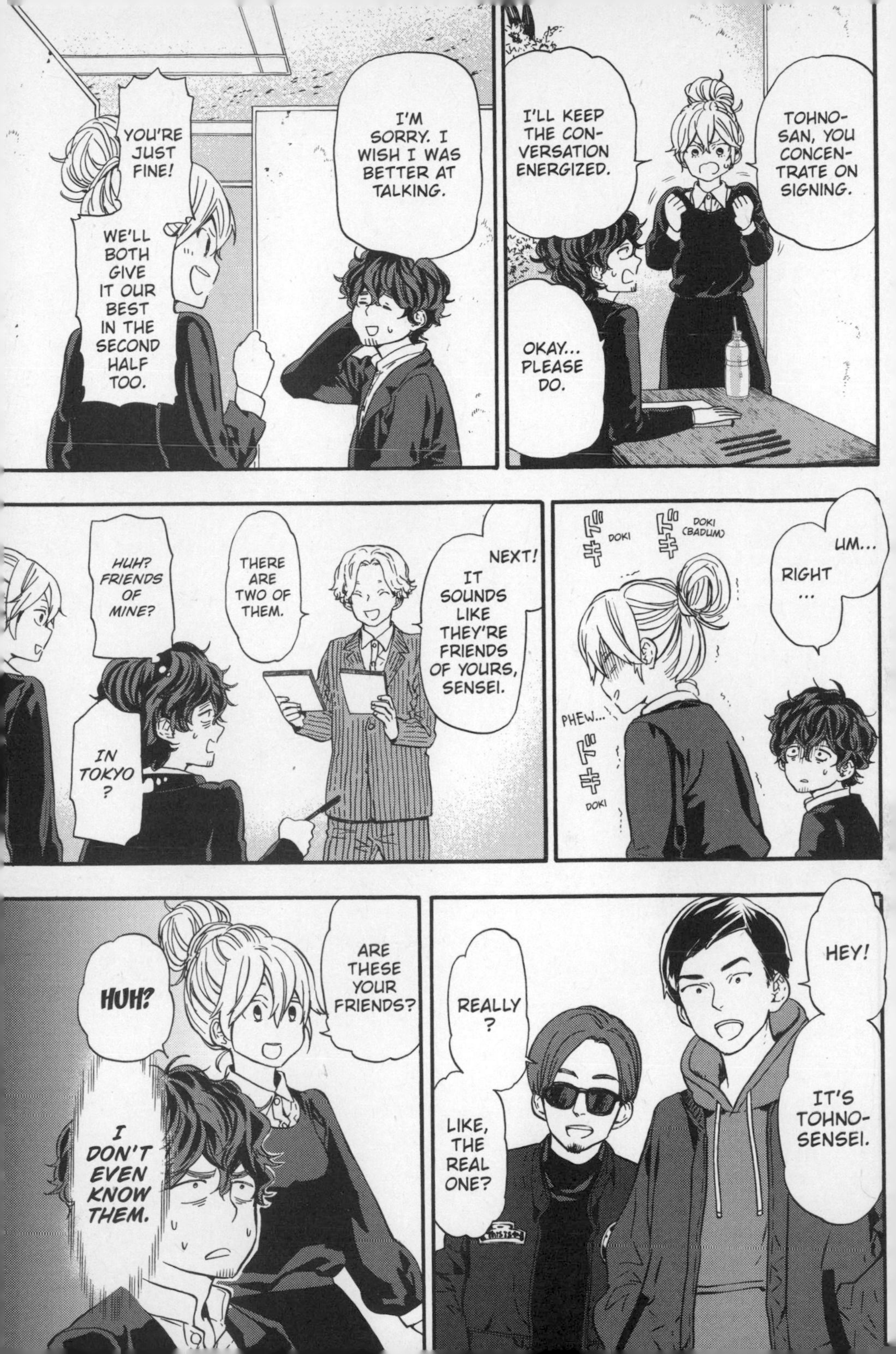
TOHNO-SAN, YOU CONCENTRATE ON SIGNING.
I'LL KEEP THE CONVERSATION ENERGIZED.
OKAY... PLEASE DO.
I'M SORRY. I WISH I WAS BETTER AT TALKING.
YOU'RE JUST FINE!
WE'LL BOTH GIVE IT OUR BEST IN THE SECOND HALF TOO.
UM... RIGHT...
ドキ DOKI (BADUM)
ドキ DOKI
PHEW...
ドキ DOKI
NEXT!
IT SOUNDS LIKE THEY'RE FRIENDS OF YOURS, SENSEI.
THERE ARE TWO OF THEM.
HUH? FRIENDS OF MINE?
IN TOKYO?
HEY!
IT'S TOHNO-SENSEI.
REALLY?
LIKE, THE REAL ONE?
ARE THESE YOUR FRIENDS?
HUH?
I DON'T EVEN KNOW THEM.

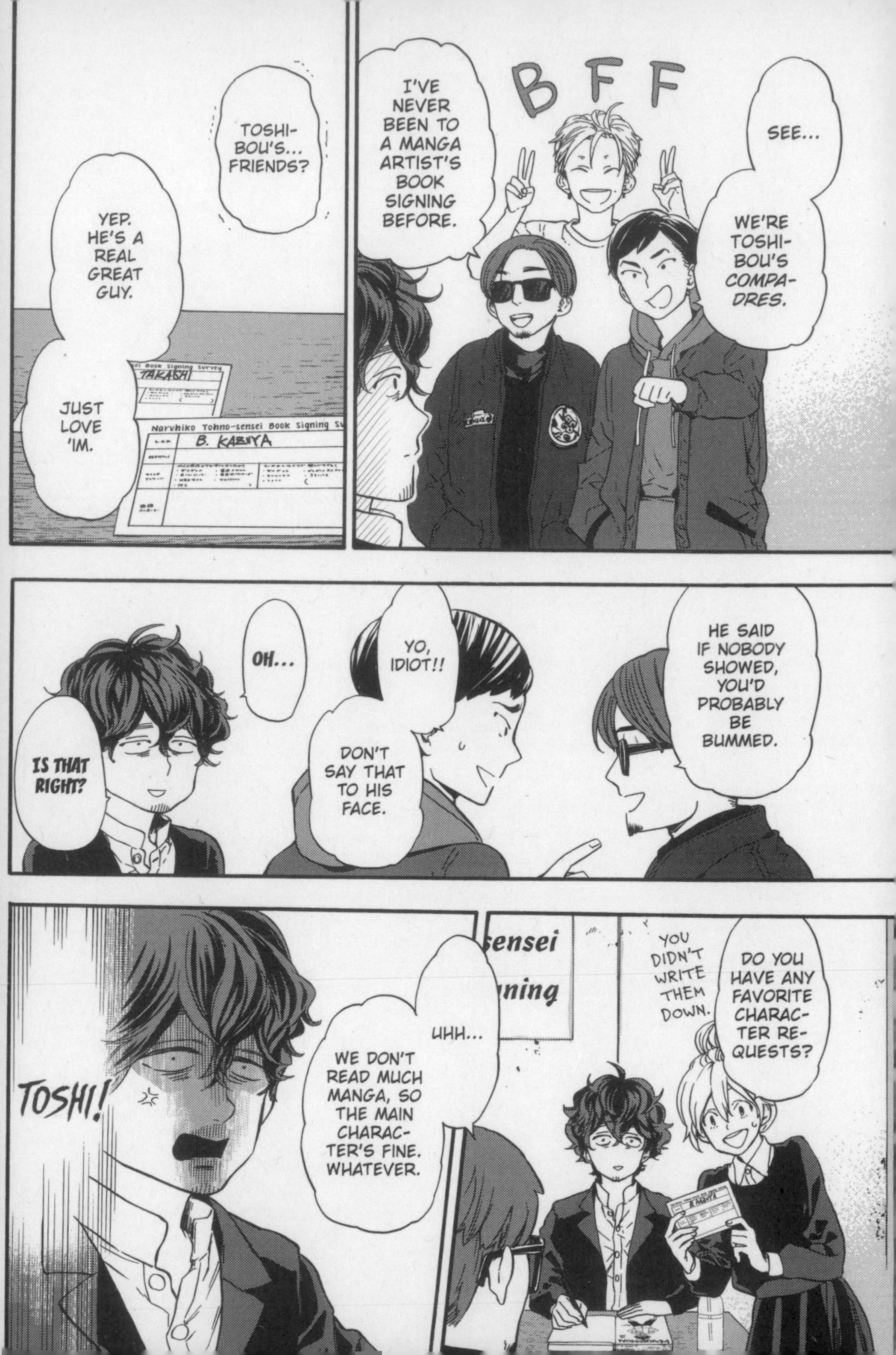
SEE...
WE'RE TOSHI-BOU'S COMPADRES.
BFF
I'VE NEVER BEEN TO A MANGA ARTIST'S BOOK SIGNING BEFORE.
TOSHI-BOU'S... FRIENDS?
YEP. HE'S A REAL GREAT GUY.
JUST LOVE 'IM.
TAKASHI
B. KABUYA
HE SAID IF NOBODY SHOWED, YOU'D PROBABLY BE BUMMED.
YO, IDIOT!!
DON'T SAY THAT TO HIS FACE.
OH...
IS THAT RIGHT?
DO YOU HAVE ANY FAVORITE CHARACTER REQUESTS?
YOU DIDN'T WRITE THEM DOWN.
sensei
UHH...
WE DON'T READ MUCH MANGA, SO THE MAIN CHARACTER'S FINE. WHATEVER.
TOSHI!

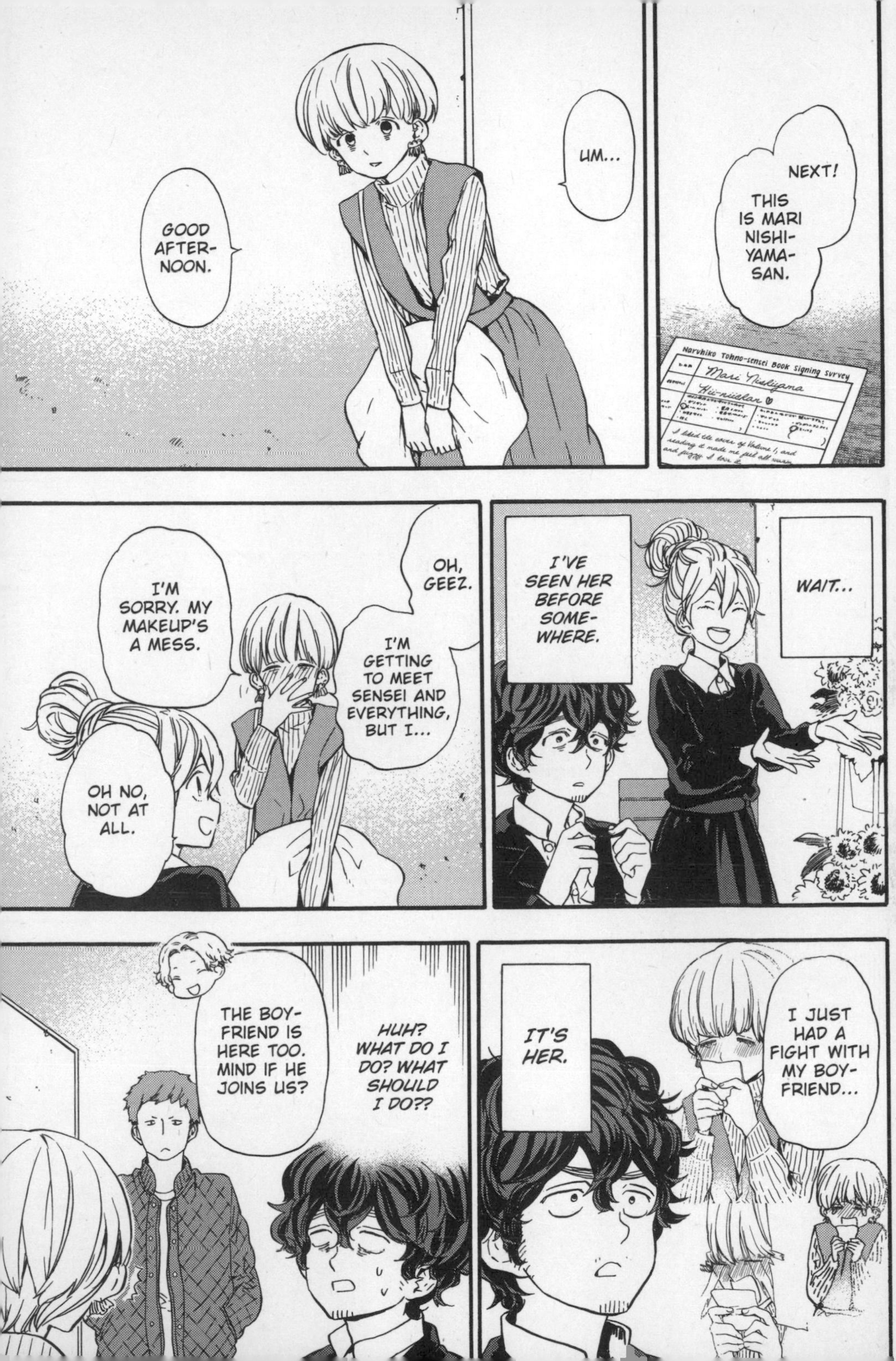
NEXT! THIS IS MARI NISHI-YAMA-SAN.
Naruhiko Tohno-sensei Book Signing Survey
Mari Nishiyama
UM...
GOOD AFTER-NOON.
WAIT...
I'VE SEEN HER BEFORE SOME-WHERE.
OH, GEEZ.
I'M GETTING TO MEET SENSEI AND EVERYTHING, BUT I...
I'M SORRY. MY MAKEUP'S A MESS.
OH NO, NOT AT ALL.
I JUST HAD A FIGHT WITH MY BOY-FRIEND...
IT'S HER.
HUH? WHAT DO I DO? WHAT SHOULD I DO??
THE BOY-FRIEND IS HERE TOO. MIND IF HE JOINS US?

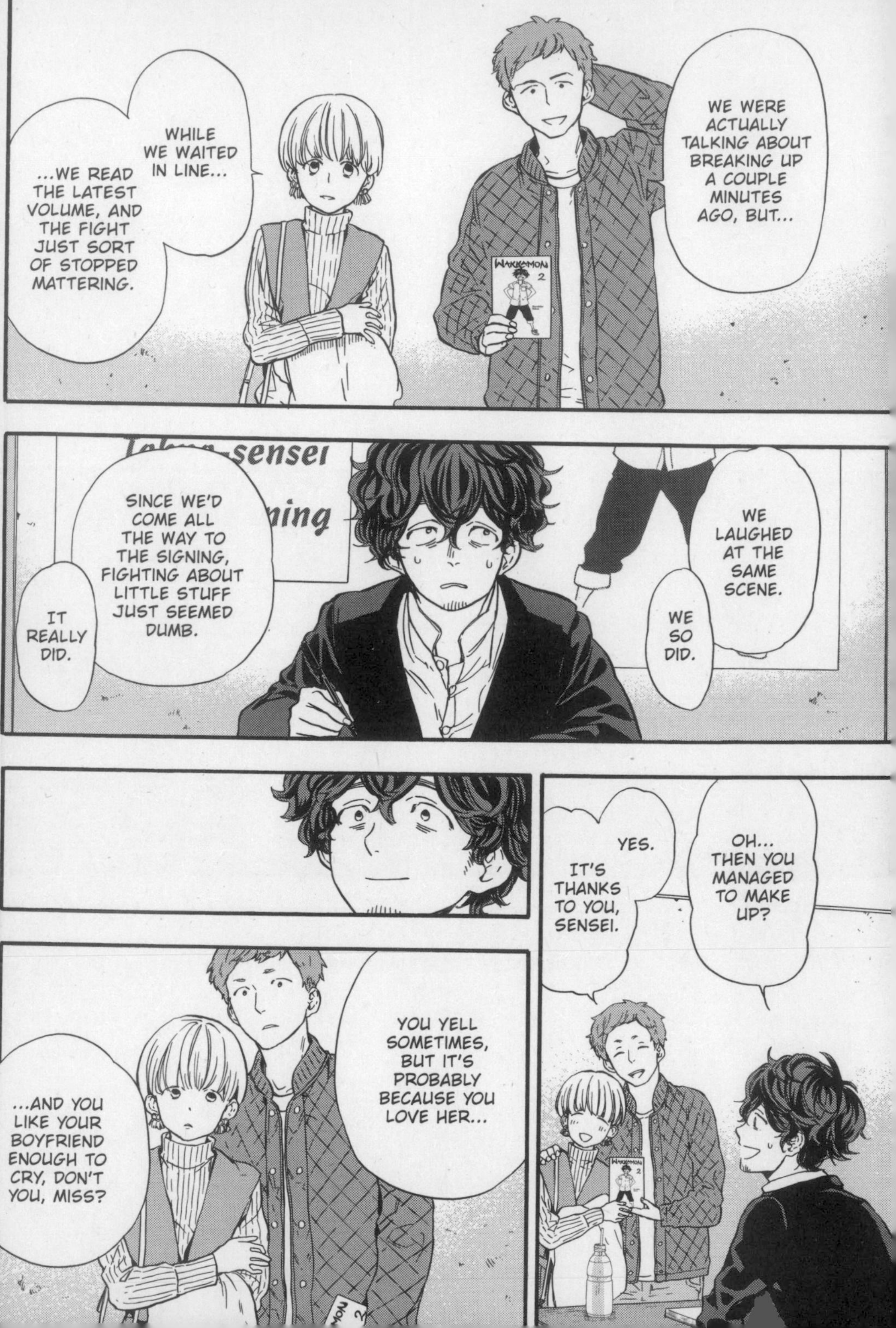
WE WERE ACTUALLY TALKING ABOUT BREAKING UP A COUPLE MINUTES AGO, BUT...
WAKAMON 2
WHILE WE WAITED IN LINE...
...WE READ THE LATEST VOLUME, AND THE FIGHT JUST SORT OF STOPPED MATTERING.
WE LAUGHED AT THE SAME SCENE.
WE SO DID.
SINCE WE'D COME ALL THE WAY TO THE SIGNING, FIGHTING ABOUT LITTLE STUFF JUST SEEMED DUMB.
IT REALLY DID.
OH... THEN YOU MANAGED TO MAKE UP?
YES.
IT'S THANKS TO YOU, SENSEI.
YOU YELL SOMETIMES, BUT IT'S PROBABLY BECAUSE YOU LOVE HER...
...AND YOU LIKE YOUR BOYFRIEND ENOUGH TO CRY, DON'T YOU, MISS?

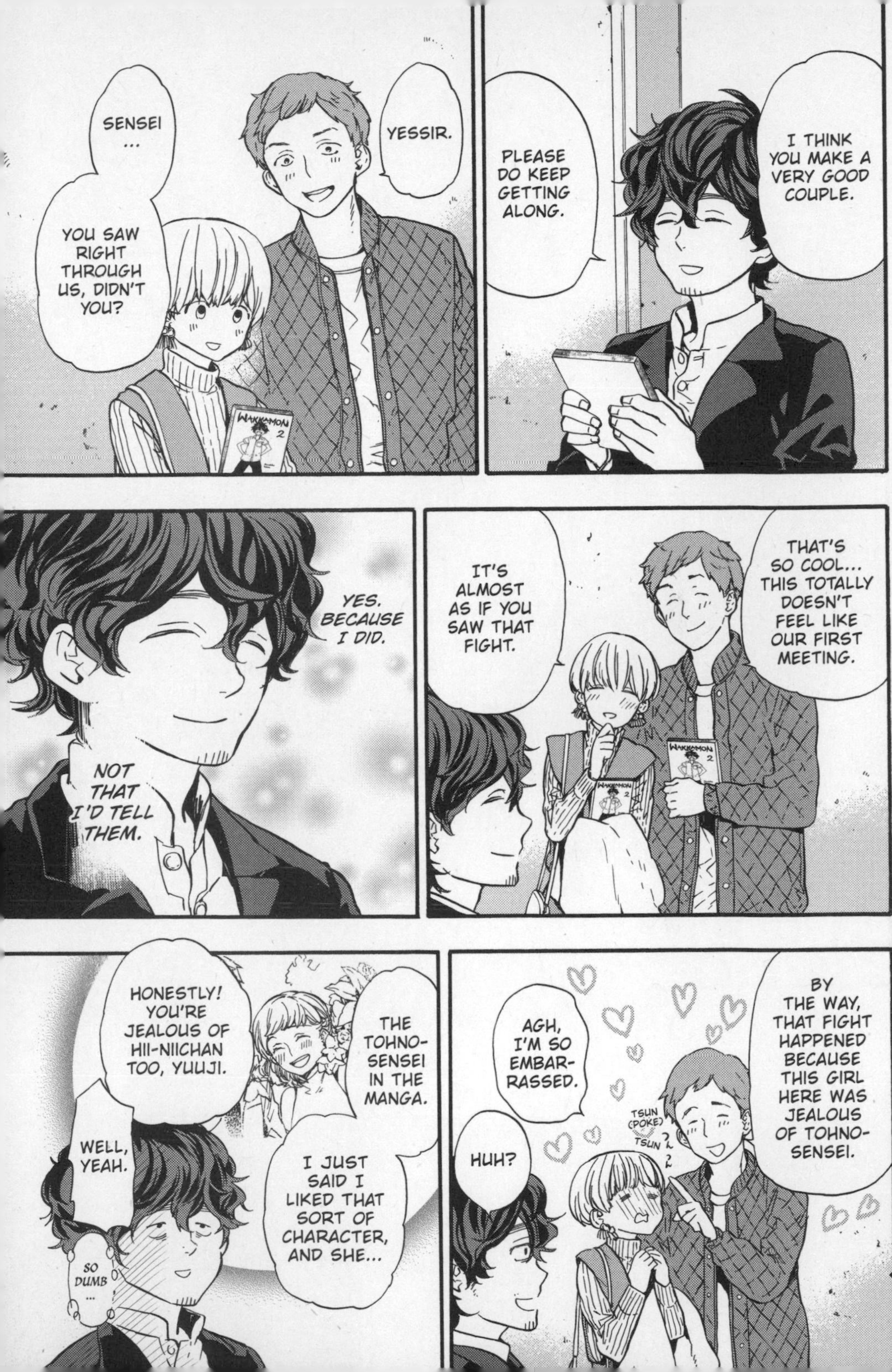
I THINK YOU MAKE A VERY GOOD COUPLE.
PLEASE DO KEEP GETTING ALONG.
YESSIR.
SENSEI ...
YOU SAW RIGHT THROUGH US, DIDN'T YOU?
THAT'S SO COOL... THIS TOTALLY DOESN'T FEEL LIKE OUR FIRST MEETING.
IT'S ALMOST AS IF YOU SAW THAT FIGHT.
YES. BECAUSE I DID.
NOT THAT I'D TELL THEM.
BY THE WAY, THAT FIGHT HAPPENED BECAUSE THIS GIRL HERE WAS JEALOUS OF TOHNO-SENSEI.
AGH, I'M SO EMBAR-RASSED.
TSUN (POKE) TSUN
HUH?
THE TOHNO-SENSEI IN THE MANGA.
HONESTLY! YOU'RE JEALOUS OF HII-NIICHAN TOO, YUUJI.
I JUST SAID I LIKED THAT SORT OF CHARACTER, AND SHE...
WELL, YEAH.
SO DUMB ...

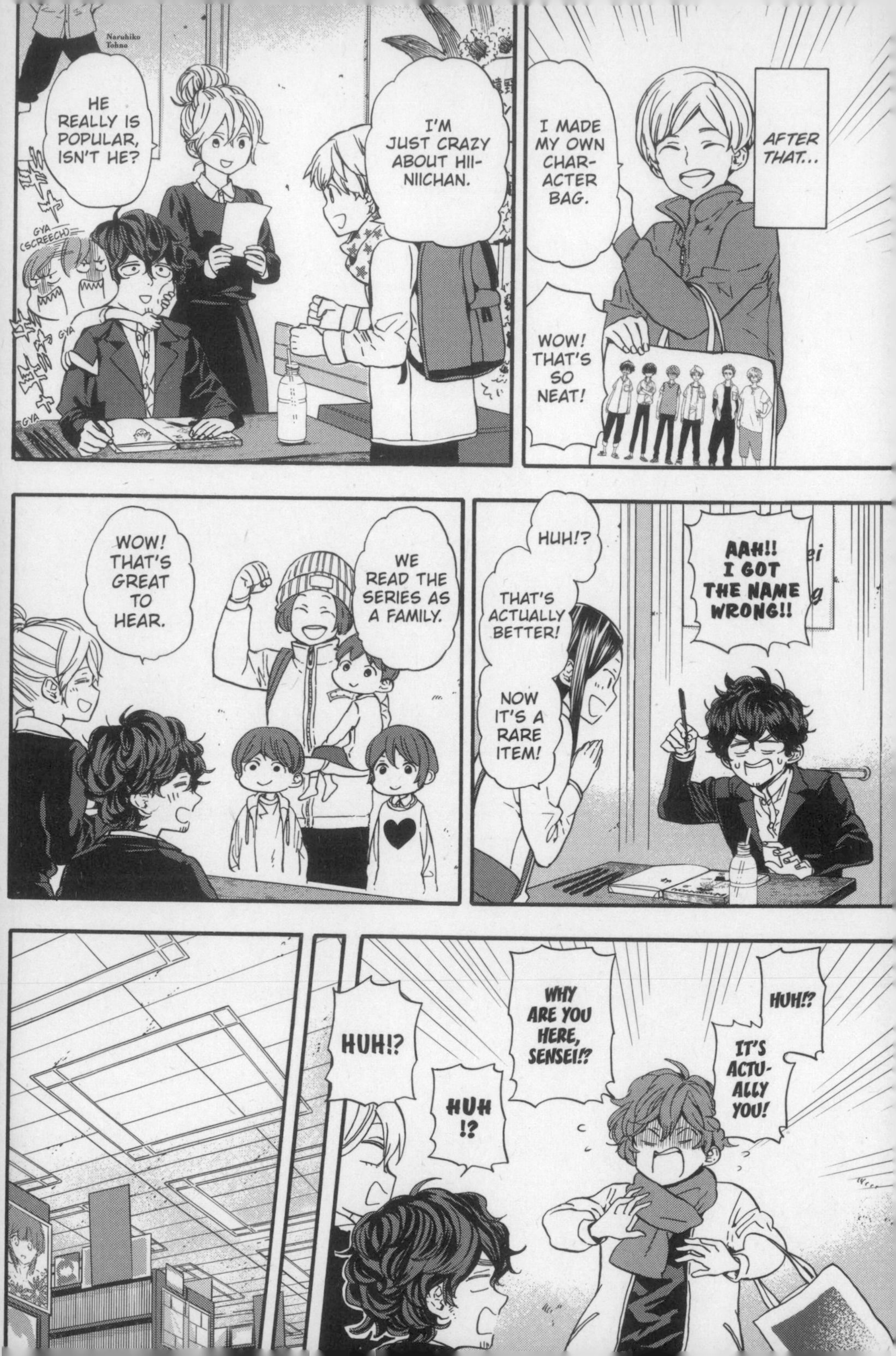
AFTER THAT...
I MADE MY OWN CHAR-ACTER BAG.
WOW! THAT'S SO NEAT!
I'M JUST CRAZY ABOUT HII-NIICHAN.
Naruhiko Tohno
HE REALLY IS POPULAR, ISN'T HE?
GYA (SCREECH)
GYA
GYA
AAH!! I GOT THE NAME WRONG!!
HUH!?
THAT'S ACTUALLY BETTER!
NOW IT'S A RARE ITEM!
WE READ THE SERIES AS A FAMILY.
WOW! THAT'S GREAT TO HEAR.
HUH!?
IT'S ACTU-ALLY YOU!
WHY ARE YOU HERE, SENSEI!?
HUH !?
HUH!?

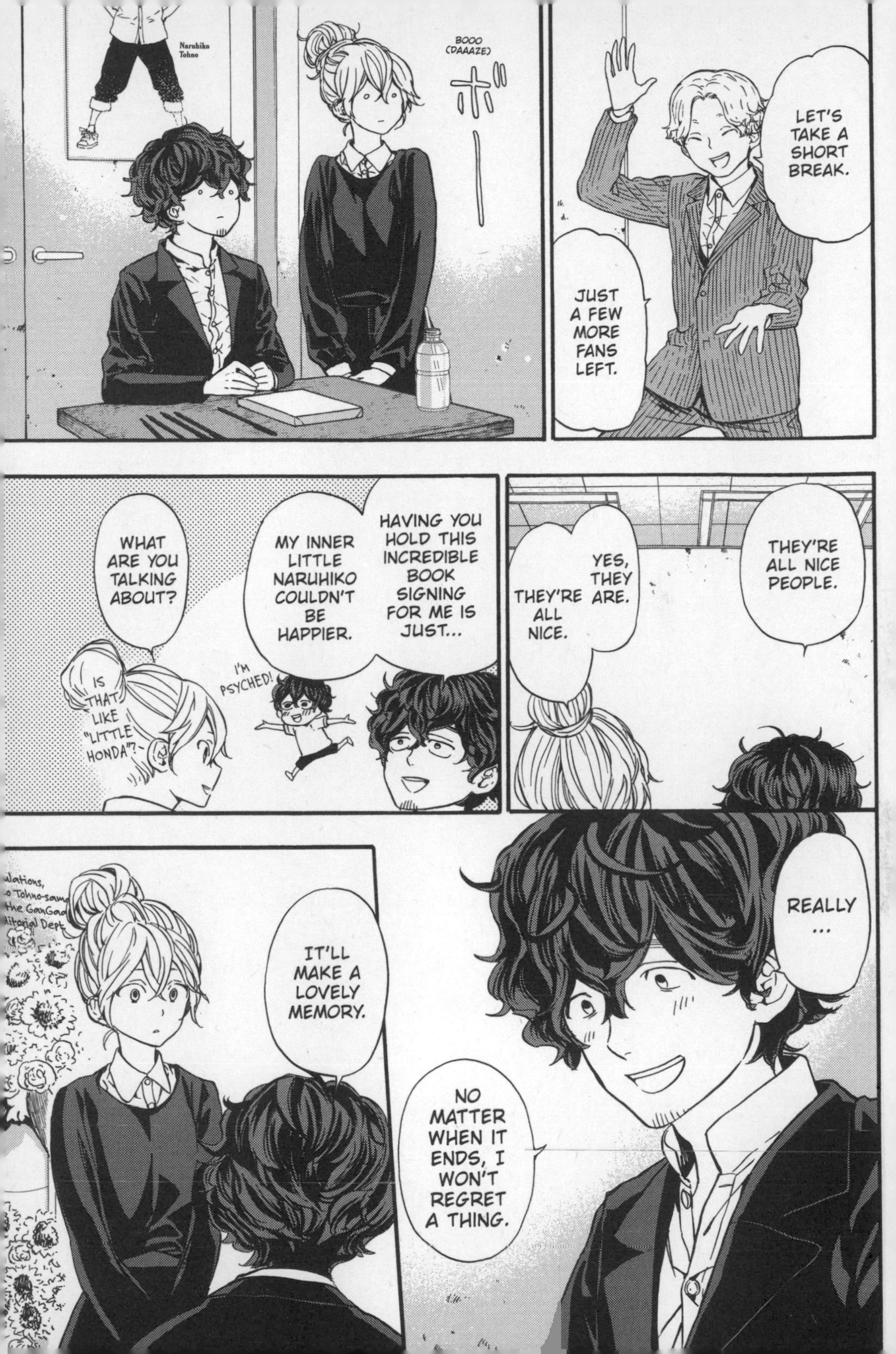
LET'S TAKE A SHORT BREAK.
JUST A FEW MORE FANS LEFT.
Naruhiko Tohno
BOOO (DAAAZE)
ボー
THEY'RE ALL NICE PEOPLE.
YES, THEY ARE.
THEY'RE ALL NICE.
HAVING YOU HOLD THIS INCREDIBLE BOOK SIGNING FOR ME IS JUST...
MY INNER LITTLE NARUHIKO COULDN'T BE HAPPIER.
I'M PSYCHED!
WHAT ARE YOU TALKING ABOUT?
IS THAT LIKE "LITTLE HONDA"?
REALLY ...
NO MATTER WHEN IT ENDS, I WON'T REGRET A THING.
IT'LL MAKE A LOVELY MEMORY.

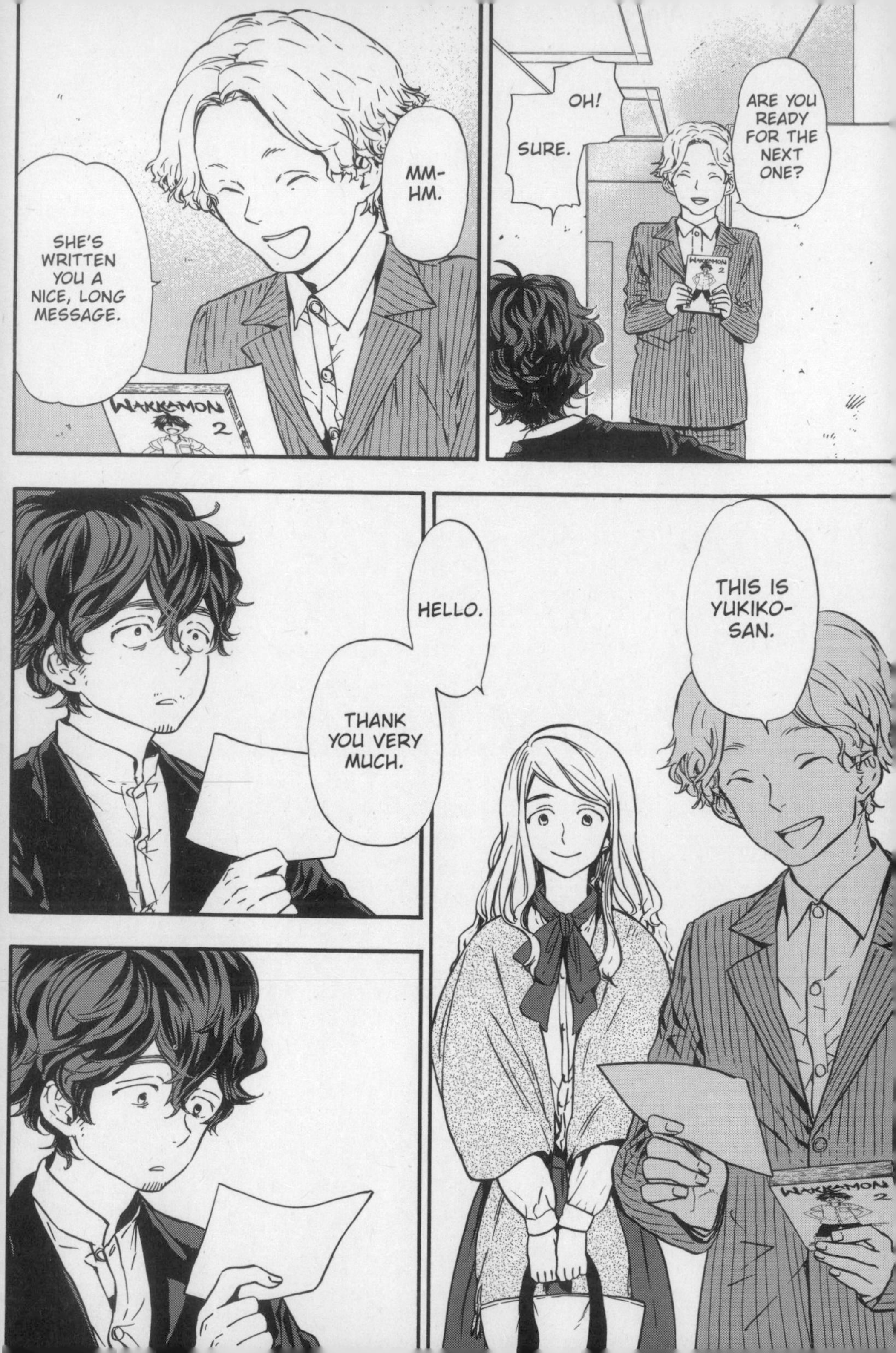
ARE YOU READY FOR THE NEXT ONE?
OH!
SURE.
MM-HM.
SHE'S WRITTEN YOU A NICE, LONG MESSAGE.
THIS IS YUKIKO-SAN.
HELLO.
THANK YOU VERY MUCH.

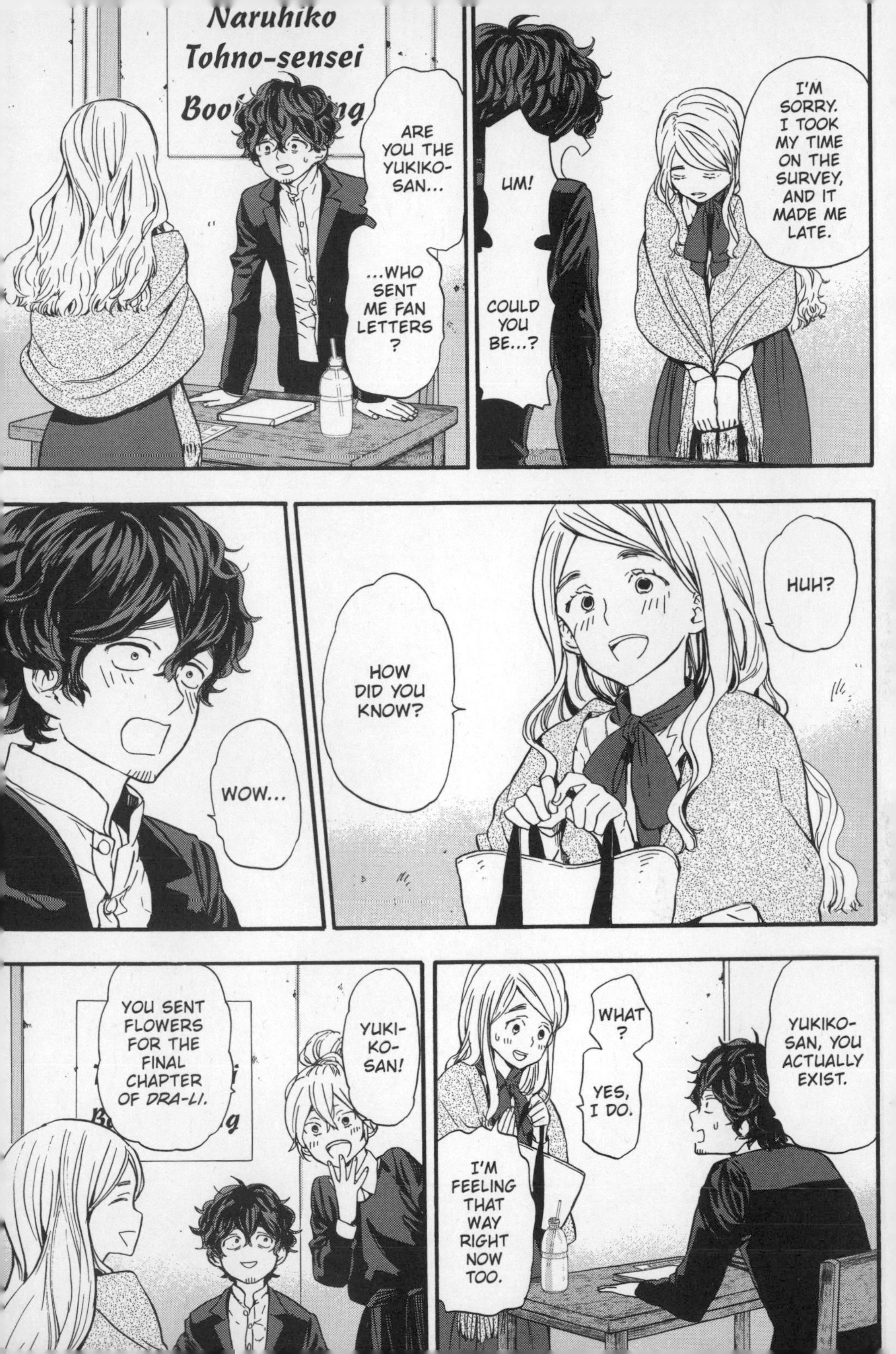
I'M SORRY. I TOOK MY TIME ON THE SURVEY, AND IT MADE ME LATE.
UM!
COULD YOU BE...?
Naruhiko Tohno-sensei
ARE YOU THE YUKIKO-SAN...
...WHO SENT ME FAN LETTERS?
HUH?
HOW DID YOU KNOW?
WOW...
YUKIKO-SAN, YOU ACTUALLY EXIST.
WHAT?
YES, I DO.
I'M FEELING THAT WAY RIGHT NOW TOO.
YUKI-KO-SAN!
YOU SENT FLOWERS FOR THE FINAL CHAPTER OF *DRA-LI.*

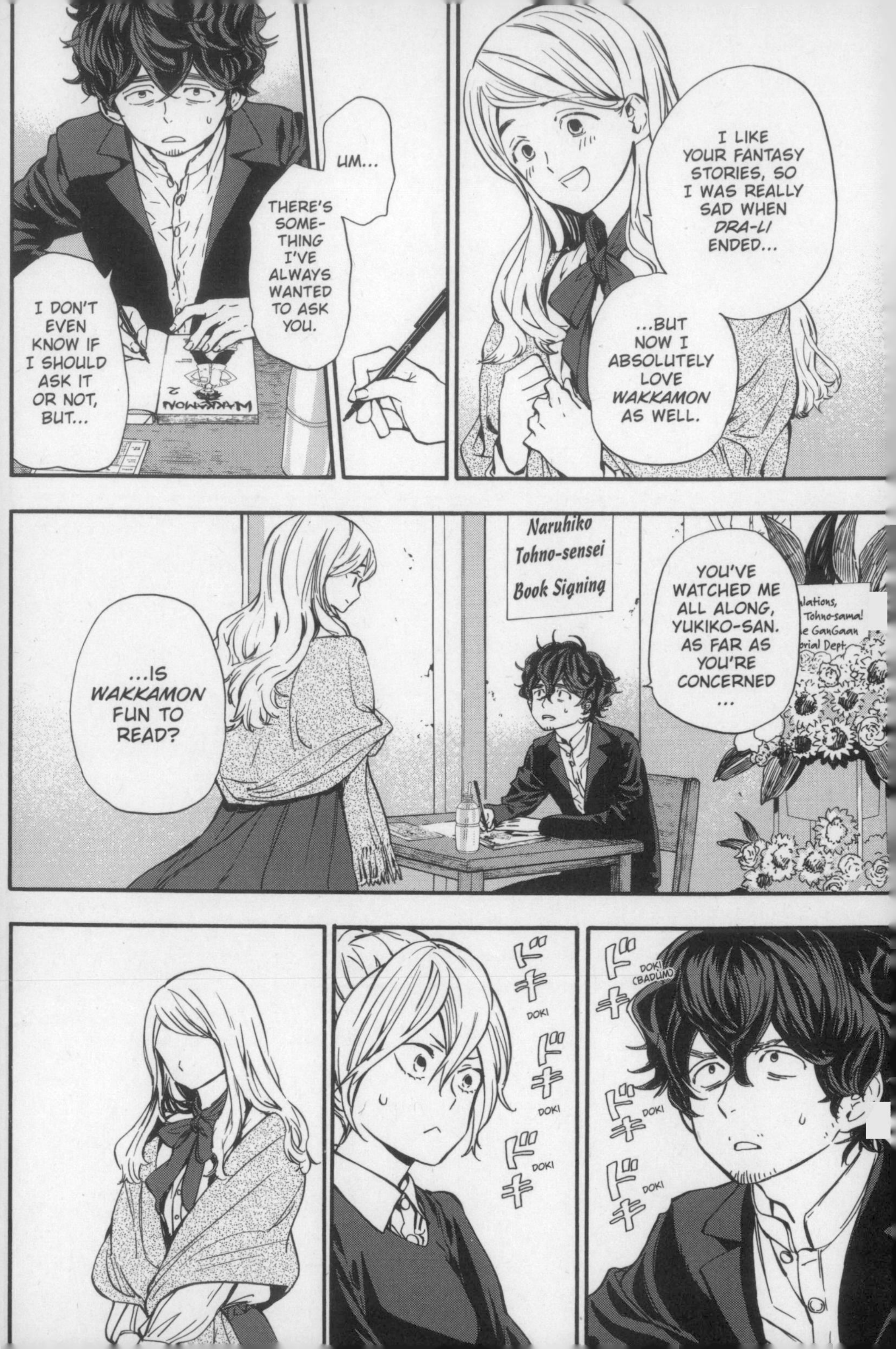
I LIKE YOUR FANTASY STORIES, SO I WAS REALLY SAD WHEN *DRA-LI* ENDED...
...BUT NOW I ABSOLUTELY LOVE *WAKKAMON* AS WELL.
UM...
THERE'S SOMETHING I'VE ALWAYS WANTED TO ASK YOU.
I DON'T EVEN KNOW IF I SHOULD ASK IT OR NOT, BUT...
WAKKAMON 2
Naruhiko Tohno-sensei Book Signing
YOU'VE WATCHED ME ALL ALONG, YUKIKO-SAN. AS FAR AS YOU'RE CONCERNED ...
...IS *WAKKAMON* FUN TO READ?
ドキ DOKI (BADUM)
ドキ DOKI
ドキ DOKI
ドキ DOKI
ドキ DOKI
ドキ DOKI

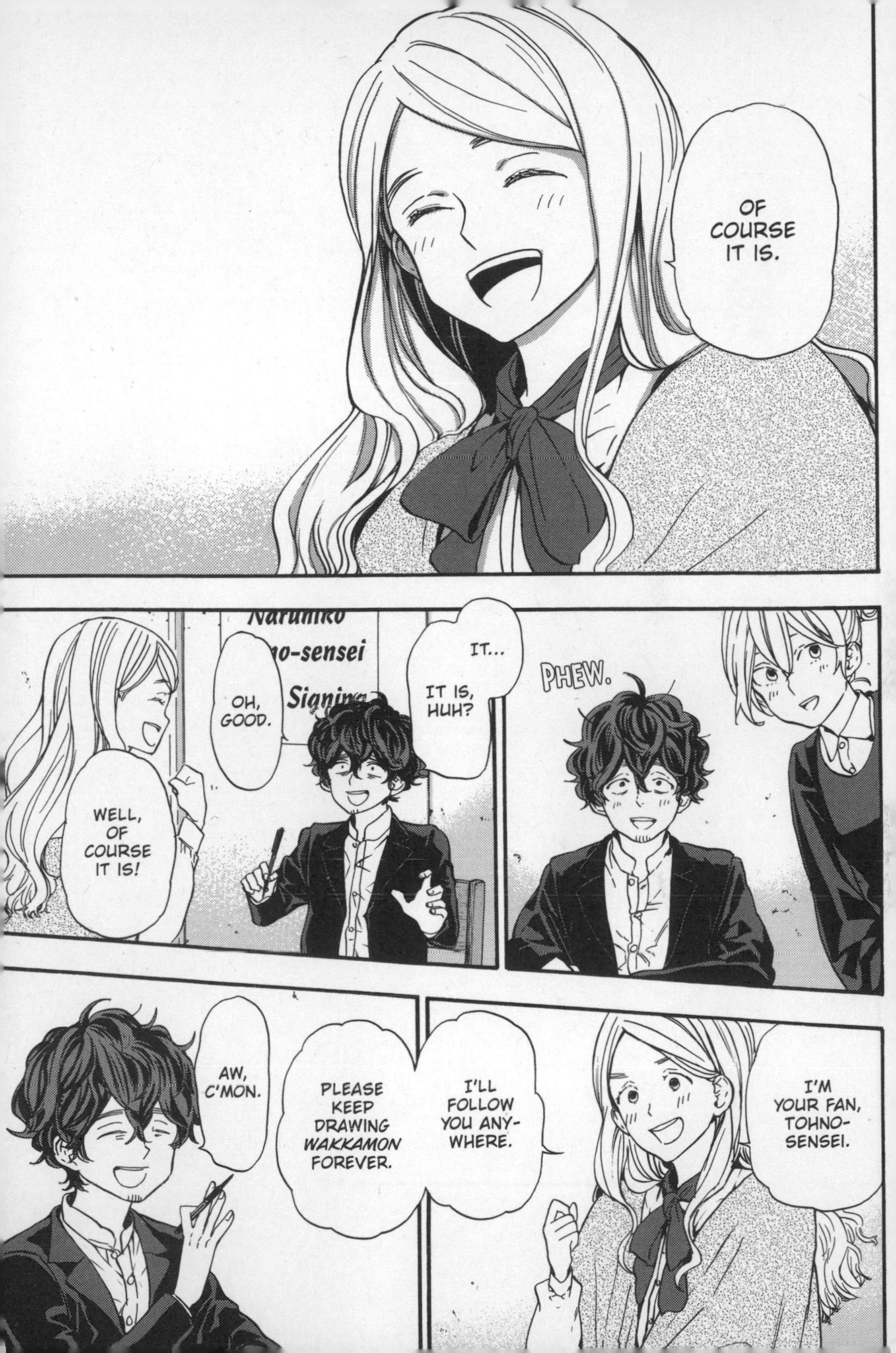
OF COURSE IT IS.
PHEW.
IT... IT IS, HUH?
OH, GOOD.
WELL, OF COURSE IT IS!
I'M YOUR FAN, TOHNO-SENSEI.
I'LL FOLLOW YOU ANY-WHERE.
PLEASE KEEP DRAWING *WAKKAMON* FOREVER.
AW, C'MON.

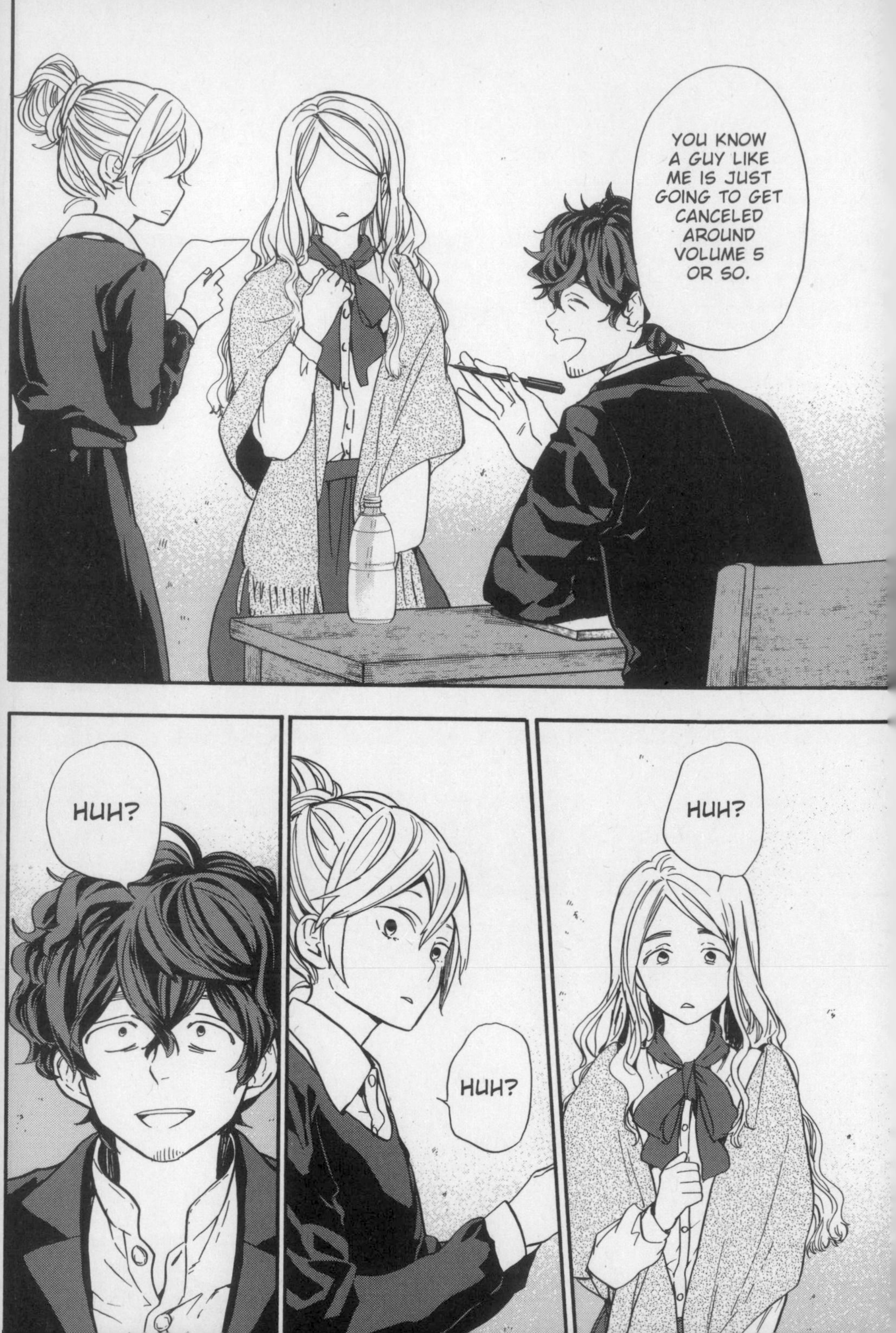
YOU KNOW A GUY LIKE ME IS JUST GOING TO GET CANCELED AROUND VOLUME 5 OR SO.
HUH?
HUH?
HUH?

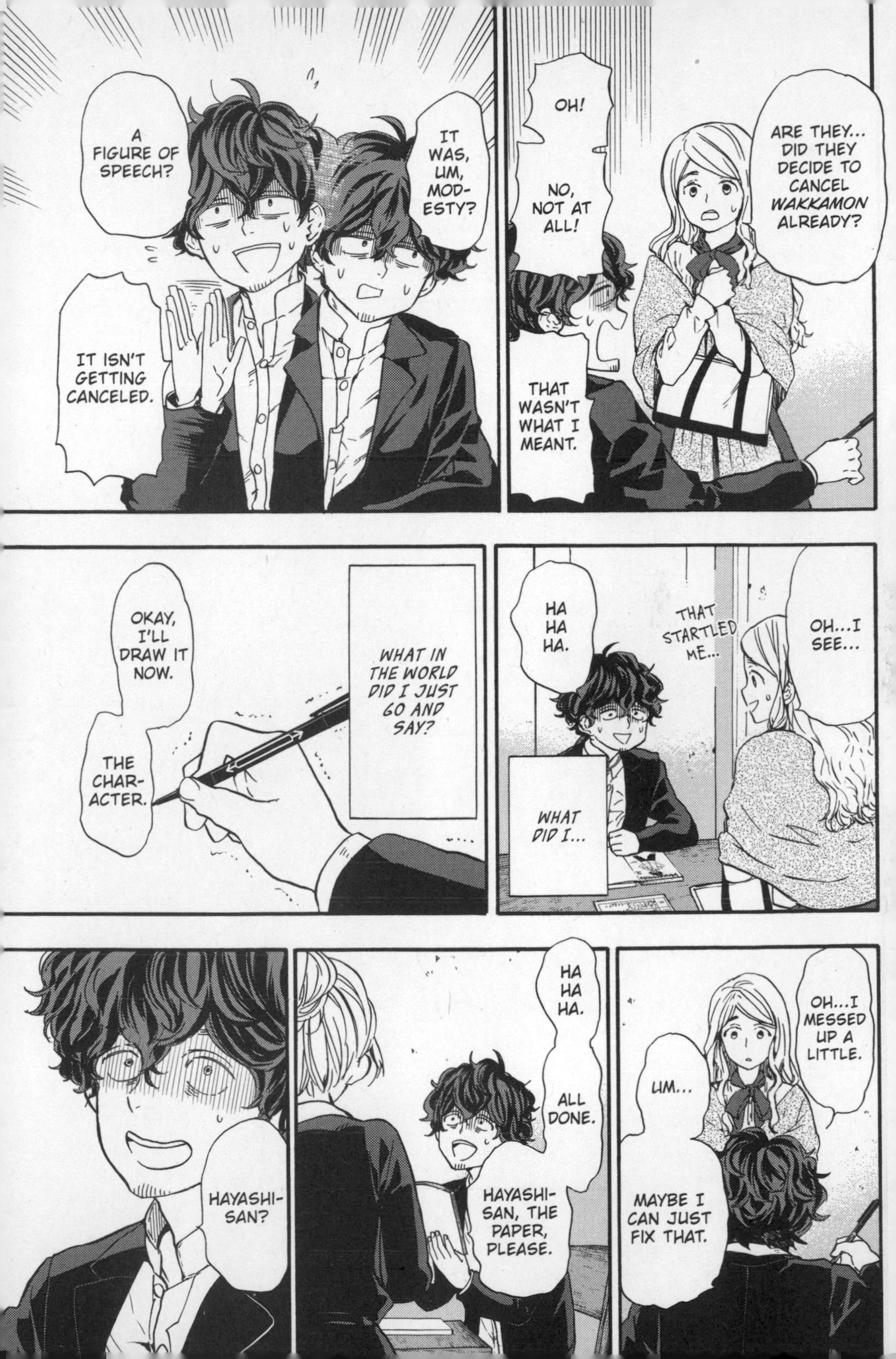
ARE THEY... DID THEY DECIDE TO CANCEL *WAKKAMON* ALREADY?
OH!
NO, NOT AT ALL!
THAT WASN'T WHAT I MEANT.
IT WAS, UM, MOD-ESTY?
A FIGURE OF SPEECH?
IT ISN'T GETTING CANCELED.
OH...I SEE...
THAT STARTLED ME...
HA HA HA.
WHAT DID I...
WHAT IN THE WORLD DID I JUST GO AND SAY?
OKAY, I'LL DRAW IT NOW.
THE CHAR-ACTER.
OH...I MESSED UP A LITTLE.
UM...
MAYBE I CAN JUST FIX THAT.
HA HA HA.
ALL DONE.
HAYASHI-SAN, THE PAPER, PLEASE.
HAYASHI-SAN?

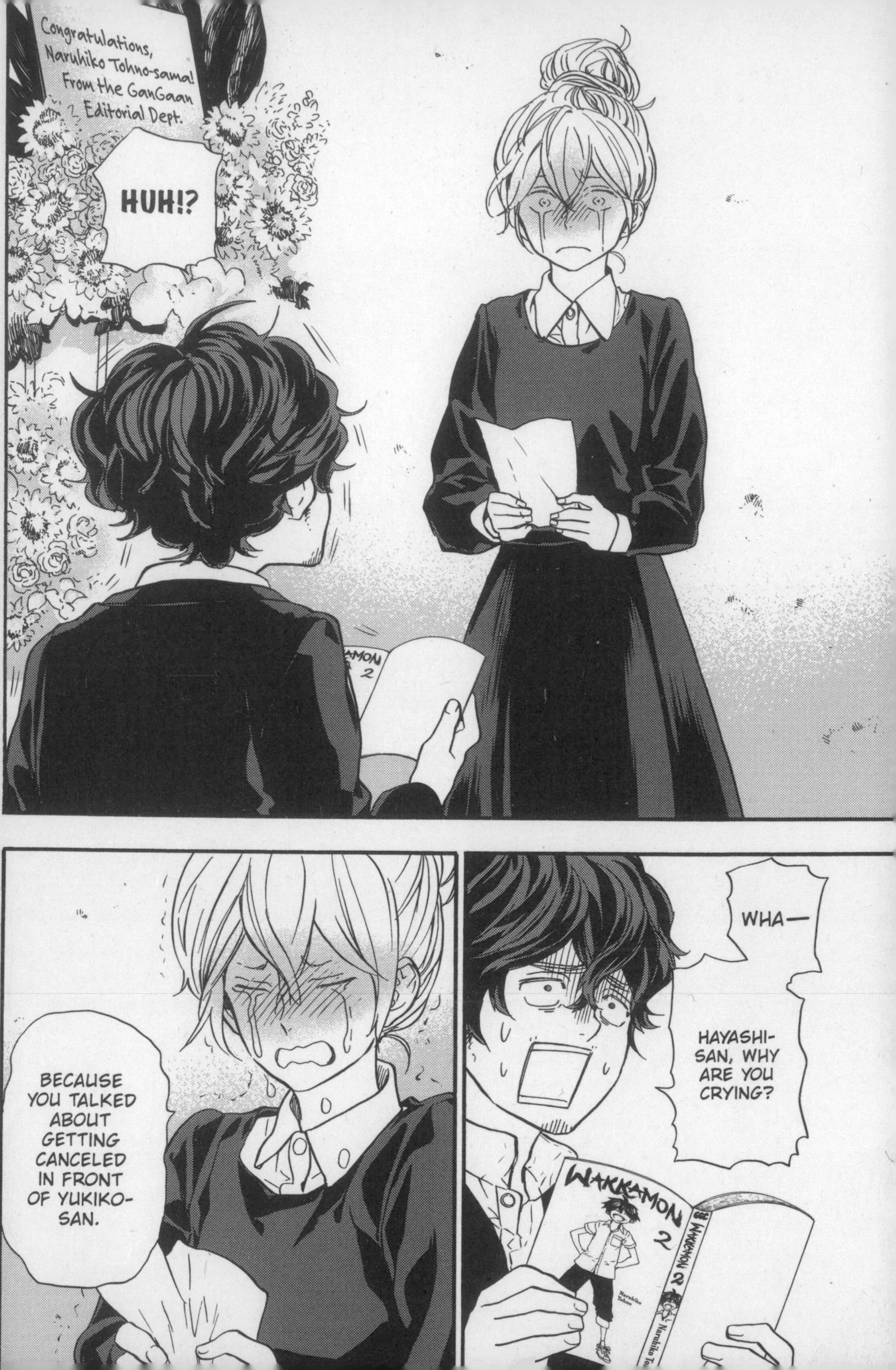
Congratulations, Naruhiko Tohno-sama! From the GanGaan Editorial Dept.
HUH!?
WHA—
HAYASHI-SAN, WHY ARE YOU CRYING?
WAKKAMON 2
BECAUSE YOU TALKED ABOUT GETTING CANCELED IN FRONT OF YUKIKO-SAN.

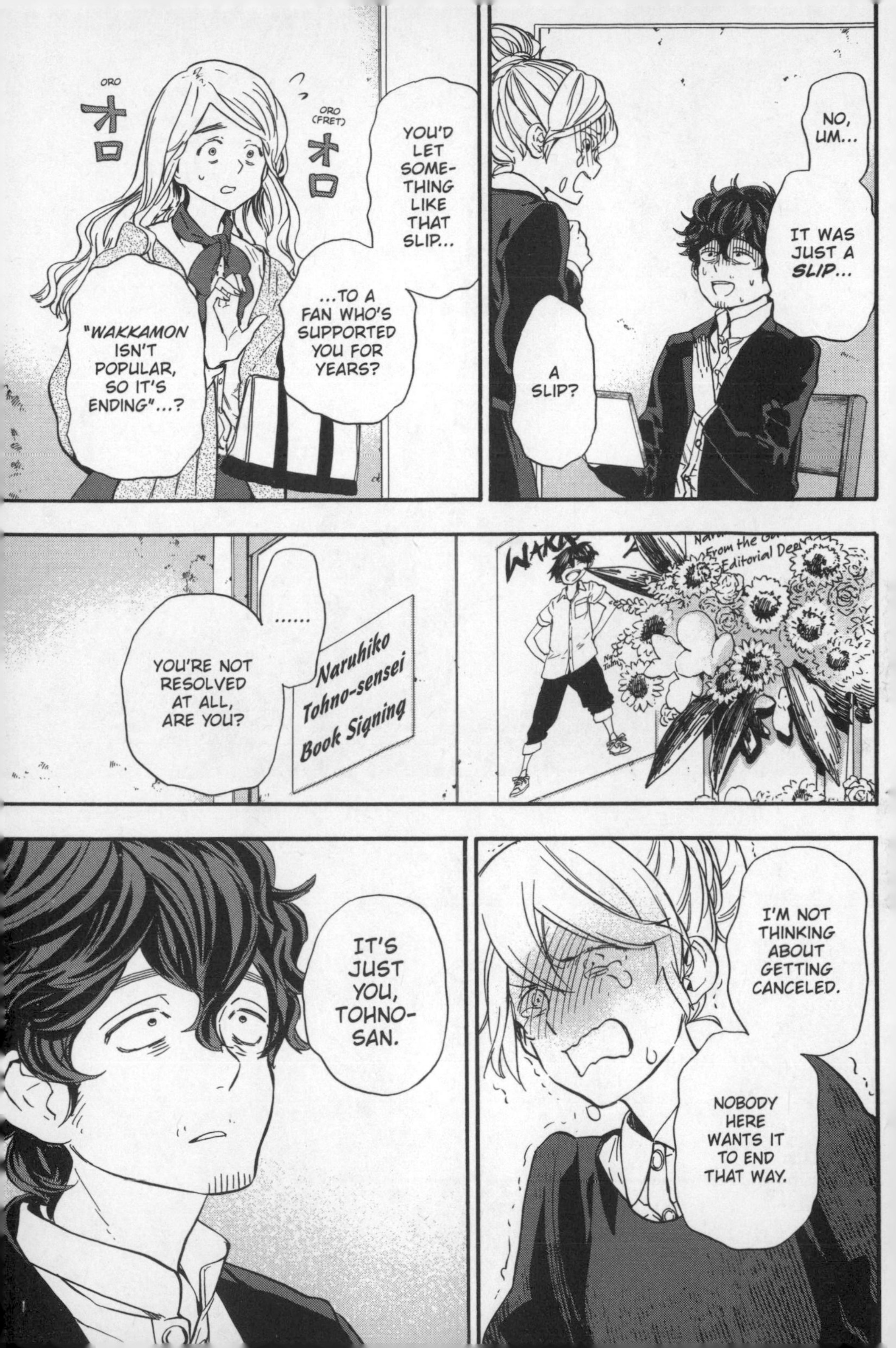
NO, UM...
IT WAS JUST A *SLIP*...
A SLIP?
YOU'D LET SOME-THING LIKE THAT SLIP...
ORO (FRET) オロ
ORO オロ
...TO A FAN WHO'S SUPPORTED YOU FOR YEARS?
"*WAKKAMON* ISN'T POPULAR, SO IT'S ENDING"...?
......
Naruhiko Tohno-sensei Book Signing
YOU'RE NOT RESOLVED AT ALL, ARE YOU?
I'M NOT THINKING ABOUT GETTING CANCELED.
NOBODY HERE WANTS IT TO END THAT WAY.
IT'S JUST YOU, TOHNO-SAN.

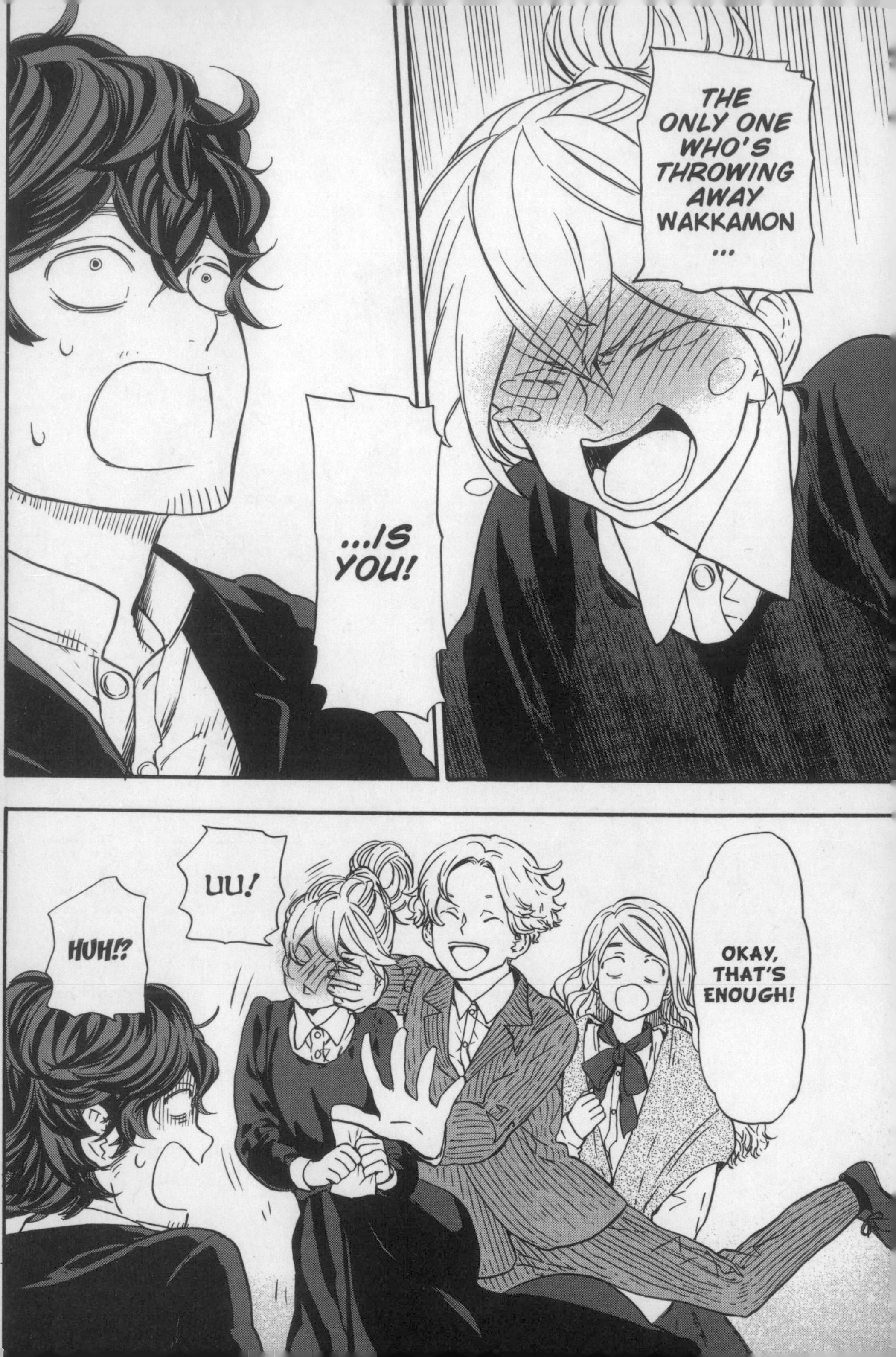

THE ONLY ONE WHO'S THROWING AWAY WAKKAMON ...
...IS YOU!
OKAY, THAT'S ENOUGH!
UU!
HUH!?

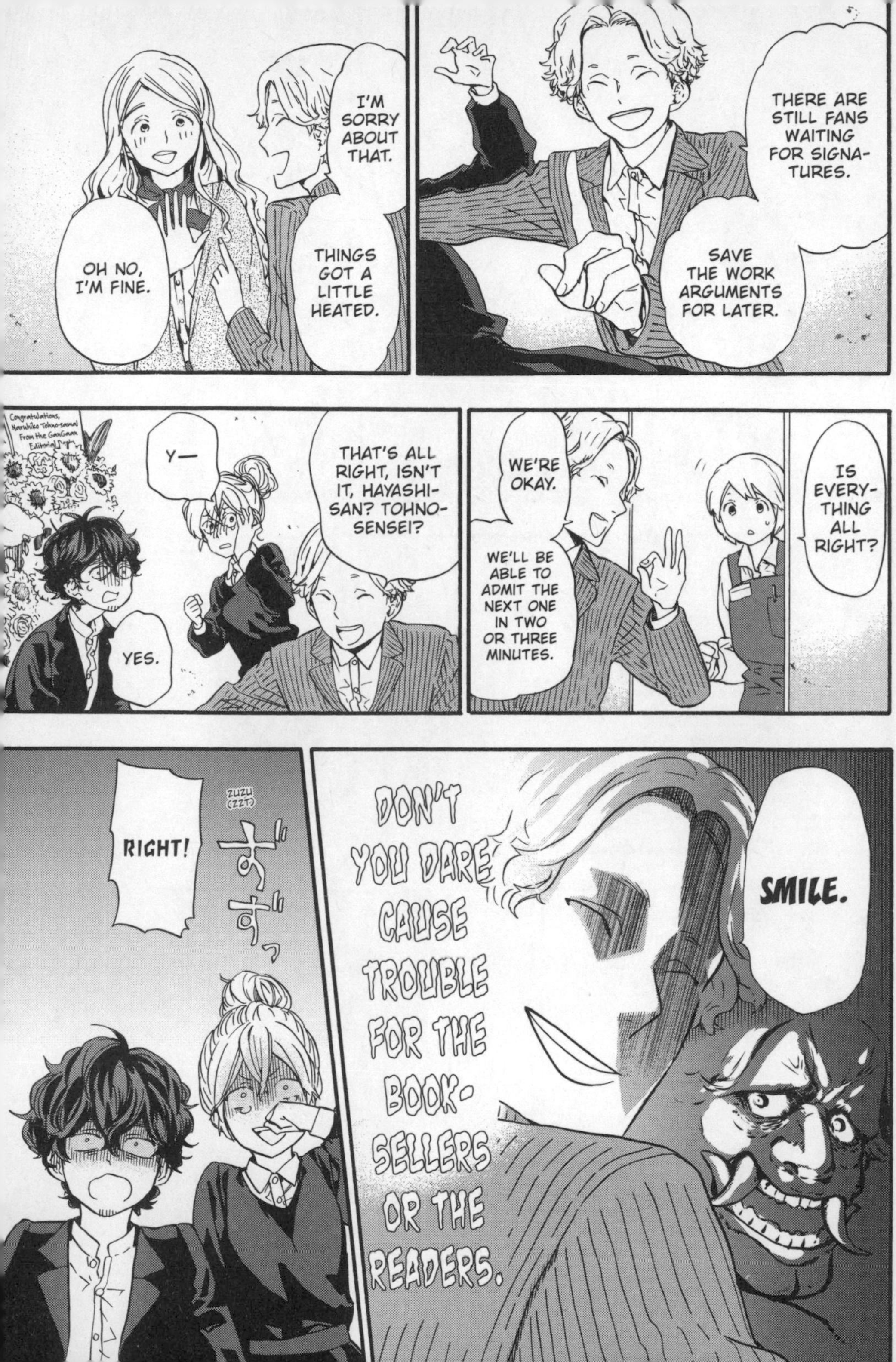

THERE ARE STILL FANS WAITING FOR SIGNATURES.
SAVE THE WORK ARGUMENTS FOR LATER.
I'M SORRY ABOUT THAT.
THINGS GOT A LITTLE HEATED.
OH NO, I'M FINE.
IS EVERYTHING ALL RIGHT?
WE'RE OKAY.
WE'LL BE ABLE TO ADMIT THE NEXT ONE IN TWO OR THREE MINUTES.
THAT'S ALL RIGHT, ISN'T IT, HAYASHI-SAN? TOHNO-SENSEI?
Congratulations, Naruhiko Tohno-sama! From the GanGan Editorial Dept.
Y—
YES.
SMILE.
DON'T YOU DARE CAUSE TROUBLE FOR THE BOOKSELLERS OR THE READERS.
ZUZU (ZZT)
ずずっ
RIGHT!

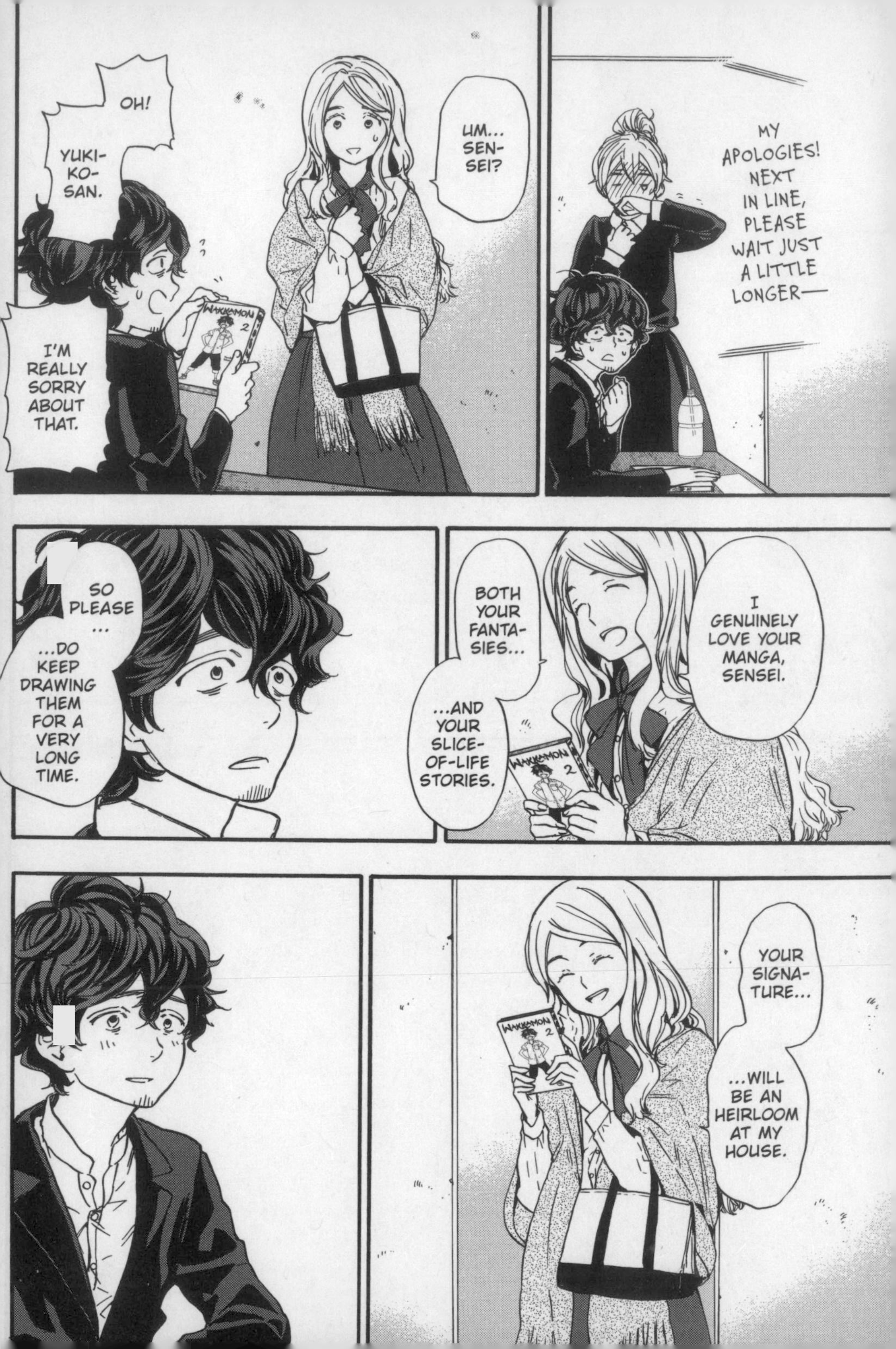
MY APOLOGIES! NEXT IN LINE, PLEASE WAIT JUST A LITTLE LONGER—
UM... SEN-SEI?
OH!
YUKI-KO-SAN.
I'M REALLY SORRY ABOUT THAT.
I GENUINELY LOVE YOUR MANGA, SENSEI.
BOTH YOUR FANTA-SIES...
...AND YOUR SLICE-OF-LIFE STORIES.
SO PLEASE ...
...DO KEEP DRAWING THEM FOR A VERY LONG TIME.
YOUR SIGNA-TURE...
...WILL BE AN HEIRLOOM AT MY HOUSE.

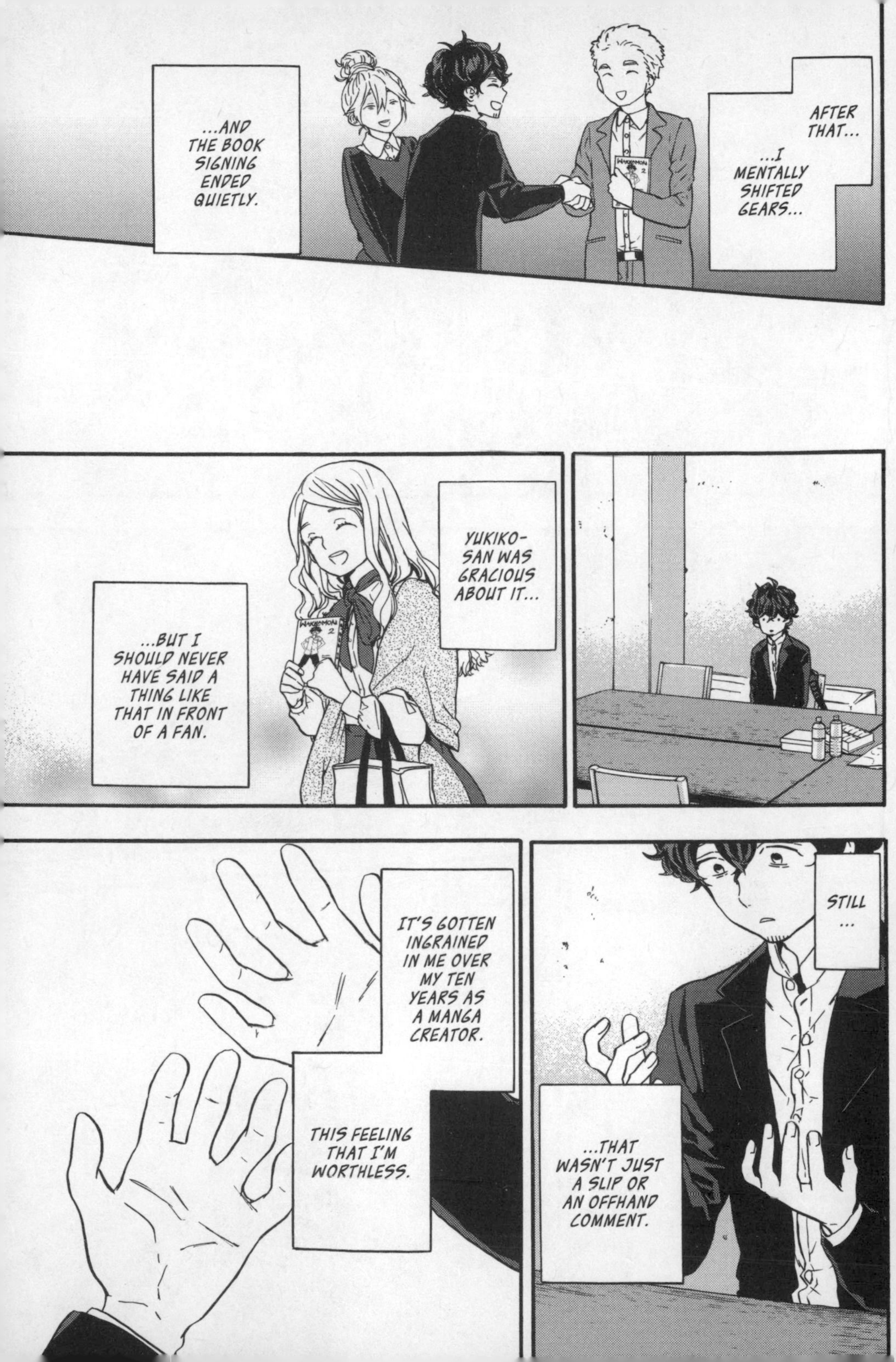
AFTER THAT...
...I MENTALLY SHIFTED GEARS...
...AND THE BOOK SIGNING ENDED QUIETLY.
YUKIKO-SAN WAS GRACIOUS ABOUT IT...
...BUT I SHOULD NEVER HAVE SAID A THING LIKE THAT IN FRONT OF A FAN.
STILL...
...THAT WASN'T JUST A SLIP OR AN OFFHAND COMMENT.
IT'S GOTTEN INGRAINED IN ME OVER MY TEN YEARS AS A MANGA CREATOR.
THIS FEELING THAT I'M WORTHLESS.

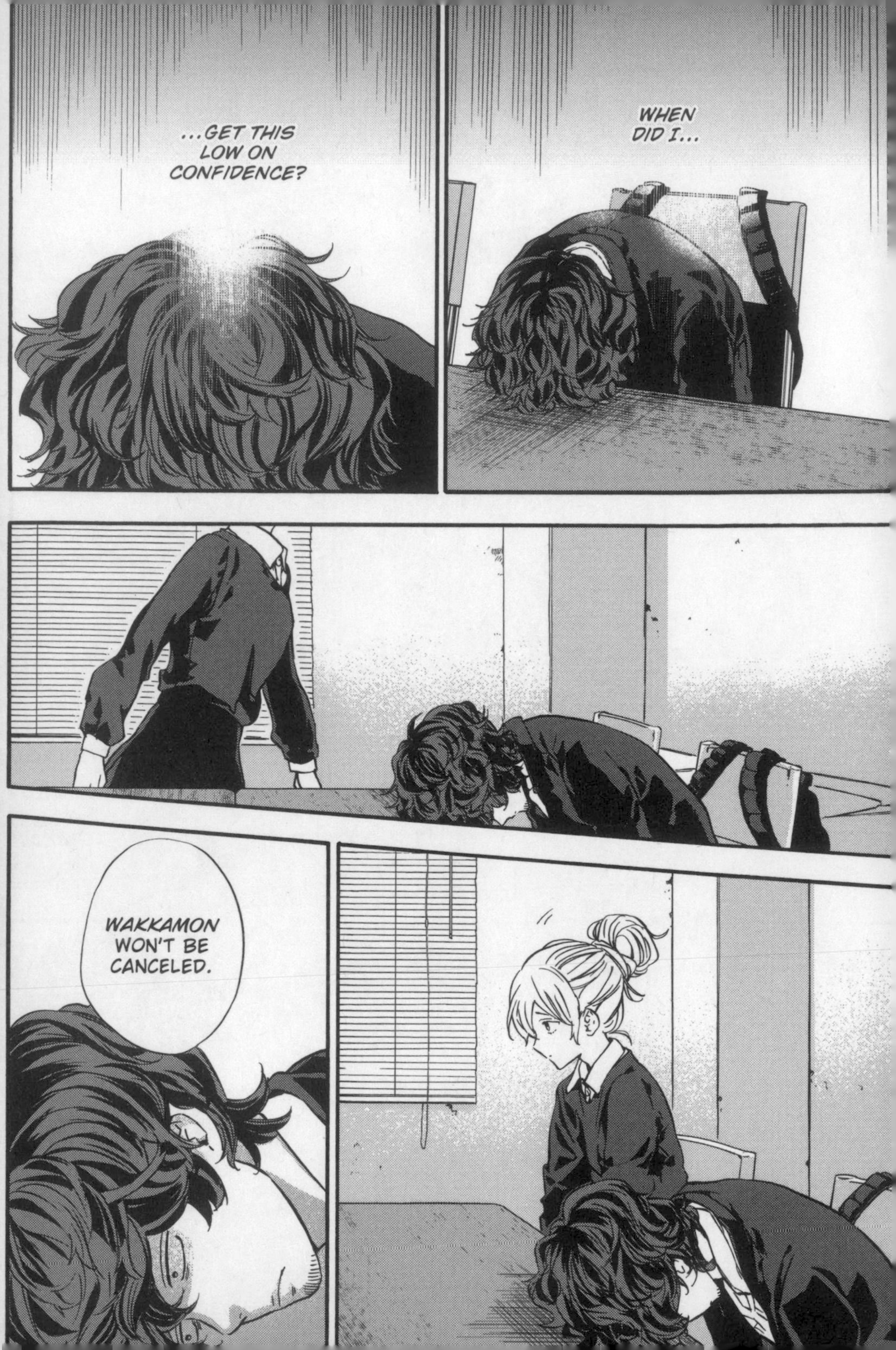
WHEN DID I...
...GET THIS LOW ON CONFIDENCE?
WAKKAMON WON'T BE CANCELED.

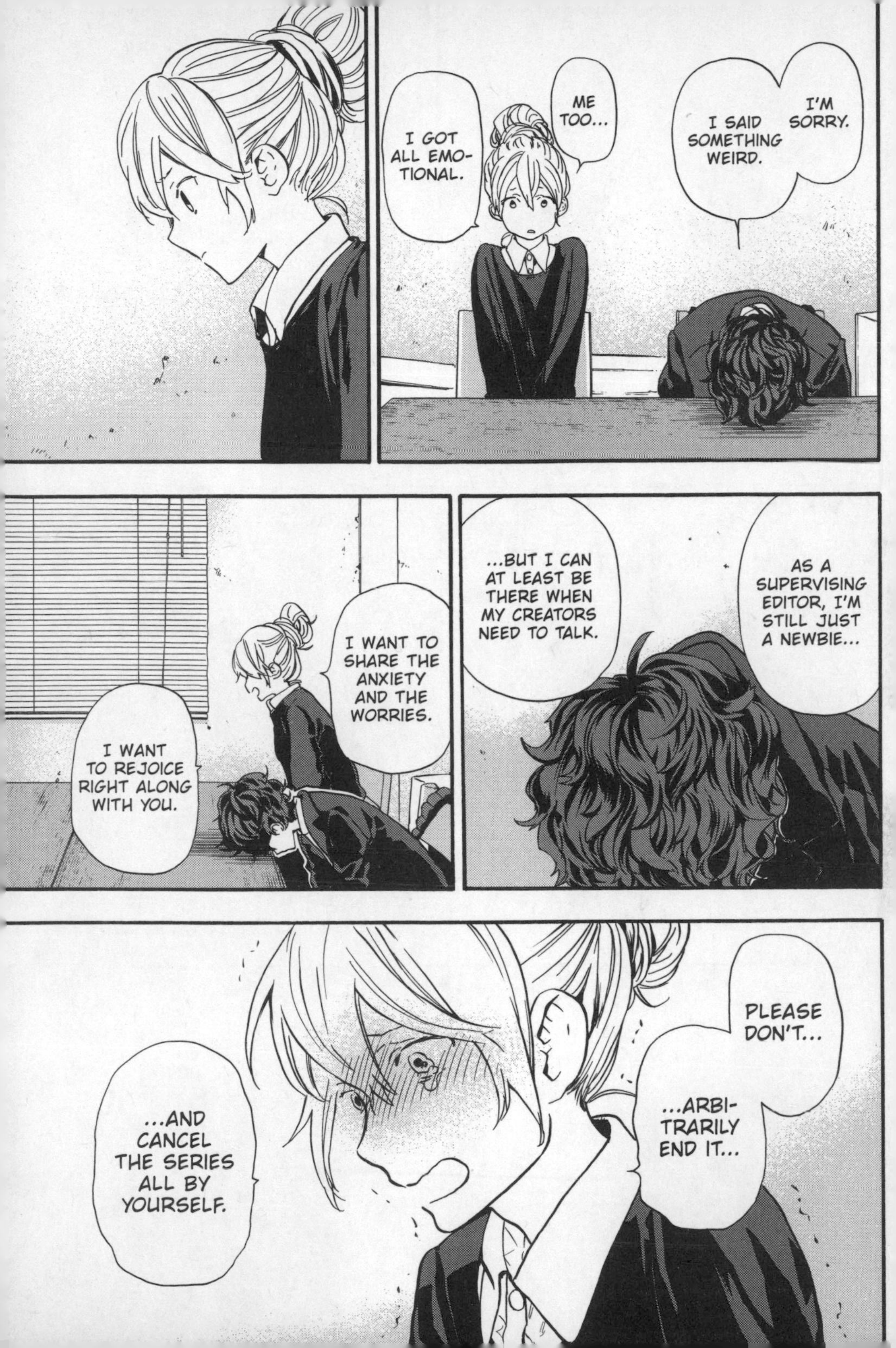
I'M SORRY.
I SAID SOMETHING WEIRD.
ME TOO...
I GOT ALL EMO-TIONAL.
AS A SUPERVISING EDITOR, I'M STILL JUST A NEWBIE...
...BUT I CAN AT LEAST BE THERE WHEN MY CREATORS NEED TO TALK.
I WANT TO SHARE THE ANXIETY AND THE WORRIES.
I WANT TO REJOICE RIGHT ALONG WITH YOU.
PLEASE DON'T...
...ARBI-TRARILY END IT...
...AND CANCEL THE SERIES ALL BY YOURSELF.

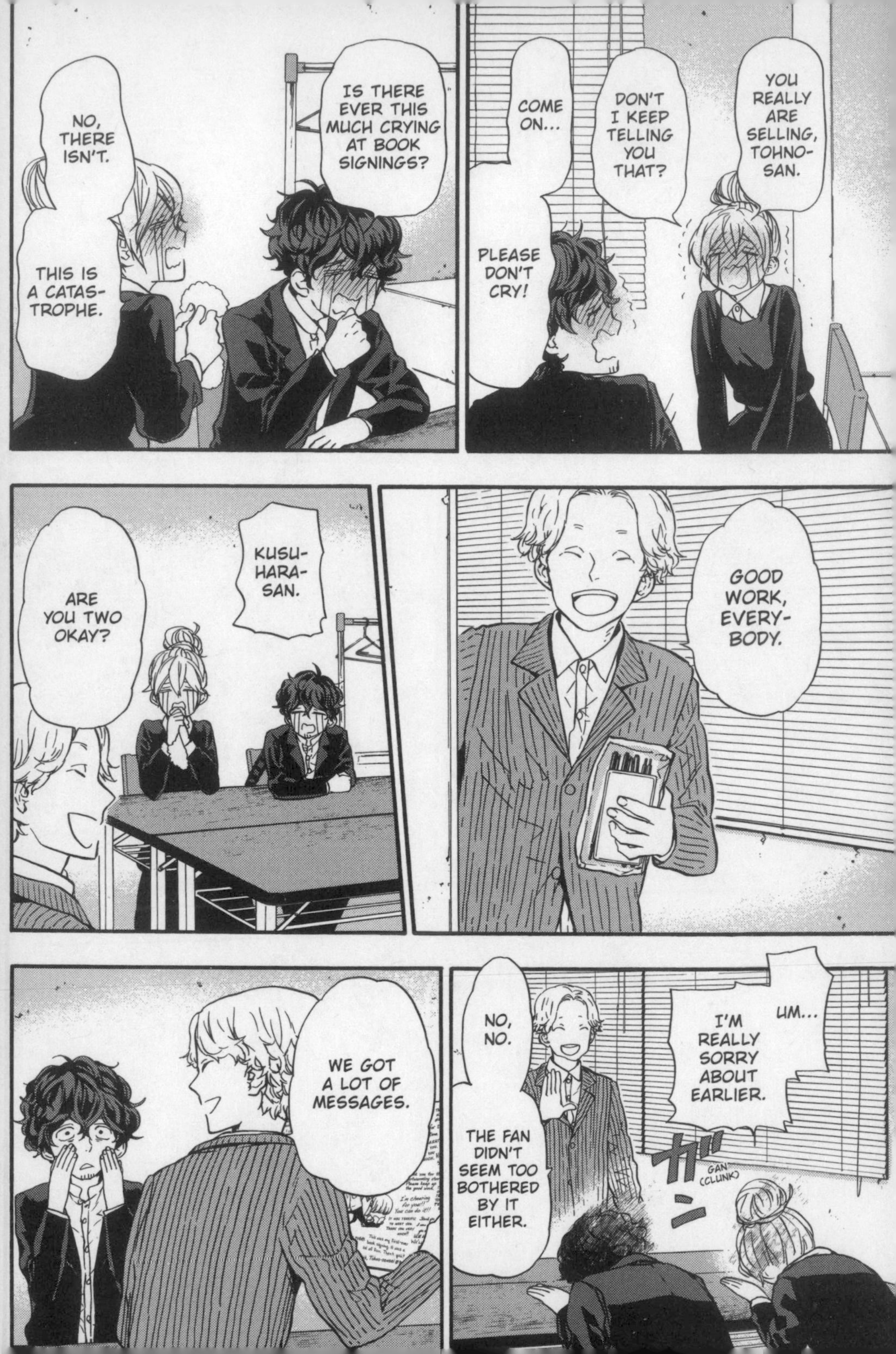
YOU REALLY ARE SELLING, TOHNO-SAN.
DON'T I KEEP TELLING YOU THAT?
COME ON...
PLEASE DON'T CRY!
IS THERE EVER THIS MUCH CRYING AT BOOK SIGNINGS?
NO, THERE ISN'T.
THIS IS A CATASTROPHE.
GOOD WORK, EVERYBODY.
KUSUHARA-SAN.
ARE YOU TWO OKAY?
UM...
I'M REALLY SORRY ABOUT EARLIER.
GAN (CLUNK)
NO, NO.
THE FAN DIDN'T SEEM TOO BOTHERED BY IT EITHER.
WE GOT A LOT OF MESSAGES.

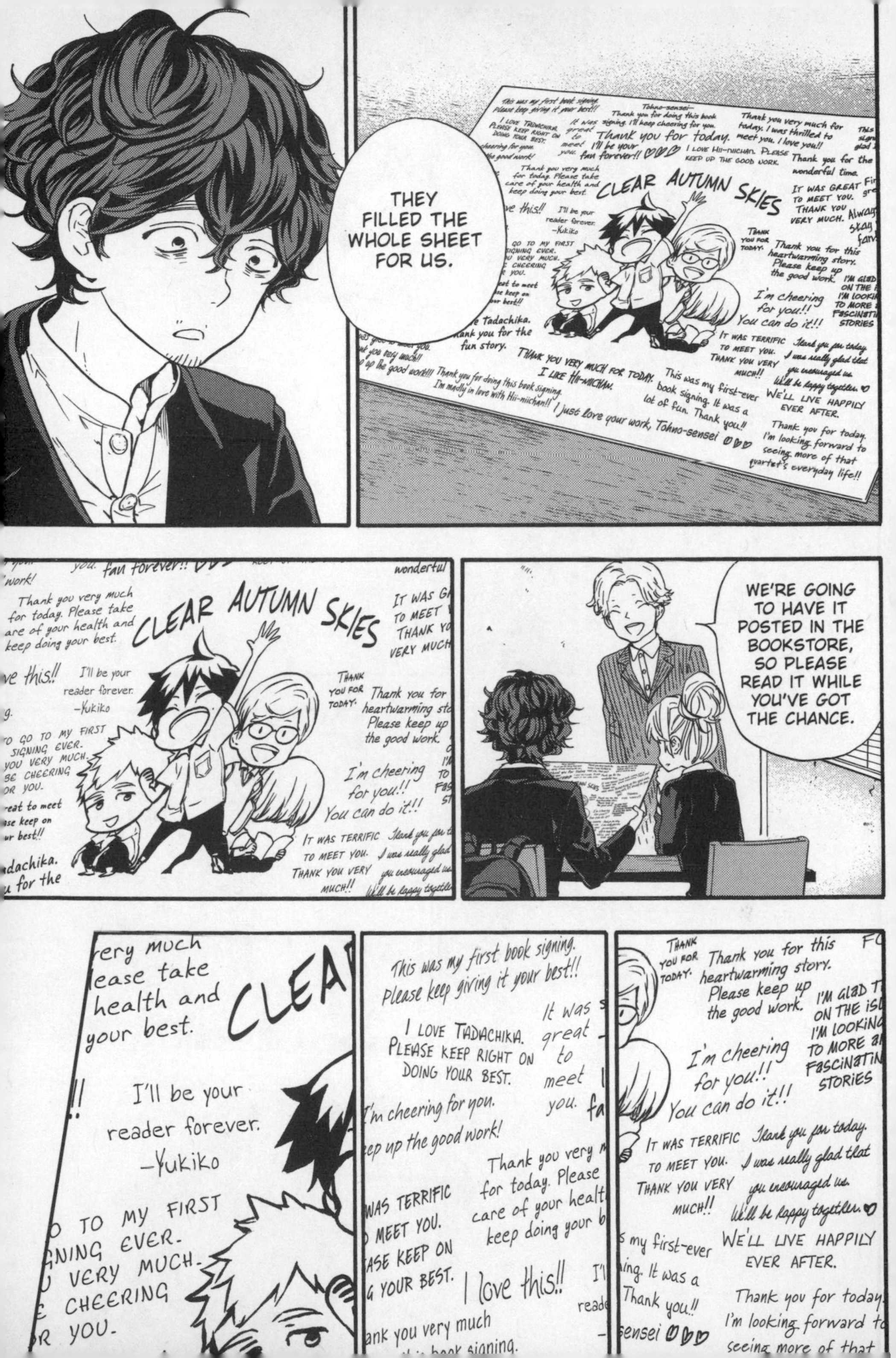

CLEAR AUTUMN SKIES
This was my first book signing. Please keep giving it your best!!
I LOVE TADACHIKA. PLEASE KEEP RIGHT ON DOING YOUR BEST.
It was great to meet you.
Tohno-sensei—Thank you for doing this book signing. I'll keep cheering for you.
Thank you for today.
I'll be your fan forever!!
I LOVE HII-NIICHAN. PLEASE KEEP UP THE GOOD WORK.
Thank you very much for today. I was thrilled to meet you. I love you!!
Thank you for the wonderful time.
IT WAS GREAT TO MEET YOU. THANK YOU VERY MUCH.
Thank you very much for today. Please take care of your health and keep doing your best.
I'll be your reader forever. —Yukiko
THANK YOU FOR TODAY.
Thank you for this heartwarming story. Please keep up the good work.
I'M GLAD TO MORE FASCINATING STORIES
I'm cheering for you!! You can do it!!
IT WAS TERRIFIC TO MEET YOU. THANK YOU VERY MUCH!!
Thank you for today. I was really glad that you encouraged us. We'll be happy together.
WE'LL LIVE HAPPILY EVER AFTER.
THANK YOU VERY MUCH FOR TODAY. I LIKE HII-NIICHAN.
Thank you for doing this book signing. I'm madly in love with Hii-niichan!!
This was my first-ever book signing. It was a lot of fun. Thank you!!
I just love your work, Tohno-sensei
Thank you for today. I'm looking forward to seeing more of that quartet's everyday life!!
I love this!!
THEY FILLED THE WHOLE SHEET FOR US.
WE'RE GOING TO HAVE IT POSTED IN THE BOOKSTORE, SO PLEASE READ IT WHILE YOU'VE GOT THE CHANCE.

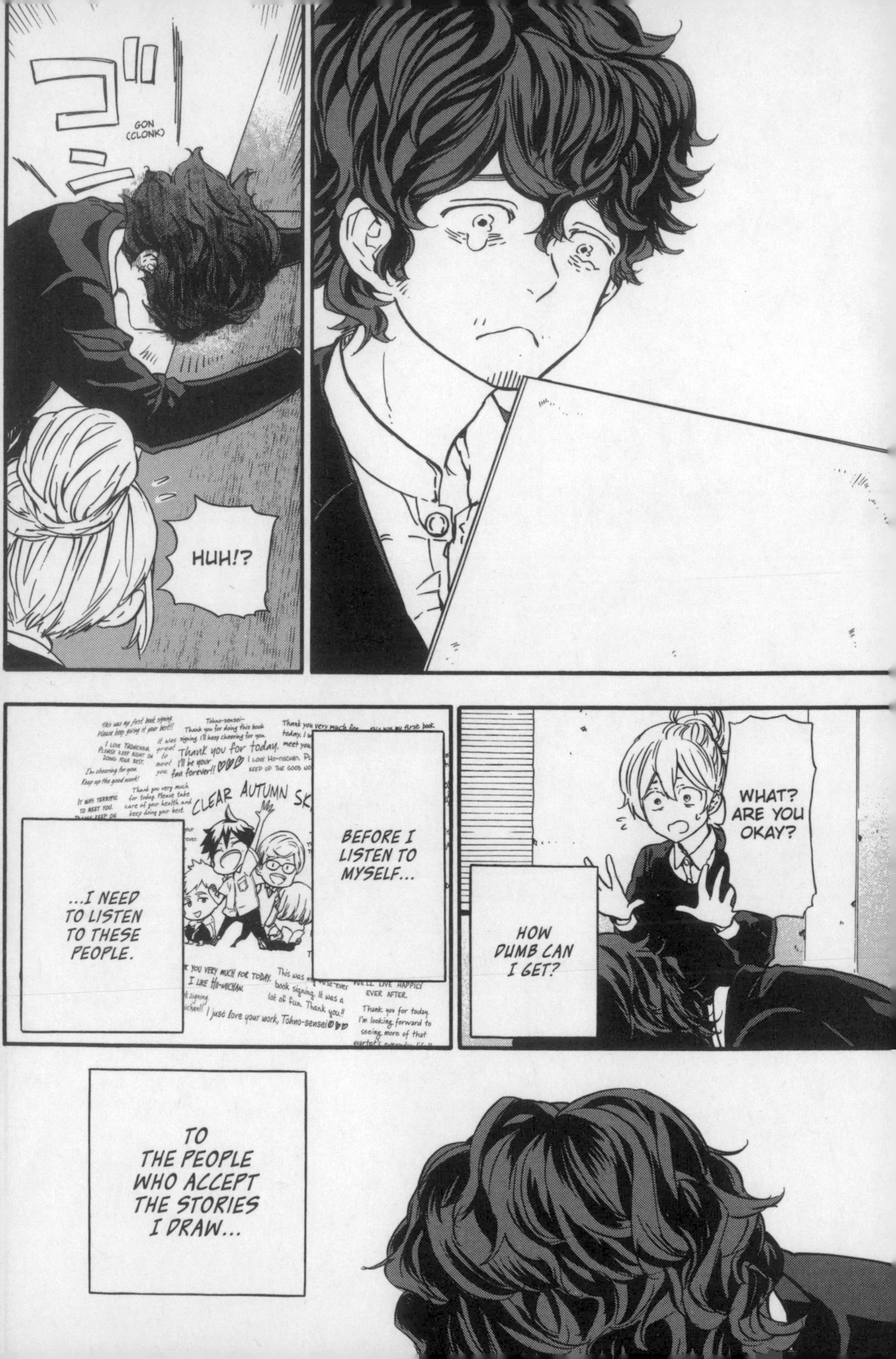
GON (CLONK)
HUH!?
WHAT? ARE YOU OKAY?
HOW DUMB CAN I GET?
BEFORE I LISTEN TO MYSELF...
Tohno-sensei— Thank you for doing this book signing. I'll keep cheering for you.
This was my first book signing. Please keep giving it your best!!
I LOVE TADACHIKA. PLEASE KEEP RIGHT ON DOING YOUR BEST.
I'm cheering for you. Keep up the good work!
Thank you for today. I'll be your fan forever!!
Thank you very much for today. Please take care of your health and keep doing your best.
I just love your work, Tohno-sensei
...I NEED TO LISTEN TO THESE PEOPLE.
TO THE PEOPLE WHO ACCEPT THE STORIES I DRAW...

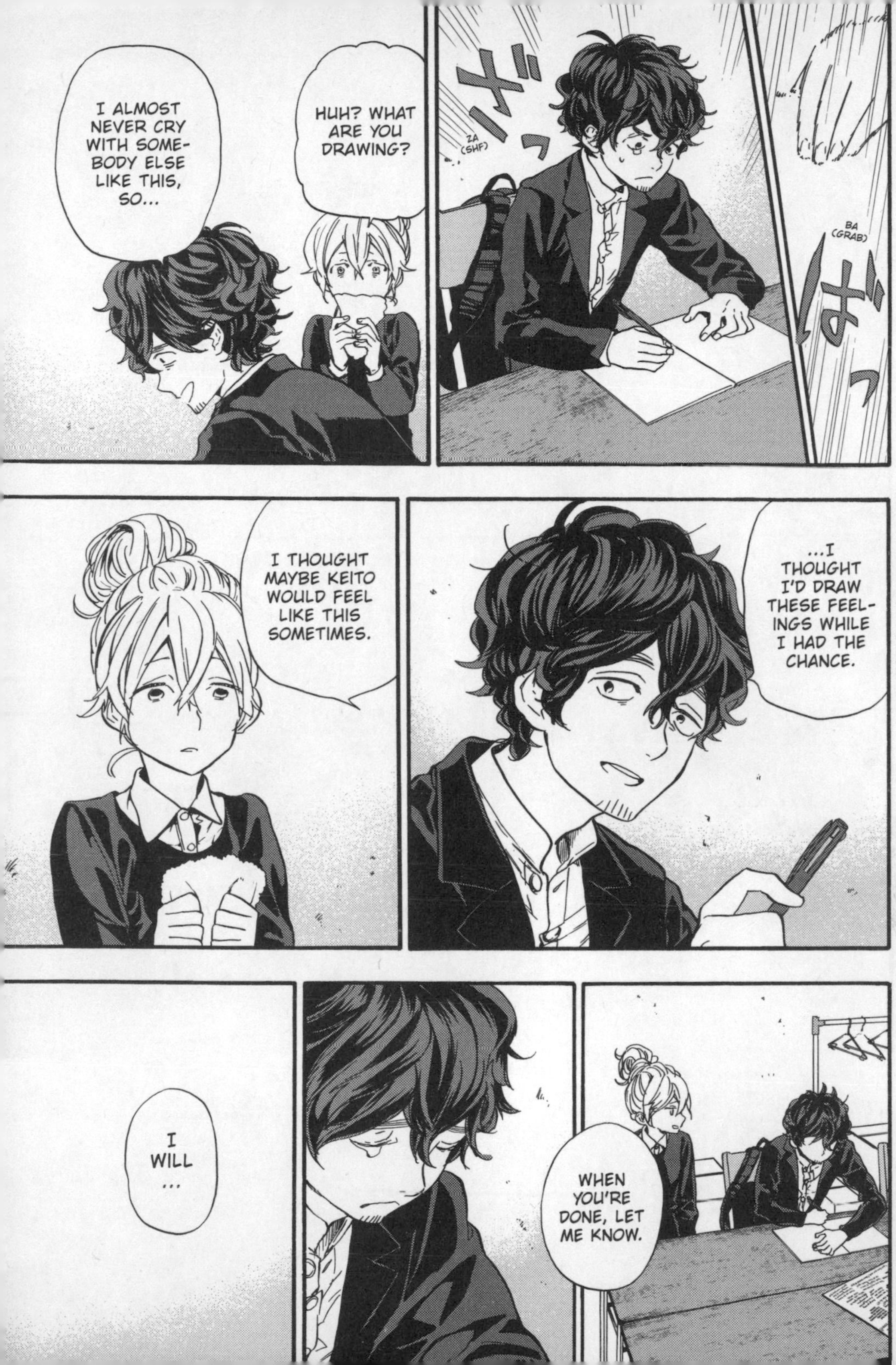
BA (GRAB)
ばっ
ZA (SHF)
ざっ
HUH? WHAT ARE YOU DRAWING?
I ALMOST NEVER CRY WITH SOME-BODY ELSE LIKE THIS, SO...
...I THOUGHT I'D DRAW THESE FEEL-INGS WHILE I HAD THE CHANCE.
I THOUGHT MAYBE KEITO WOULD FEEL LIKE THIS SOMETIMES.
WHEN YOU'RE DONE, LET ME KNOW.
I WILL ...

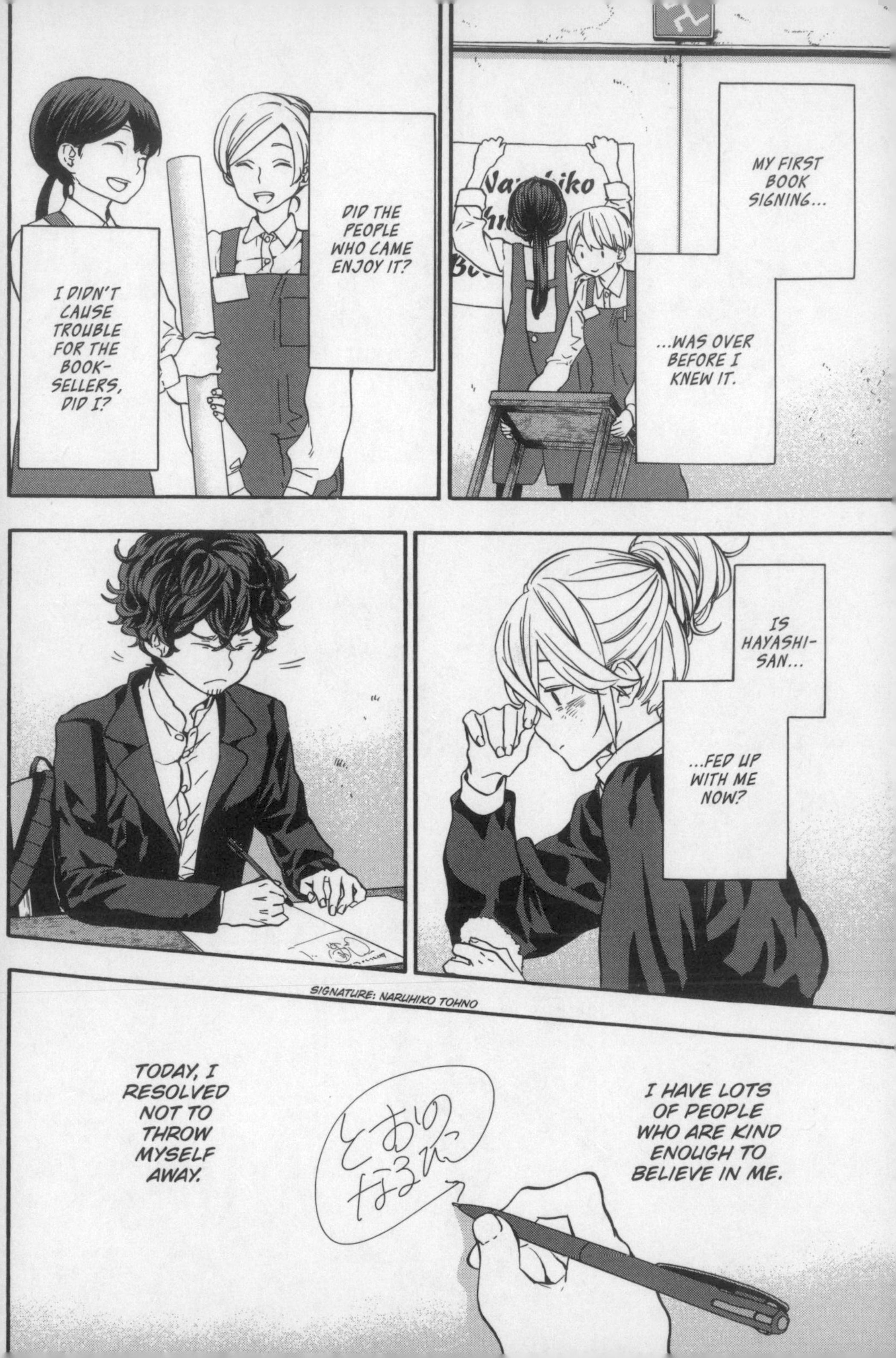
MY FIRST BOOK SIGNING...
...WAS OVER BEFORE I KNEW IT.
DID THE PEOPLE WHO CAME ENJOY IT?
I DIDN'T CAUSE TROUBLE FOR THE BOOK-SELLERS, DID I?
IS HAYASHI-SAN...
...FED UP WITH ME NOW?
SIGNATURE: NARUHIKO TOHNO
I HAVE LOTS OF PEOPLE WHO ARE KIND ENOUGH TO BELIEVE IN ME.
TODAY, I RESOLVED NOT TO THROW MYSELF AWAY.

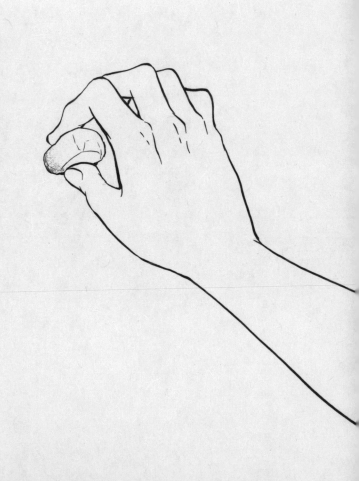

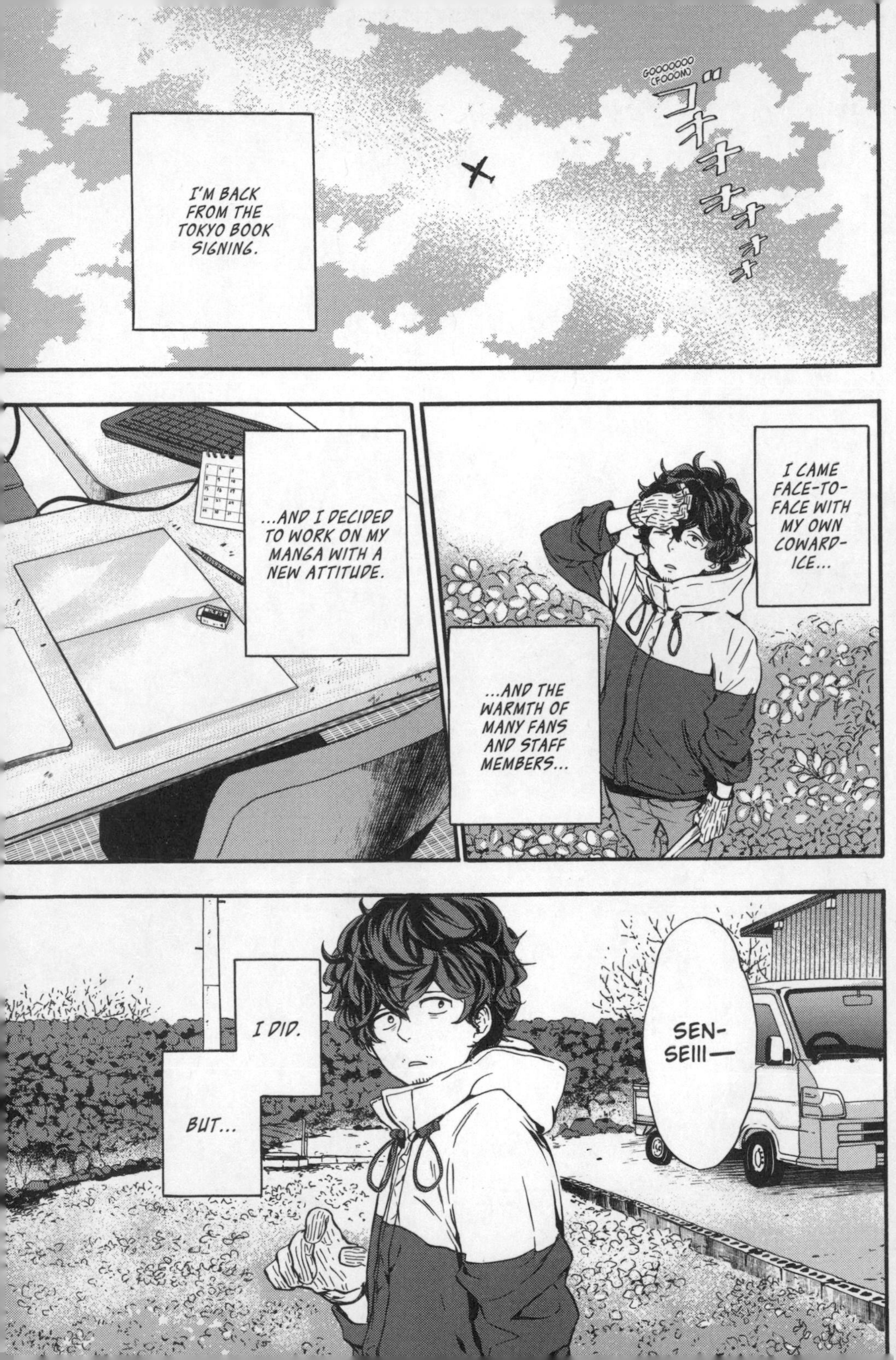
GOOOOOOO (FOOOM)
I'M BACK FROM THE TOKYO BOOK SIGNING.
I CAME FACE-TO-FACE WITH MY OWN COWARD-ICE...
...AND THE WARMTH OF MANY FANS AND STAFF MEMBERS...
...AND I DECIDED TO WORK ON MY MANGA WITH A NEW ATTITUDE.
SEN-SEIII—
I DID.
BUT...

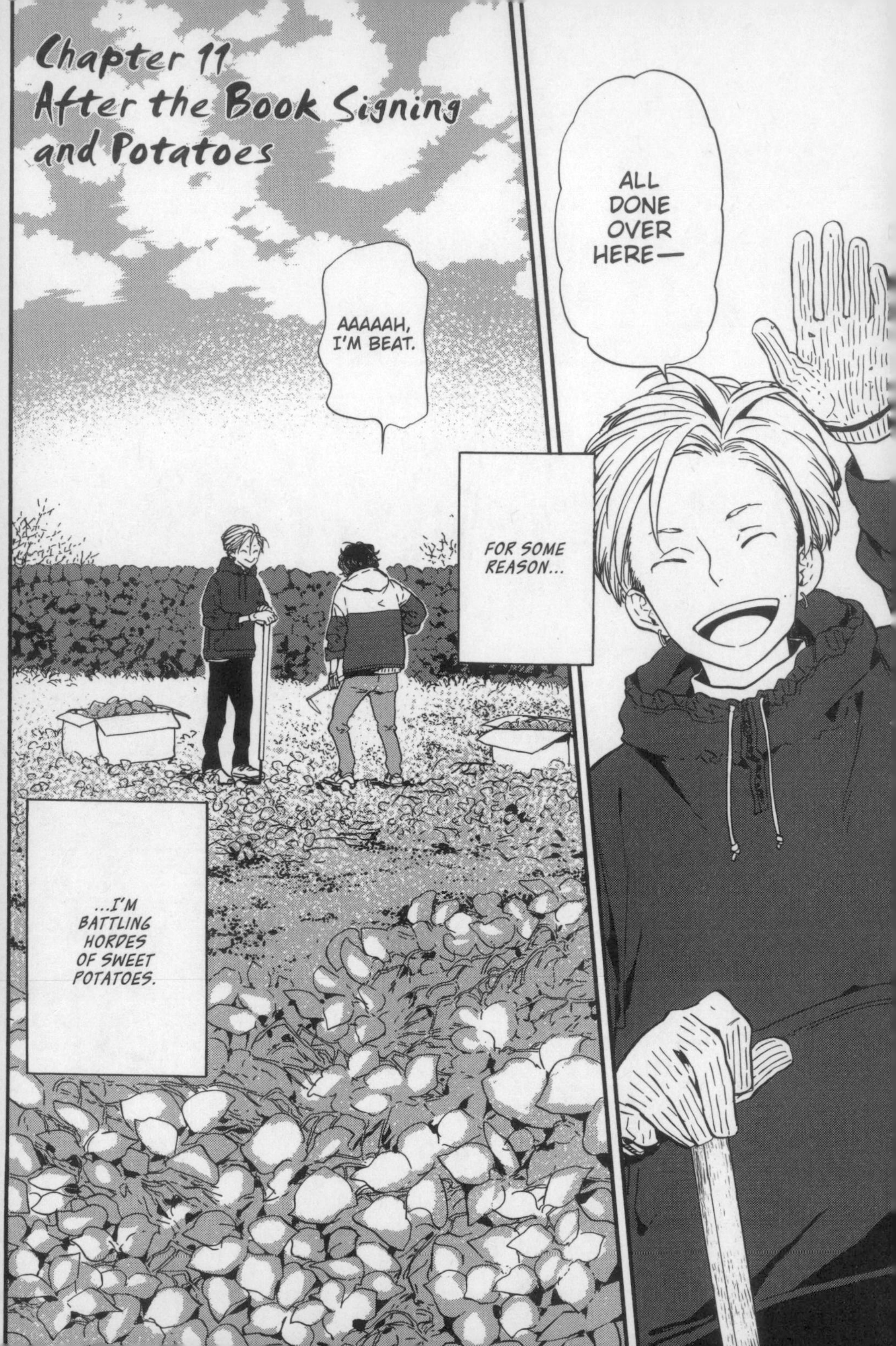
ALL DONE OVER HERE—
FOR SOME REASON...
Chapter 11 After the Book Signing and Potatoes
AAAAAH, I'M BEAT.
...I'M BATTLING HORDES OF SWEET POTATOES.

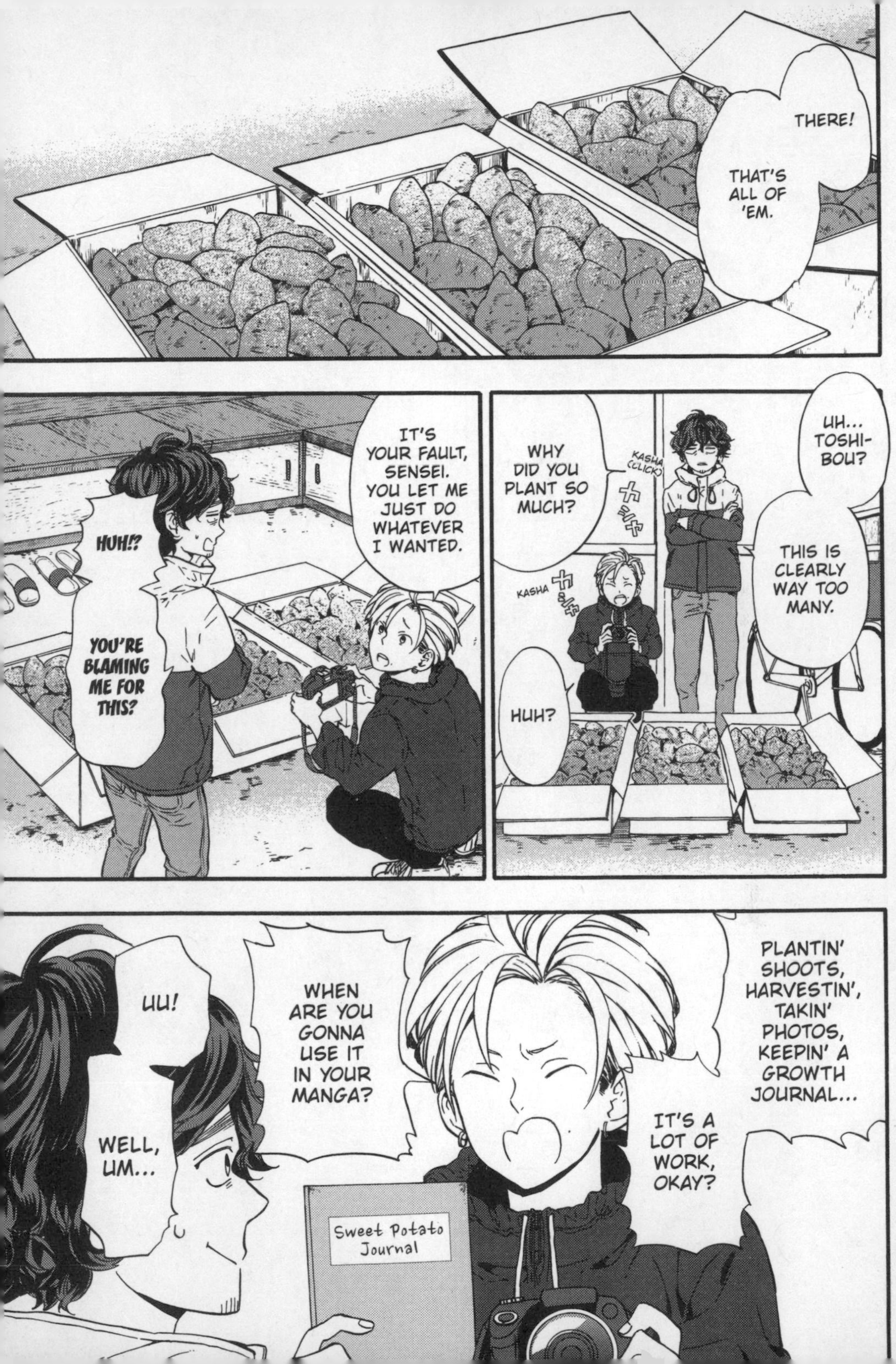
THERE!
THAT'S ALL OF 'EM.
UH... TOSHI-BOU?
THIS IS CLEARLY WAY TOO MANY.
WHY DID YOU PLANT SO MUCH?
KASHA (CLICK)
HUH?
KASHA
IT'S YOUR FAULT, SENSEI. YOU LET ME JUST DO WHATEVER I WANTED.
HUH!?
YOU'RE BLAMING ME FOR THIS?
PLANTIN' SHOOTS, HARVESTIN', TAKIN' PHOTOS, KEEPIN' A GROWTH JOURNAL...
IT'S A LOT OF WORK, OKAY?
WHEN ARE YOU GONNA USE IT IN YOUR MANGA?
UU!
WELL, UM...
Sweet Potato Journal

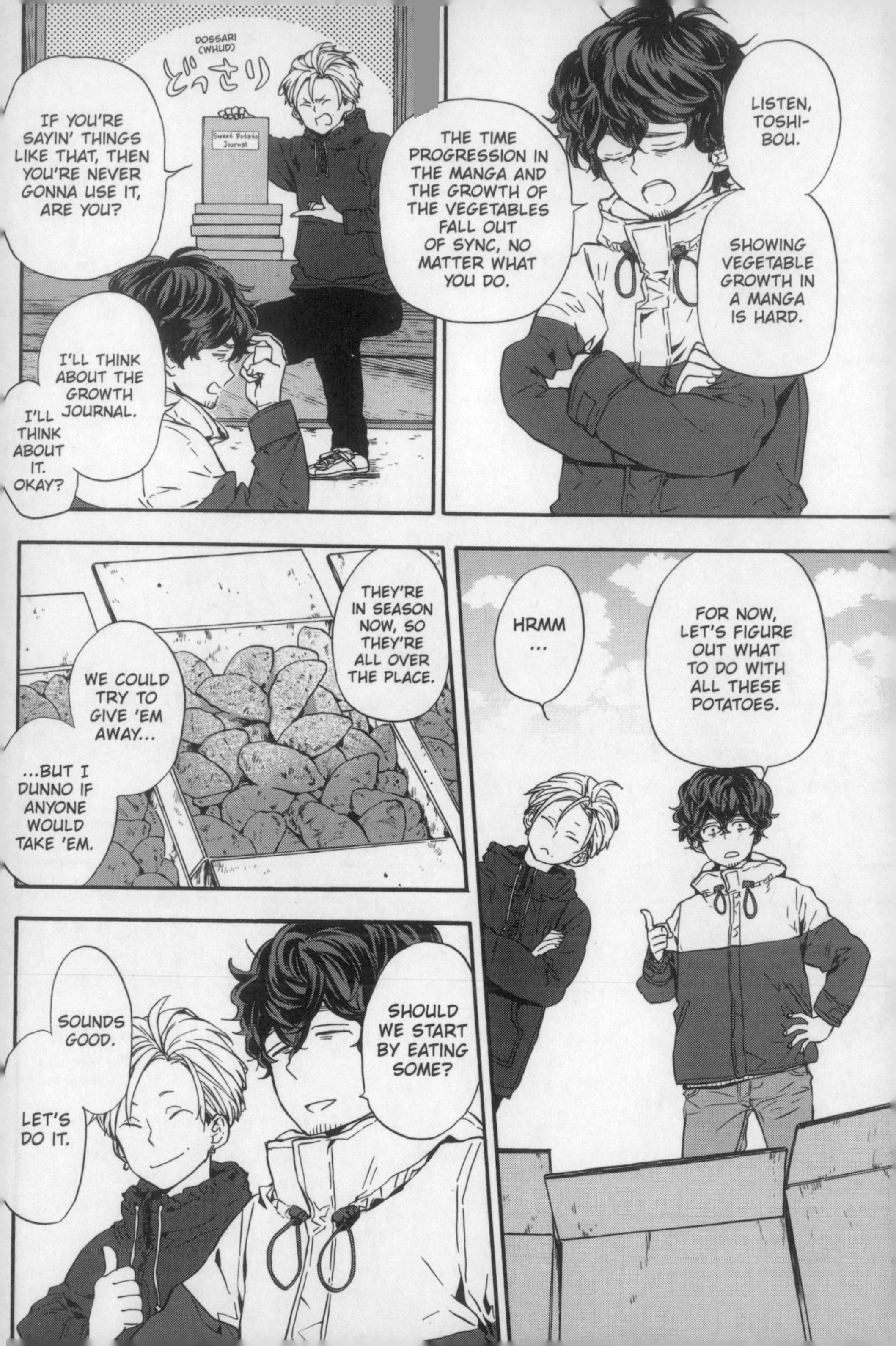
LISTEN, TOSHI-BOU.
SHOWING VEGETABLE GROWTH IN A MANGA IS HARD.
THE TIME PROGRESSION IN THE MANGA AND THE GROWTH OF THE VEGETABLES FALL OUT OF SYNC, NO MATTER WHAT YOU DO.
DOSSARI (WHUD)
どっさり
Sweet Potato Journal
IF YOU'RE SAYIN' THINGS LIKE THAT, THEN YOU'RE NEVER GONNA USE IT, ARE YOU?
I'LL THINK ABOUT THE GROWTH JOURNAL.
I'LL THINK ABOUT IT. OKAY?
FOR NOW, LET'S FIGURE OUT WHAT TO DO WITH ALL THESE POTATOES.
HRMM ...
THEY'RE IN SEASON NOW, SO THEY'RE ALL OVER THE PLACE.
WE COULD TRY TO GIVE 'EM AWAY...
...BUT I DUNNO IF ANYONE WOULD TAKE 'EM.
SHOULD WE START BY EATING SOME?
SOUNDS GOOD.
LET'S DO IT.

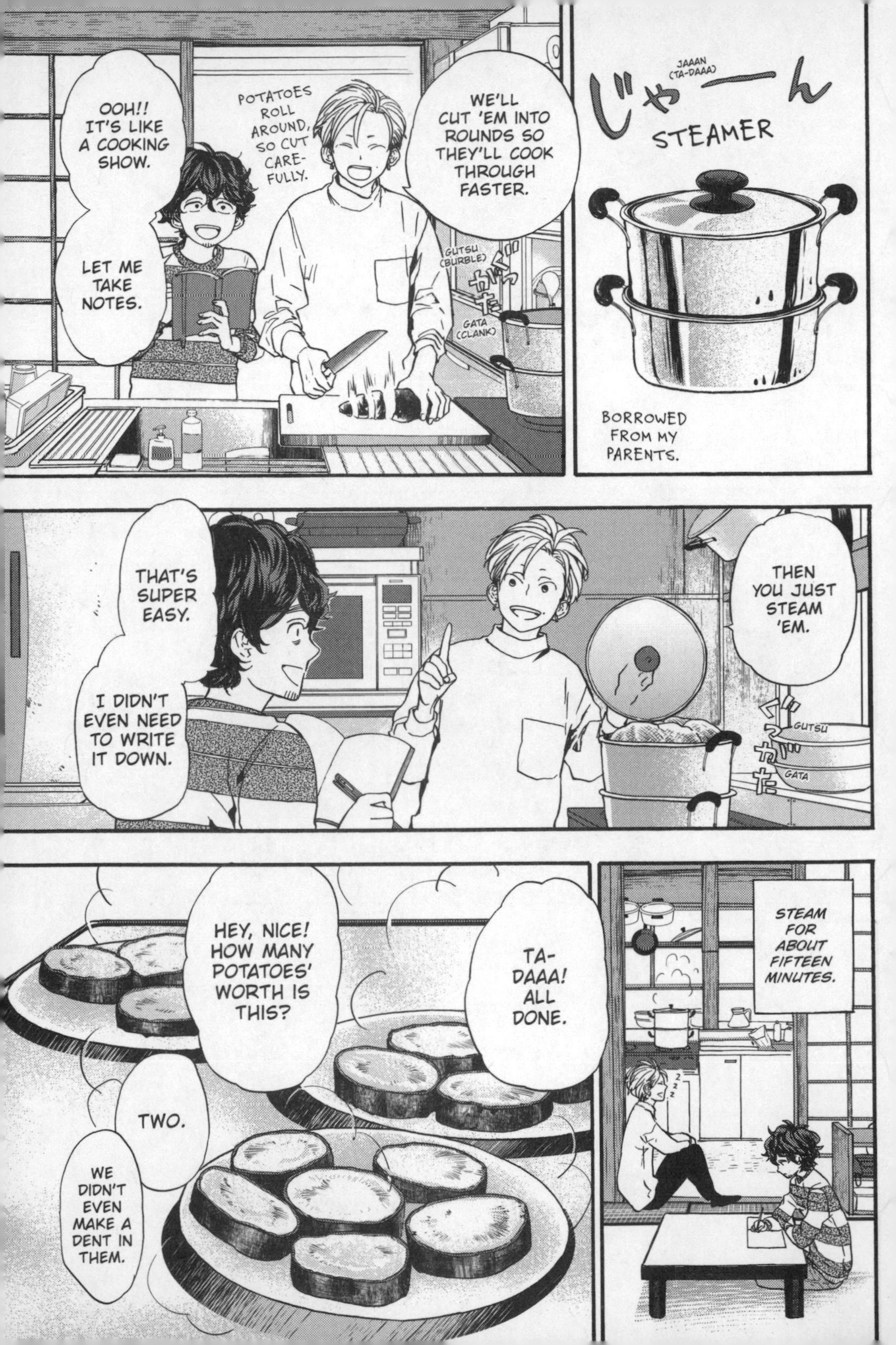
JAAAN (TA-DAAA)
じゃーん
STEAMER
BORROWED FROM MY PARENTS.
WE'LL CUT 'EM INTO ROUNDS SO THEY'LL COOK THROUGH FASTER.
POTATOES ROLL AROUND, SO CUT CAREFULLY.
GUTSU (BURBLE)
GATA (CLANK)
OOH!! IT'S LIKE A COOKING SHOW.
LET ME TAKE NOTES.
THEN YOU JUST STEAM 'EM.
GUTSU
GATA
THAT'S SUPER EASY.
I DIDN'T EVEN NEED TO WRITE IT DOWN.
STEAM FOR ABOUT FIFTEEN MINUTES.
TA-DAAA! ALL DONE.
HEY, NICE! HOW MANY POTATOES' WORTH IS THIS?
TWO.
WE DIDN'T EVEN MAKE A DENT IN THEM.

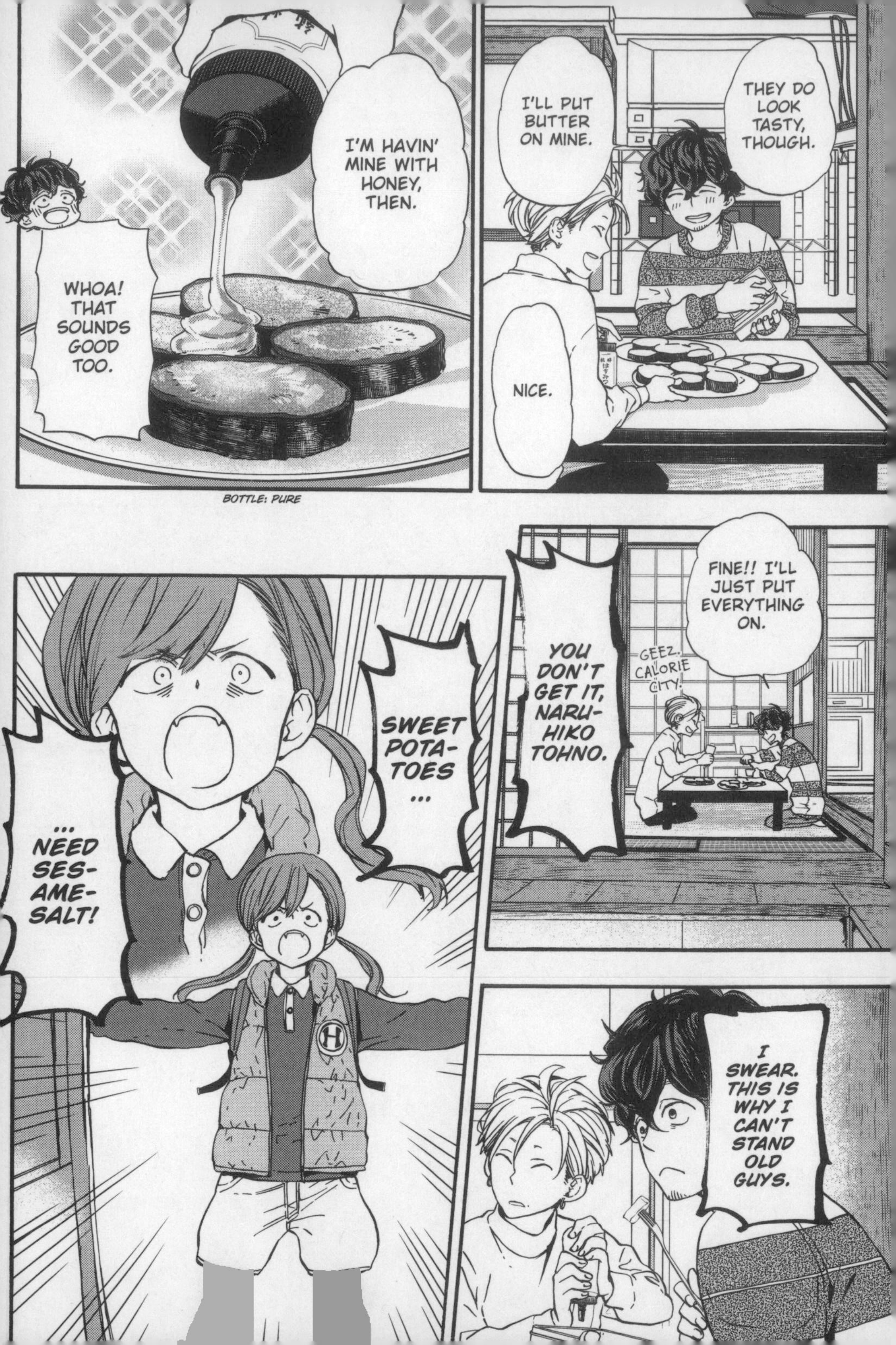
THEY DO LOOK TASTY, THOUGH.
I'LL PUT BUTTER ON MINE.
NICE.
I'M HAVIN' MINE WITH HONEY, THEN.
WHOA! THAT SOUNDS GOOD TOO.
BOTTLE: PURE
FINE!! I'LL JUST PUT EVERYTHING ON.
GEEZ. CALORIE CITY.
YOU DON'T GET IT, NARUHIKO TOHNO.
I SWEAR. THIS IS WHY I CAN'T STAND OLD GUYS.
SWEET POTATOES ...
... NEED SESAME-SALT!

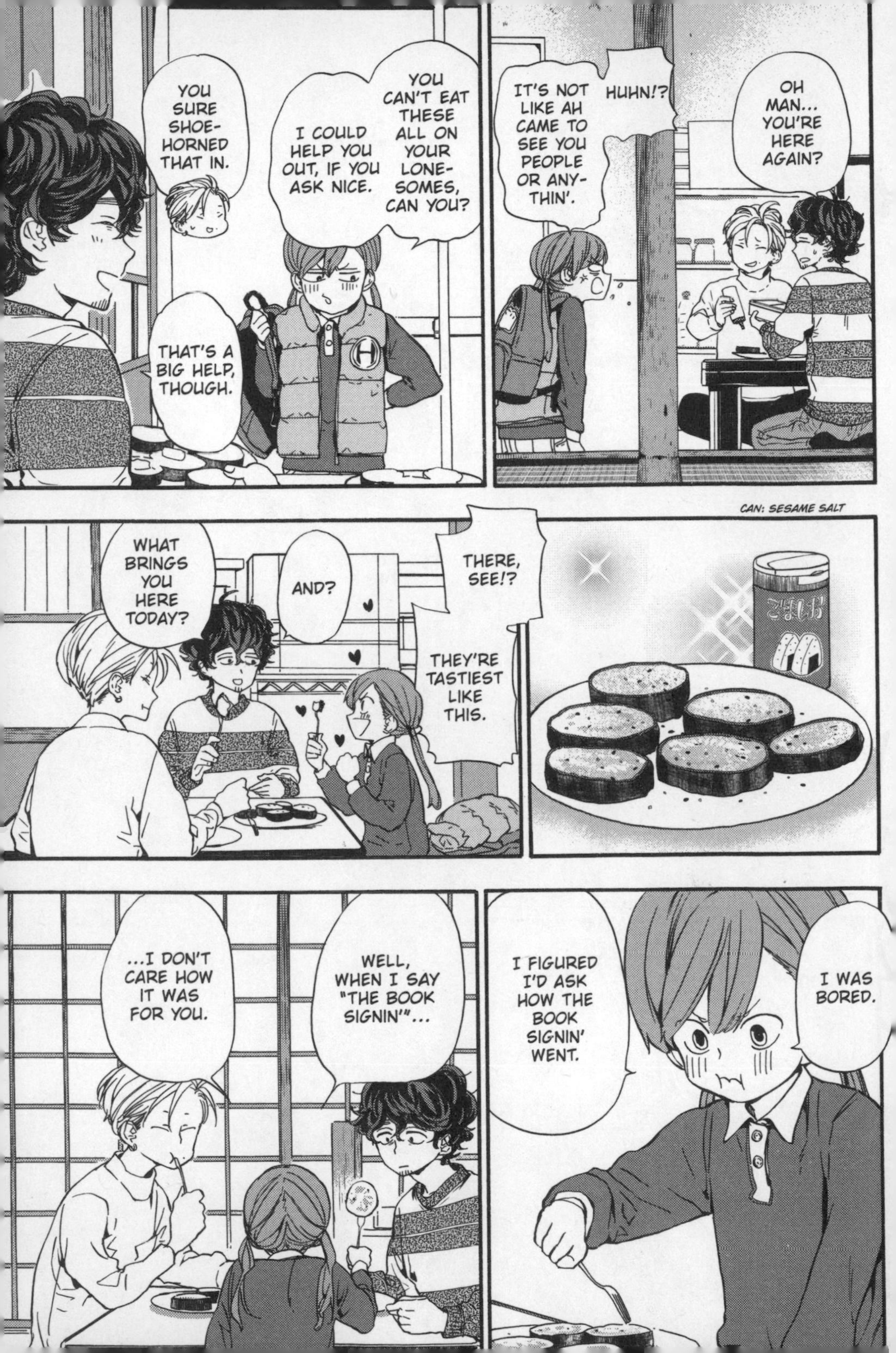
OH MAN... YOU'RE HERE AGAIN?
HUHN!?
IT'S NOT LIKE AH CAME TO SEE YOU PEOPLE OR ANYTHIN'.
YOU CAN'T EAT THESE ALL ON YOUR LONESOMES, CAN YOU?
I COULD HELP YOU OUT, IF YOU ASK NICE.
YOU SURE SHOEHORNED THAT IN.
THAT'S A BIG HELP, THOUGH.
CAN: SESAME SALT
ごましお
THERE, SEE!?
THEY'RE TASTIEST LIKE THIS.
AND?
WHAT BRINGS YOU HERE TODAY?
I WAS BORED.
I FIGURED I'D ASK HOW THE BOOK SIGNIN' WENT.
WELL, WHEN I SAY "THE BOOK SIGNIN'"...
...I DON'T CARE HOW IT WAS FOR YOU.

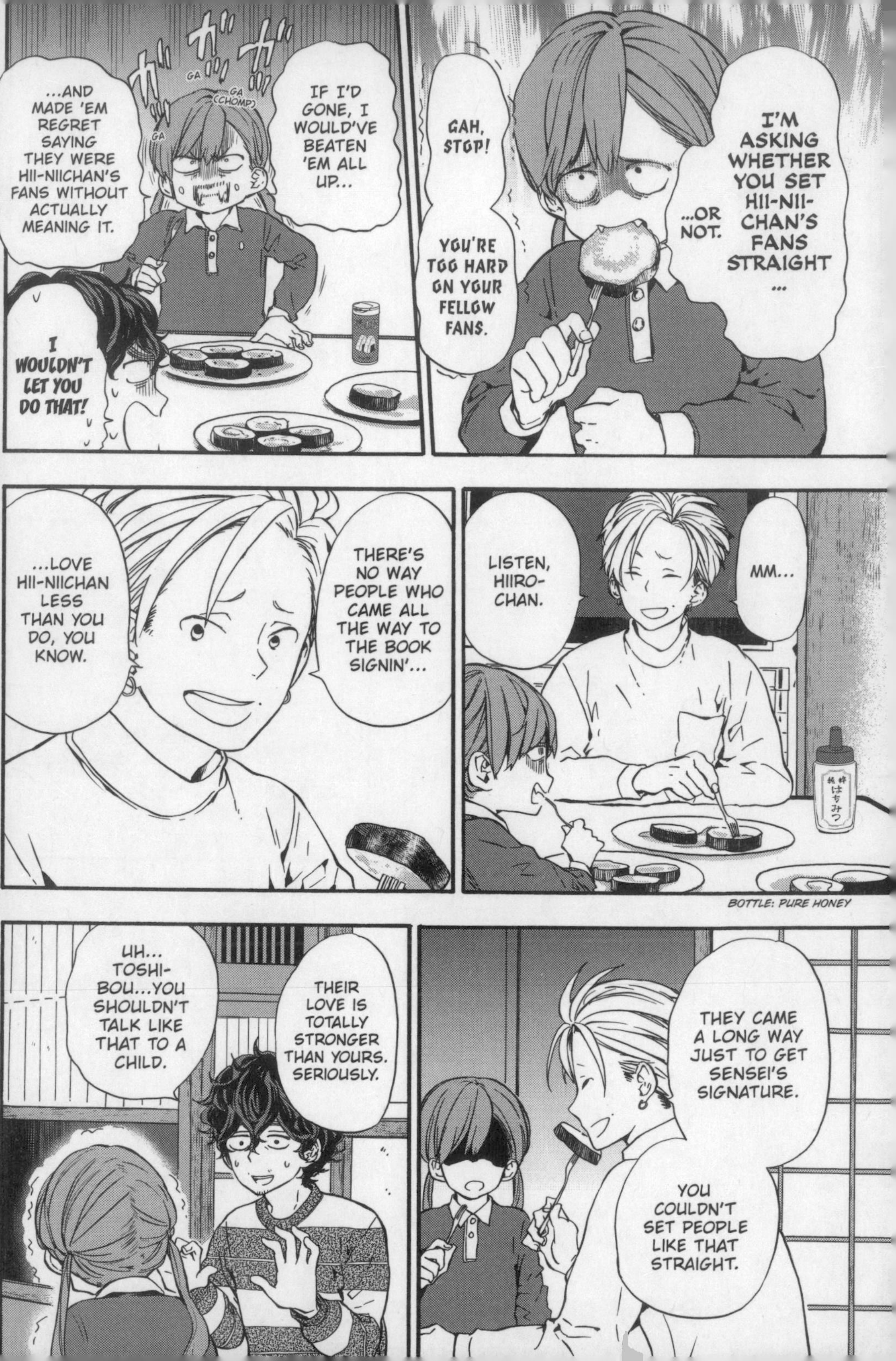
I'M ASKING WHETHER YOU SET HII-NIICHAN'S FANS STRAIGHT...
...OR NOT.
GAH, STOP!
YOU'RE TOO HARD ON YOUR FELLOW FANS.
IF I'D GONE, I WOULD'VE BEATEN 'EM ALL UP...
GA
GA (CHOMP)
GA
...AND MADE 'EM REGRET SAYING THEY WERE HII-NIICHAN'S FANS WITHOUT ACTUALLY MEANING IT.
I WOULDN'T LET YOU DO THAT!
MM...
LISTEN, HIIRO-CHAN.
BOTTLE: PURE HONEY
THERE'S NO WAY PEOPLE WHO CAME ALL THE WAY TO THE BOOK SIGNIN'...
...LOVE HII-NIICHAN LESS THAN YOU DO, YOU KNOW.
THEY CAME A LONG WAY JUST TO GET SENSEI'S SIGNATURE.
YOU COULDN'T SET PEOPLE LIKE THAT STRAIGHT.
THEIR LOVE IS TOTALLY STRONGER THAN YOURS. SERIOUSLY.
UH... TOSHI-BOU...YOU SHOULDN'T TALK LIKE THAT TO A CHILD.

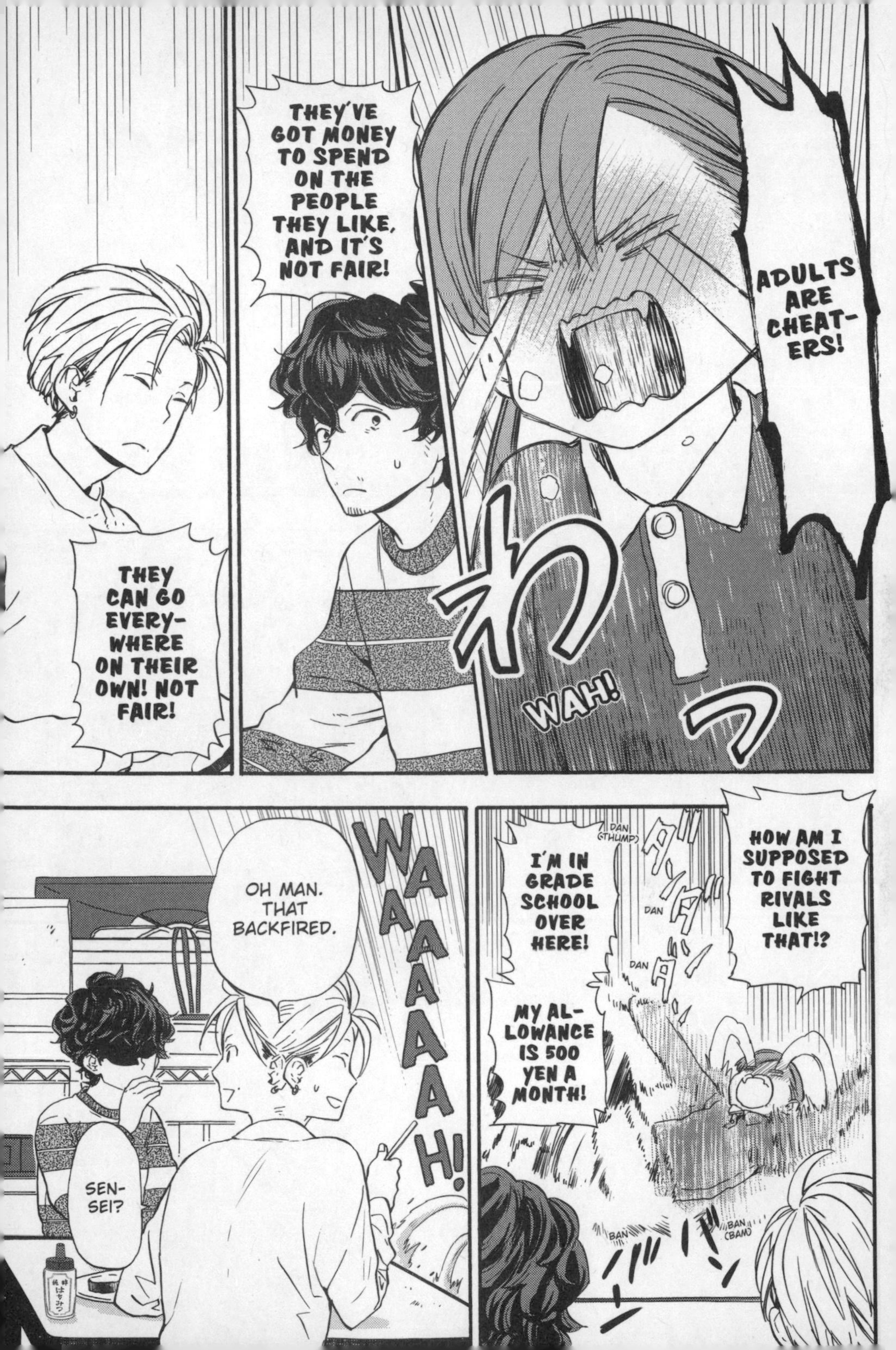
ADULTS ARE CHEAT-ERS!
WAH!
THEY'VE GOT MONEY TO SPEND ON THE PEOPLE THEY LIKE, AND IT'S NOT FAIR!
THEY CAN GO EVERY-WHERE ON THEIR OWN! NOT FAIR!
HOW AM I SUPPOSED TO FIGHT RIVALS LIKE THAT!?
DAN (THUMP)
DAN
DAN
I'M IN GRADE SCHOOL OVER HERE!
MY AL-LOWANCE IS 500 YEN A MONTH!
BAN (BAN)
BAN
WAAAAAAAH!
OH MAN. THAT BACKFIRED.
SEN-SEI?

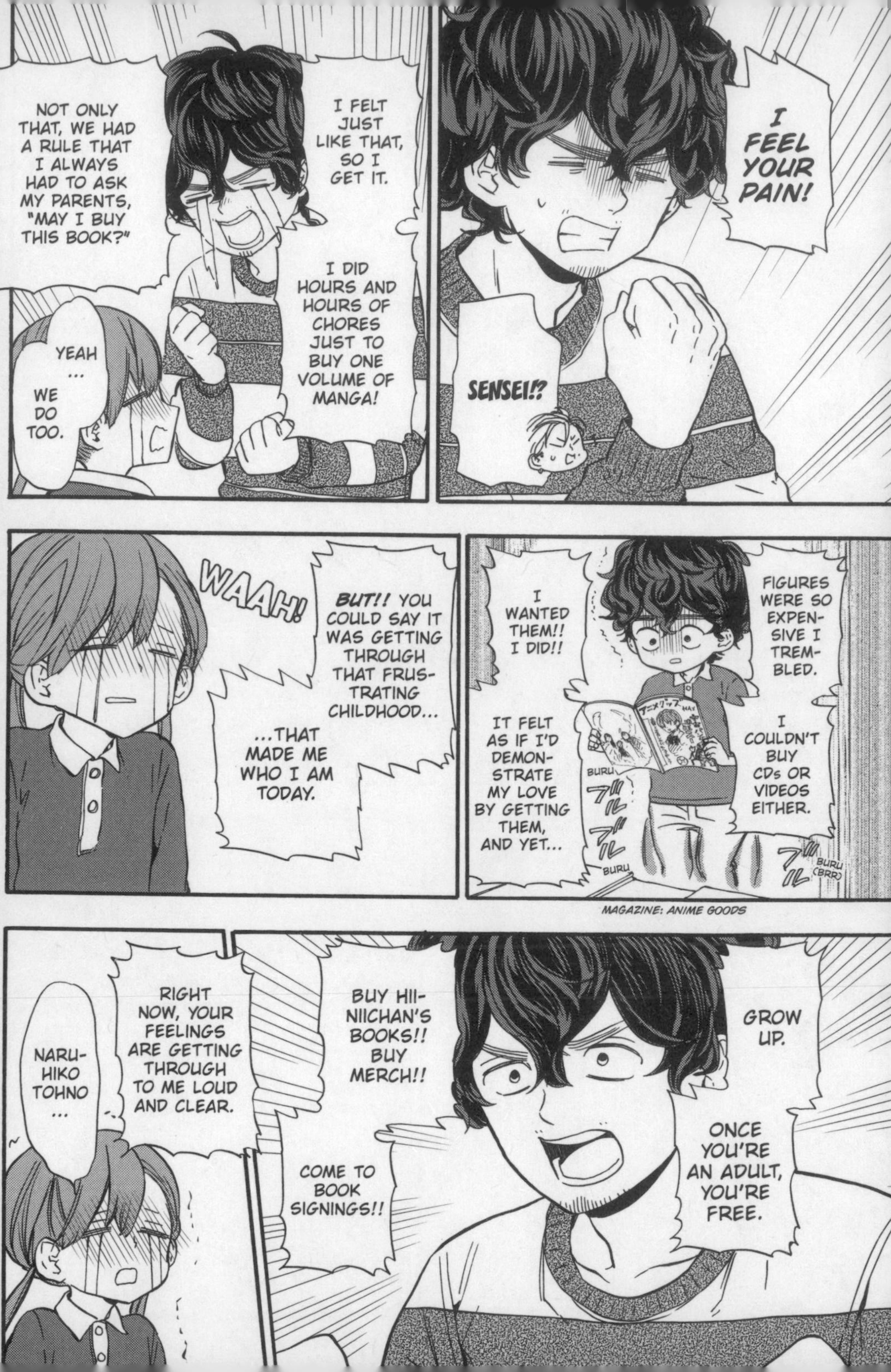

I FEEL YOUR PAIN!
SENSEI!?
I FELT JUST LIKE THAT, SO I GET IT.
NOT ONLY THAT, WE HAD A RULE THAT I ALWAYS HAD TO ASK MY PARENTS, "MAY I BUY THIS BOOK?"
I DID HOURS AND HOURS OF CHORES JUST TO BUY ONE VOLUME OF MANGA!
YEAH... WE DO TOO.
FIGURES WERE SO EXPEN-SIVE I TREM-BLED.
I WANTED THEM!! I DID!!
I COULDN'T BUY CDs OR VIDEOS EITHER.
IT FELT AS IF I'D DEMON-STRATE MY LOVE BY GETTING THEM, AND YET...
BURU
BURU
BURU (BRR)
MAGAZINE: ANIME GOODS
WAAAH!
BUT!! YOU COULD SAY IT WAS GETTING THROUGH THAT FRUS-TRATING CHILDHOOD...
...THAT MADE ME WHO I AM TODAY.
GROW UP.
ONCE YOU'RE AN ADULT, YOU'RE FREE.
BUY HII-NIICHAN'S BOOKS!! BUY MERCH!!
COME TO BOOK SIGNINGS!!
RIGHT NOW, YOUR FEELINGS ARE GETTING THROUGH TO ME LOUD AND CLEAR.
NARU-HIKO TOHNO...

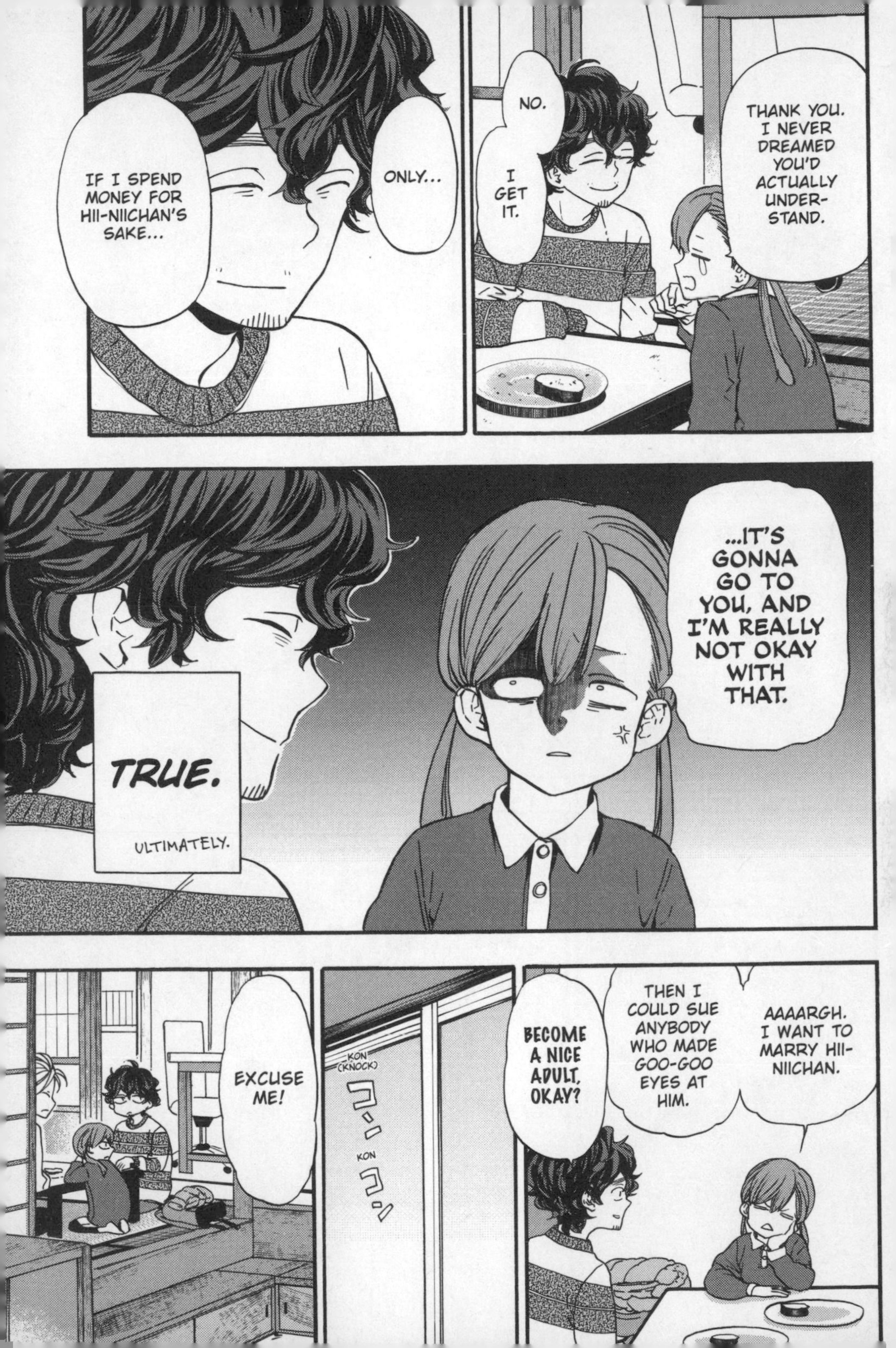
THANK YOU. I NEVER DREAMED YOU'D ACTUALLY UNDER-STAND.
NO.
I GET IT.
ONLY...
IF I SPEND MONEY FOR HII-NIICHAN'S SAKE...
...IT'S GONNA GO TO YOU, AND I'M REALLY NOT OKAY WITH THAT.
TRUE.
ULTIMATELY.
AAAARGH. I WANT TO MARRY HII-NIICHAN.
THEN I COULD SUE ANYBODY WHO MADE GOO-GOO EYES AT HIM.
BECOME A NICE ADULT, OKAY?
KON (KNOCK)
KON
EXCUSE ME!

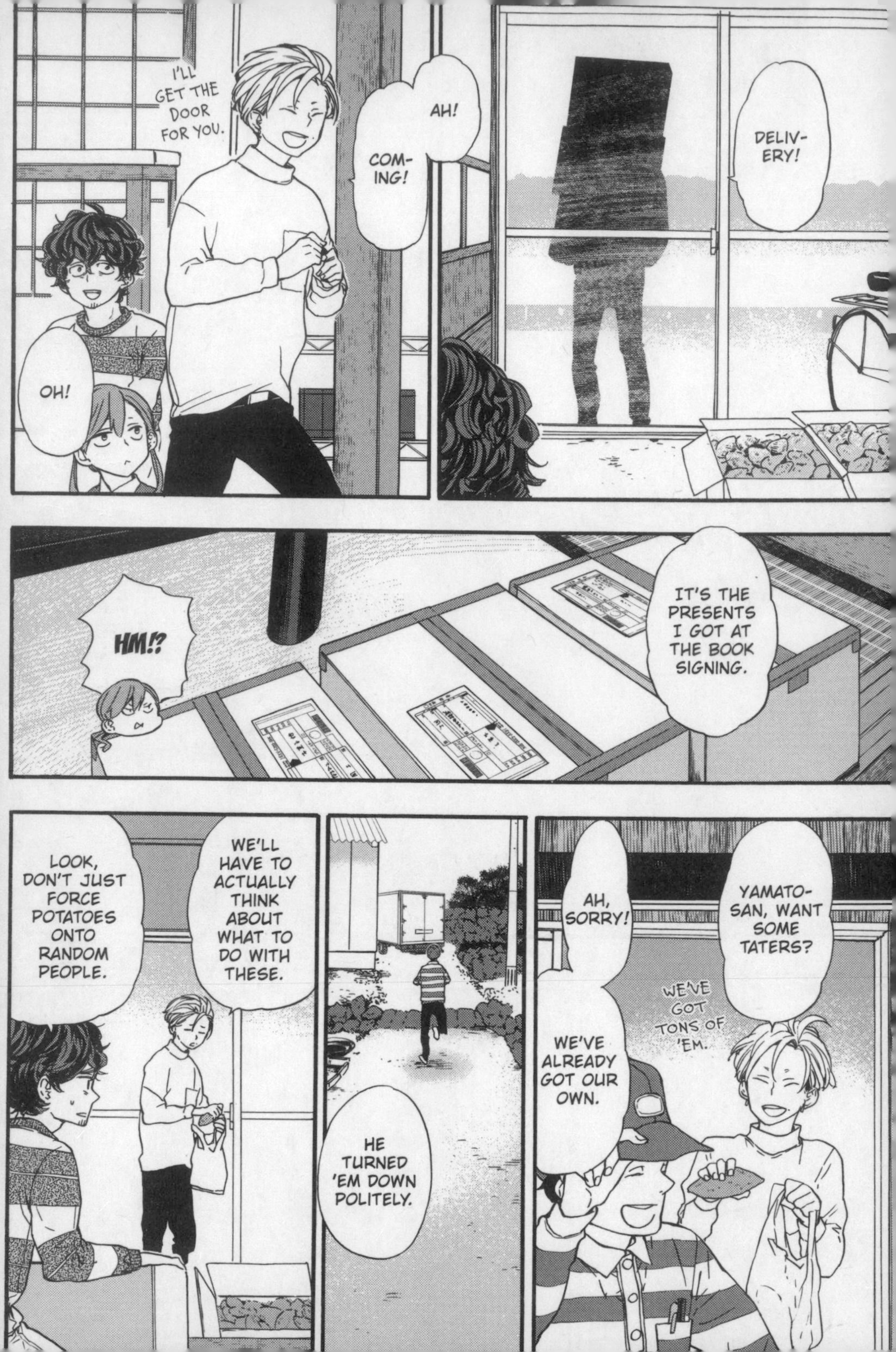
DELIV-ERY!
AH!
COM-ING!
I'LL GET THE DOOR FOR YOU.
OH!
IT'S THE PRESENTS I GOT AT THE BOOK SIGNING.
HM!?
YAMATO-SAN, WANT SOME TATERS?
WE'VE GOT TONS OF 'EM.
AH, SORRY!
WE'VE ALREADY GOT OUR OWN.
HE TURNED 'EM DOWN POLITELY.
WE'LL HAVE TO ACTUALLY THINK ABOUT WHAT TO DO WITH THESE.
LOOK, DON'T JUST FORCE POTATOES ONTO RANDOM PEOPLE.

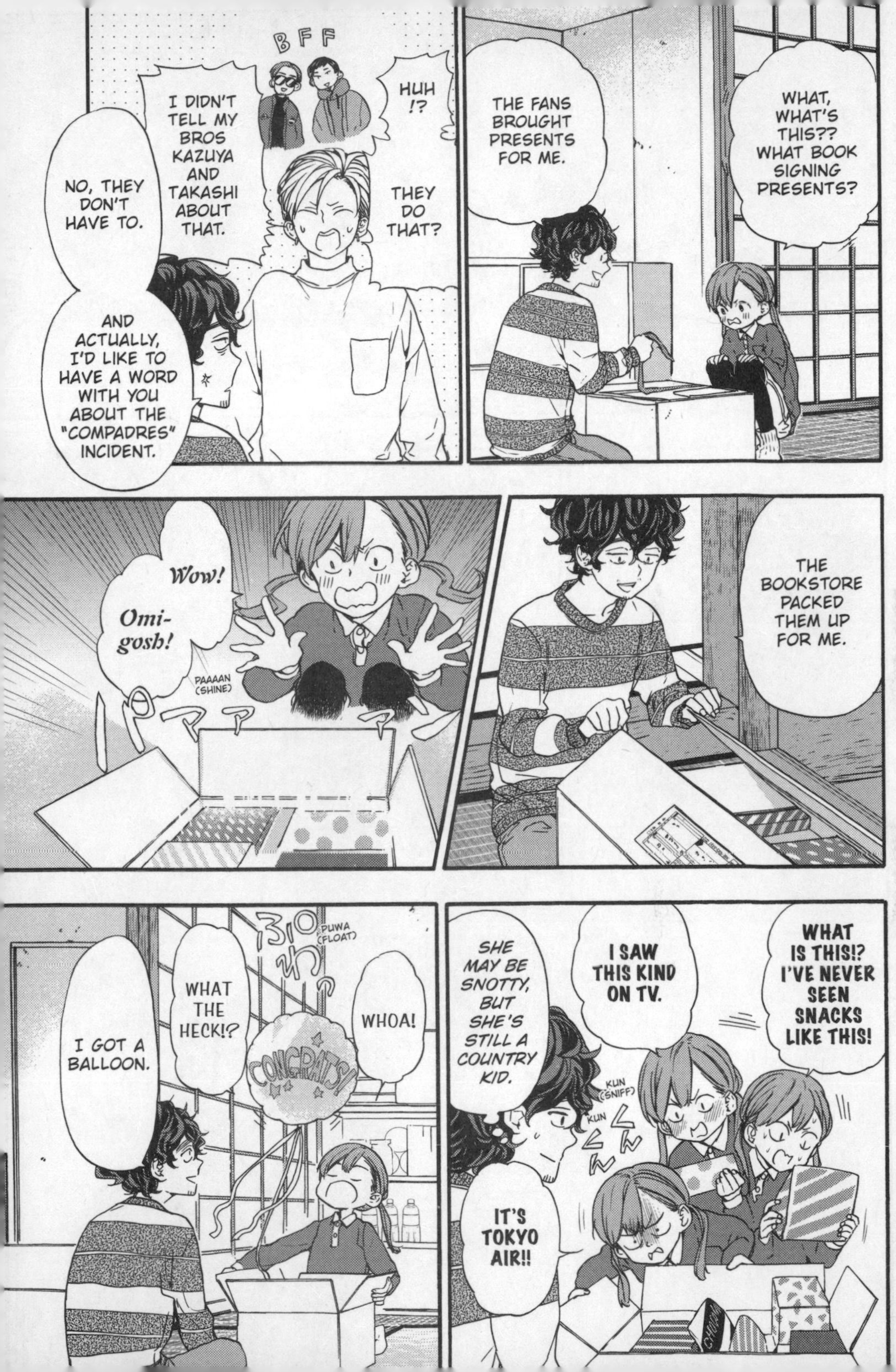
WHAT, WHAT'S THIS?? WHAT BOOK SIGNING PRESENTS?
THE FANS BROUGHT PRESENTS FOR ME.
HUH!?
THEY DO THAT?
I DIDN'T TELL MY BROS KAZUYA AND TAKASHI ABOUT THAT.
BFF
NO, THEY DON'T HAVE TO.
AND ACTUALLY, I'D LIKE TO HAVE A WORD WITH YOU ABOUT THE "COMPADRES" INCIDENT.
THE BOOKSTORE PACKED THEM UP FOR ME.
Wow!
Omi-gosh!
PAAAAN (SHINE)
WHAT IS THIS!? I'VE NEVER SEEN SNACKS LIKE THIS!
I SAW THIS KIND ON TV.
SHE MAY BE SNOTTY, BUT SHE'S STILL A COUNTRY KID.
KUN (SNIFF)
KUN
IT'S TOKYO AIR!!
PUWA (FLOAT)
WHOA!
WHAT THE HECK!?
CONGRATS!
I GOT A BALLOON.

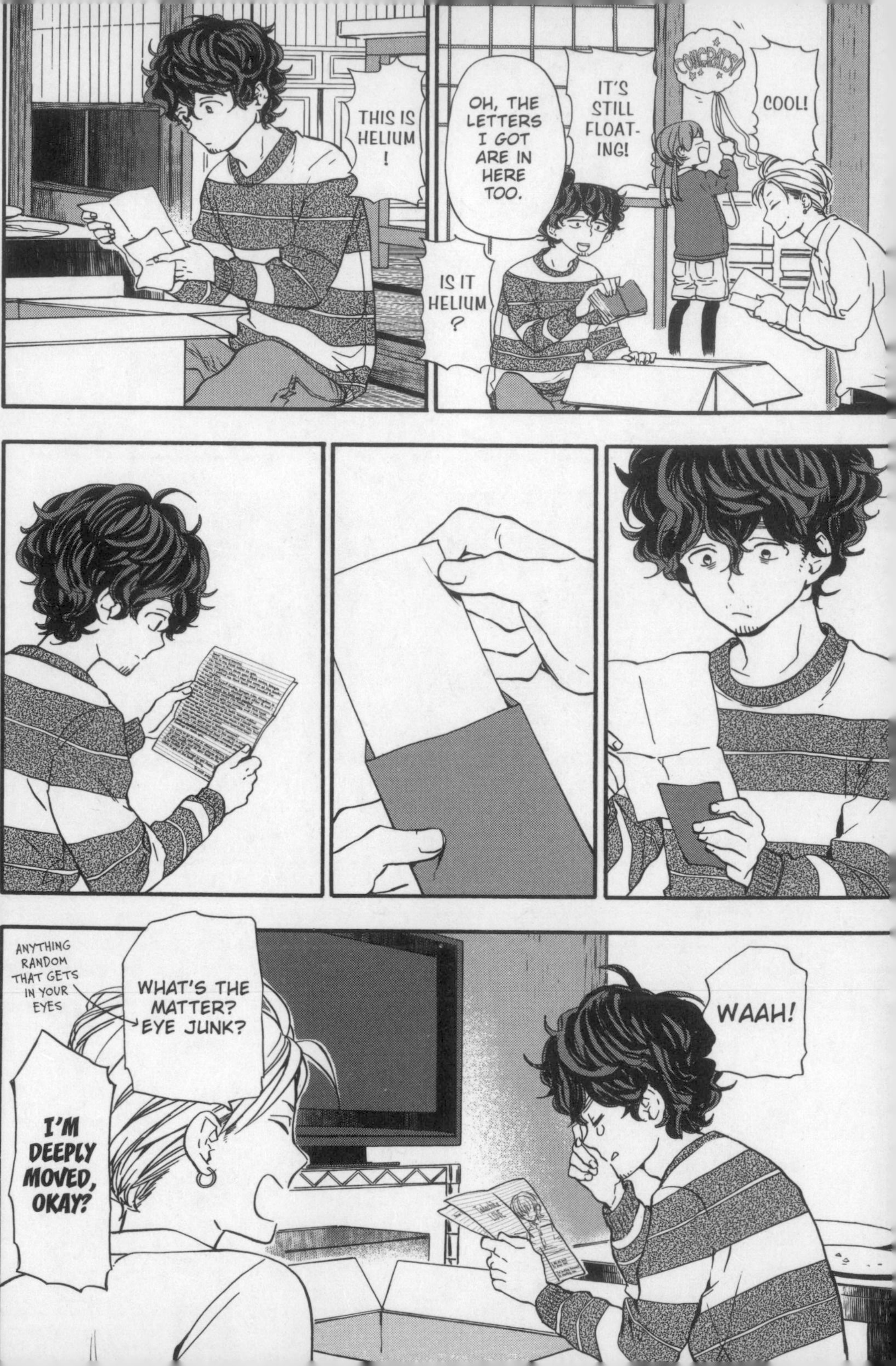
CONGRATS!
COOL!
IT'S STILL FLOAT-ING!
OH, THE LETTERS I GOT ARE IN HERE TOO.
IS IT HELIUM?
THIS IS HELIUM!
WAAH!
WHAT'S THE MATTER? EYE JUNK?
ANYTHING RANDOM THAT GETS IN YOUR EYES
I'M DEEPLY MOVED, OKAY?

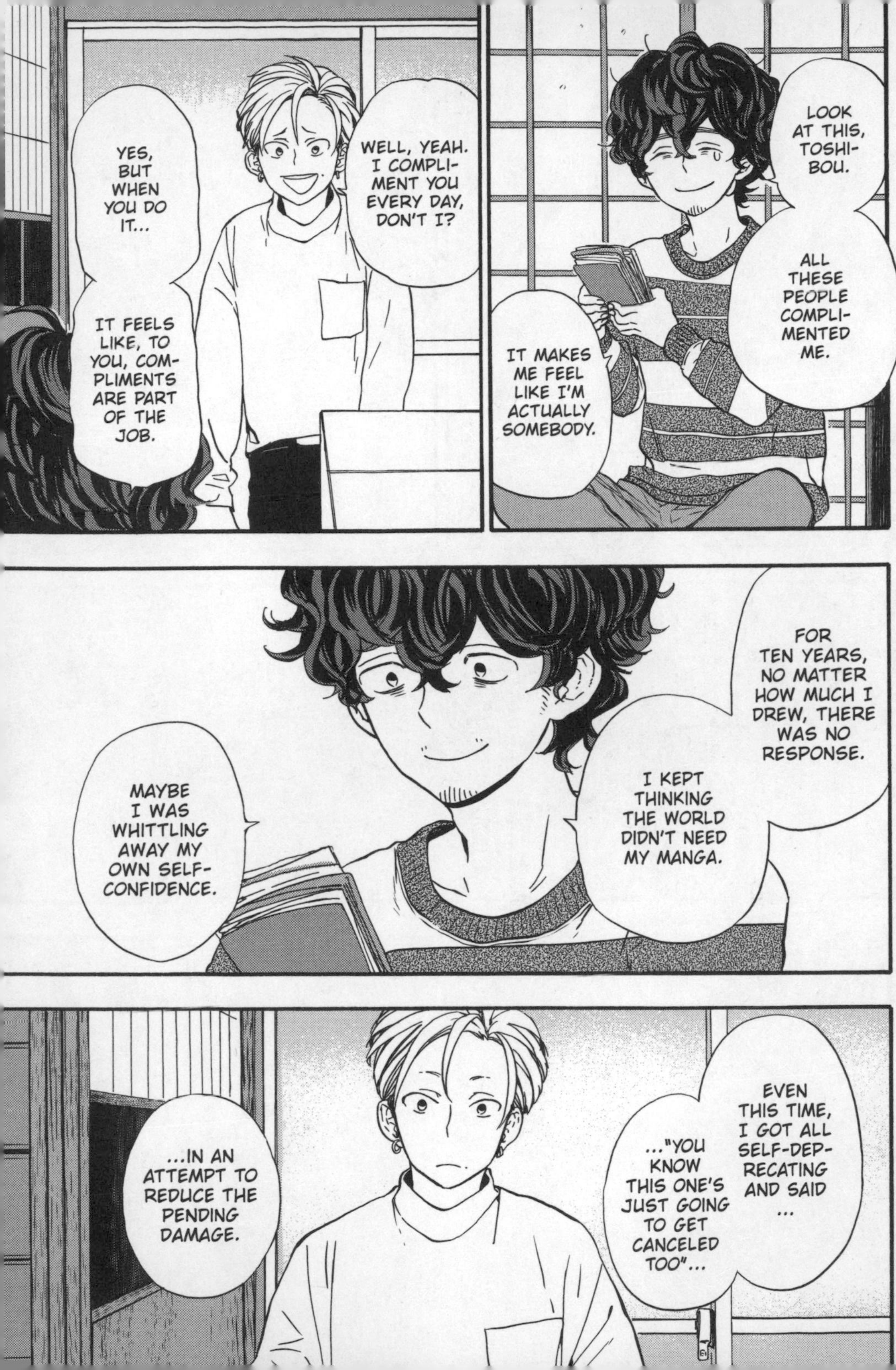
LOOK AT THIS, TOSHIBOU.
ALL THESE PEOPLE COMPLIMENTED ME.
IT MAKES ME FEEL LIKE I'M ACTUALLY SOMEBODY.
WELL, YEAH. I COMPLIMENT YOU EVERY DAY, DON'T I?
YES, BUT WHEN YOU DO IT...
IT FEELS LIKE, TO YOU, COMPLIMENTS ARE PART OF THE JOB.
FOR TEN YEARS, NO MATTER HOW MUCH I DREW, THERE WAS NO RESPONSE.
I KEPT THINKING THE WORLD DIDN'T NEED MY MANGA.
MAYBE I WAS WHITTLING AWAY MY OWN SELF-CONFIDENCE.
EVEN THIS TIME, I GOT ALL SELF-DEPRECATING AND SAID...
..."YOU KNOW THIS ONE'S JUST GOING TO GET CANCELED TOO"...
...IN AN ATTEMPT TO REDUCE THE PENDING DAMAGE.

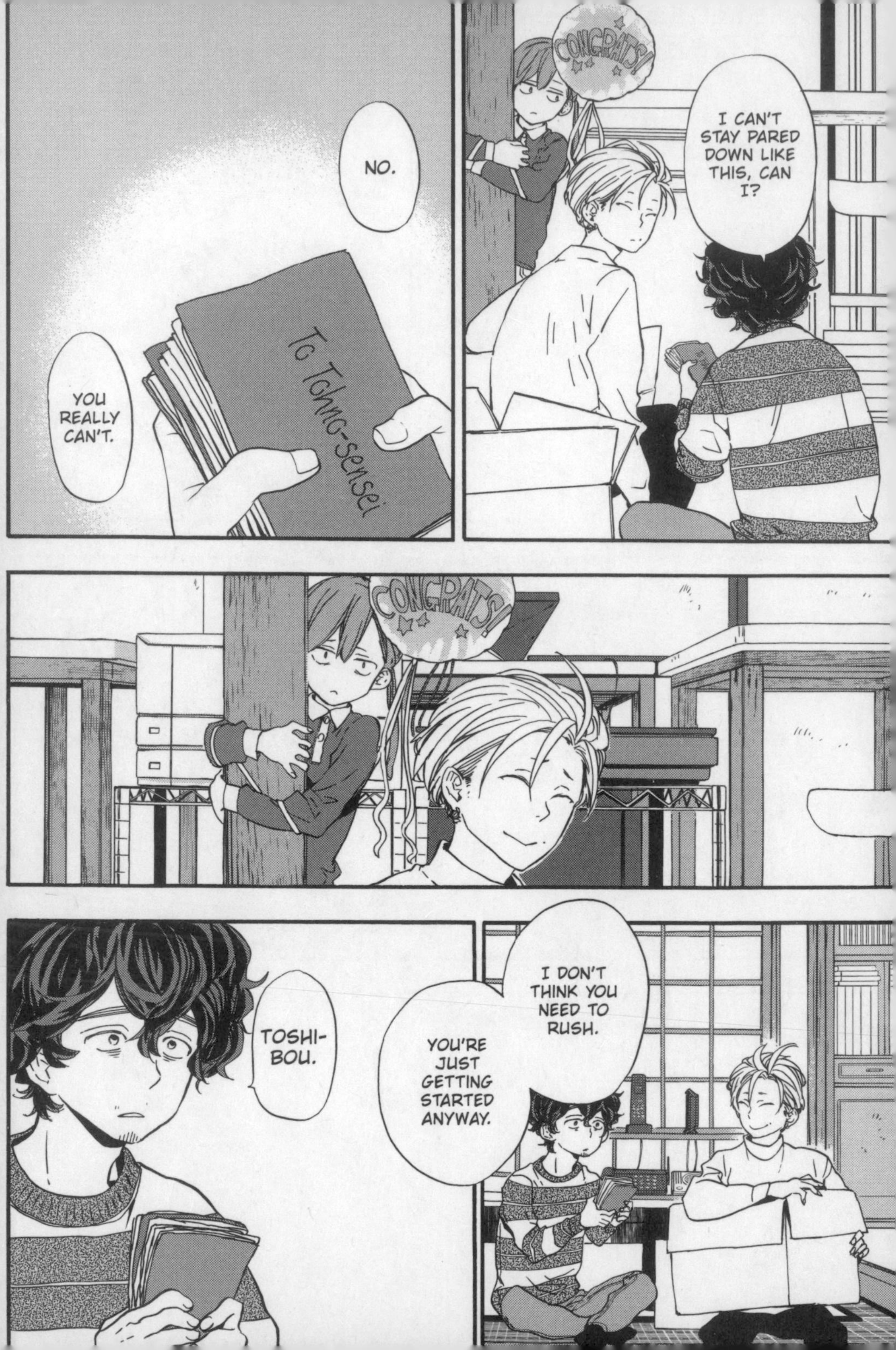
CONGRATS!
I CAN'T STAY PARED DOWN LIKE THIS, CAN I?
NO.
YOU REALLY CAN'T.
CONGRATS!
I DON'T THINK YOU NEED TO RUSH.
YOU'RE JUST GETTING STARTED ANYWAY.
TOSHI-BOU.

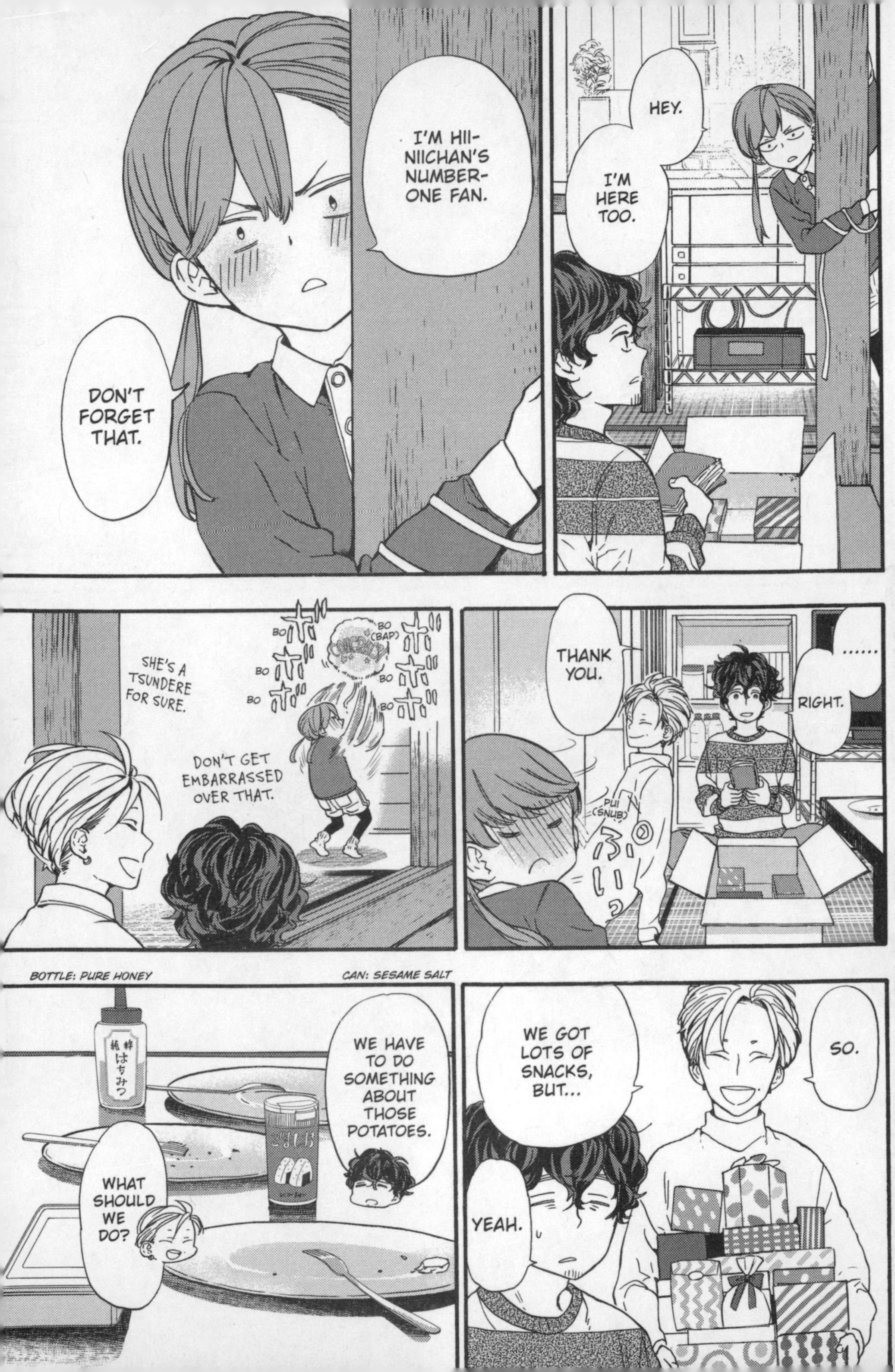
HEY.
I'M HERE TOO.
I'M HII-NIICHAN'S NUMBER-ONE FAN.
DON'T FORGET THAT.
......
RIGHT.
THANK YOU.
PUI (SNUB)
BO (BAP)
BO
BO
BO
BO
BO
SHE'S A TSUNDERE FOR SURE.
DON'T GET EMBARRASSED OVER THAT.
BOTTLE: PURE HONEY
CAN: SESAME SALT
SO.
WE GOT LOTS OF SNACKS, BUT...
YEAH.
WE HAVE TO DO SOMETHING ABOUT THOSE POTATOES.
WHAT SHOULD WE DO?

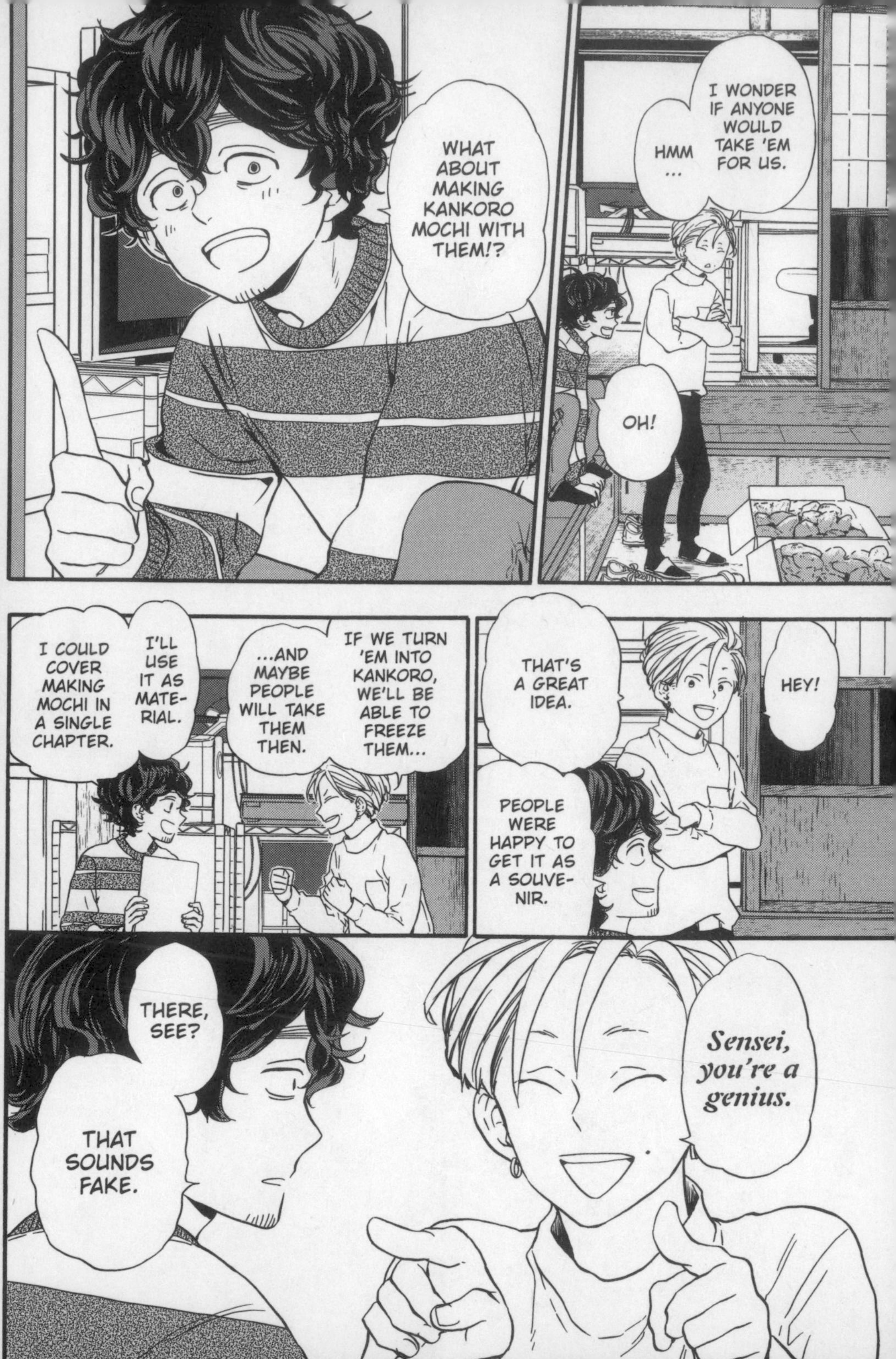
I WONDER IF ANYONE WOULD TAKE 'EM FOR US.
HMM ...
OH!
WHAT ABOUT MAKING KANKORO MOCHI WITH THEM!?
HEY!
THAT'S A GREAT IDEA.
PEOPLE WERE HAPPY TO GET IT AS A SOUVENIR.
IF WE TURN 'EM INTO KANKORO, WE'LL BE ABLE TO FREEZE THEM...
...AND MAYBE PEOPLE WILL TAKE THEM THEN.
I'LL USE IT AS MATERIAL.
I COULD COVER MAKING MOCHI IN A SINGLE CHAPTER.
Sensei, you're a genius.
THERE, SEE?
THAT SOUNDS FAKE.

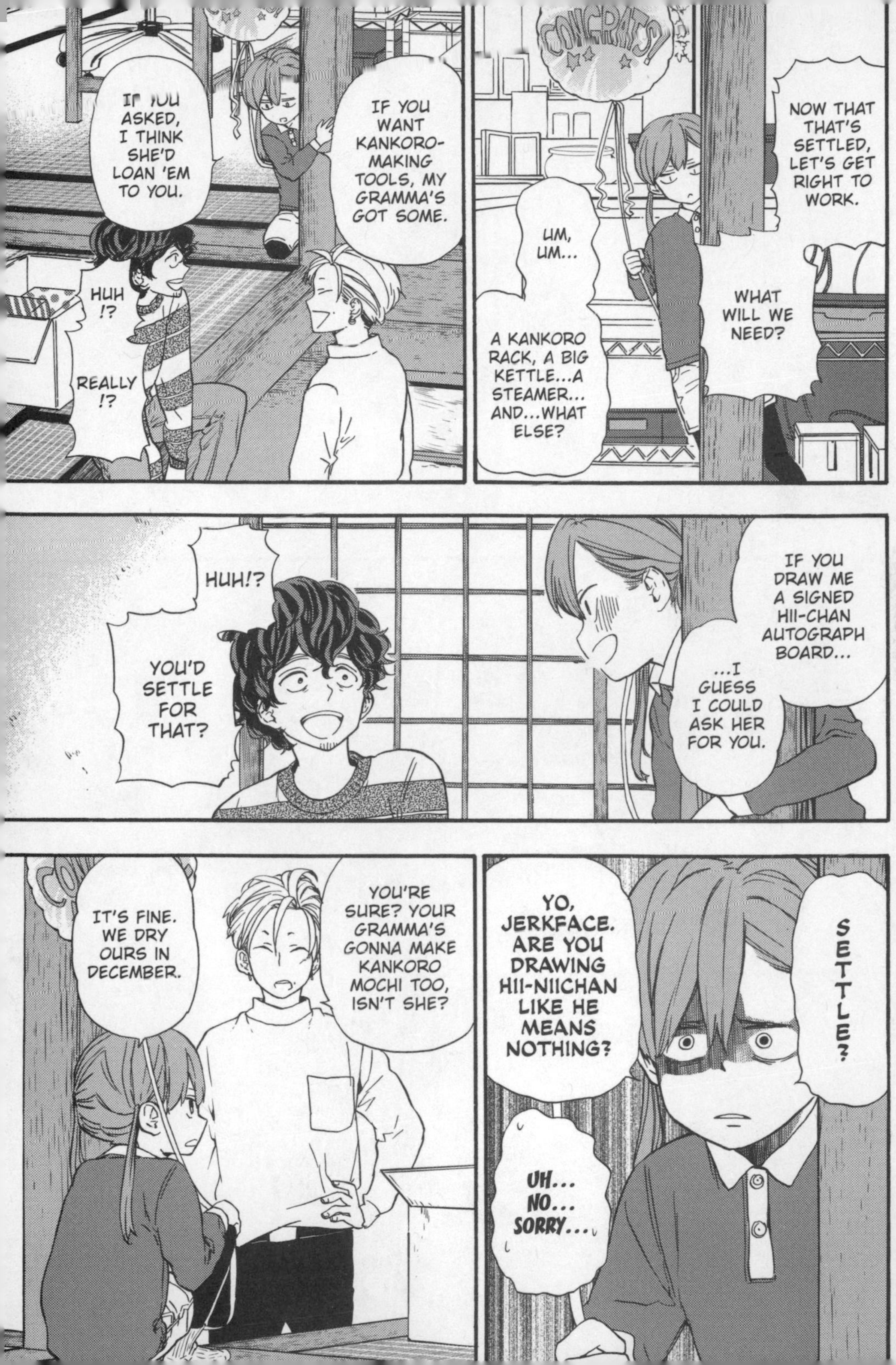
NOW THAT THAT'S SETTLED, LET'S GET RIGHT TO WORK.
WHAT WILL WE NEED?
UM, UM...
A KANKORO RACK, A BIG KETTLE...A STEAMER... AND...WHAT ELSE?
IF YOU WANT KANKORO-MAKING TOOLS, MY GRAMMA'S GOT SOME.
IF YOU ASKED, I THINK SHE'D LOAN 'EM TO YOU.
HUH!?
REALLY!?
IF YOU DRAW ME A SIGNED HII-CHAN AUTOGRAPH BOARD...
...I GUESS I COULD ASK HER FOR YOU.
HUH!?
YOU'D SETTLE FOR THAT?
SETTLE?
YO, JERKFACE. ARE YOU DRAWING HII-NIICHAN LIKE HE MEANS NOTHING?
UH... NO... SORRY...
YOU'RE SURE? YOUR GRAMMA'S GONNA MAKE KANKORO MOCHI TOO, ISN'T SHE?
IT'S FINE. WE DRY OURS IN DECEMBER.

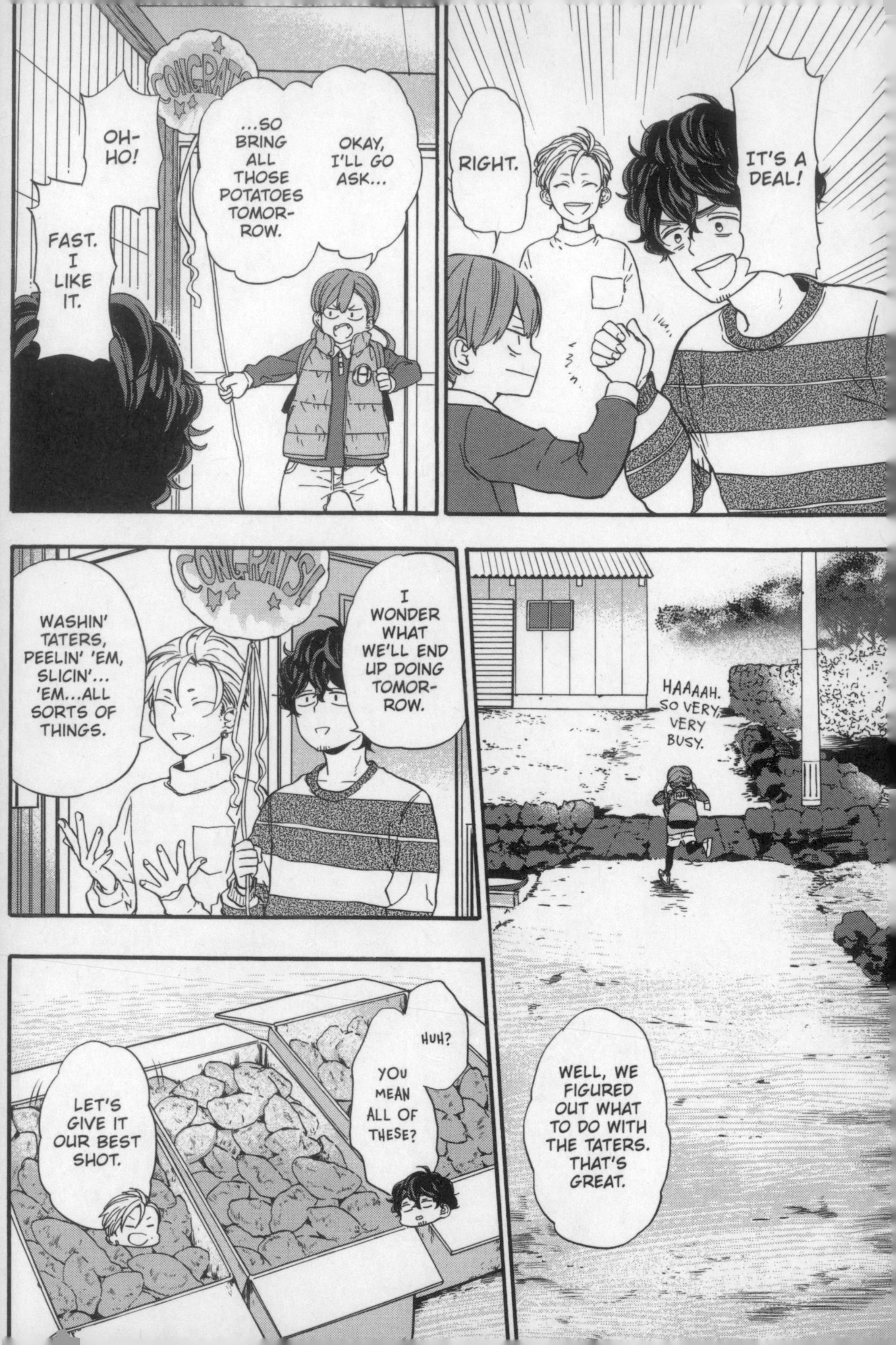
IT'S A DEAL!
RIGHT.
OKAY, I'LL GO ASK...
...SO BRING ALL THOSE POTATOES TOMORROW.
OH-HO!
FAST. I LIKE IT.
HAAAAH. SO VERY, VERY BUSY.
WELL, WE FIGURED OUT WHAT TO DO WITH THE TATERS. THAT'S GREAT.
I WONDER WHAT WE'LL END UP DOING TOMORROW.
WASHIN' TATERS, PEELIN' 'EM, SLICIN' 'EM...ALL SORTS OF THINGS.
HUH?
YOU MEAN ALL OF THESE?
LET'S GIVE IT OUR BEST SHOT.
CONGRATS!

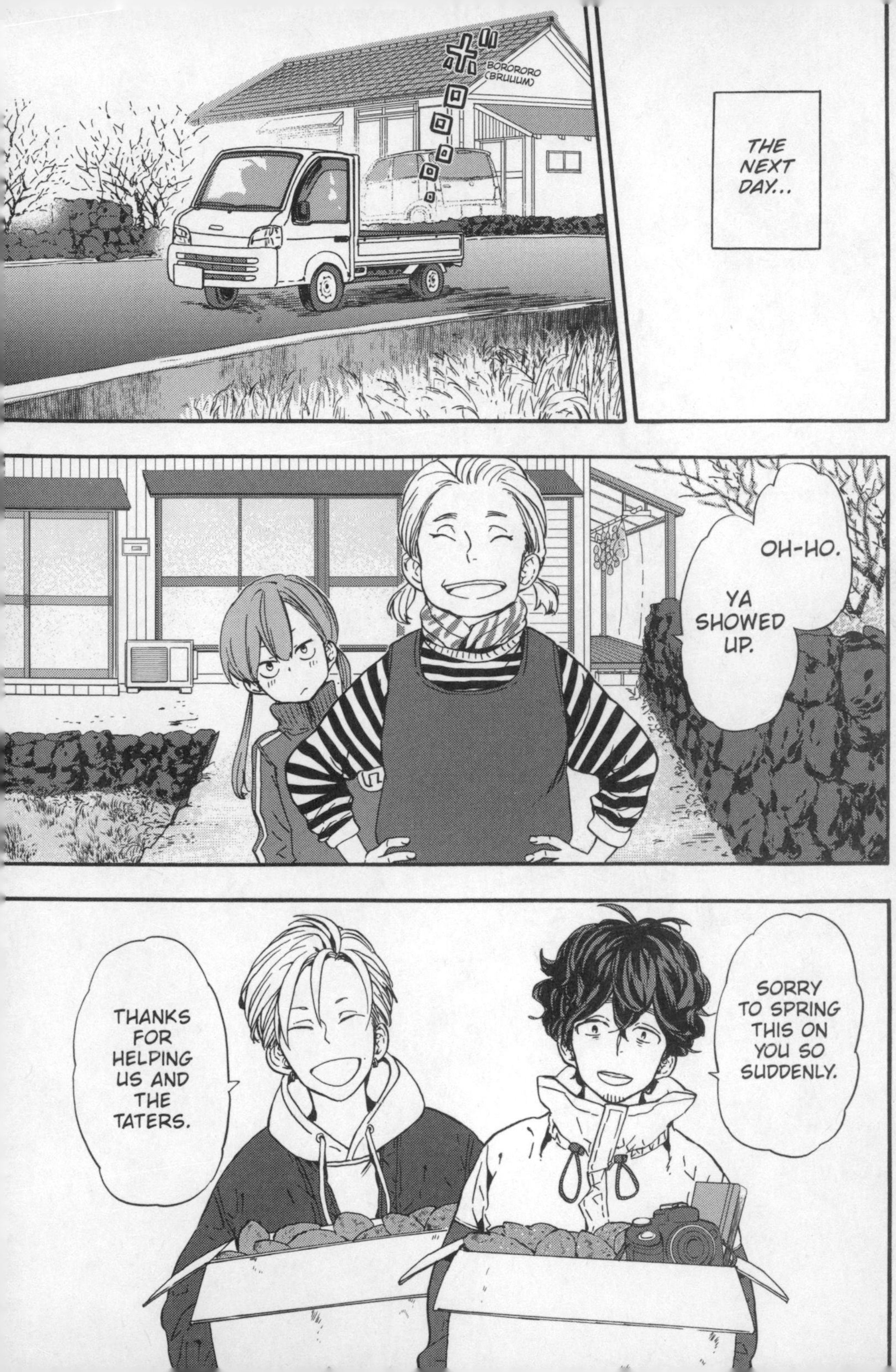
THE NEXT DAY...
BORORORO (BRUUUM)
OH-HO.
YA SHOWED UP.
SORRY TO SPRING THIS ON YOU SO SUDDENLY.
THANKS FOR HELPING US AND THE TATERS.

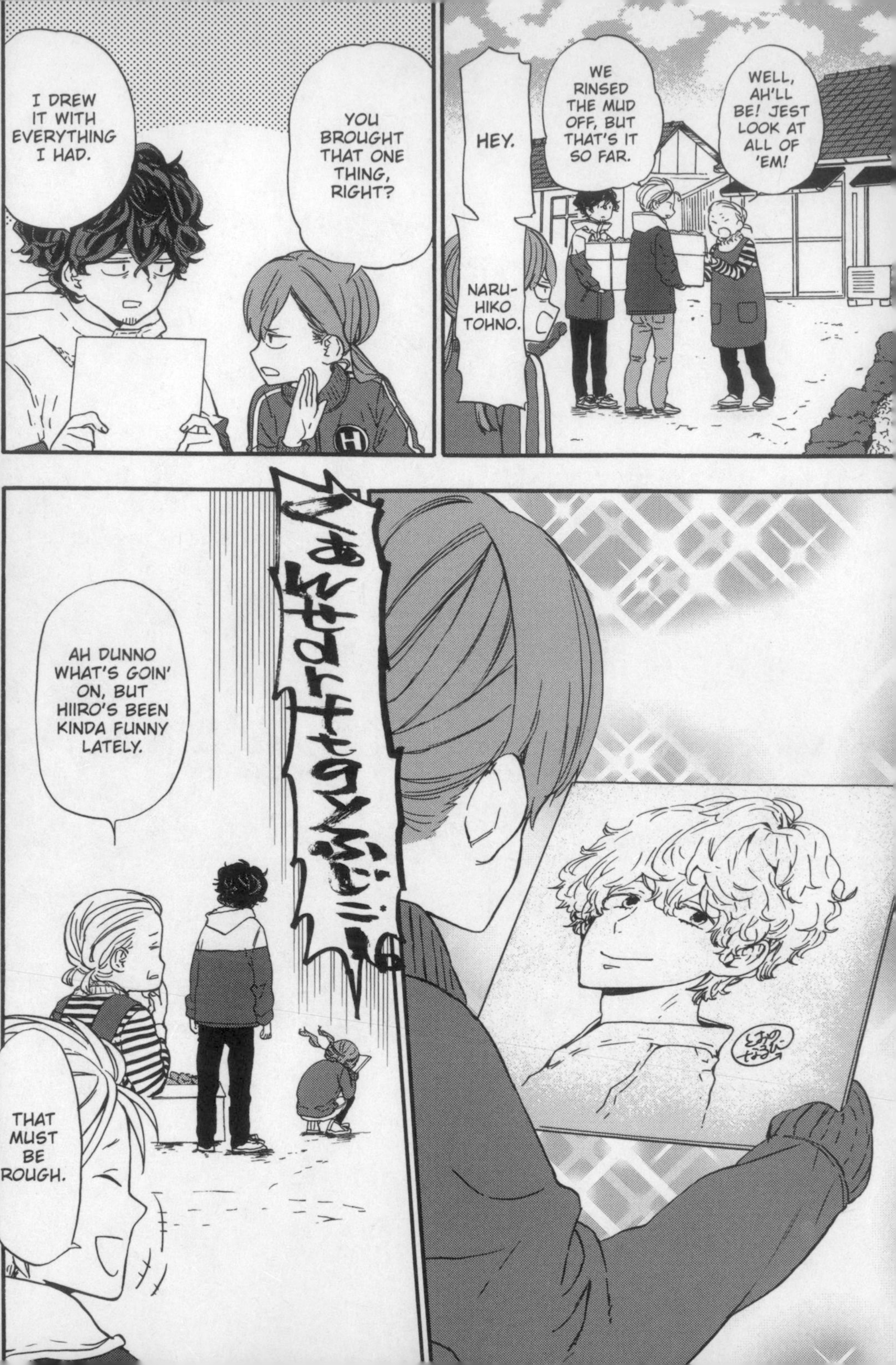
WELL, AH'LL BE! JEST LOOK AT ALL OF 'EM!
WE RINSED THE MUD OFF, BUT THAT'S IT SO FAR.
HEY.
NARUHIKO TOHNO.
YOU BROUGHT THAT ONE THING, RIGHT?
I DREW IT WITH EVERYTHING I HAD.
AH DUNNO WHAT'S GOIN' ON, BUT HIIRO'S BEEN KINDA FUNNY LATELY.
THAT MUST BE ROUGH.

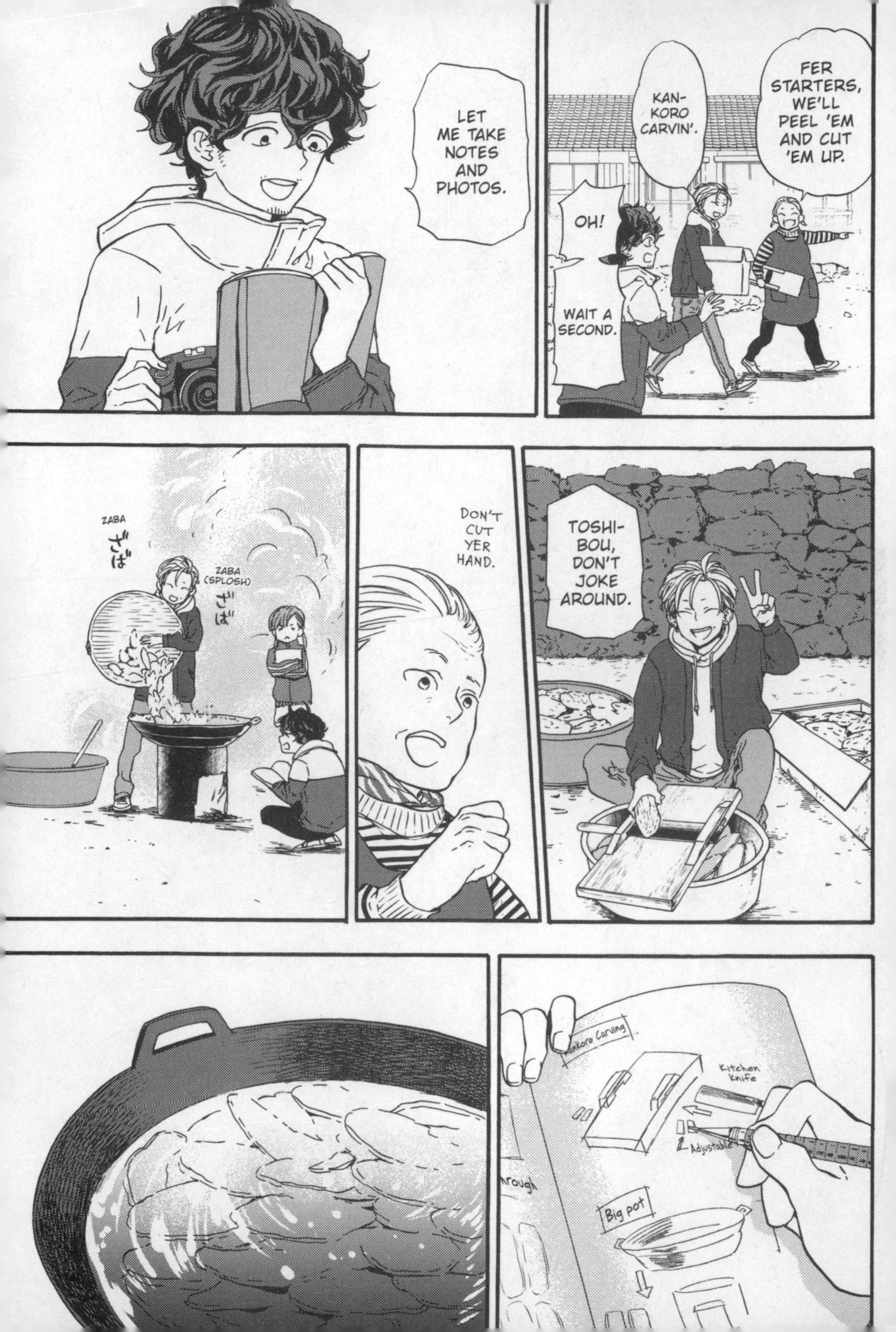
FER STARTERS, WE'LL PEEL 'EM AND CUT 'EM UP.
KAN-KORO CARVIN'.
OH!
WAIT A SECOND.
LET ME TAKE NOTES AND PHOTOS.
TOSHI-BOU, DON'T JOKE AROUND.
DON'T CUT YER HAND.
ZABA (SPLOSH)
ざば
ZABA
ざば
ankoro Carving
Kitchen knife
Adjustable
rough
Big pot

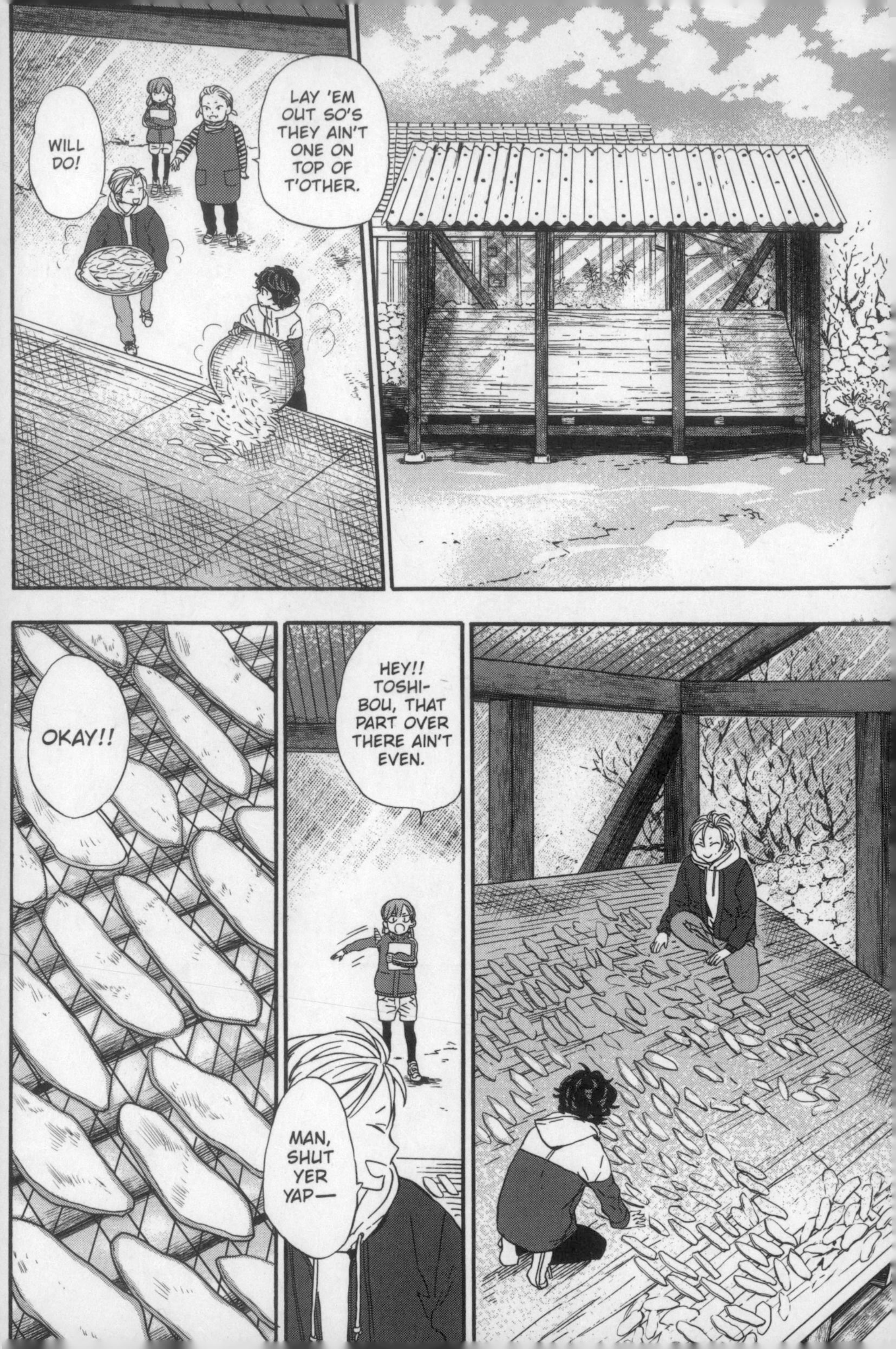
LAY 'EM OUT SO'S THEY AIN'T ONE ON TOP OF T'OTHER.
WILL DO!
HEY!! TOSHI-BOU, THAT PART OVER THERE AIN'T EVEN.
MAN, SHUT YER YAP—
OKAY!!

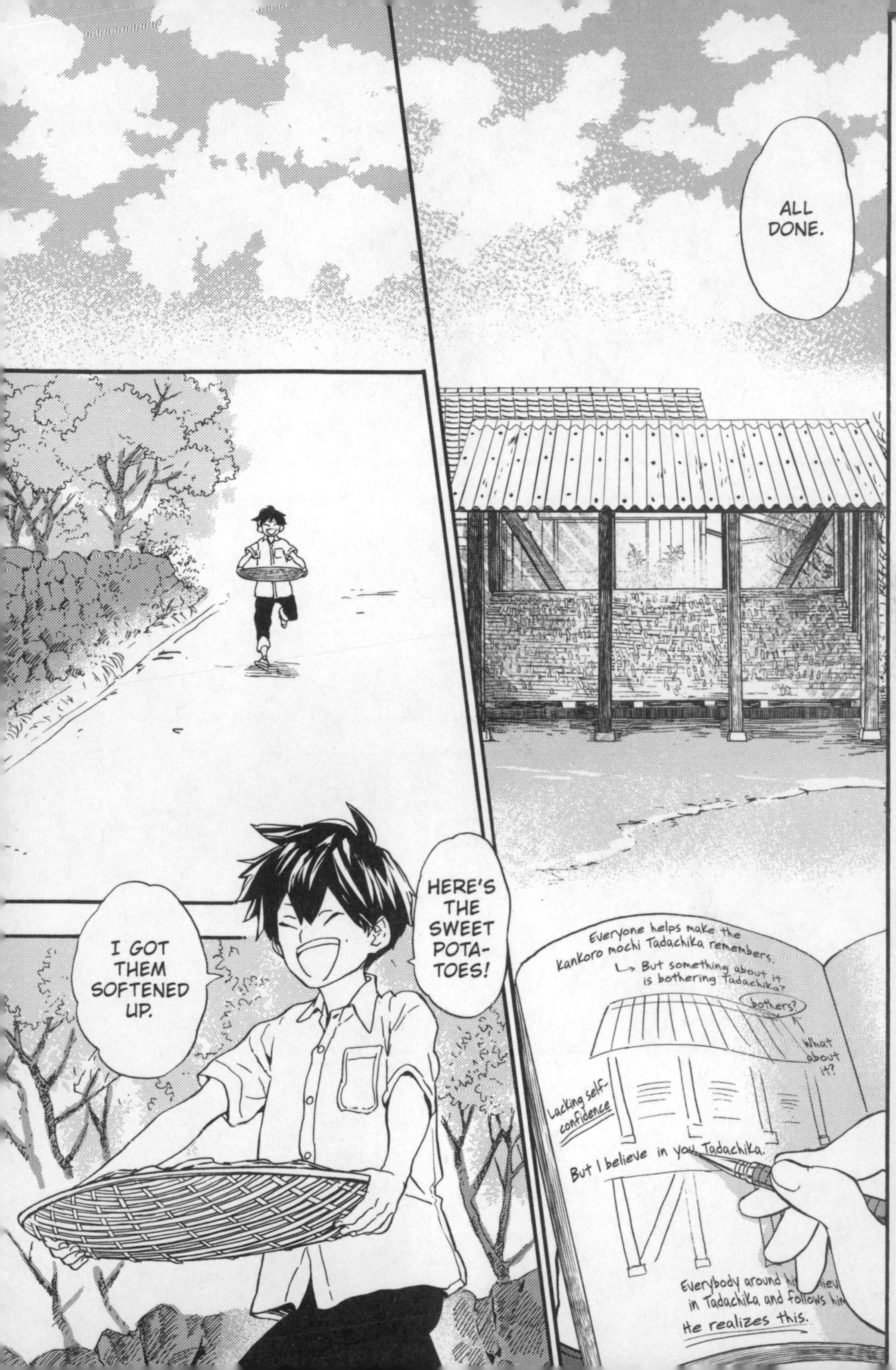
ALL DONE.
Everyone helps make the kankoro mochi Tadachika remembers.
↳ But something about it is bothering Tadachika?
bothers?
What about it?
Lacking self-confidence
But I believe in you, Tadachika.
Everybody around
in Tadachika and follows
He realizes this.
HERE'S THE SWEET POTATOES!
I GOT THEM SOFTENED UP.

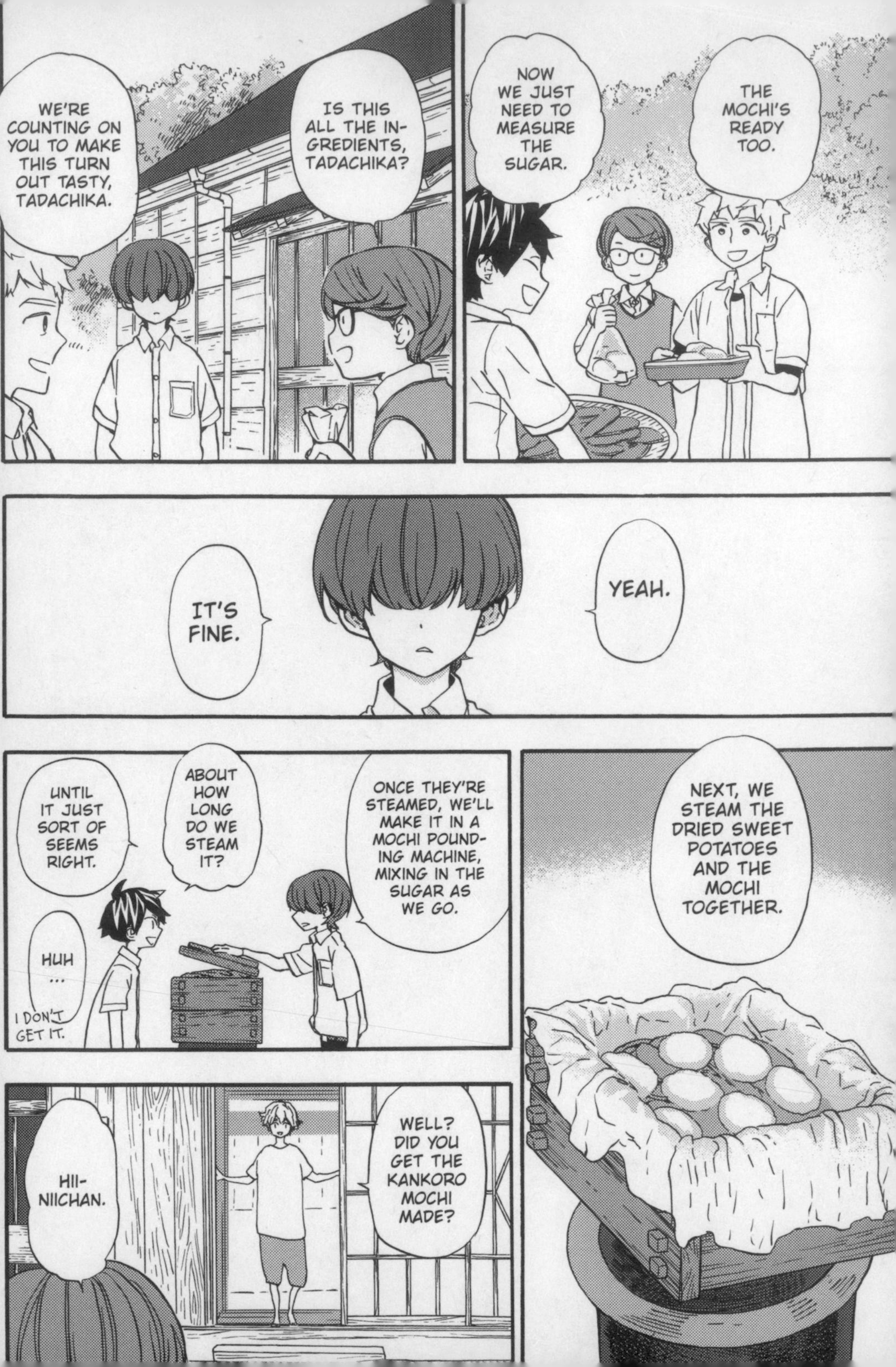
THE MOCHI'S READY TOO.
NOW WE JUST NEED TO MEASURE THE SUGAR.
IS THIS ALL THE INGREDIENTS, TADACHIKA?
WE'RE COUNTING ON YOU TO MAKE THIS TURN OUT TASTY, TADACHIKA.
YEAH.
IT'S FINE.
NEXT, WE STEAM THE DRIED SWEET POTATOES AND THE MOCHI TOGETHER.
ONCE THEY'RE STEAMED, WE'LL MAKE IT IN A MOCHI POUNDING MACHINE, MIXING IN THE SUGAR AS WE GO.
ABOUT HOW LONG DO WE STEAM IT?
UNTIL IT JUST SORT OF SEEMS RIGHT.
HUH...
I DON'T GET IT.
WELL? DID YOU GET THE KANKORO MOCHI MADE?
HII-NIICHAN.

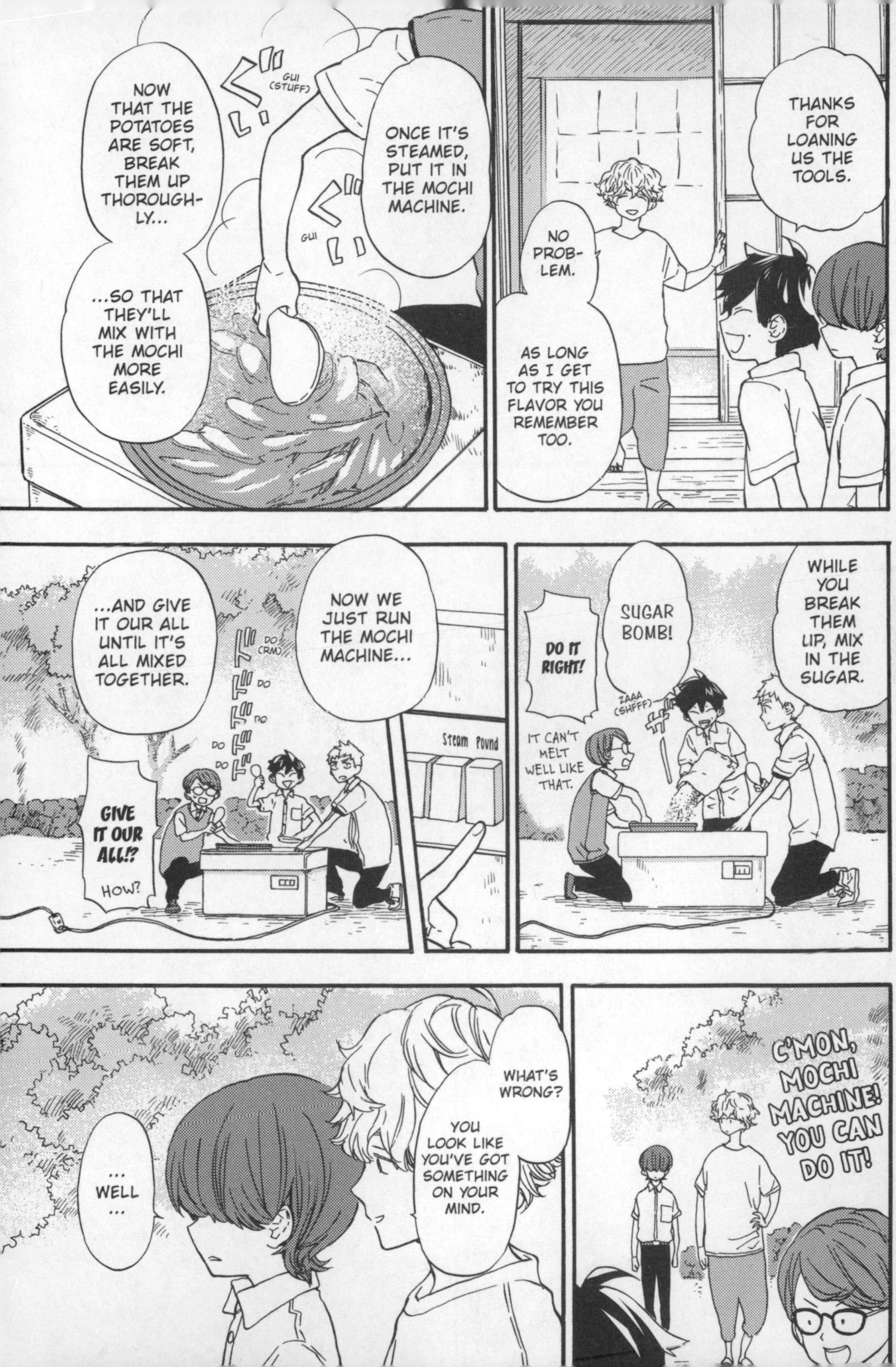
THANKS FOR LOANING US THE TOOLS.
NO PROBLEM.
AS LONG AS I GET TO TRY THIS FLAVOR YOU REMEMBER TOO.
ONCE IT'S STEAMED, PUT IT IN THE MOCHI MACHINE.
GUI (STUFF)
GUI
NOW THAT THE POTATOES ARE SOFT, BREAK THEM UP THOROUGHLY...
...SO THAT THEY'LL MIX WITH THE MOCHI MORE EASILY.
WHILE YOU BREAK THEM UP, MIX IN THE SUGAR.
SUGAR BOMB!
DO IT RIGHT!
ZAAA (SHFFF)
IT CAN'T MELT WELL LIKE THAT.
NOW WE JUST RUN THE MOCHI MACHINE...
...AND GIVE IT OUR ALL UNTIL IT'S ALL MIXED TOGETHER.
DO (RM)
DO
DO
DO
DO
Steam Pound
GIVE IT OUR ALL!?
HOW?
C'MON, MOCHI MACHINE! YOU CAN DO IT!
WHAT'S WRONG?
YOU LOOK LIKE YOU'VE GOT SOMETHING ON YOUR MIND.
... WELL ...

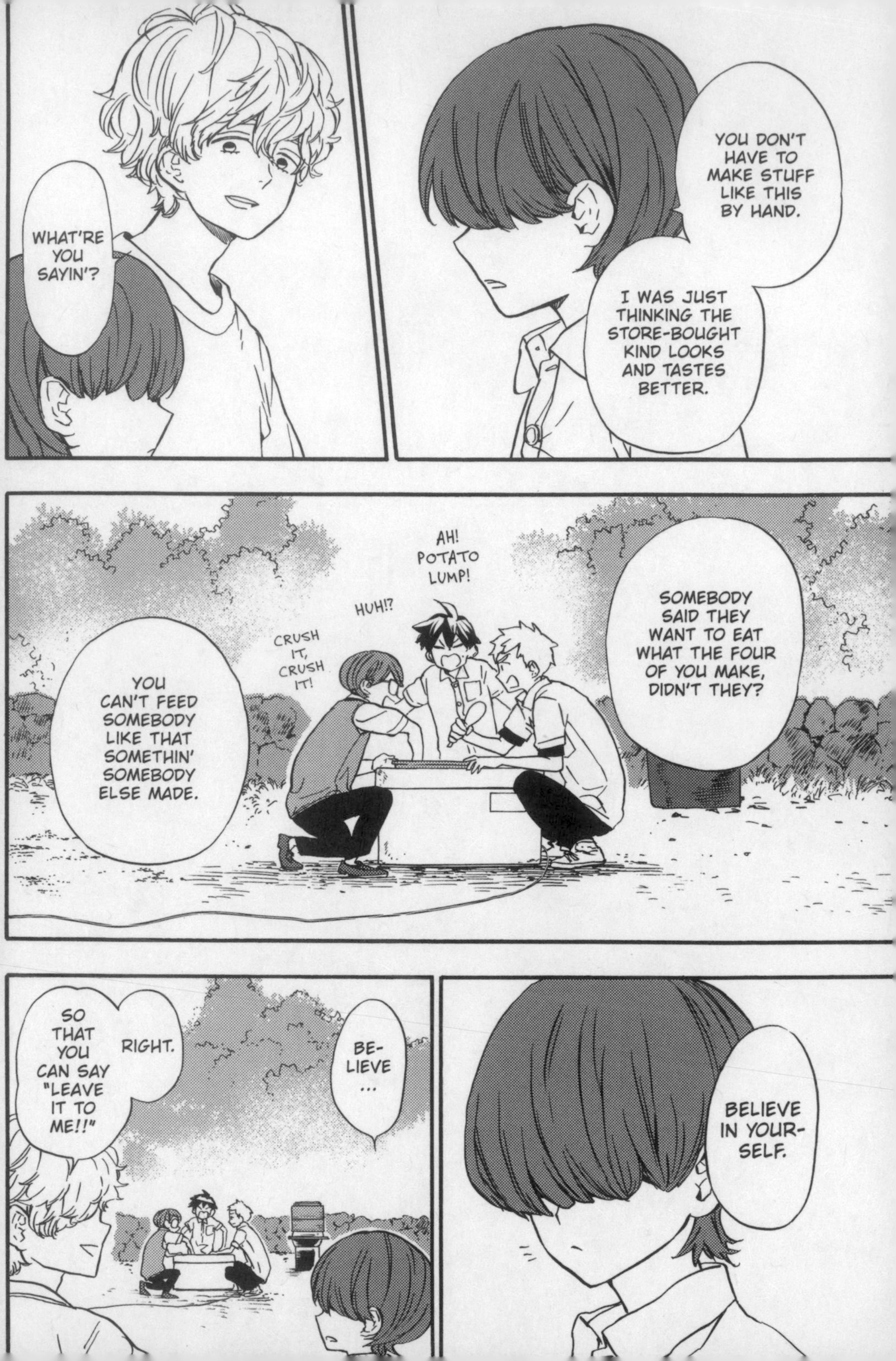
YOU DON'T HAVE TO MAKE STUFF LIKE THIS BY HAND.
I WAS JUST THINKING THE STORE-BOUGHT KIND LOOKS AND TASTES BETTER.
WHAT'RE YOU SAYIN'?
SOMEBODY SAID THEY WANT TO EAT WHAT THE FOUR OF YOU MAKE, DIDN'T THEY?
AH! POTATO LUMP!
HUH!?
CRUSH IT, CRUSH IT!
YOU CAN'T FEED SOMEBODY LIKE THAT SOMETHIN' SOMEBODY ELSE MADE.
BELIEVE IN YOURSELF.
BE-LIEVE ...
RIGHT.
SO THAT YOU CAN SAY "LEAVE IT TO ME!!"

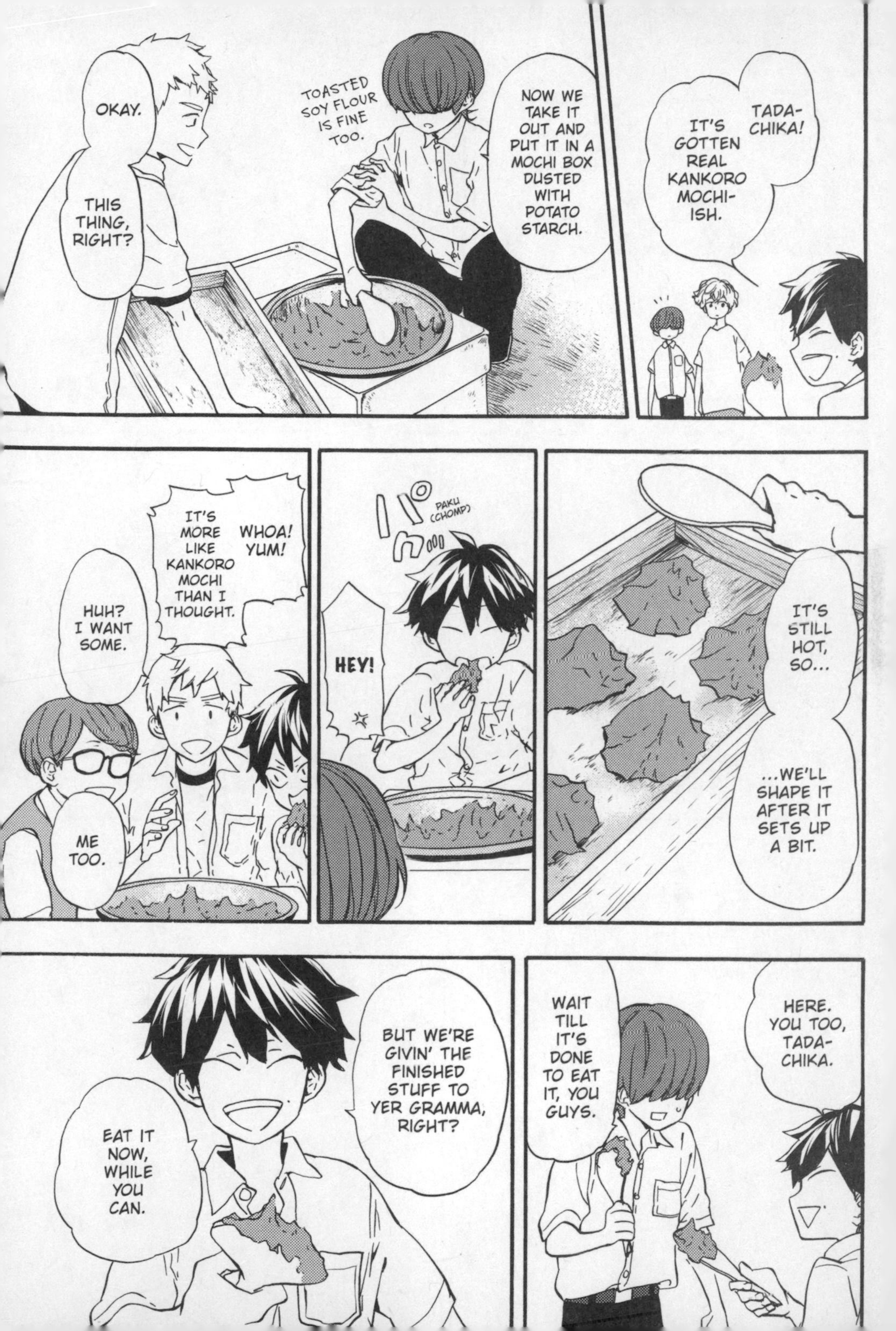
TADA-CHIKA!
IT'S GOTTEN REAL KANKORO MOCHI-ISH.
NOW WE TAKE IT OUT AND PUT IT IN A MOCHI BOX DUSTED WITH POTATO STARCH.
TOASTED SOY FLOUR IS FINE TOO.
OKAY.
THIS THING, RIGHT?
IT'S STILL HOT, SO...
...WE'LL SHAPE IT AFTER IT SETS UP A BIT.
パク
PAKU (CHOMP)
HEY!
WHOA! YUM!
IT'S MORE LIKE KANKORO MOCHI THAN I THOUGHT.
HUH? I WANT SOME.
ME TOO.
HERE. YOU TOO, TADA-CHIKA.
WAIT TILL IT'S DONE TO EAT IT, YOU GUYS.
BUT WE'RE GIVIN' THE FINISHED STUFF TO YER GRAMMA, RIGHT?
EAT IT NOW, WHILE YOU CAN.

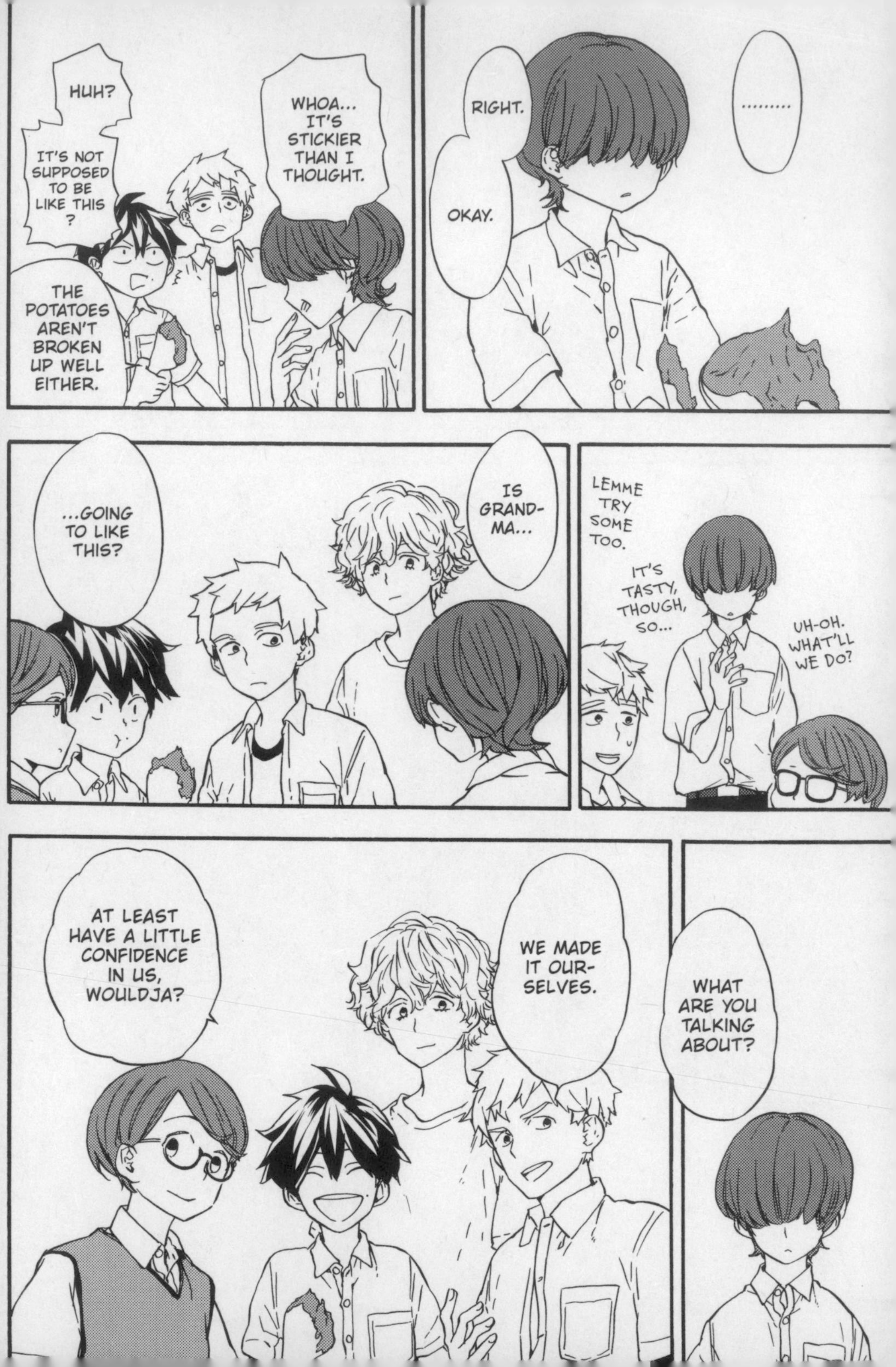
....
RIGHT.
OKAY.
WHOA... IT'S STICKIER THAN I THOUGHT.
HUH?
IT'S NOT SUPPOSED TO BE LIKE THIS?
THE POTATOES AREN'T BROKEN UP WELL EITHER.
LEMME TRY SOME TOO.
IT'S TASTY, THOUGH, SO...
UH-OH. WHAT'LL WE DO?
IS GRAND-MA...
...GOING TO LIKE THIS?
WHAT ARE YOU TALKING ABOUT?
WE MADE IT OUR-SELVES.
AT LEAST HAVE A LITTLE CONFIDENCE IN US, WOULDJA?

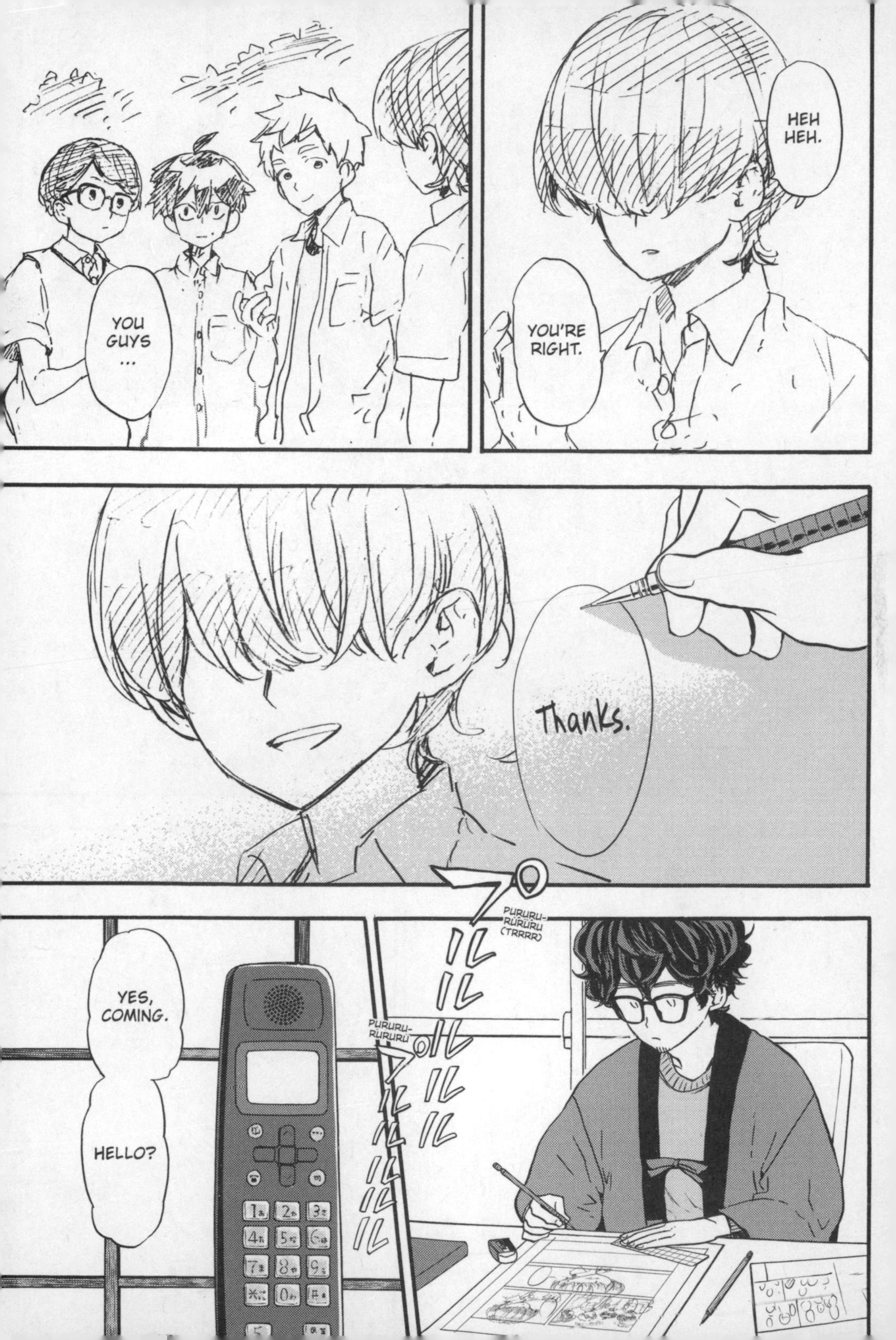
HEH HEH.
YOU'RE RIGHT.
YOU GUYS ...
Thanks.
PURURU-RURURU (TRRRR)
PURURU-RURURU
YES, COMING.
HELLO?

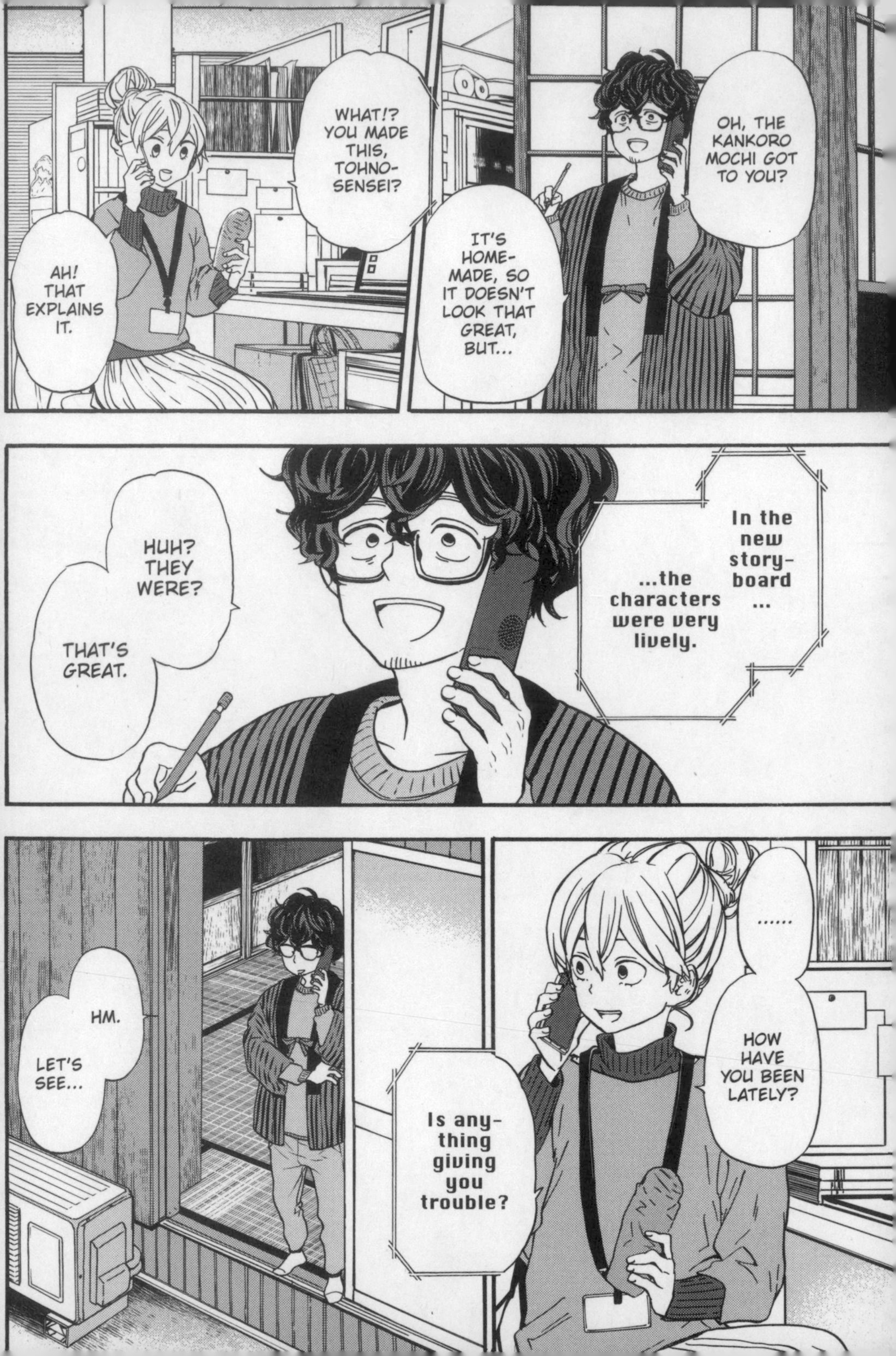
OH, THE KANKORO MOCHI GOT TO YOU?
IT'S HOME-MADE, SO IT DOESN'T LOOK THAT GREAT, BUT...
WHAT!? YOU MADE THIS, TOHNO-SENSEI?
AH! THAT EXPLAINS IT.
In the new story-board...
...the characters were very lively.
HUH? THEY WERE?
THAT'S GREAT.
......
HOW HAVE YOU BEEN LATELY?
Is any-thing giving you trouble?
HM.
LET'S SEE...

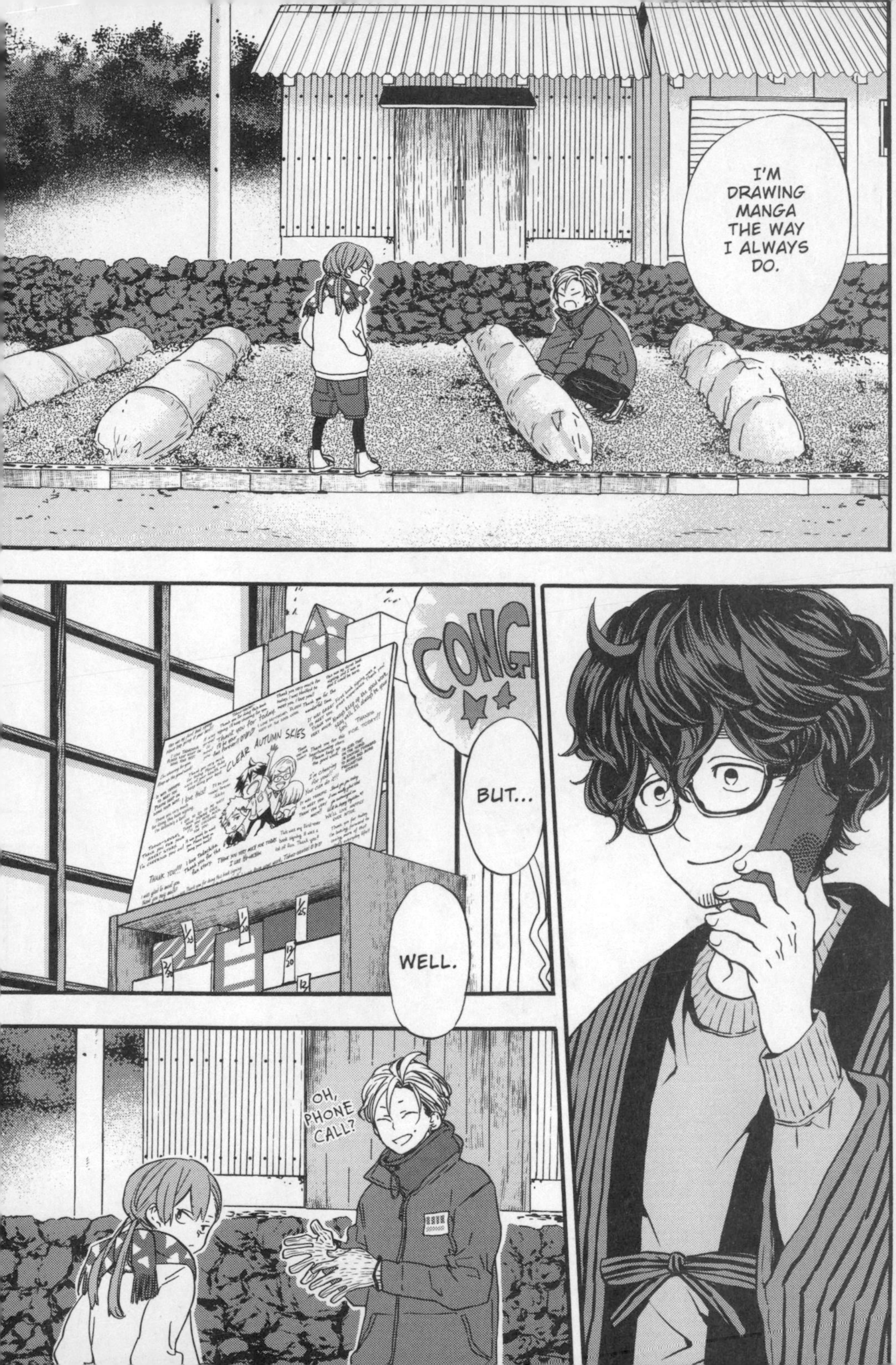
I'M DRAWING MANGA THE WAY I ALWAYS DO.
BUT...
WELL.
CONG
CLEAR AUTUMN SKIES
OH, PHONE CALL?

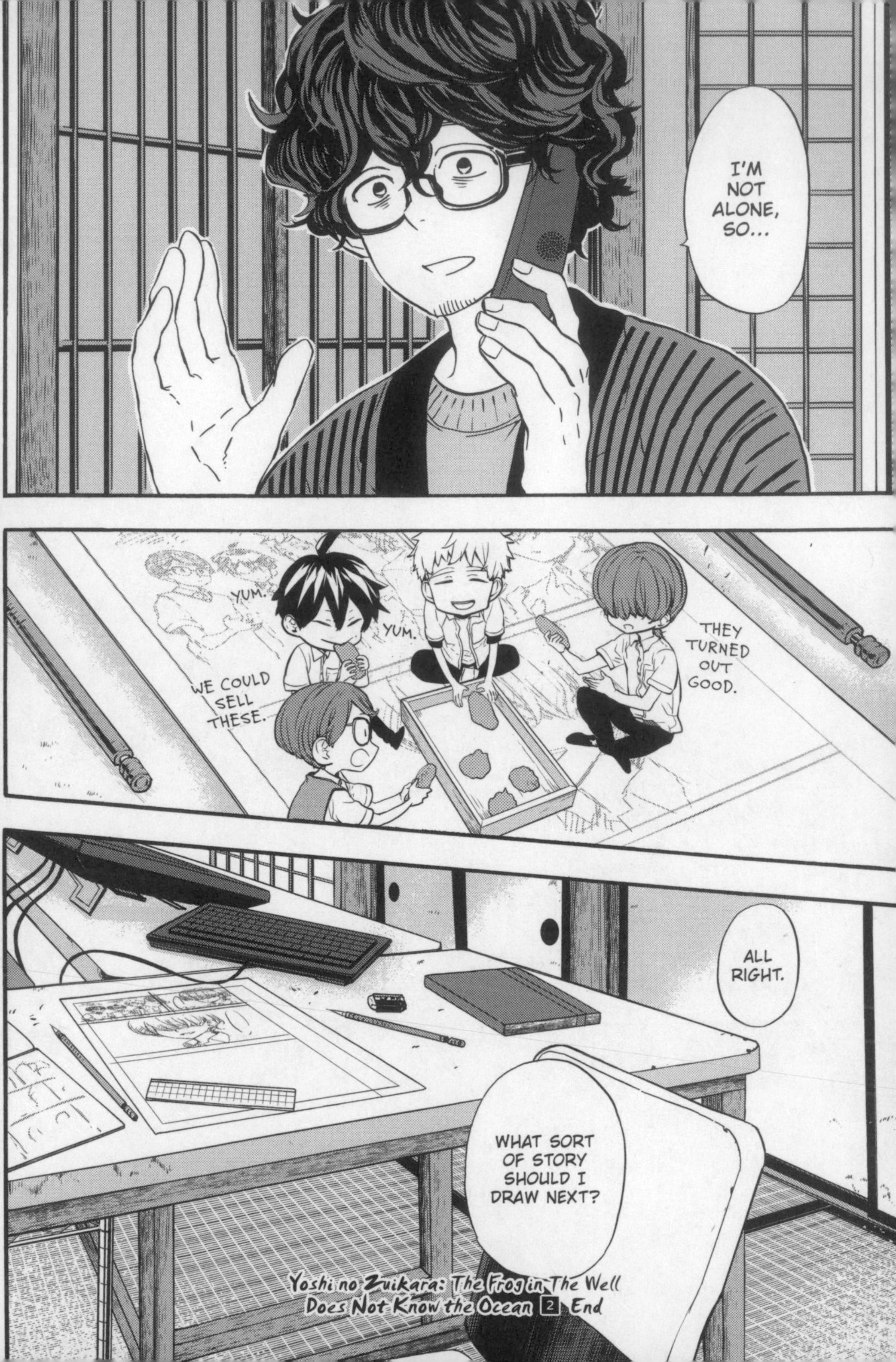
I'M NOT ALONE, SO...
THEY TURNED OUT GOOD.
YUM.
YUM.
WE COULD SELL THESE.
ALL RIGHT.
WHAT SORT OF STORY SHOULD I DRAW NEXT?
Yoshi no Zuikara: The Frog in The Well Does Not Know the Ocean 2 End

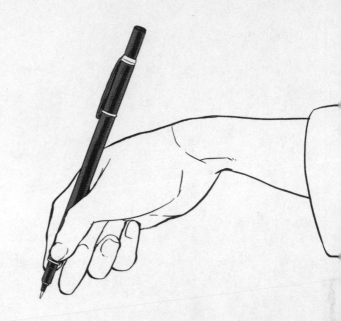

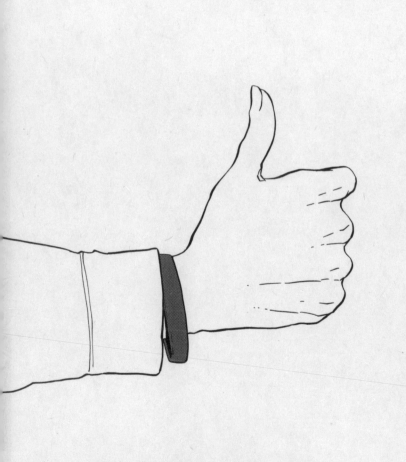

YOSHI NO ZUIKARA

- EVERYDAY STORIES -

THE "TOHNO WRAP PARTY" VOLUME

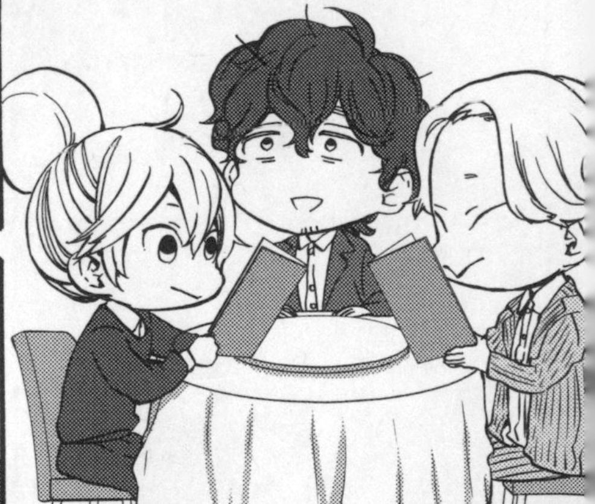

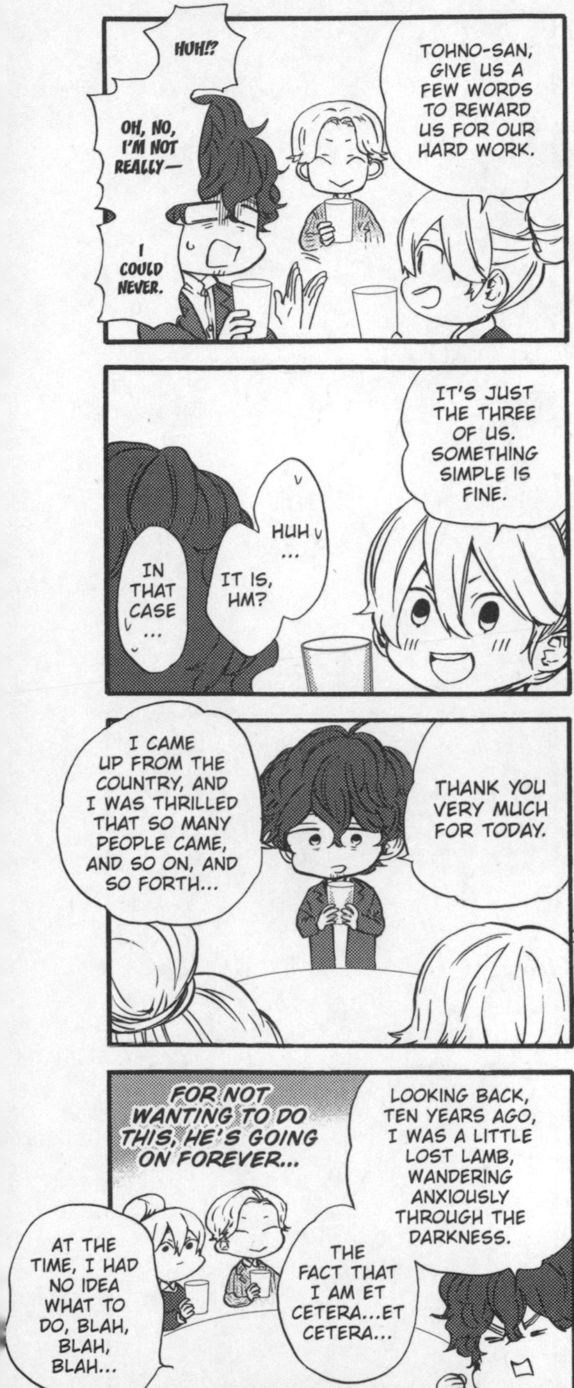
TOHNO-SAN, GIVE US A FEW WORDS TO REWARD US FOR OUR HARD WORK.
HUH!?
OH, NO, I'M NOT REALLY—
I COULD NEVER.
IT'S JUST THE THREE OF US. SOMETHING SIMPLE IS FINE.
HUH...
IT IS, HM?
IN THAT CASE...
THANK YOU VERY MUCH FOR TODAY.
I CAME UP FROM THE COUNTRY, AND I WAS THRILLED THAT SO MANY PEOPLE CAME, AND SO ON, AND SO FORTH...
LOOKING BACK, TEN YEARS AGO, I WAS A LITTLE LOST LAMB, WANDERING ANXIOUSLY THROUGH THE DARKNESS.
FOR NOT WANTING TO DO THIS, HE'S GOING ON FOREVER...
THE FACT THAT I AM ET CETERA...ET CETERA...
AT THE TIME, I HAD NO IDEA WHAT TO DO, BLAH, BLAH, BLAH...

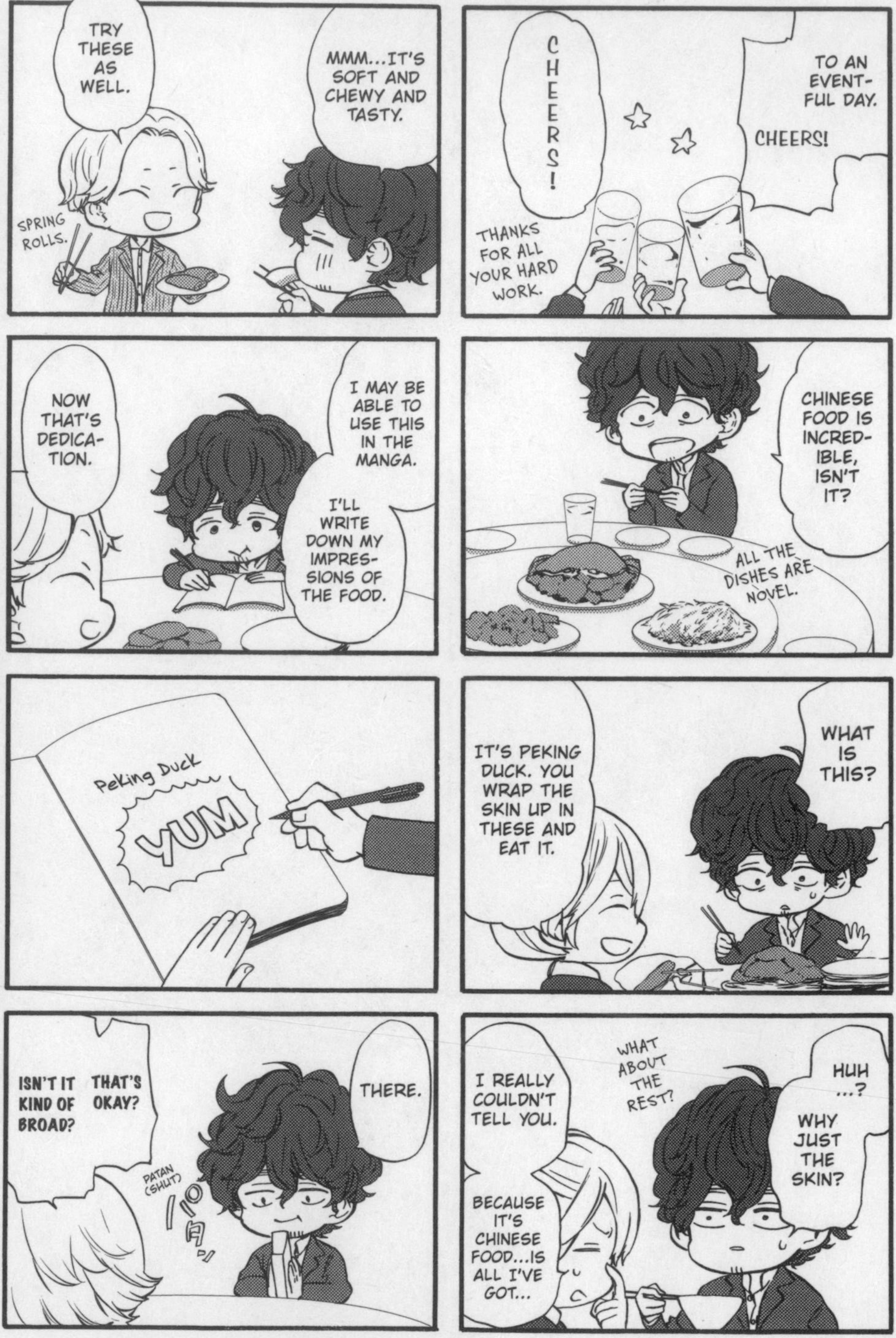
TO AN EVENTFUL DAY.
CHEERS!
CHEERS!
THANKS FOR ALL YOUR HARD WORK.
MMM...IT'S SOFT AND CHEWY AND TASTY.
TRY THESE AS WELL.
SPRING ROLLS.
CHINESE FOOD IS INCREDIBLE, ISN'T IT?
ALL THE DISHES ARE NOVEL.
I MAY BE ABLE TO USE THIS IN THE MANGA.
I'LL WRITE DOWN MY IMPRESSIONS OF THE FOOD.
NOW THAT'S DEDICATION.
WHAT IS THIS?
IT'S PEKING DUCK. YOU WRAP THE SKIN UP IN THESE AND EAT IT.
Peking Duck
YUM
HUH...?
WHY JUST THE SKIN?
WHAT ABOUT THE REST?
I REALLY COULDN'T TELL YOU.
BECAUSE IT'S CHINESE FOOD...IS ALL I'VE GOT...
THERE.
THAT'S OKAY?
ISN'T IT KIND OF BROAD?
PATAN (SHUT)

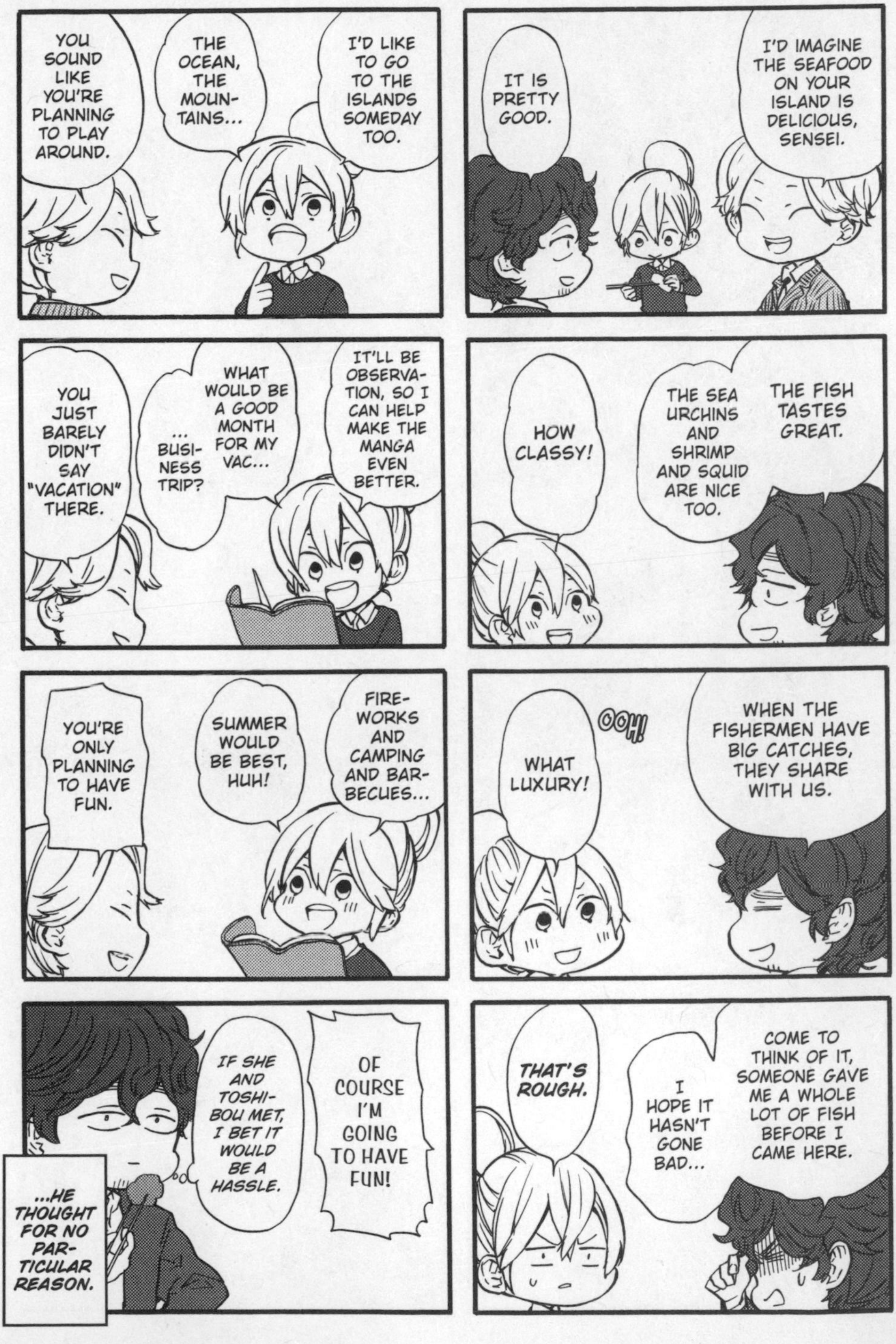
I'D IMAGINE THE SEAFOOD ON YOUR ISLAND IS DELICIOUS, SENSEI.
IT IS PRETTY GOOD.
I'D LIKE TO GO TO THE ISLANDS SOMEDAY TOO.
THE OCEAN, THE MOUNTAINS...
YOU SOUND LIKE YOU'RE PLANNING TO PLAY AROUND.
THE FISH TASTES GREAT.
THE SEA URCHINS AND SHRIMP AND SQUID ARE NICE TOO.
HOW CLASSY!
IT'LL BE OBSERVATION, SO I CAN HELP MAKE THE MANGA EVEN BETTER.
WHAT WOULD BE A GOOD MONTH FOR MY VAC...
...BUSINESS TRIP?
YOU JUST BARELY DIDN'T SAY "VACATION" THERE.
WHEN THE FISHERMEN HAVE BIG CATCHES, THEY SHARE WITH US.
OOH!
WHAT LUXURY!
FIREWORKS AND CAMPING AND BARBECUES...
SUMMER WOULD BE BEST, HUH!
YOU'RE ONLY PLANNING TO HAVE FUN.
COME TO THINK OF IT, SOMEONE GAVE ME A WHOLE LOT OF FISH BEFORE I CAME HERE.
I HOPE IT HASN'T GONE BAD...
THAT'S ROUGH.
OF COURSE I'M GOING TO HAVE FUN!
IF SHE AND TOSHIBOU MET, I BET IT WOULD BE A HASSLE.
...HE THOUGHT FOR NO PARTICULAR REASON.

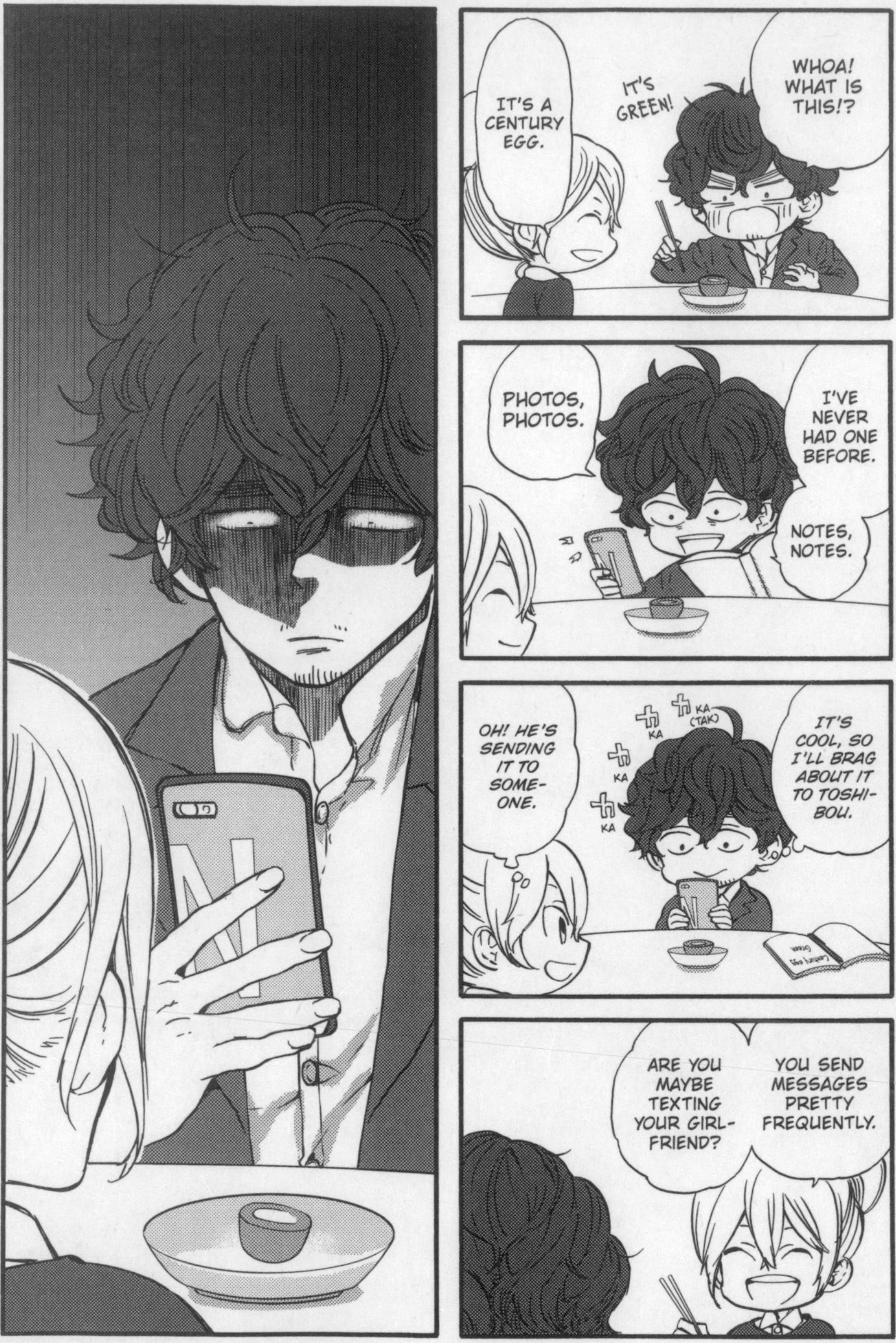
WHOA! WHAT IS THIS!?
IT'S GREEN!
IT'S A CENTURY EGG.
I'VE NEVER HAD ONE BEFORE.
NOTES, NOTES.
PHOTOS, PHOTOS.
IT'S COOL, SO I'LL BRAG ABOUT IT TO TOSHI-BOU.
KA (TAK)
KA
KA
KA
OH! HE'S SENDING IT TO SOME-ONE.
YOU SEND MESSAGES PRETTY FREQUENTLY.
ARE YOU MAYBE TEXTING YOUR GIRL-FRIEND?

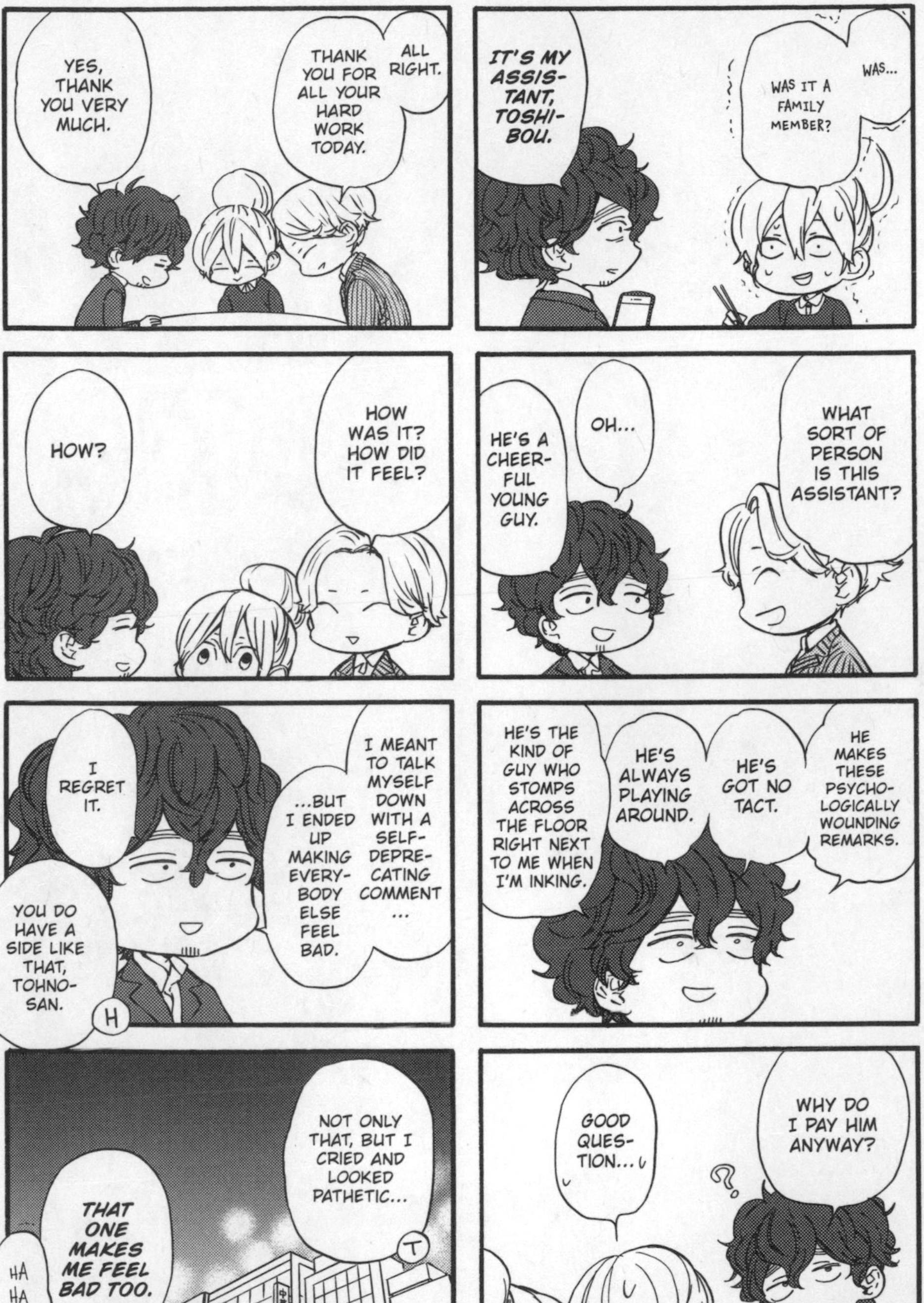
WAS...
WAS IT A FAMILY MEMBER?
IT'S MY ASSISTANT, TOSHIBOU.
WHAT SORT OF PERSON IS THIS ASSISTANT?
OH...
HE'S A CHEERFUL YOUNG GUY.
HE MAKES THESE PSYCHOLOGICALLY WOUNDING REMARKS.
HE'S GOT NO TACT.
HE'S ALWAYS PLAYING AROUND.
HE'S THE KIND OF GUY WHO STOMPS ACROSS THE FLOOR RIGHT NEXT TO ME WHEN I'M INKING.
WHY DO I PAY HIM ANYWAY?
GOOD QUESTION...
ALL RIGHT.
THANK YOU FOR ALL YOUR HARD WORK TODAY.
YES, THANK YOU VERY MUCH.
HOW WAS IT? HOW DID IT FEEL?
HOW?
I MEANT TO TALK MYSELF DOWN WITH A SELF-DEPRECATING COMMENT...
...BUT I ENDED UP MAKING EVERYBODY ELSE FEEL BAD.
I REGRET IT.
YOU DO HAVE A SIDE LIKE THAT, TOHNO-SAN.
H
NOT ONLY THAT, BUT I CRIED AND LOOKED PATHETIC...
T
THAT ONE MAKES ME FEEL BAD TOO.
H
HA HA HA.

YOSHI NO ZUIKARA

- EVERYDAY STORIES -

THE "TOHNO GOES HOME" VOLUME

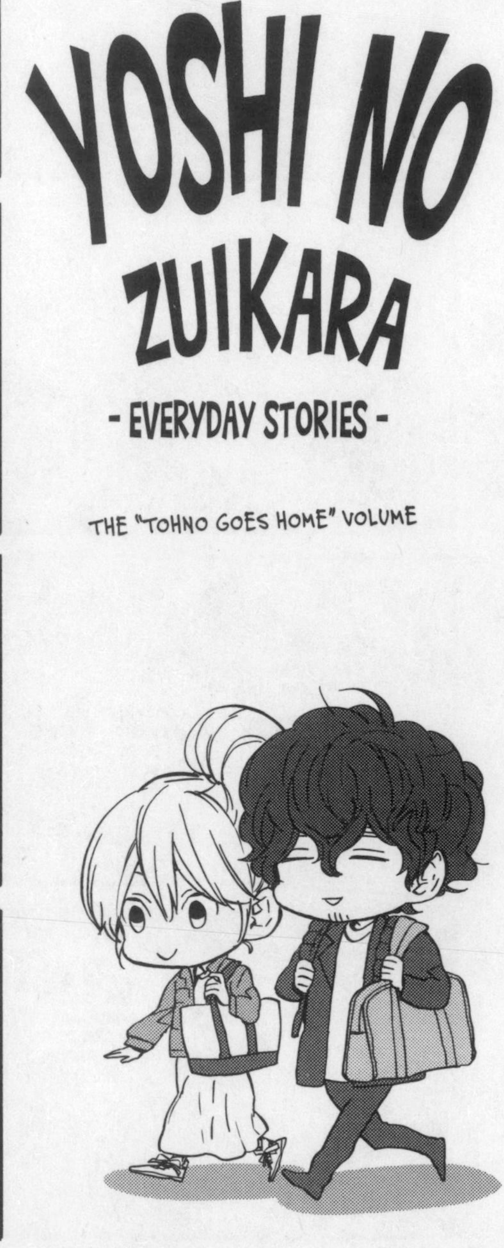

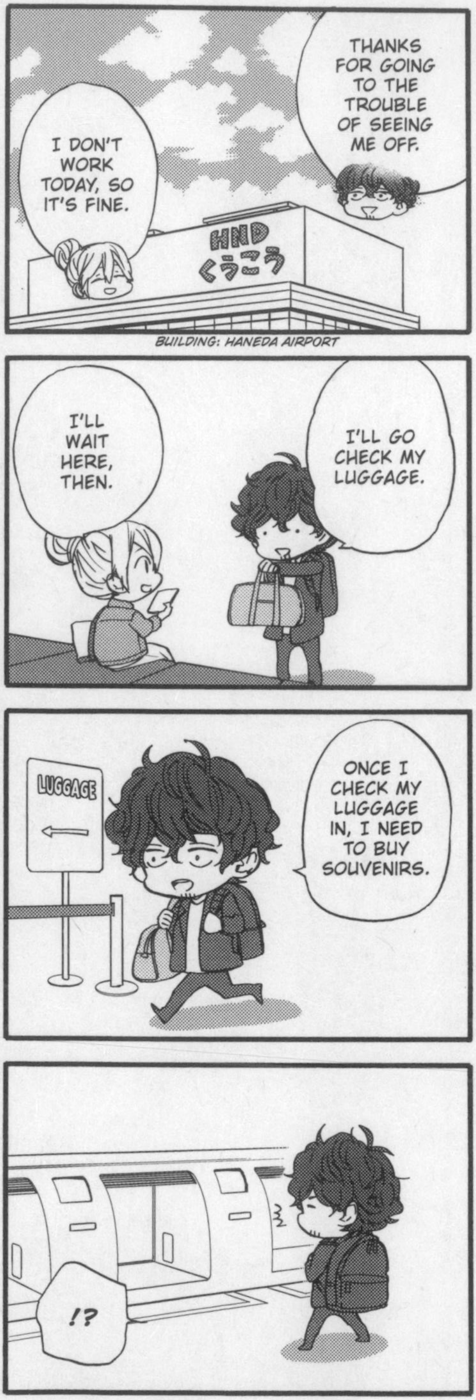

THANKS FOR GOING TO THE TROUBLE OF SEEING ME OFF.
I DON'T WORK TODAY, SO IT'S FINE.
HND
くうこう
BUILDING: HANEDA AIRPORT
I'LL GO CHECK MY LUGGAGE.
I'LL WAIT HERE, THEN.
ONCE I CHECK MY LUGGAGE IN, I NEED TO BUY SOUVENIRS.
LUGGAGE
!?

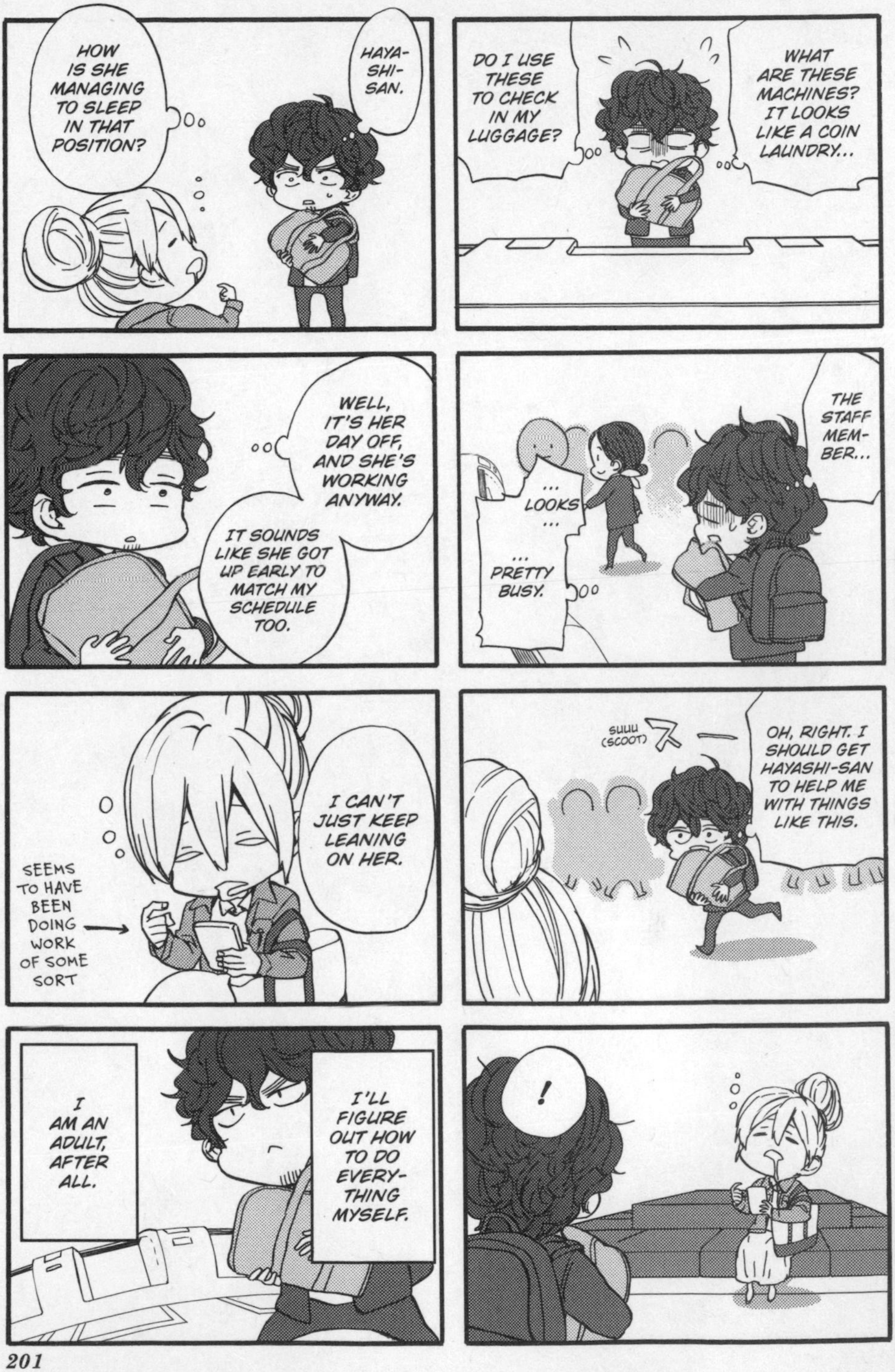

WHAT ARE THESE MACHINES? IT LOOKS LIKE A COIN LAUNDRY...
DO I USE THESE TO CHECK IN MY LUGGAGE?
HAYA-SHI-SAN.
HOW IS SHE MANAGING TO SLEEP IN THAT POSITION?
THE STAFF MEMBER...
...LOOKS... ...PRETTY BUSY.
WELL, IT'S HER DAY OFF, AND SHE'S WORKING ANYWAY.
IT SOUNDS LIKE SHE GOT UP EARLY TO MATCH MY SCHEDULE TOO.
OH, RIGHT. I SHOULD GET HAYASHI-SAN TO HELP ME WITH THINGS LIKE THIS.
スー
SUUU (SCOOT)
I CAN'T JUST KEEP LEANING ON HER.
SEEMS TO HAVE BEEN DOING WORK OF SOME SORT
!
I'LL FIGURE OUT HOW TO DO EVERY-THING MYSELF.
I AM AN ADULT, AFTER ALL.

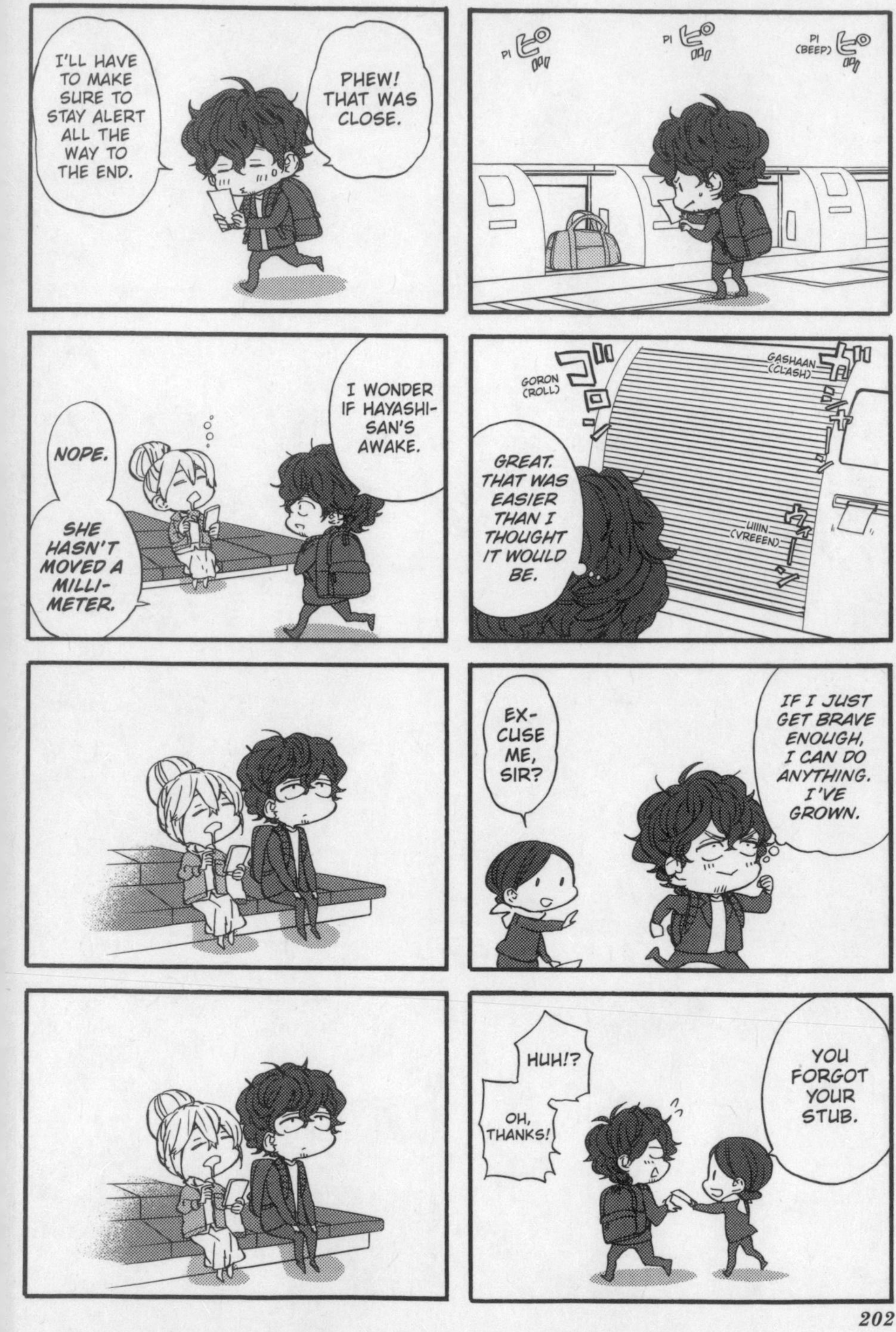
PI
PI
PI (BEEP)
PHEW! THAT WAS CLOSE.
I'LL HAVE TO MAKE SURE TO STAY ALERT ALL THE WAY TO THE END.
GASHAAN (CLASH)
GORON (ROLL)
UIIIN (VREEEN)
GREAT. THAT WAS EASIER THAN I THOUGHT IT WOULD BE.
I WONDER IF HAYASHI-SAN'S AWAKE.
NOPE.
SHE HASN'T MOVED A MILLI-METER.
IF I JUST GET BRAVE ENOUGH, I CAN DO ANYTHING. I'VE GROWN.
EX-CUSE ME, SIR?
YOU FORGOT YOUR STUB.
HUH!?
OH, THANKS!

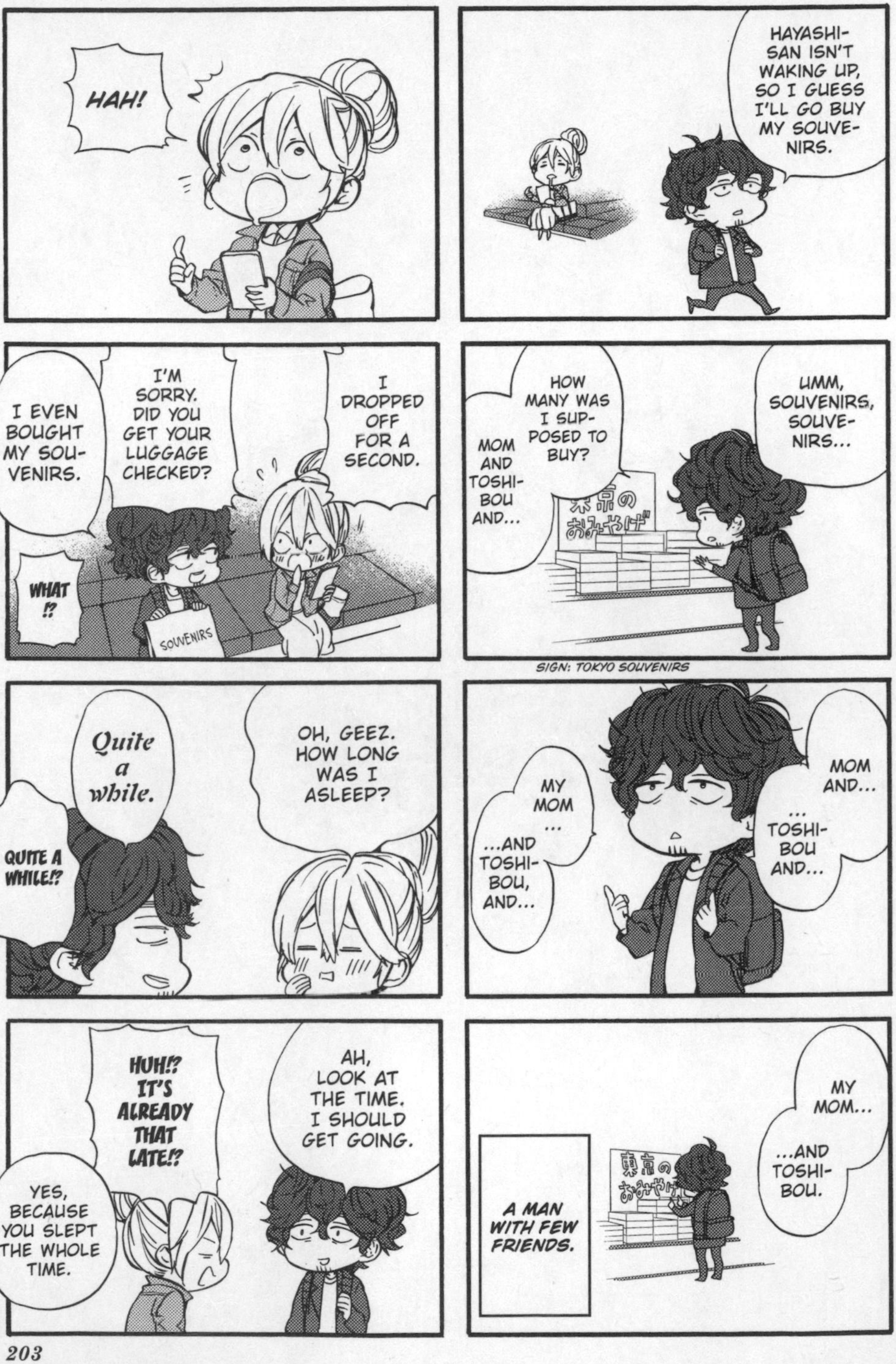
HAYASHI-SAN ISN'T WAKING UP, SO I GUESS I'LL GO BUY MY SOUVENIRS.
HAH!
UMM, SOUVENIRS, SOUVENIRS...
HOW MANY WAS I SUPPOSED TO BUY?
MOM AND TOSHIBOU AND...
SIGN: TOKYO SOUVENIRS
I DROPPED OFF FOR A SECOND.
I'M SORRY. DID YOU GET YOUR LUGGAGE CHECKED?
I EVEN BOUGHT MY SOUVENIRS.
WHAT!?
SOUVENIRS
MOM AND...
...TOSHIBOU AND...
MY MOM...
...AND TOSHIBOU, AND...
OH, GEEZ. HOW LONG WAS I ASLEEP?
Quite a while.
QUITE A WHILE!?
MY MOM...
...AND TOSHIBOU.
A MAN WITH FEW FRIENDS.
AH, LOOK AT THE TIME. I SHOULD GET GOING.
HUH!? IT'S ALREADY THAT LATE!?
YES, BECAUSE YOU SLEPT THE WHOLE TIME.

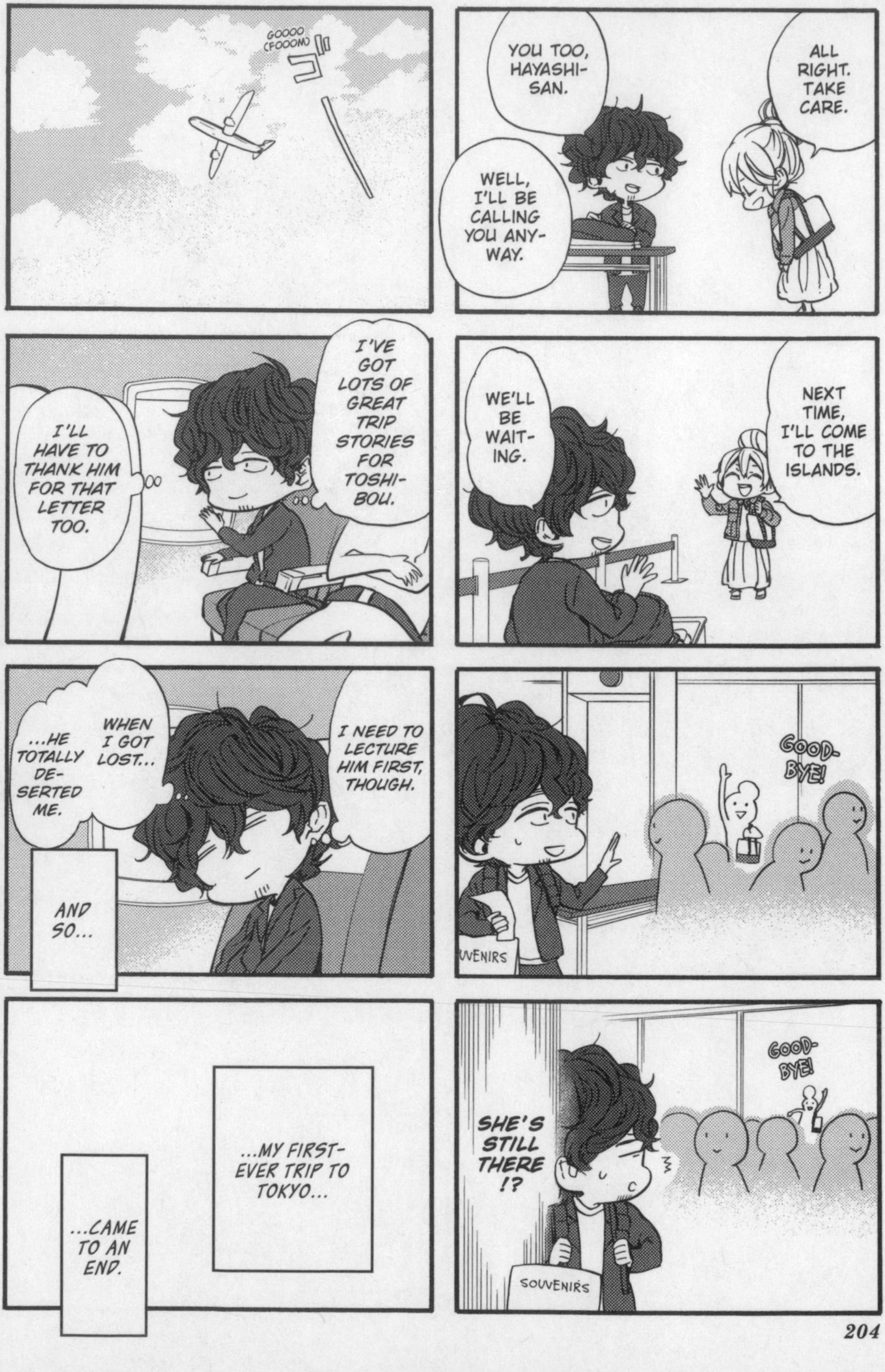
ALL RIGHT. TAKE CARE.
YOU TOO, HAYASHI-SAN.
WELL, I'LL BE CALLING YOU ANYWAY.
GOOOO (FOOOM)
NEXT TIME, I'LL COME TO THE ISLANDS.
WE'LL BE WAITING.
I'VE GOT LOTS OF GREAT TRIP STORIES FOR TOSHIBOU.
I'LL HAVE TO THANK HIM FOR THAT LETTER TOO.
GOOD-BYE!
SOUVENIRS
I NEED TO LECTURE HIM FIRST, THOUGH.
WHEN I GOT LOST...
...HE TOTALLY DESERTED ME.
AND SO...
GOOD-BYE!
SHE'S STILL THERE!?
SOUVENIRS
...MY FIRST-EVER TRIP TO TOKYO...
...CAME TO AN END.

Yoshi no Zuikara
The Frog in the Well Does Not Know the Ocean

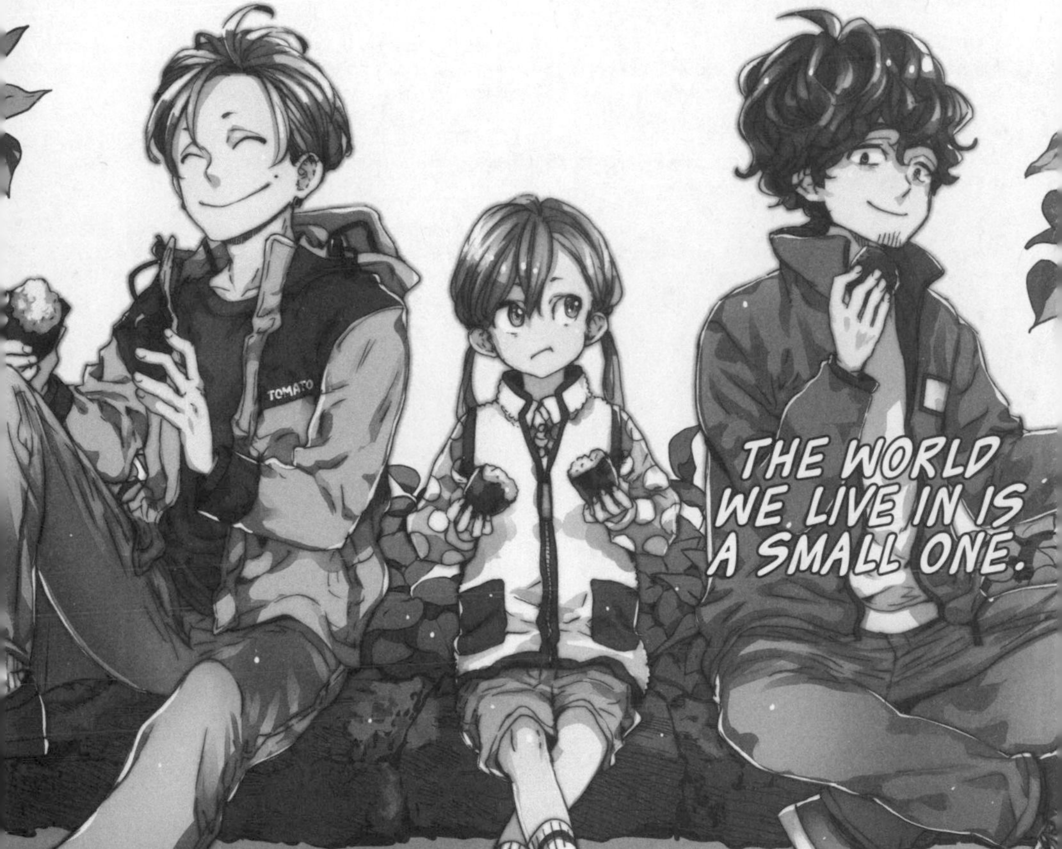
THE WORLD WE LIVE IN IS A SMALL ONE.

Volume 3
Coming next year!

COMMON HONORIFICS

no honorific: Indicates familiarity or closeness; if used without permission or reason, addressing someone in this manner would constitute an insult.

-san: The Japanese equivalent of Mr./Mrs./Miss. If a situation calls for politeness, this is the fail-safe honorific.

-sama: Conveys great respect; may also indicate that the social status of the speaker is lower than that of the addressee.

-kun: Used most often when referring to boys, this indicates affection or familiarity. Occasionally used by older men among their peers, but it may also be used by anyone referring to a person of lower standing.

-chan: An affectionate honorific indicating familiarity used mostly in reference to girls; also used in reference to cute persons or animals of either gender.

-sensei: A Japanese term of respect commonly used for teachers, but can also refer to doctors, writers, and artists.

PAGE 3
While **crow gourds** are actually called "Japanese snake gourds" in English, their ability to attract snakes is likely nonexistent.

PAGE 6
Niichan is a common way for kids to refer to an older boy, especially one they're very familiar with.

PAGE 7
Obachan is a typical way of addressing a middle-aged woman, and much like *niichan*, it gives off a friendly, familiar vibe.

PAGE 13
Ecchi girl: In Japanese, "H," pronounced *ecchi*, is slang for sex. It comes from the first letter in *hentai*.

PAGE 14
"-bou" is a suffix meaning "kid"; Toshi-bou is about a decade younger than Tohno.

PAGE 15
Hiiro-chan chooses to call Naruhiko by his full name, yet omits the *sensei* suffix typically afforded to manga creators — not quite polite, but not entirely casual either.

PAGE 16
Tsundere is a portmanteau of two sound effect words: *tsun-tsun*, meaning "prickly" or "cold," and *dere-dere*, meaning "lovestruck." It's one of the most well-known tropes in anime and is generally used to describe a character who's too proud to admit their love and pushes the object of their affection away with their harsh attitude.

PAGE 36
The **big silhouette** style is all about large, baggy clothes, such as oversized shirts and other loose-fitting apparel.

PAGE 46
As Naruhiko said, "Shinjuku" appears in the names of many stations in Tokyo, which can be very confusing to visitors. *Nishi* and *higashi* mean "west" and "east," respectively.

PAGE 38
Sanappe is likely "striped beakfish" in the local dialect.

Hahakata Salt: This is almost certainly a pun on "Hakata Salt," a very common Japanese brand. In Japan, salt is thrown to drive away evil and, by extension, unwanted guests (although it's not usually done literally in that situation).

PAGE 50
In their classic form, **Tokyo Bananas** are Twinkie-like sponge cakes filled with banana custard cream. They're Tokyo's most iconic official souvenir sweet.

PAGE 53
In the 1986 Hayao Miyazaki movie *Tenkuu no Shiro Rapyuta*, released in English as *Castle in the Sky*, **Laputa** is a legendary floating castle that the movie's protagonists are searching for.

PAGE 61
IC card: "IC" stands for "Integrated Circuit." Similar cards are known as "smart cards" in the U.S. While many types of cards use this format, the one Tohno's buying is used for prepaid train travel.

PAGE 63
Yokohama is in the exact opposite direction from Higashi-Shinjuku.

PAGE 75
Hayashi is referring to the fact that Naruhiko's old signature was written in *kanji*, or Chinese characters, whereas the new one uses *hiragana*, a simpler, exclusively Japanese writing system that should make it much quicker to write.

PAGE 80
Tempura is a Japanese dish easily identifiable by its deep-fried shell of batter, which can contain all sorts of seafood, meat, and vegetables. In this case, the batter is being used to make fried ice cream.

PAGE 76
Kankoro mochi: *Kankoro* is a Gotou dialect term for sweet potatoes that have been cut into rounds, then dried in the sun. It only refers to sweet potatoes in this state.

PAGE 94
Mercari is an e-commerce marketplace, like eBay. Three hundred yen is about three dollars, or roughly half the price of the new (unsigned) manga.

PAGE 101
Drink sizes: While the 8 oz. "short" doesn't appear on U.S. Starbucks menus, the size is one of the basic options at Japanese Starbucks (and is actually still available in the U.S. if you ask for it), so a "tall" is indeed the medium size.

PAGE 107
Junpudo: This is a send-up of the humongous Junkudo bookstore in Ikebukuro. The building is identical.

PAGE 112
Group letter: The term Tohno actually uses is *yose-gaki*, or "collective writing"; the filled-in message board that appears on page 153 is a prime example. It's similar to a yearbook or card where everyone signs it and leaves a comment for the person they're giving it to.

PAGE 137
Little Honda: Keisuke Honda is a Japanese soccer player who plays for AC Milan. When asked why he joined the club, he said "the Little Honda in my heart told me to." This was later riffed on in a series of Pepsi commercials in which he and Little Honda co-starred, and that's probably what Hayashi's referring to.

PAGE 164
Sesame salt, or *gomashio*, is exactly what it sounds like—a mixture of salt and toasted sesame seeds.

PAGE 170
Although it's written with different characters, it's worth noting that **Yamato Transport** is one of Japan's major delivery services, so naming the delivery guy "Yamato" is a casual joke.

PAGE 196
Peking duck is traditionally served in three stages. First, the skin is served by itself with a dipping sauce. Next, the meat is wrapped in pancakes with sauce and vegetables and eaten, and finally, the bones are either made into broth, stir-fried or sautéed with the remaining meat, or packed up to be taken home by the diners. Authentic versions apparently serve mostly the skin and very little meat, and there seems to be an urban legend in Japan that the rest of the meat is thrown away, but it actually is just an urban legend.

INSIDE COVER
Potato stamp: It's supposed to say "Tohno," but various pieces of the characters are flipped or scrambled.

Yoshi no Zuikara
The Frog in the Well Does Not Know the Ocean

SATSUKI YOSHINO

TRANSLATOR:
Taylor Engel

LETTERER:
Lys Blakeslee

YOSHINOZUIKARA vol. 2
© 2019 Satsuki Yoshino/SQUARE ENIX CO., LTD.
First published in Japan in 2019 by SQUARE ENIX CO., LTD. English translation rights arranged with SQUARE ENIX CO., LTD. and Yen Press, LLC through Tuttle-Mori Agency, Inc.

English translation © 2020 by SQUARE ENIX CO., LTD.

Yen Press
150 West 30th Street, 19th Floor
New York, NY 10001

Visit us at yenpress.com
facebook.com/yenpress
twitter.com/yenpress
yenpress.tumblr.com
instagram.com/yenpress

First Yen Press Edition: November 2020

Yen Press is an imprint of Yen Press, LLC.
The Yen Press name and logo are trademarks of Yen Press, LLC.

The publisher is not responsible for websites (or their content) that are not owned by the publisher.

Library of Congress Control Number: 2020940867

ISBNs: 978-1-9753-1742-3 (paperback)
         978-1-9753-1743-0 (ebook)

10 9 8 7 6 5 4 3 2 1

WOR

Printed in the United States of America